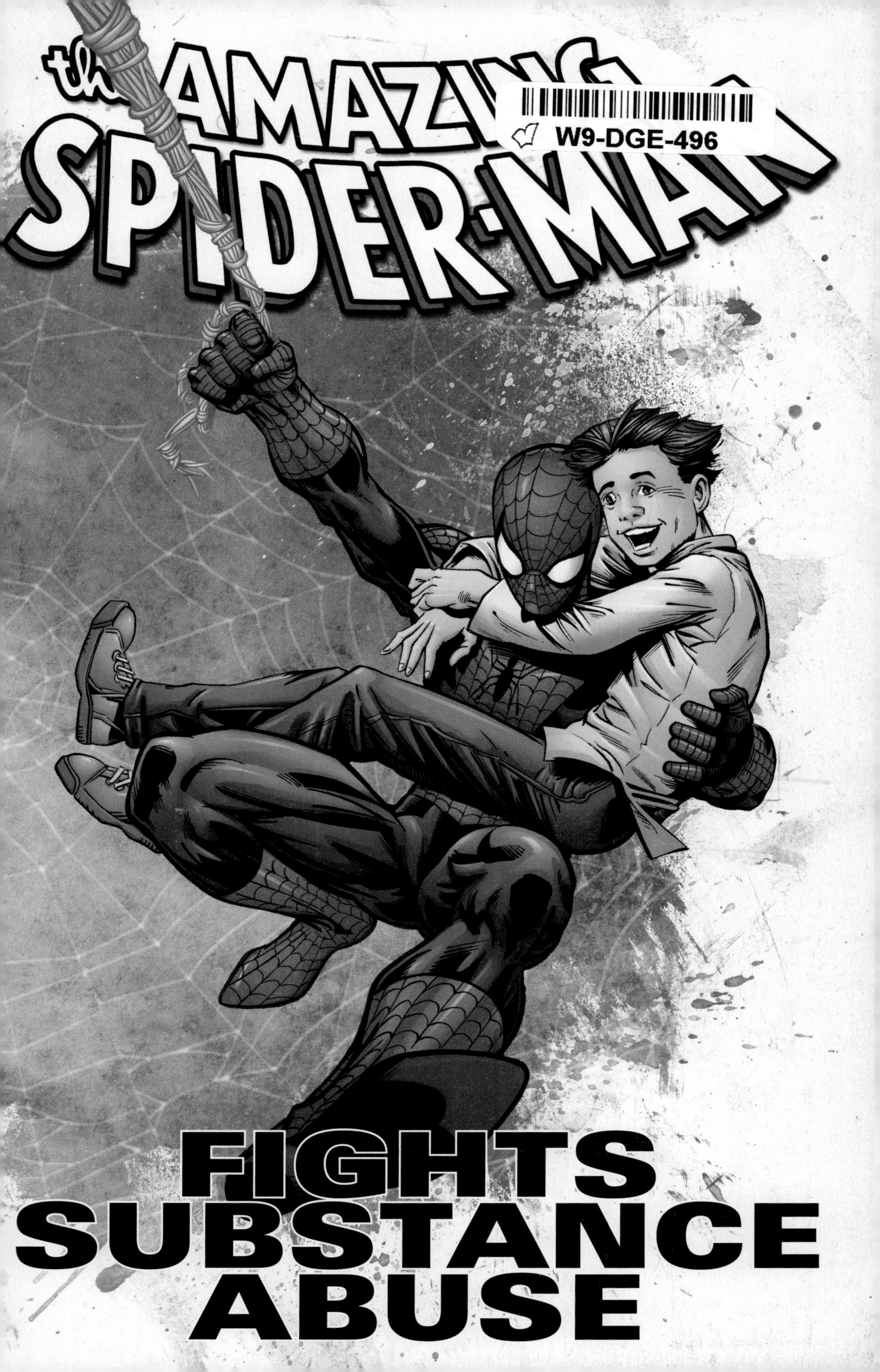
the AMAZING
SPIDER-MAN
FIGHTS
SUBSTANCE
ABUSE

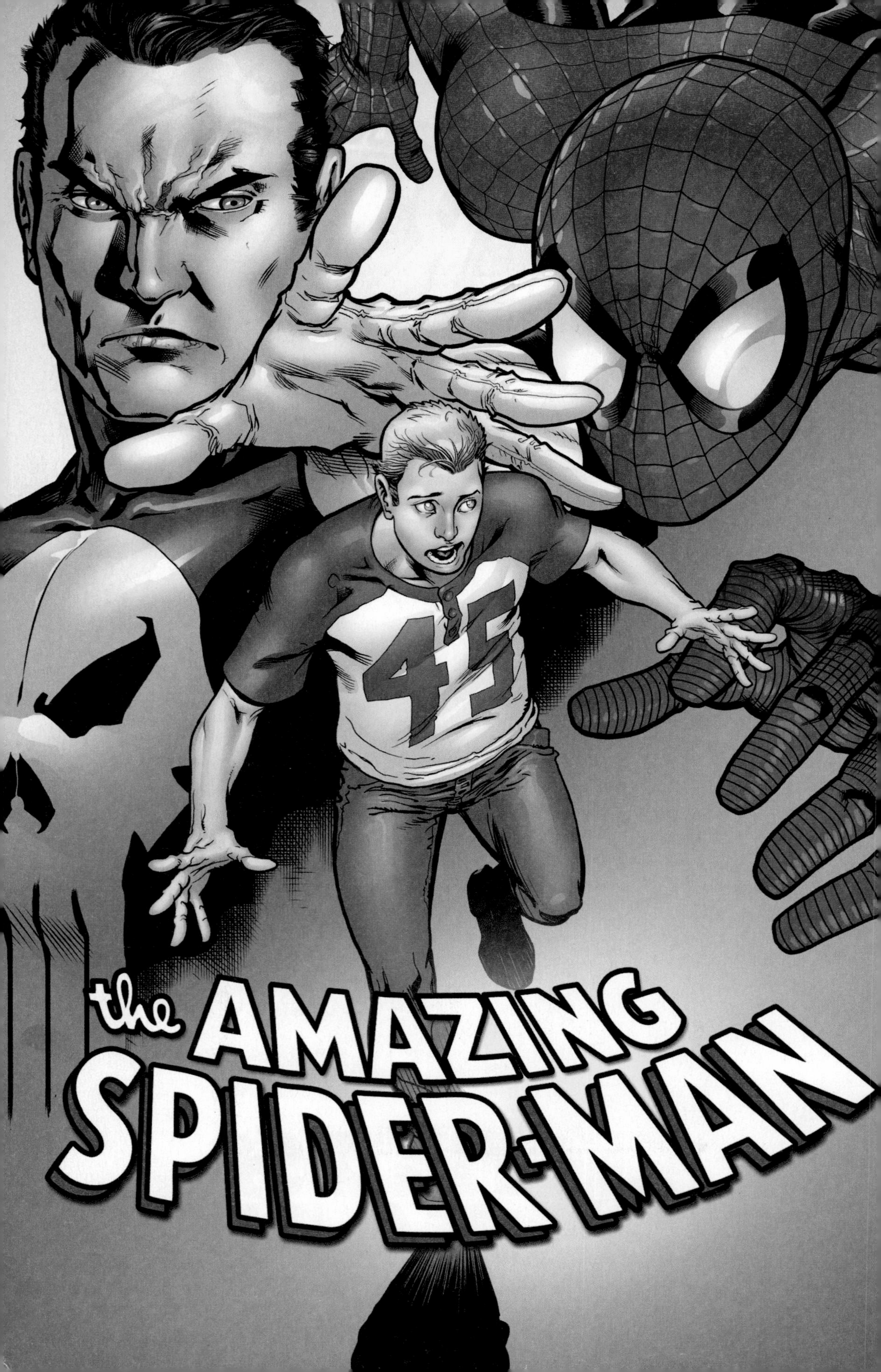

45
the AMAZING
SPIDER-MAN

FIGHTS SUBSTANCE ABUSE

WRITERS:
Stan Lee, Dwayne McDuffie,
Glenn Herdling & John Ostrander

PENCILERS:
Gil Kane, Alex Saviuk, Herb Trimpe,
Gregg Schigiel, Michael Ryan
& Todd Nauck

INKERS:
John Romita, Frank Giacoia,
Chris Ivy, Richard Case, Mark
Pennington & Victor Olazaba
with Tony Mortellaro

COLORISTS:
Gregory Wright, Paul Mounts &
Ian Hannin

LETTERERS:
Artie Simek, Sam Rosen,
Rick Parker, Chris Dickey &
Virtual Calligraphy's Joe Sabino

The creators of **Spider-Man, Storm and Power Man** are unknown.

EDITORS: Stan Lee, Glenn Herdling, Michael Stewart, Steve Behling & Stephen Wacker
FRONT COVER ARTISTS: Todd McFarlane & Chris Sotomayor
BACK COVER ARTISTS: John Romita & Morry Hollowell

EDITOR'S NOTE: The information presented in this volume may be out of date, including the contact information for the various sponsor organizations, and should be viewed in a historical context only.

COLLECTION EDITOR:
Mark D. Beazley
ASSISTANT EDITORS:
Alex Starbuck & Nelson Ribeiro
MASTERWORKS EDITOR:
Cory Sedlmeier
EDITOR, SPECIAL PROJECTS:
Jennifer Grünwald
SENIOR EDITOR, SPECIAL PROJECTS:
Jeff Youngquist
RESEARCH:
Jacob Rougemont & Jeph York
LAYOUT:
Jeph York
PRODUCTION:
ColorTek & Joe Frontirre

BOOK DESIGNER:
Rodolfo Muraguchi
SENIOR VICE PRESIDENT OF SALES:
David Gabriel
SVP OF BRAND PLANNING & COMMUNICATIONS:
Michael Pasciullo

EDITOR IN CHIEF:
Axel Alonso
CHIEF CREATIVE OFFICER:
Joe Quesada
PUBLISHER:
Dan Buckley
EXECUTIVE PRODUCER:
Alan Fine

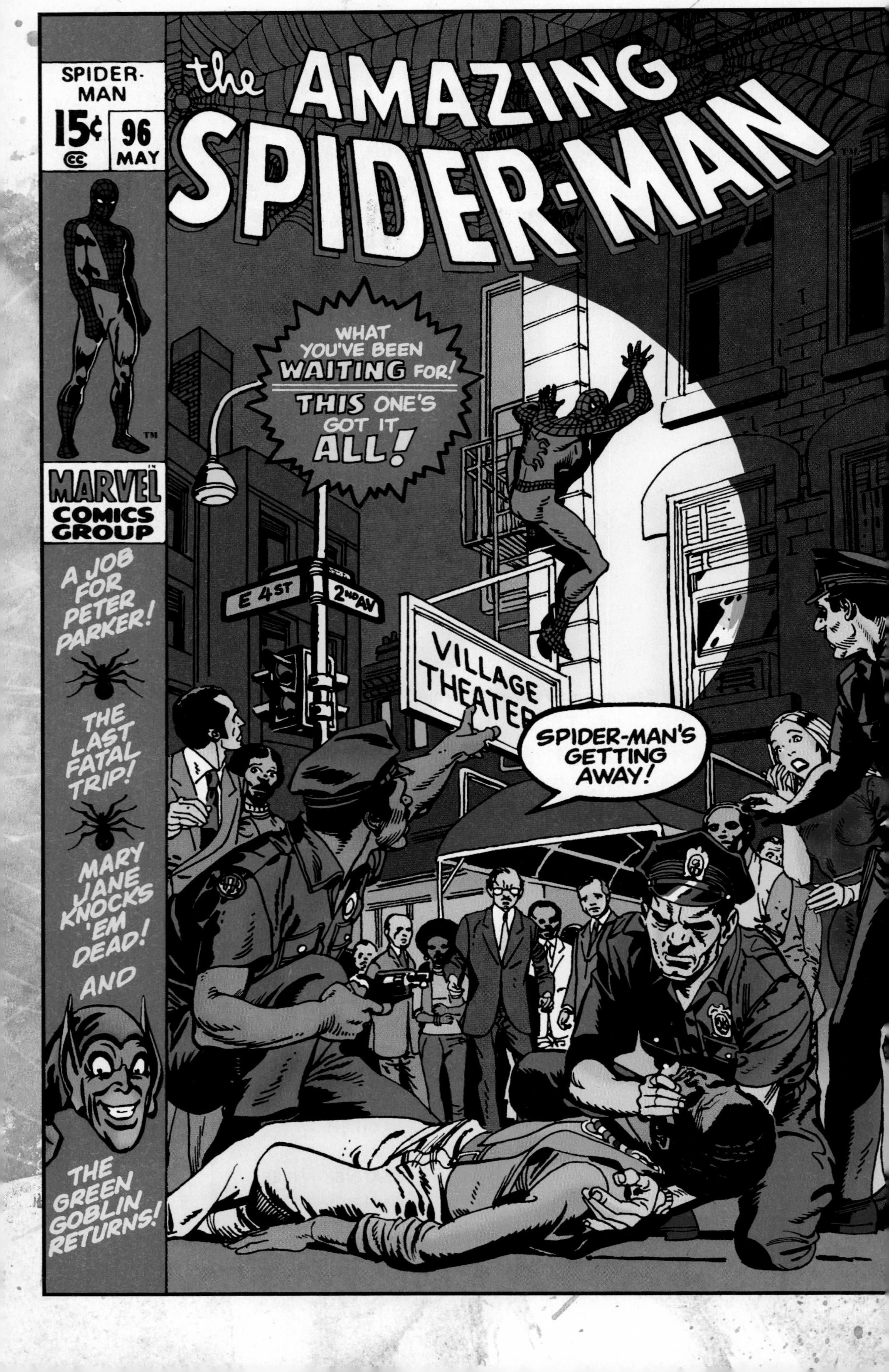

SPIDER-MAN
15¢
96
MAY
the AMAZING SPIDER-MAN
MARVEL COMICS GROUP
A JOB FOR PETER PARKER!
THE LAST FATAL TRIP!
MARY JANE KNOCKS 'EM DEAD!
AND
THE GREEN GOBLIN RETURNS!
WHAT YOU'VE BEEN WAITING FOR!
THIS ONE'S GOT IT ALL!
E 4ST
2ND AV
VILLAGE THEATER
SPIDER-MAN'S GETTING AWAY!

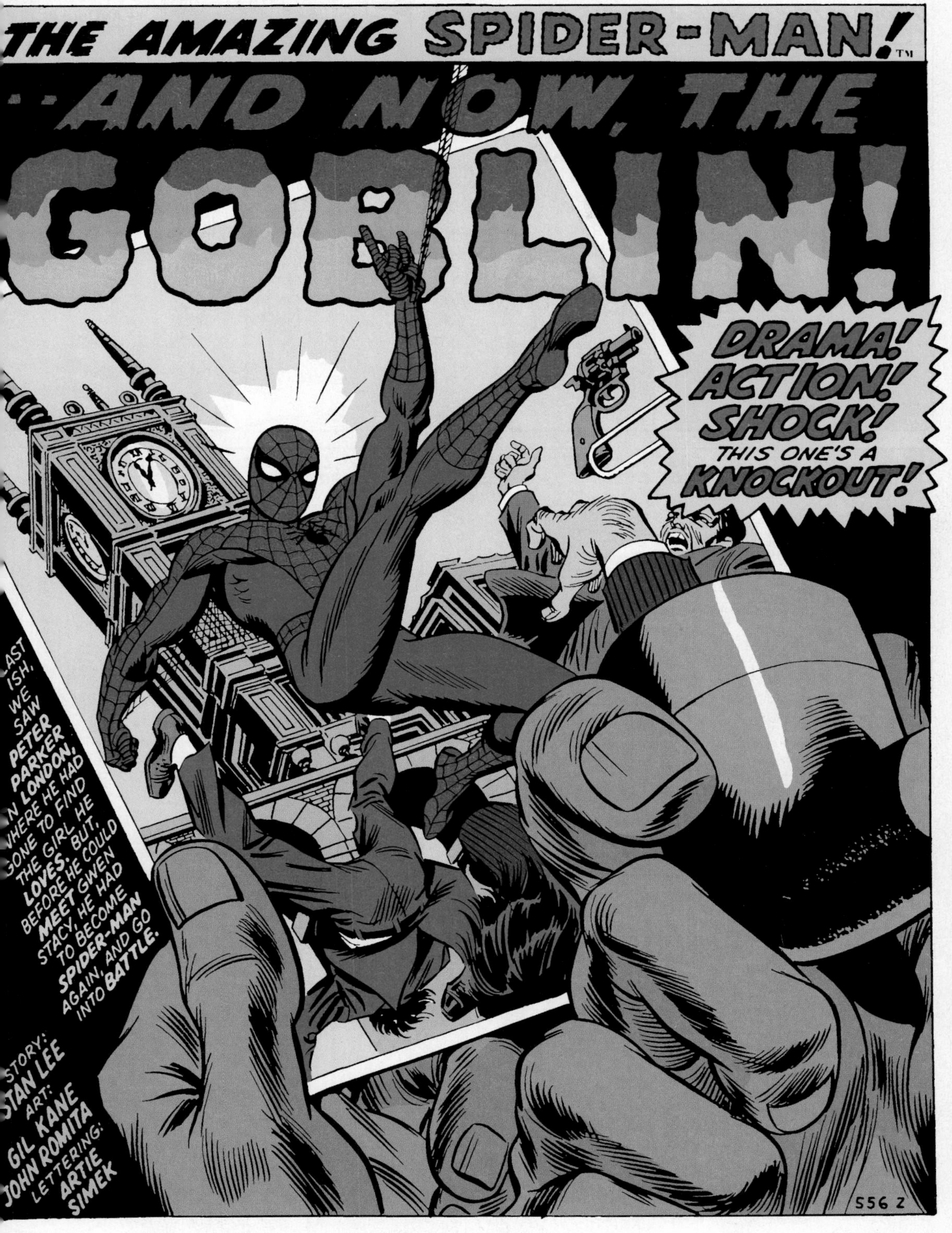
THE AMAZING SPIDER-MAN!™
--AND NOW, THE GOBLIN!
DRAMA! ACTION! SHOCK! THIS ONE'S A KNOCKOUT!
LAST ISH, WE SAW PETER PARKER IN LONDON, WHERE HE HAD GONE TO FIND THE GIRL HE LOVES. BUT, BEFORE HE COULD MEET GWEN STACY, HE HAD TO BECOME SPIDER-MAN AGAIN, AND GO INTO BATTLE.
STORY: STAN LEE ART: GIL KANE JOHN ROMITA LETTERING: ARTIE SIMEK
556 2

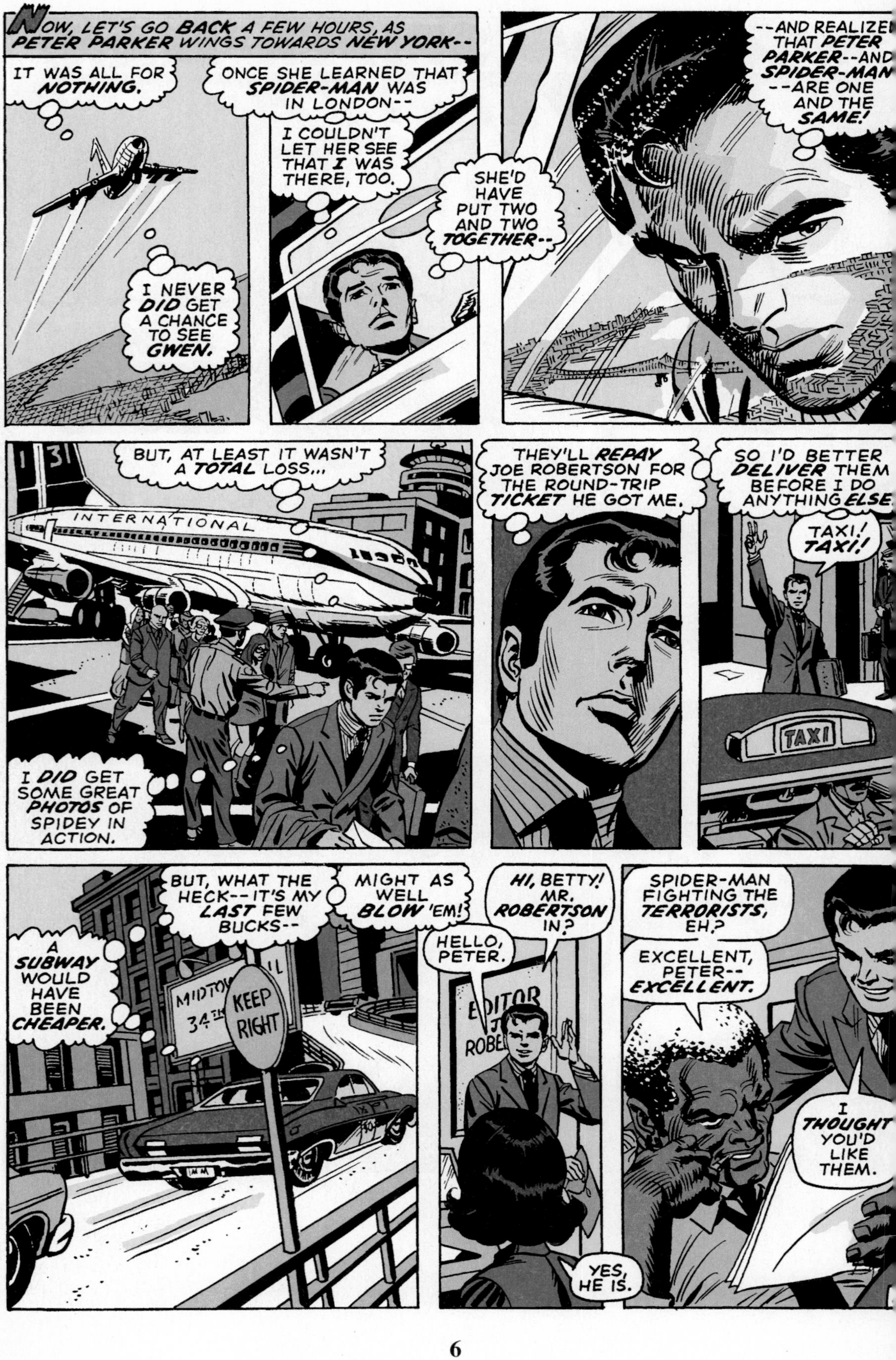

NOW, LET'S GO BACK A FEW HOURS, AS PETER PARKER WINGS TOWARDS NEW YORK--
IT WAS ALL FOR NOTHING.
I NEVER DID GET A CHANCE TO SEE GWEN.
ONCE SHE LEARNED THAT SPIDER-MAN WAS IN LONDON--
I COULDN'T LET HER SEE THAT I WAS THERE, TOO.
SHE'D HAVE PUT TWO AND TWO TOGETHER--
--AND REALIZE THAT PETER PARKER--AND SPIDER-MAN --ARE ONE AND THE SAME!
BUT, AT LEAST IT WASN'T A TOTAL LOSS...
INTERNATIONAL
I DID GET SOME GREAT PHOTOS OF SPIDEY IN ACTION.
THEY'LL REPAY JOE ROBERTSON FOR THE ROUND-TRIP TICKET HE GOT ME.
SO I'D BETTER DELIVER THEM BEFORE I DO ANYTHING ELSE.
TAXI! TAXI!
TAXI
A SUBWAY WOULD HAVE BEEN CHEAPER.
BUT, WHAT THE HECK--IT'S MY LAST FEW BUCKS--
MIGHT AS WELL BLOW 'EM!
KEEP RIGHT
HI, BETTY! MR. ROBERTSON IN?
HELLO, PETER.
YES, HE IS.
SPIDER-MAN FIGHTING THE TERRORISTS, EH?
EXCELLENT, PETER-- EXCELLENT.
I THOUGHT YOU'D LIKE THEM.

YOU WERE **LUCKY** TO GET THESE.

WHAT DOES HE **MEAN** BY THAT? WHY'S HE **LOOKING** AT THEM SO LONG? CAN HE BE THINKING-- WHAT I'M **AFRAID** HE'S THINKING?

I WAS A **FOOL**! I WAS SO BUSY WORRYING ABOUT **GWEN** LEARNING MY SECRET--

--I DIDN'T STOP TO THINK ABOUT **ROBBIE**.

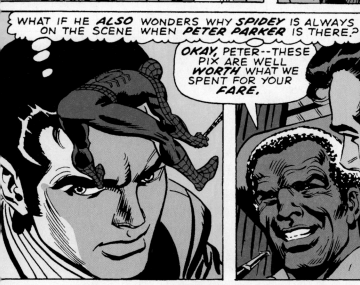

WHAT IF HE **ALSO** WONDERS WHY **SPIDEY** IS ALWAYS ON THE SCENE WHEN **PETER PARKER** IS THERE?

OKAY, PETER--THESE PIX ARE WELL **WORTH** WHAT WE SPENT FOR YOUR **FARE**.

I **KNEW** YOU WOULDN'T LET ME DOWN, SON.

I WONDER-- HOW MUCH **MORE** THAN THAT HE KNOWS?

BUT, MAYBE I'M **OVERLY** SUSPICIOUS! AFTER ALL, HE HASN'T **SAID** ANYTHING.

MY BEST BET IS TO PLAY IT **COOL**.

--WHILE I **CAN**.

THE NEXT DAY, AT GOOD OLD E. S. U.--

IT FEELS **FUNNY**, GETTING BACK TO THE OLD ROUTINE.

HEY, **PETE**! I'VE BEEN **LOOKING** FOR YOU.

THE GANG'S GOING TO THE **THEATRE** TONIGHT.

SORRY, HARRY-- COUNT ME **OUT**.

I'M **BROKE**.

3.

7

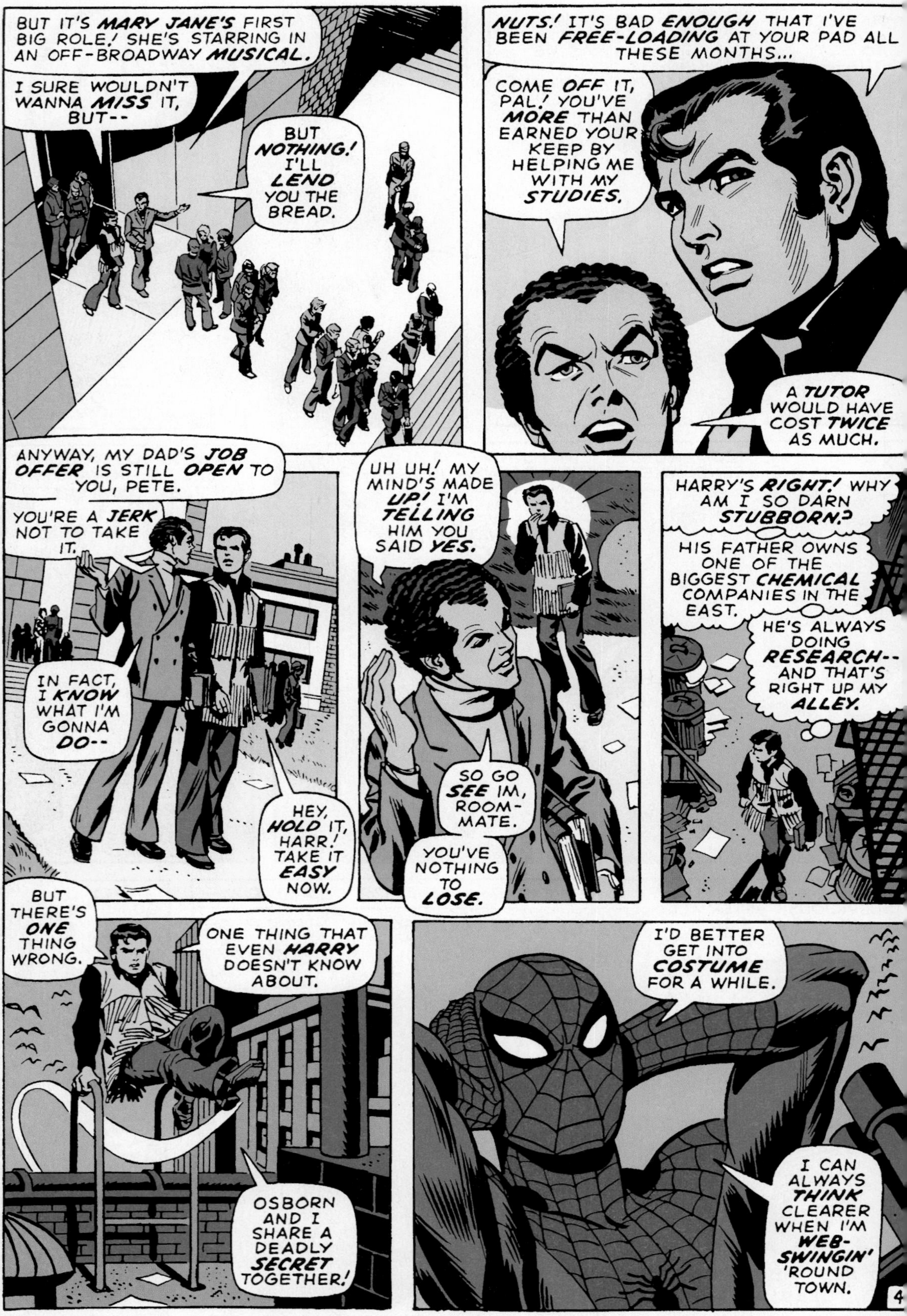
BUT IT'S MARY JANE'S FIRST BIG ROLE! SHE'S STARRING IN AN OFF-BROADWAY MUSICAL.
I SURE WOULDN'T WANNA MISS IT, BUT--
BUT NOTHING! I'LL LEND YOU THE BREAD.
NUTS! IT'S BAD ENOUGH THAT I'VE BEEN FREE-LOADING AT YOUR PAD ALL THESE MONTHS...
COME OFF IT, PAL! YOU'VE MORE THAN EARNED YOUR KEEP BY HELPING ME WITH MY STUDIES.
A TUTOR WOULD HAVE COST TWICE AS MUCH.
ANYWAY, MY DAD'S JOB OFFER IS STILL OPEN TO YOU, PETE.
YOU'RE A JERK NOT TO TAKE IT.
IN FACT, I KNOW WHAT I'M GONNA DO--
HEY, HOLD IT, HARR! TAKE IT EASY NOW.
UH UH! MY MIND'S MADE UP! I'M TELLING HIM YOU SAID YES.
SO GO SEE IM, ROOM-MATE.
YOU'VE NOTHING TO LOSE.
HARRY'S RIGHT! WHY AM I SO DARN STUBBORN?
HIS FATHER OWNS ONE OF THE BIGGEST CHEMICAL COMPANIES IN THE EAST.
HE'S ALWAYS DOING RESEARCH-- AND THAT'S RIGHT UP MY ALLEY.
BUT THERE'S ONE THING WRONG.
ONE THING THAT EVEN HARRY DOESN'T KNOW ABOUT.
OSBORN AND I SHARE A DEADLY SECRET TOGETHER!
I'D BETTER GET INTO COSTUME FOR A WHILE.
I CAN ALWAYS THINK CLEARER WHEN I'M WEB-SWINGIN' 'ROUND TOWN.
4

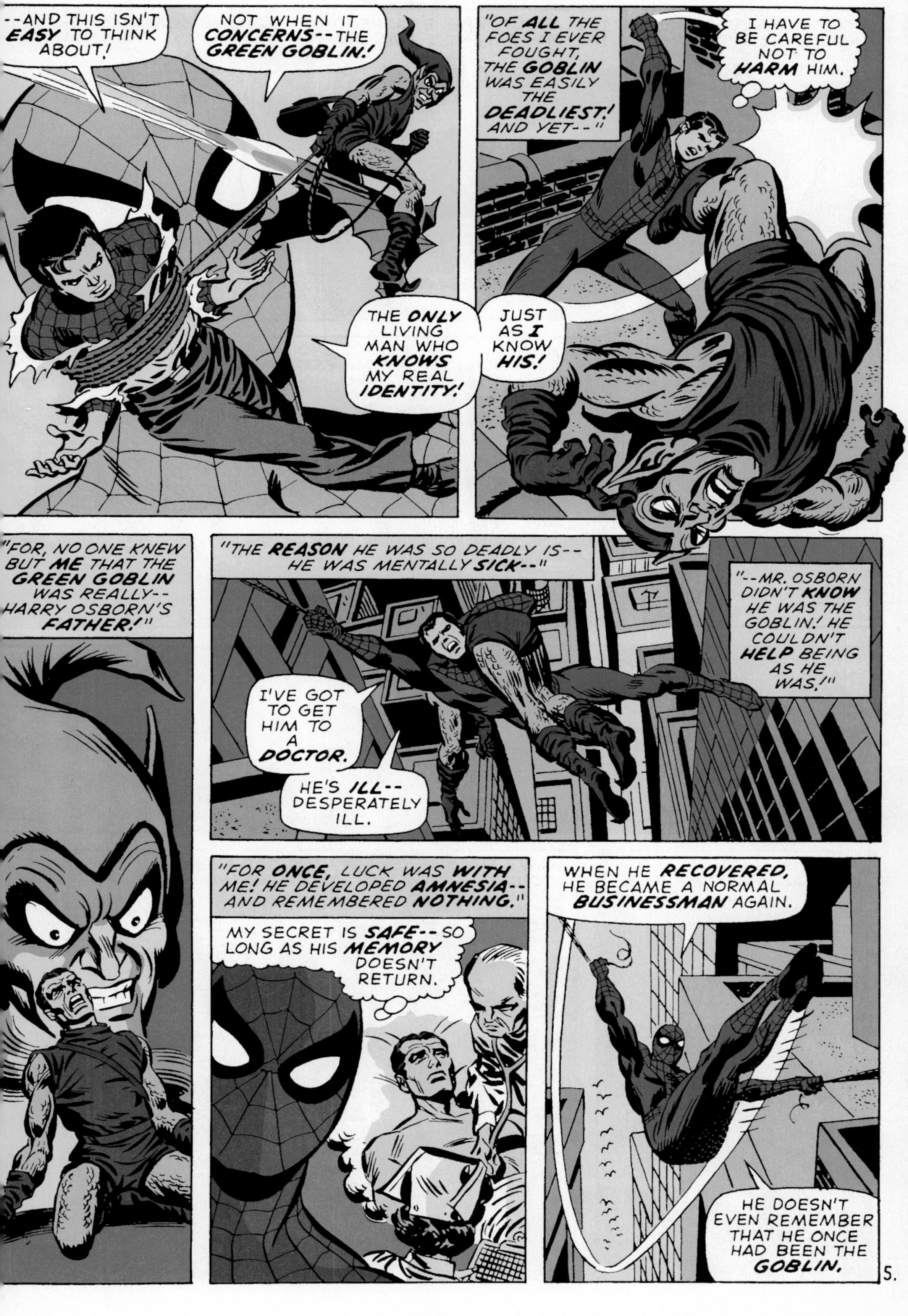
--AND THIS ISN'T EASY TO THINK ABOUT!
NOT WHEN IT CONCERNS--THE GREEN GOBLIN!
THE ONLY LIVING MAN WHO KNOWS MY REAL IDENTITY!
JUST AS I KNOW HIS!
"OF ALL THE FOES I EVER FOUGHT, THE GOBLIN WAS EASILY THE DEADLIEST! AND YET--"
I HAVE TO BE CAREFUL NOT TO HARM HIM.
"FOR, NO ONE KNEW BUT ME THAT THE GREEN GOBLIN WAS REALLY--HARRY OSBORN'S FATHER!"
"THE REASON HE WAS SO DEADLY IS--HE WAS MENTALLY SICK--"
"--MR. OSBORN DIDN'T KNOW HE WAS THE GOBLIN! HE COULDN'T HELP BEING AS HE WAS!"
I'VE GOT TO GET HIM TO A DOCTOR.
HE'S ILL--DESPERATELY ILL.
"FOR ONCE, LUCK WAS WITH ME! HE DEVELOPED AMNESIA--AND REMEMBERED NOTHING."
MY SECRET IS SAFE--SO LONG AS HIS MEMORY DOESN'T RETURN.
WHEN HE RECOVERED, HE BECAME A NORMAL BUSINESSMAN AGAIN.
HE DOESN'T EVEN REMEMBER THAT HE ONCE HAD BEEN THE GOBLIN.
5.

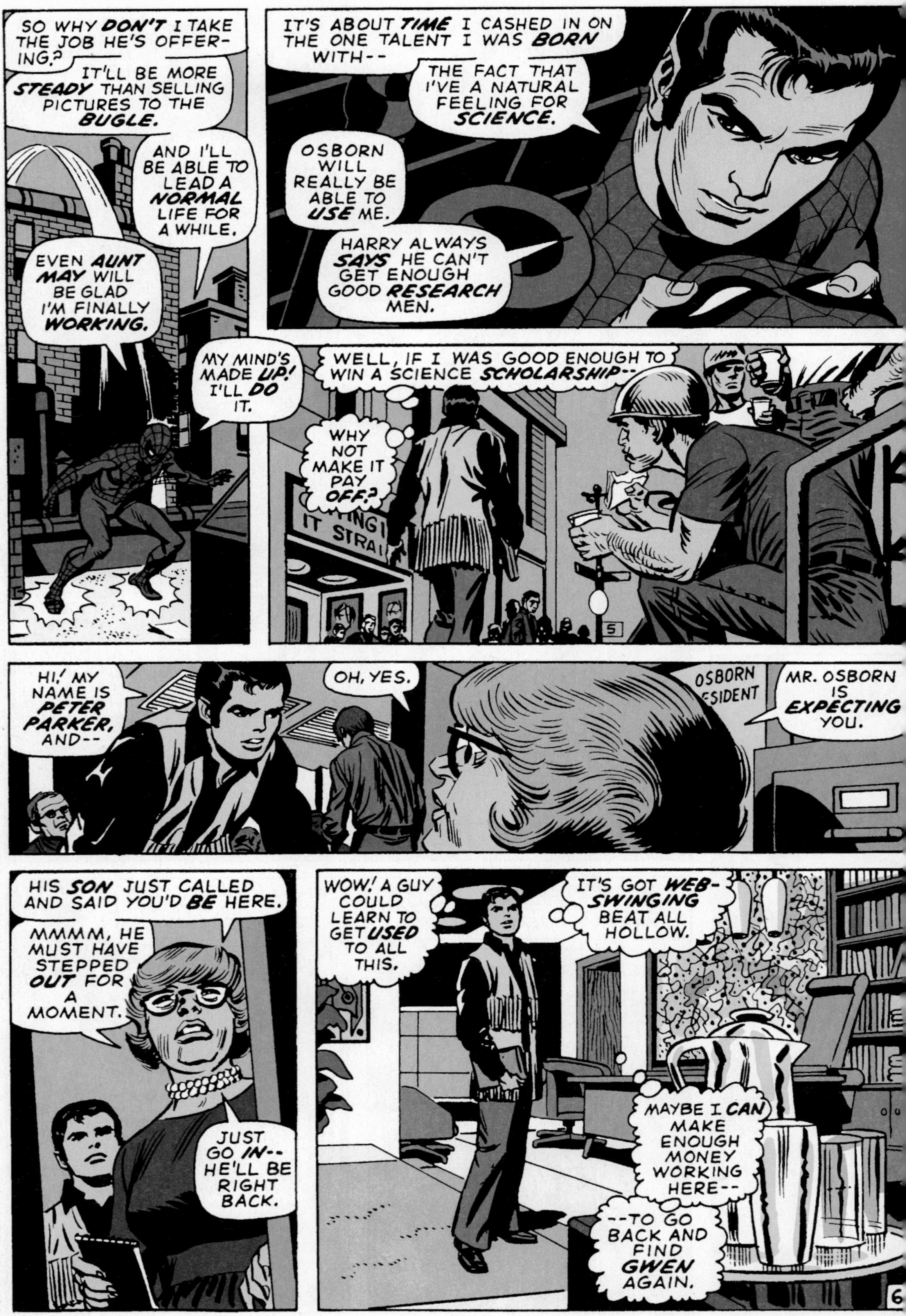
SO WHY DON'T I TAKE THE JOB HE'S OFFERING?
IT'LL BE MORE STEADY THAN SELLING PICTURES TO THE BUGLE.
AND I'LL BE ABLE TO LEAD A NORMAL LIFE FOR A WHILE.
EVEN AUNT MAY WILL BE GLAD I'M FINALLY WORKING.
IT'S ABOUT TIME I CASHED IN ON THE ONE TALENT I WAS BORN WITH--
THE FACT THAT I'VE A NATURAL FEELING FOR SCIENCE.
OSBORN WILL REALLY BE ABLE TO USE ME.
HARRY ALWAYS SAYS HE CAN'T GET ENOUGH GOOD RESEARCH MEN.
MY MIND'S MADE UP! I'LL DO IT.
WELL, IF I WAS GOOD ENOUGH TO WIN A SCIENCE SCHOLARSHIP--
WHY NOT MAKE IT PAY OFF?
5
HI! MY NAME IS PETER PARKER, AND--
OH, YES.
OSBORN
ESIDENT
MR. OSBORN IS EXPECTING YOU.
HIS SON JUST CALLED AND SAID YOU'D BE HERE.
MMMM, HE MUST HAVE STEPPED OUT FOR A MOMENT.
JUST GO IN-- HE'LL BE RIGHT BACK.
WOW! A GUY COULD LEARN TO GET USED TO ALL THIS.
IT'S GOT WEB-SWINGING BEAT ALL HOLLOW.
MAYBE I CAN MAKE ENOUGH MONEY WORKING HERE--
--TO GO BACK AND FIND GWEN AGAIN.
6

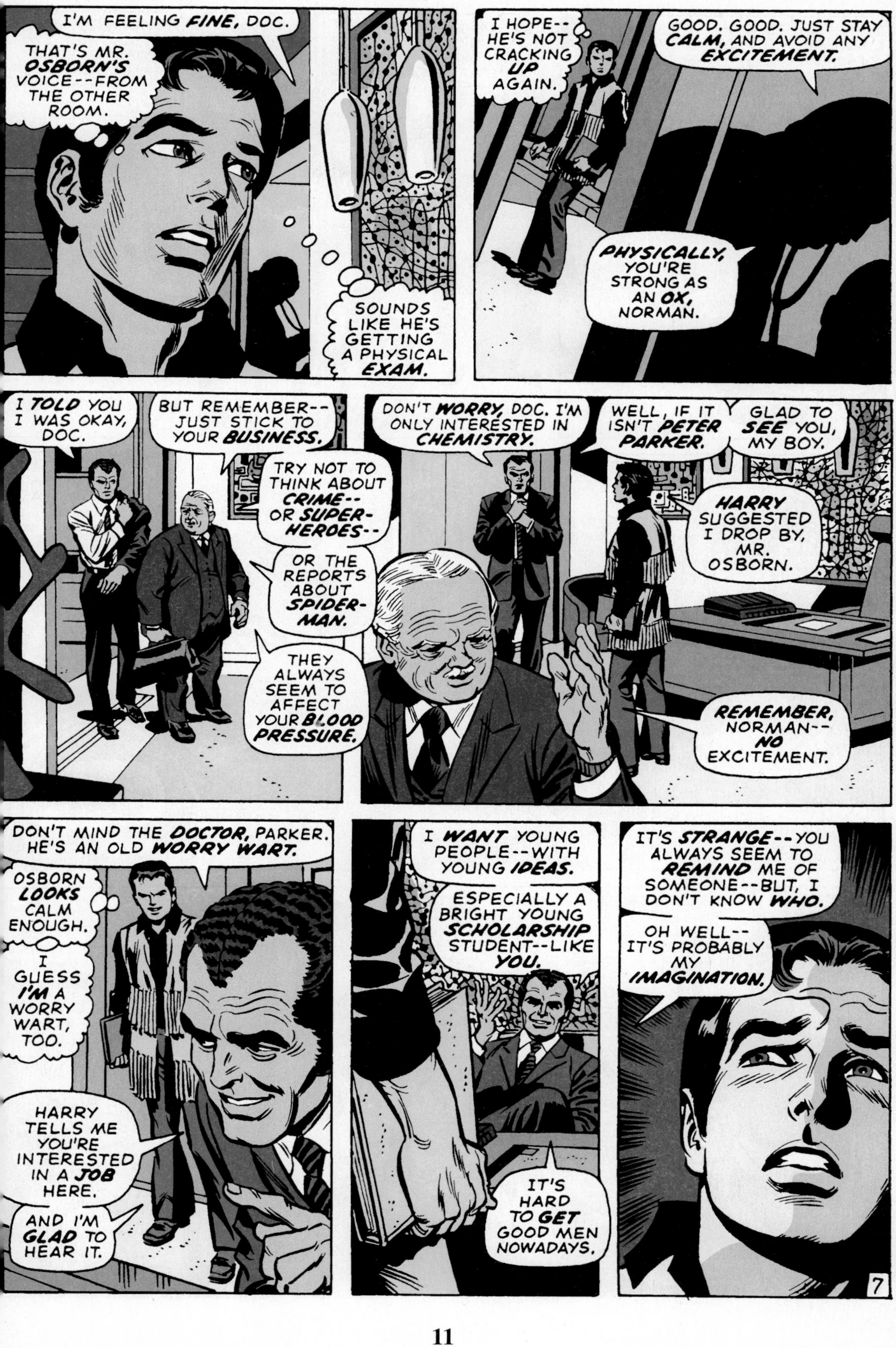
I'M FEELING FINE, DOC.
THAT'S MR. OSBORN'S VOICE--FROM THE OTHER ROOM.
SOUNDS LIKE HE'S GETTING A PHYSICAL EXAM.
I HOPE--HE'S NOT CRACKING UP AGAIN.
GOOD. GOOD. JUST STAY CALM, AND AVOID ANY EXCITEMENT.
PHYSICALLY, YOU'RE STRONG AS AN OX, NORMAN.
I TOLD YOU I WAS OKAY, DOC.
BUT REMEMBER--JUST STICK TO YOUR BUSINESS.
TRY NOT TO THINK ABOUT CRIME--OR SUPER-HEROES--
OR THE REPORTS ABOUT SPIDER-MAN.
THEY ALWAYS SEEM TO AFFECT YOUR BLOOD PRESSURE.
DON'T WORRY, DOC. I'M ONLY INTERESTED IN CHEMISTRY.
WELL, IF IT ISN'T PETER PARKER.
GLAD TO SEE YOU, MY BOY.
HARRY SUGGESTED I DROP BY, MR. OSBORN.
REMEMBER, NORMAN--NO EXCITEMENT.
DON'T MIND THE DOCTOR, PARKER. HE'S AN OLD WORRY WART.
OSBORN LOOKS CALM ENOUGH.
I GUESS I'M A WORRY WART, TOO.
HARRY TELLS ME YOU'RE INTERESTED IN A JOB HERE.
AND I'M GLAD TO HEAR IT.
I WANT YOUNG PEOPLE--WITH YOUNG IDEAS.
ESPECIALLY A BRIGHT YOUNG SCHOLARSHIP STUDENT--LIKE YOU.
IT'S HARD TO GET GOOD MEN NOWADAYS.
IT'S STRANGE--YOU ALWAYS SEEM TO REMIND ME OF SOMEONE--BUT, I DON'T KNOW WHO.
OH WELL--IT'S PROBABLY MY IMAGINATION.
7

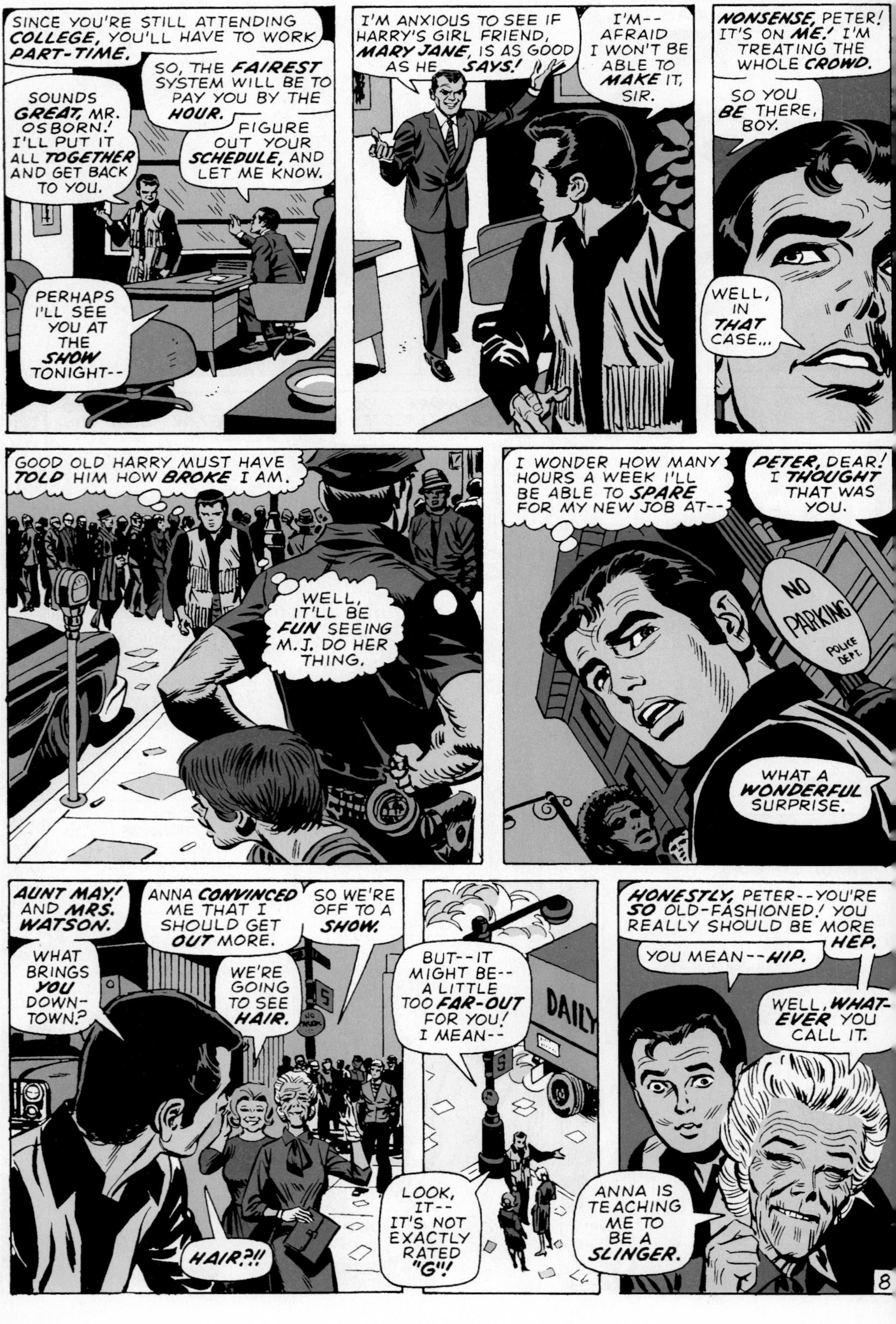
SINCE YOU'RE STILL ATTENDING COLLEGE, YOU'LL HAVE TO WORK PART-TIME.
SO, THE FAIREST SYSTEM WILL BE TO PAY YOU BY THE HOUR.
SOUNDS GREAT, MR. OSBORN! I'LL PUT IT ALL TOGETHER AND GET BACK TO YOU.
FIGURE OUT YOUR SCHEDULE, AND LET ME KNOW.
PERHAPS I'LL SEE YOU AT THE SHOW TONIGHT--
I'M ANXIOUS TO SEE IF HARRY'S GIRL FRIEND, MARY JANE, IS AS GOOD AS HE SAYS!
I'M--AFRAID I WON'T BE ABLE TO MAKE IT, SIR.
NONSENSE, PETER! IT'S ON ME! I'M TREATING THE WHOLE CROWD.
SO YOU BE THERE, BOY.
WELL, IN THAT CASE...
GOOD OLD HARRY MUST HAVE TOLD HIM HOW BROKE I AM.
WELL, IT'LL BE FUN SEEING M.J. DO HER THING.
I WONDER HOW MANY HOURS A WEEK I'LL BE ABLE TO SPARE FOR MY NEW JOB AT--
PETER, DEAR! I THOUGHT THAT WAS YOU.
NO PARKING
POLICE DEPT.
WHAT A WONDERFUL SURPRISE.
AUNT MAY! AND MRS. WATSON.
WHAT BRINGS YOU DOWN-TOWN?
ANNA CONVINCED ME THAT I SHOULD GET OUT MORE.
SO WE'RE OFF TO A SHOW.
WE'RE GOING TO SEE HAIR.
HAIR?!!
BUT--IT MIGHT BE--A LITTLE TOO FAR-OUT FOR YOU! I MEAN--
DAILY
LOOK, IT--IT'S NOT EXACTLY RATED "G"!
HONESTLY, PETER--YOU'RE SO OLD-FASHIONED! YOU REALLY SHOULD BE MORE HEP.
YOU MEAN--HIP.
WELL, WHAT-EVER YOU CALL IT.
ANNA IS TEACHING ME TO BE A SLINGER.
8

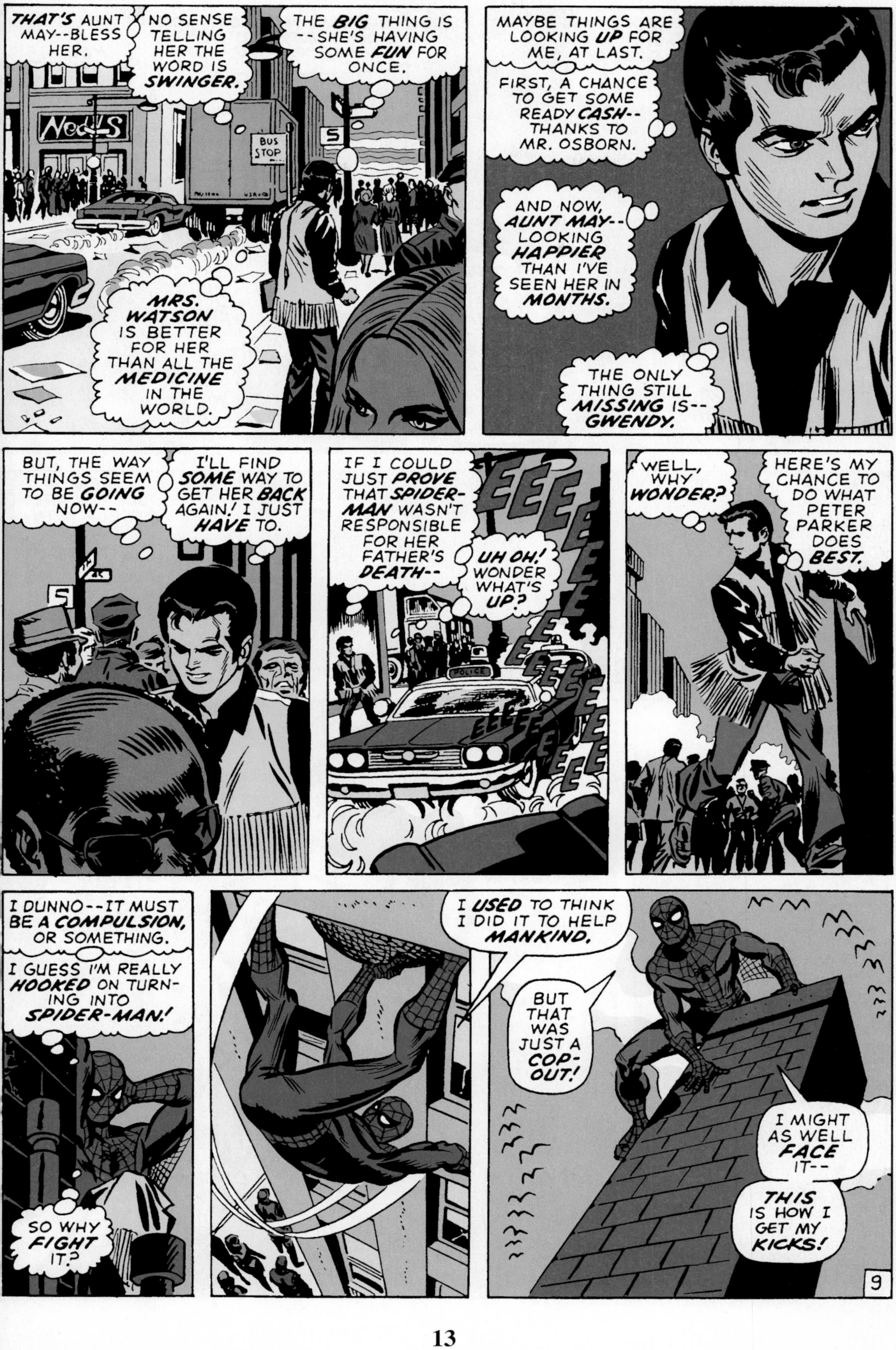
THAT'S AUNT MAY--BLESS HER.
NO SENSE TELLING HER THE WORD IS SWINGER.
THE BIG THING IS --SHE'S HAVING SOME FUN FOR ONCE.
MRS. WATSON IS BETTER FOR HER THAN ALL THE MEDICINE IN THE WORLD.
MAYBE THINGS ARE LOOKING UP FOR ME, AT LAST.
FIRST, A CHANCE TO GET SOME READY CASH-- THANKS TO MR. OSBORN.
AND NOW, AUNT MAY-- LOOKING HAPPIER THAN I'VE SEEN HER IN MONTHS.
THE ONLY THING STILL MISSING IS-- GWENDY.
BUT, THE WAY THINGS SEEM TO BE GOING NOW--
I'LL FIND SOME WAY TO GET HER BACK AGAIN! I JUST HAVE TO.
IF I COULD JUST PROVE THAT SPIDER-MAN WASN'T RESPONSIBLE FOR HER FATHER'S DEATH--
EEEEEEEEEEEEEEEE
UH OH! WONDER WHAT'S UP?
WELL, WHY WONDER?
HERE'S MY CHANCE TO DO WHAT PETER PARKER DOES BEST.
I DUNNO--IT MUST BE A COMPULSION, OR SOMETHING.
I GUESS I'M REALLY HOOKED ON TURNING INTO SPIDER-MAN!
SO WHY FIGHT IT?
I USED TO THINK I DID IT TO HELP MANKIND.
BUT THAT WAS JUST A COP-OUT!
I MIGHT AS WELL FACE IT--
THIS IS HOW I GET MY KICKS!
9

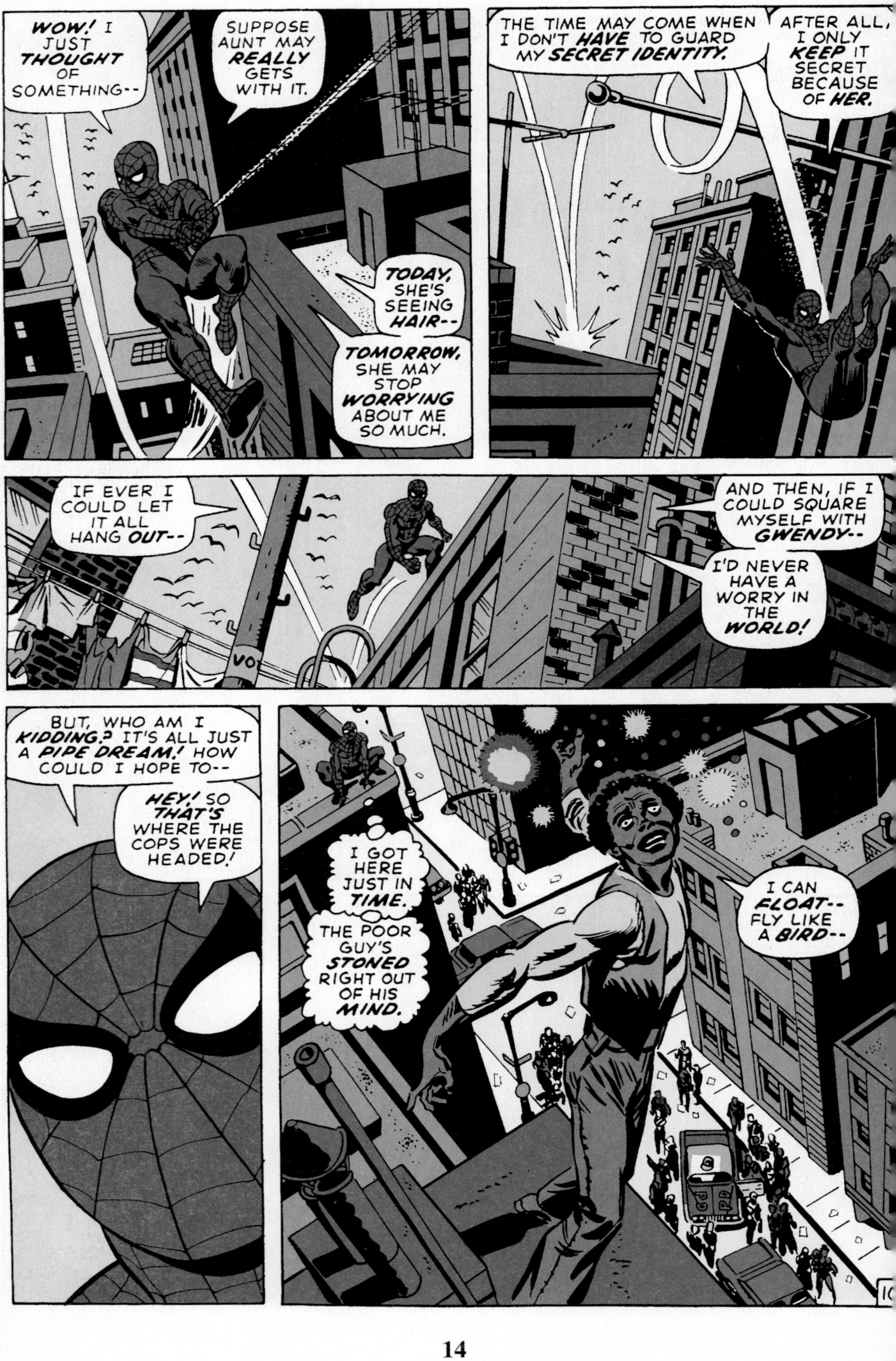
WOW! I JUST THOUGHT OF SOMETHING--
SUPPOSE AUNT MAY REALLY GETS WITH IT.
TODAY, SHE'S SEEING HAIR--
TOMORROW, SHE MAY STOP WORRYING ABOUT ME SO MUCH.
THE TIME MAY COME WHEN I DON'T HAVE TO GUARD MY SECRET IDENTITY.
AFTER ALL, I ONLY KEEP IT SECRET BECAUSE OF HER.
IF EVER I COULD LET IT ALL HANG OUT--
AND THEN, IF I COULD SQUARE MYSELF WITH GWENDY--
I'D NEVER HAVE A WORRY IN THE WORLD!
BUT, WHO AM I KIDDING? IT'S ALL JUST A PIPE DREAM! HOW COULD I HOPE TO--
HEY! SO THAT'S WHERE THE COPS WERE HEADED!
I GOT HERE JUST IN TIME.
THE POOR GUY'S STONED RIGHT OUT OF HIS MIND.
I CAN FLOAT-- FLY LIKE A BIRD--
10

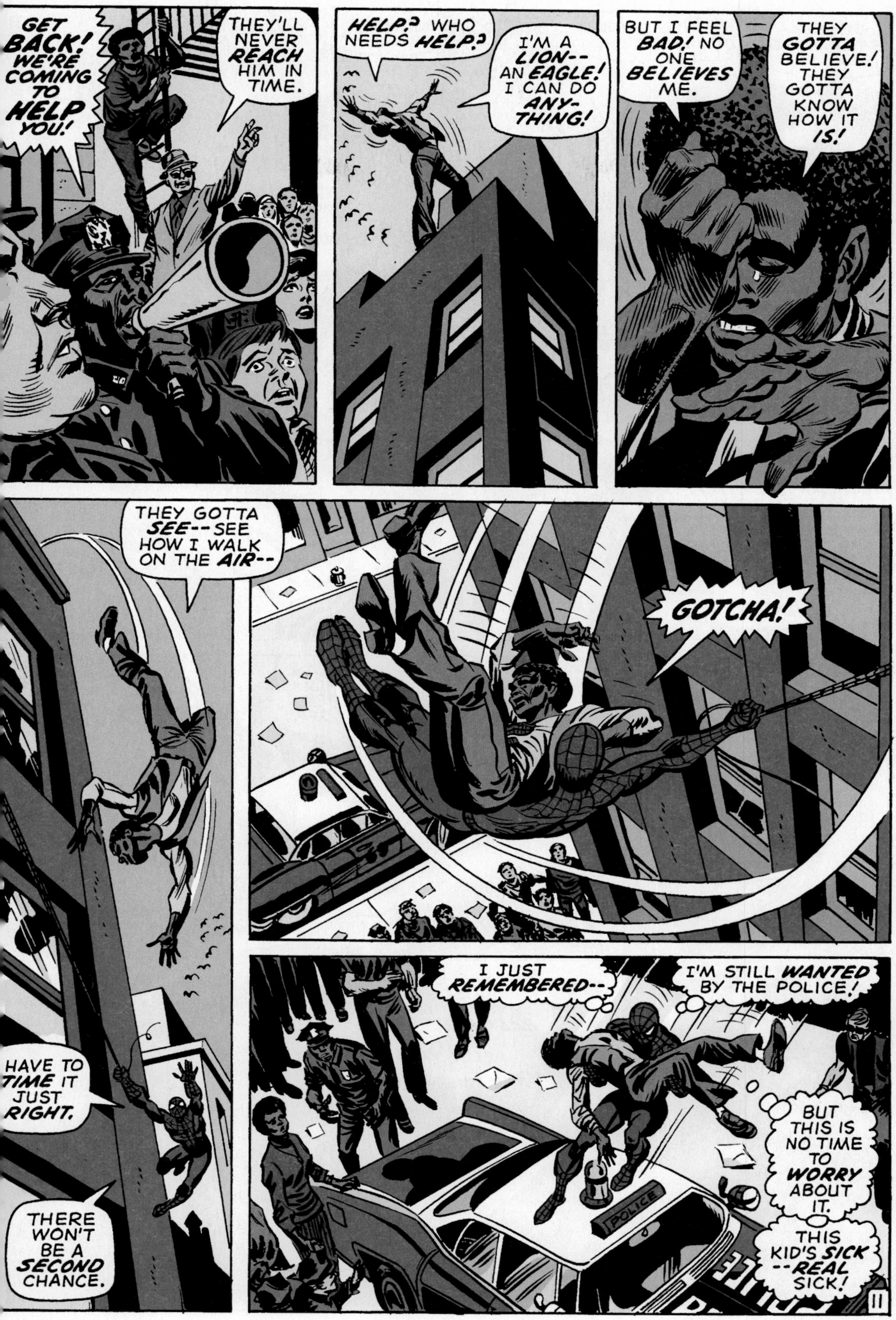
GET BACK! WE'RE COMING TO HELP YOU!
THEY'LL NEVER REACH HIM IN TIME.
HELP? WHO NEEDS HELP?
I'M A LION-- AN EAGLE! I CAN DO ANY-THING!
BUT I FEEL BAD! NO ONE BELIEVES ME.
THEY GOTTA BELIEVE! THEY GOTTA KNOW HOW IT IS!
THEY GOTTA SEE--SEE HOW I WALK ON THE AIR--
HAVE TO TIME IT JUST RIGHT.
THERE WON'T BE A SECOND CHANCE.
GOTCHA!
I JUST REMEMBERED--
I'M STILL WANTED BY THE POLICE!
BUT THIS IS NO TIME TO WORRY ABOUT IT.
THIS KID'S SICK --REAL SICK!
POLICE
11

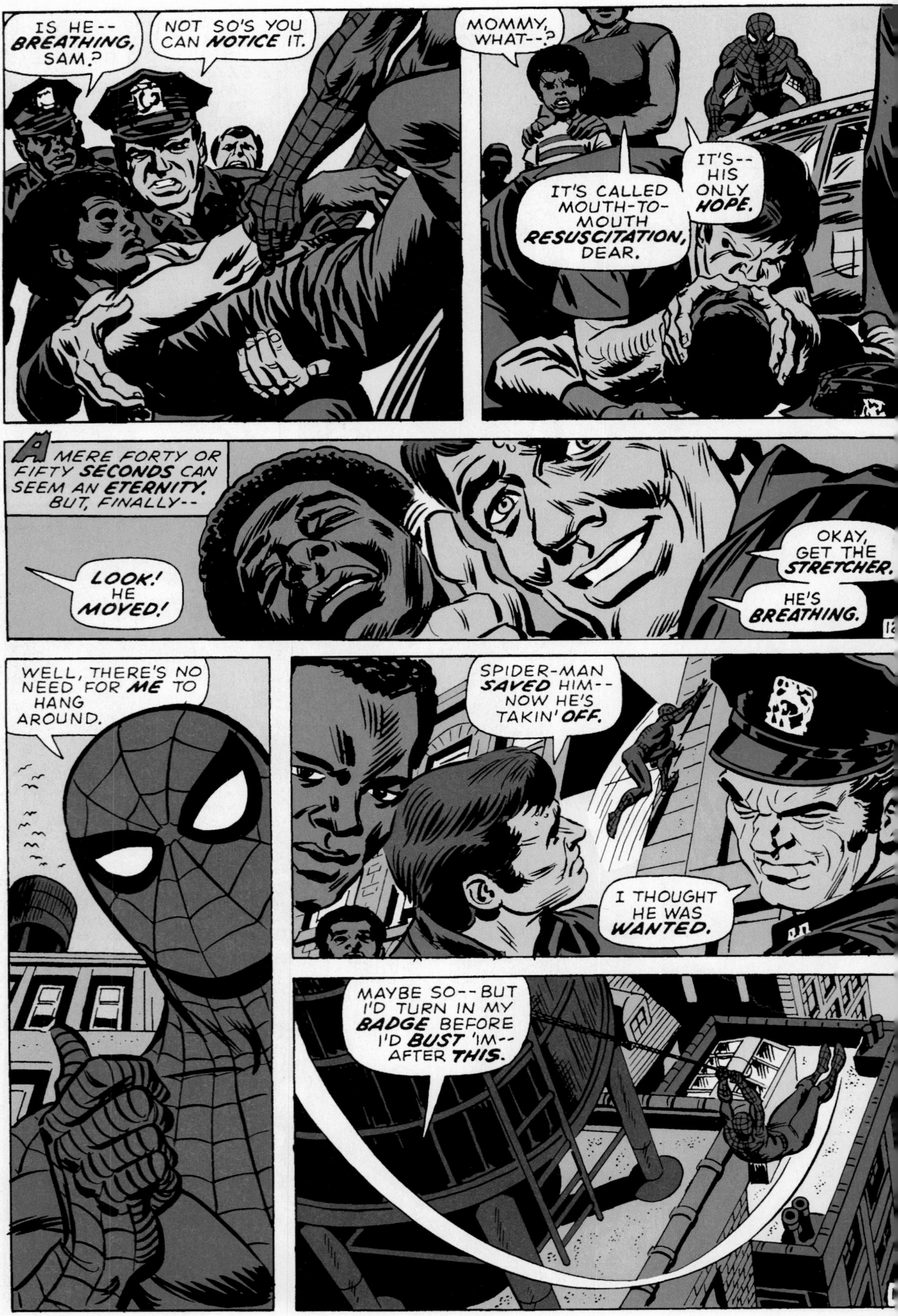
IS HE--
BREATHING, SAM?
NOT SO'S YOU CAN NOTICE IT.
MOMMY, WHAT--?
IT'S CALLED MOUTH-TO-MOUTH RESUSCITATION, DEAR.
IT'S--HIS ONLY HOPE.
A MERE FORTY OR FIFTY SECONDS CAN SEEM AN ETERNITY. BUT, FINALLY--
LOOK! HE MOVED!
OKAY, GET THE STRETCHER.
HE'S BREATHING.
12
WELL, THERE'S NO NEED FOR ME TO HANG AROUND.
SPIDER-MAN SAVED HIM--NOW HE'S TAKIN' OFF.
I THOUGHT HE WAS WANTED.
MAYBE SO--BUT I'D TURN IN MY BADGE BEFORE I'D BUST 'IM--AFTER THIS.

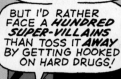

I SURE HOPE THAT POOR GUY'LL BE **ALL RIGHT.**

BUT I WOULDN'T **BET** ON IT.

ANY **DRUG** STRONG ENOUGH TO GIVE YOU **THAT** KIND OF TRIP----CAN **DAMAGE** YOUR **BRAIN**--BUT **BAD!**

BUT HOW DO YOU **WARN** THE KIDS? HOW DO YOU **REACH** THEM?

MY LIFE AS **SPIDER-MAN** IS PROBABLY AS **DANGEROUS** AS ANY---BUT I'D RATHER FACE A HUNDRED **SUPER-VILLAINS** THAN TOSS IT **AWAY** BY GETTING HOOKED ON HARD DRUGS!

--'CAUSE THAT'S **ONE** FIGHT YOU **CAN'T** WIN!

ROBBIE, AND A MILLION **OTHER** EDITORS, KEEP GRINDING OUT **EDITORIALS** AGAINST THE DRUG SCENE...

MAYBE IT'S NOT **ENOUGH!** MAYBE WE'VE GOT TO DO **MORE.**

IF ONLY **SPIDER-MAN** COULD...

FINALLY AT **SHOW-TIME--**

FOR ONCE I'M NOT **LATE!** THERE'S THE **GANG.**

BOY! THAT **THEATRE** ISN'T EXACTLY THE **MUSIC HALL!**

HOW DO YOU **LIKE** IT, ROOMMATE?

MY **DAD** ONCE OWNED THIS BUILDING.

AND **NOW,** IT'S AN OFF-BROADWAY **SHOWPLACE!**

IF IT WAS ANY **FURTHER** OFF BROADWAY --IT WOULD BE IN **HOBOKEN!**

WELCOME, TIGER.

DAD **TOLD** ME YOU TOOK THE **JOB,** PETE.

I'M REAL **GLAD** FOR YOU.

THANKS, HARRY! I HOPE IT'LL WORK OUT.

HEY! HOW ABOUT PAYING SOME ATTENTION TO THE **STAR?**

THIS IS MY BIG **BREAK,** HEAR?

SO WHEN MARVELOUS **ME** COMES ON THE STAGE, I WANNA **HEAR** IT, TROOPS!

MMMMM--REMEMBER WHEN THEY USED TO CALL YOU **PUNY PARKER?**

YOU SURE HAVE **CHANGED,** PETEY.

I NOTICE YOU DIDN'T BRING A **DATE...**

14.

17

WHAT'S MARY JANE TRYING TO *DO?*

SHE *KNOWS* HOW HARRY *FEELS* ABOUT HER! WHY'S SHE PLAYING UP TO *ME?*

IT'S GETTING *LATE.*

WHAT'RE WE *WAITING* FOR?

WE'RE JUST WAITING FOR *RANDY.*

HE'LL *BE* HERE ANY MINUTE.

HERE HE *IS!* HERE COMES RANDY *NOW!*

HEY, DIDJA HEAR WHAT *HAPPENED?*

SPIDER-MAN JUST SAVED SOME FREAKED-OUT *CAT* A FEW BLOCKS AWAY.

YEAH? HOW *ABOUT* THAT?

MAN, THIS DRUG SCENE REALLY *BUGS* ME!

WHAT DO YOU *MEAN,* RANDY?

EVERYONE FIGURES IT'S THE *BLACK* MAN'S BAG --BUT IT *AINT!*

WE'RE THE ONES WHO HATE IT THE *MOST!*

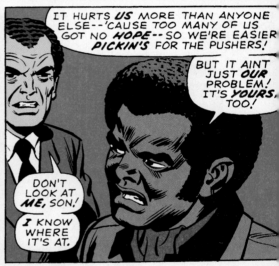

IT HURTS *US* MORE THAN ANYONE ELSE--'CAUSE TOO MANY OF US GOT NO *HOPE*--SO WE'RE EASIER *PICKIN'S* FOR THE PUSHERS!

BUT IT AINT JUST *OUR* PROBLEM! IT'S *YOURS,* TOO!

DON'T LOOK AT *ME,* SON! I KNOW WHERE IT'S AT.

YOU *DO,* HUH? YOU SIT ALL DAY IN YOUR *IVORY TOWER,* COUNTIN' YOUR *BREAD*--

I WORKED *HARD* FOR WHAT I GOT, MISTER!

SO WHAT D'YA *WANT*--A MEDAL?

EVERYBODY WORKS HARD.

ANSWER ME *THIS*--

HOW HARD ARE YOU WORKIN' FOR *PEOPLE?*

WHAT HAVE YOU DONE TO FIGHT *DRUGS?*

LOOK! I'M JUST *ONE* MAN! IT'S NOT *MY* RESPONSIBILITY.

YOU'RE *RICH!* YOU GOT *INFLUENCE!*

THAT *MAKES* IT YOUR RESPONSIBILITY.

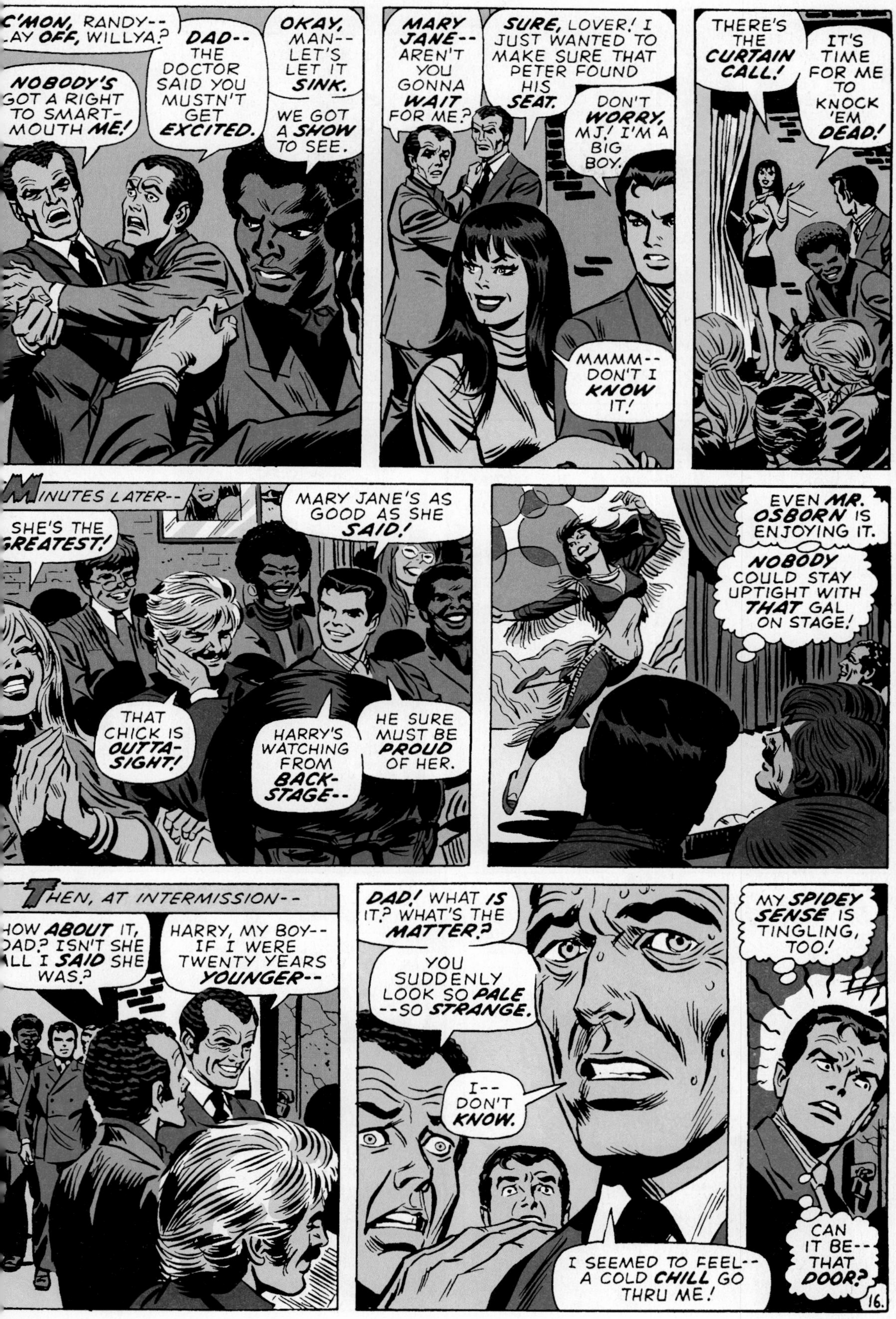
C'MON, RANDY-- LAY OFF, WILLYA?
DAD-- THE DOCTOR SAID YOU MUSTN'T GET EXCITED.
NOBODY'S GOT A RIGHT TO SMART-MOUTH ME!
OKAY, MAN-- LET'S LET IT SINK.
WE GOT A SHOW TO SEE.
MARY JANE-- AREN'T YOU GONNA WAIT FOR ME?
SURE, LOVER! I JUST WANTED TO MAKE SURE THAT PETER FOUND HIS SEAT.
DON'T WORRY, MJ! I'M A BIG BOY.
MMMM-- DON'T I KNOW IT!
THERE'S THE CURTAIN CALL!
IT'S TIME FOR ME TO KNOCK 'EM DEAD!
MINUTES LATER--
SHE'S THE GREATEST!
MARY JANE'S AS GOOD AS SHE SAID!
THAT CHICK IS OUTTA-SIGHT!
HARRY'S WATCHING FROM BACK-STAGE--
HE SURE MUST BE PROUD OF HER.
EVEN MR. OSBORN IS ENJOYING IT.
NOBODY COULD STAY UPTIGHT WITH THAT GAL ON STAGE!
THEN, AT INTERMISSION--
HOW ABOUT IT, DAD? ISN'T SHE ALL I SAID SHE WAS?
HARRY, MY BOY-- IF I WERE TWENTY YEARS YOUNGER--
DAD! WHAT IS IT? WHAT'S THE MATTER?
YOU SUDDENLY LOOK SO PALE --SO STRANGE.
I-- DON'T KNOW.
I SEEMED TO FEEL-- A COLD CHILL GO THRU ME!
MY SPIDEY SENSE IS TINGLING, TOO!
CAN IT BE-- THAT DOOR?
16.

NO TIME TO CHECK IT OUT **NOW**--

BUT I'D BETTER KEEP MY **EYE** ON HIM-- JUST IN **CASE.**

I'VE GOT TO KNOW WHAT **AFFECTED** HIM THAT WAY.

AND AS THE SHOW ROLLS ON...

BUT **THIS** TIME MR. OSBORN ISN'T **WITH** IT!

THE **LAST** ACT'S THE **BEST** OF **ALL.**

MJ IS TOO **MUCH!**

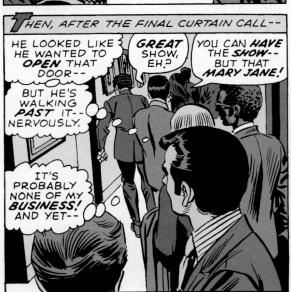

THEN, AFTER THE FINAL CURTAIN CALL--

HE LOOKED LIKE HE WANTED TO **OPEN** THAT DOOR--

BUT HE'S WALKING **PAST** IT-- NERVOUSLY.

IT'S PROBABLY NONE OF MY **BUSINESS!** AND YET--

GREAT SHOW, EH?

YOU CAN **HAVE** THE **SHOW**-- BUT THAT **MARY JANE!**

I'M TINGLING **AGAIN!**

IT **HAS** TO BE THAT **DOOR.**

I'VE **GOT** TO COME **BACK**-- AND SEE WHAT'S **INSIDE.**

HOW'D YOU **LIKE** IT? HOW **WAS** I?

DID YOU HEAR THE **CHEERS**-- AND THE **APPLAUSE?**

DID WE **HEAR** IT, HONEY? WE WERE **DOING** IT!

I TOOK A **DOZEN** CURTAIN CALLS-- AND **BOWS!**

DO YOU KNOW WHAT THAT **MEANS?**

SURE! YOU'LL HAVE A SORE **BACK** TOMORROW.

WE'VE GOT TO **CELE- BRATE,** LADY.

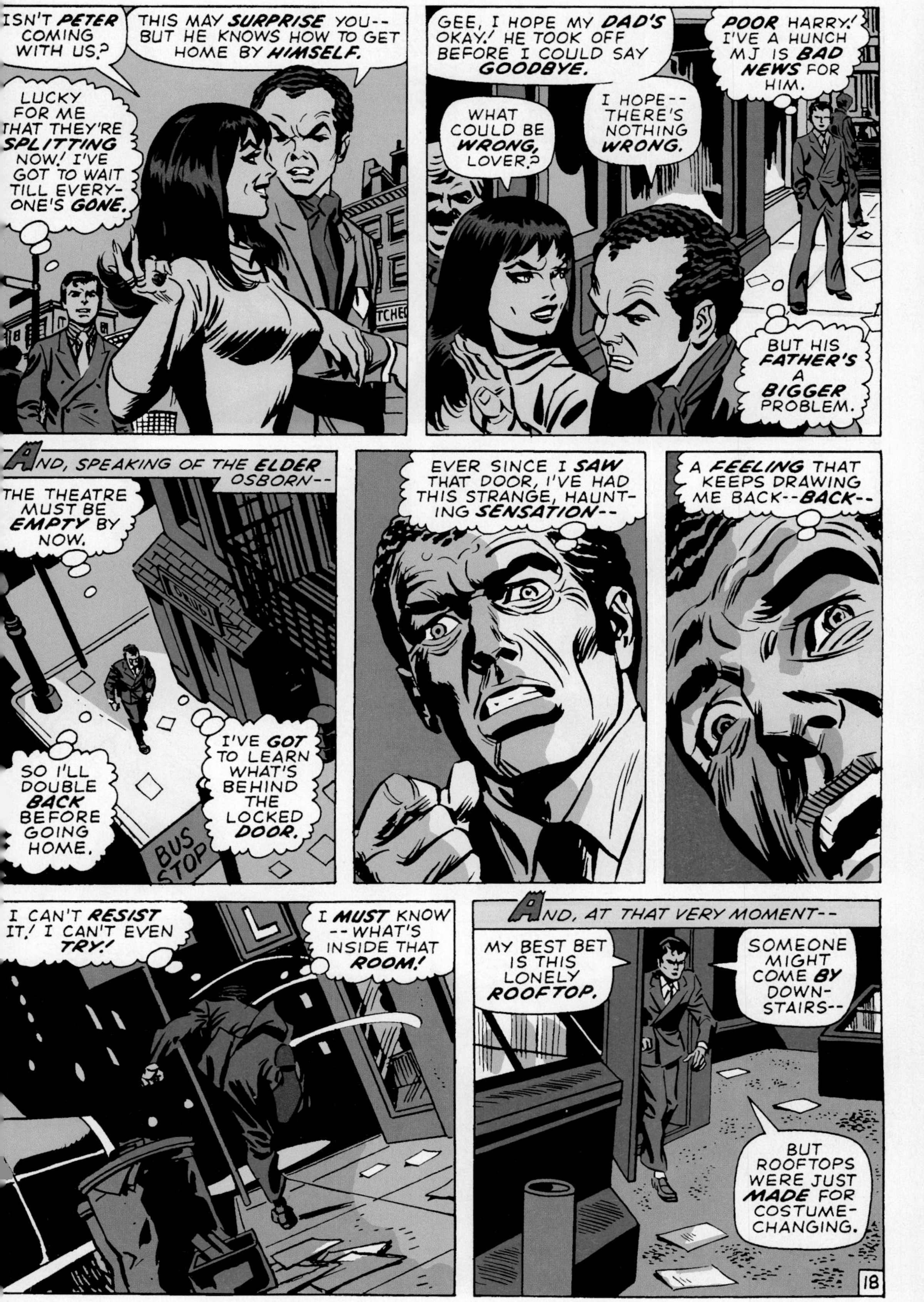
ISN'T PETER COMING WITH US?
THIS MAY SURPRISE YOU-- BUT HE KNOWS HOW TO GET HOME BY HIMSELF.
LUCKY FOR ME THAT THEY'RE SPLITTING NOW! I'VE GOT TO WAIT TILL EVERY-ONE'S GONE.
GEE, I HOPE MY DAD'S OKAY! HE TOOK OFF BEFORE I COULD SAY GOODBYE.
WHAT COULD BE WRONG, LOVER?
I HOPE--THERE'S NOTHING WRONG.
POOR HARRY! I'VE A HUNCH MJ IS BAD NEWS FOR HIM.
BUT HIS FATHER'S A BIGGER PROBLEM.
AND, SPEAKING OF THE ELDER OSBORN--
THE THEATRE MUST BE EMPTY BY NOW.
SO I'LL DOUBLE BACK BEFORE GOING HOME.
I'VE GOT TO LEARN WHAT'S BEHIND THE LOCKED DOOR.
BUS STOP
EVER SINCE I SAW THAT DOOR, I'VE HAD THIS STRANGE, HAUNTING SENSATION--
A FEELING THAT KEEPS DRAWING ME BACK--BACK--
I CAN'T RESIST IT! I CAN'T EVEN TRY!
I MUST KNOW --WHAT'S INSIDE THAT ROOM!
AND, AT THAT VERY MOMENT--
MY BEST BET IS THIS LONELY ROOFTOP.
SOMEONE MIGHT COME BY DOWN-STAIRS--
BUT ROOFTOPS WERE JUST MADE FOR COSTUME-CHANGING.
18

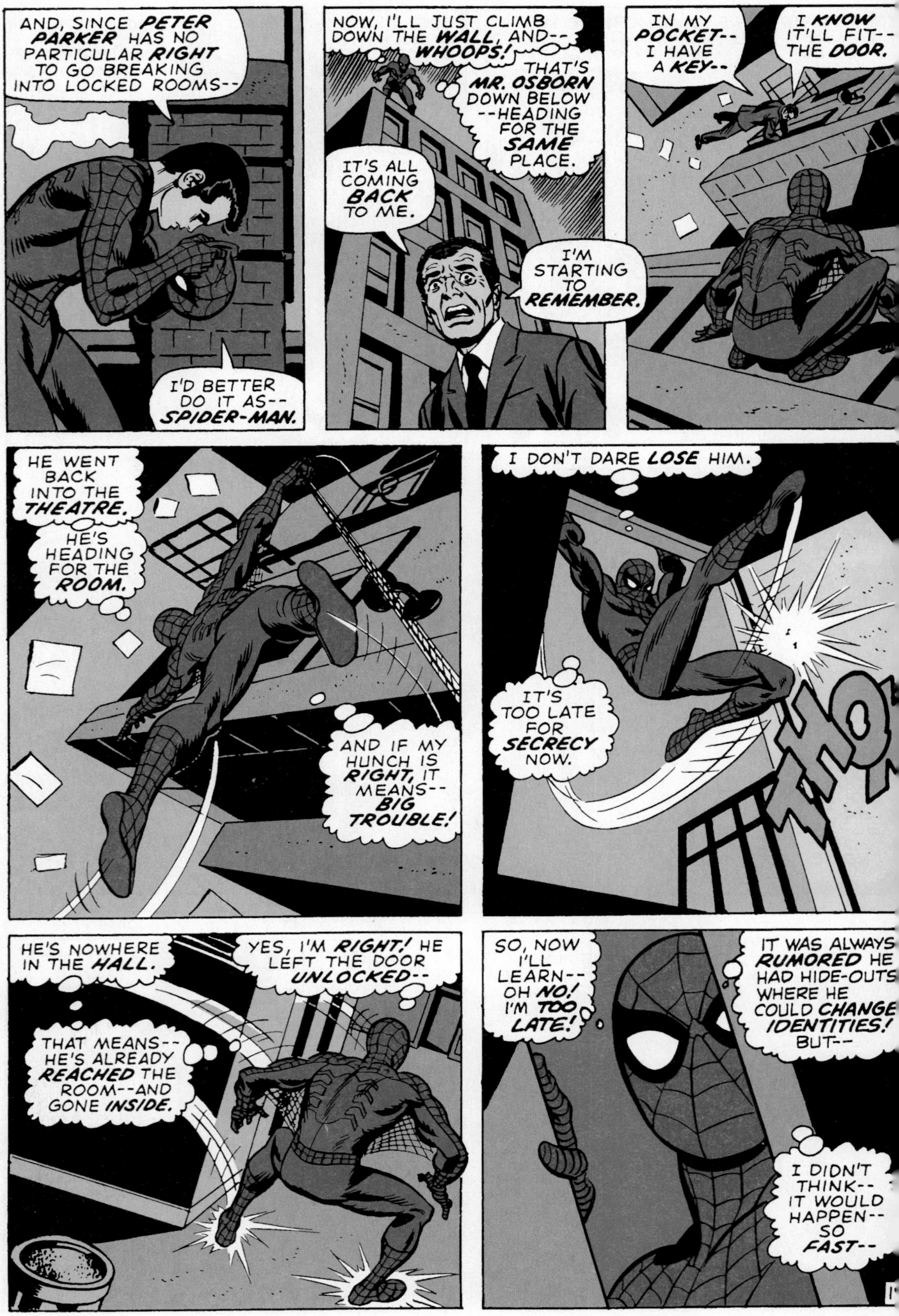
AND, SINCE PETER PARKER HAS NO PARTICULAR RIGHT TO GO BREAKING INTO LOCKED ROOMS--
I'D BETTER DO IT AS-- SPIDER-MAN.
NOW, I'LL JUST CLIMB DOWN THE WALL, AND-- WHOOPS!
THAT'S MR. OSBORN DOWN BELOW --HEADING FOR THE SAME PLACE.
IT'S ALL COMING BACK TO ME.
I'M STARTING TO REMEMBER.
IN MY POCKET-- I HAVE A KEY--
I KNOW IT'LL FIT-- THE DOOR.
HE WENT BACK INTO THE THEATRE.
HE'S HEADING FOR THE ROOM.
AND IF MY HUNCH IS RIGHT, IT MEANS-- BIG TROUBLE!
I DON'T DARE LOSE HIM.
IT'S TOO LATE FOR SECRECY NOW.
HE'S NOWHERE IN THE HALL.
YES, I'M RIGHT! HE LEFT THE DOOR UNLOCKED--
THAT MEANS-- HE'S ALREADY REACHED THE ROOM--AND GONE INSIDE.
SO, NOW I'LL LEARN-- OH NO! I'M TOO LATE!
IT WAS ALWAYS RUMORED HE HAD HIDE-OUTS WHERE HE COULD CHANGE IDENTITIES! BUT--
I DIDN'T THINK-- IT WOULD HAPPEN-- SO FAST--

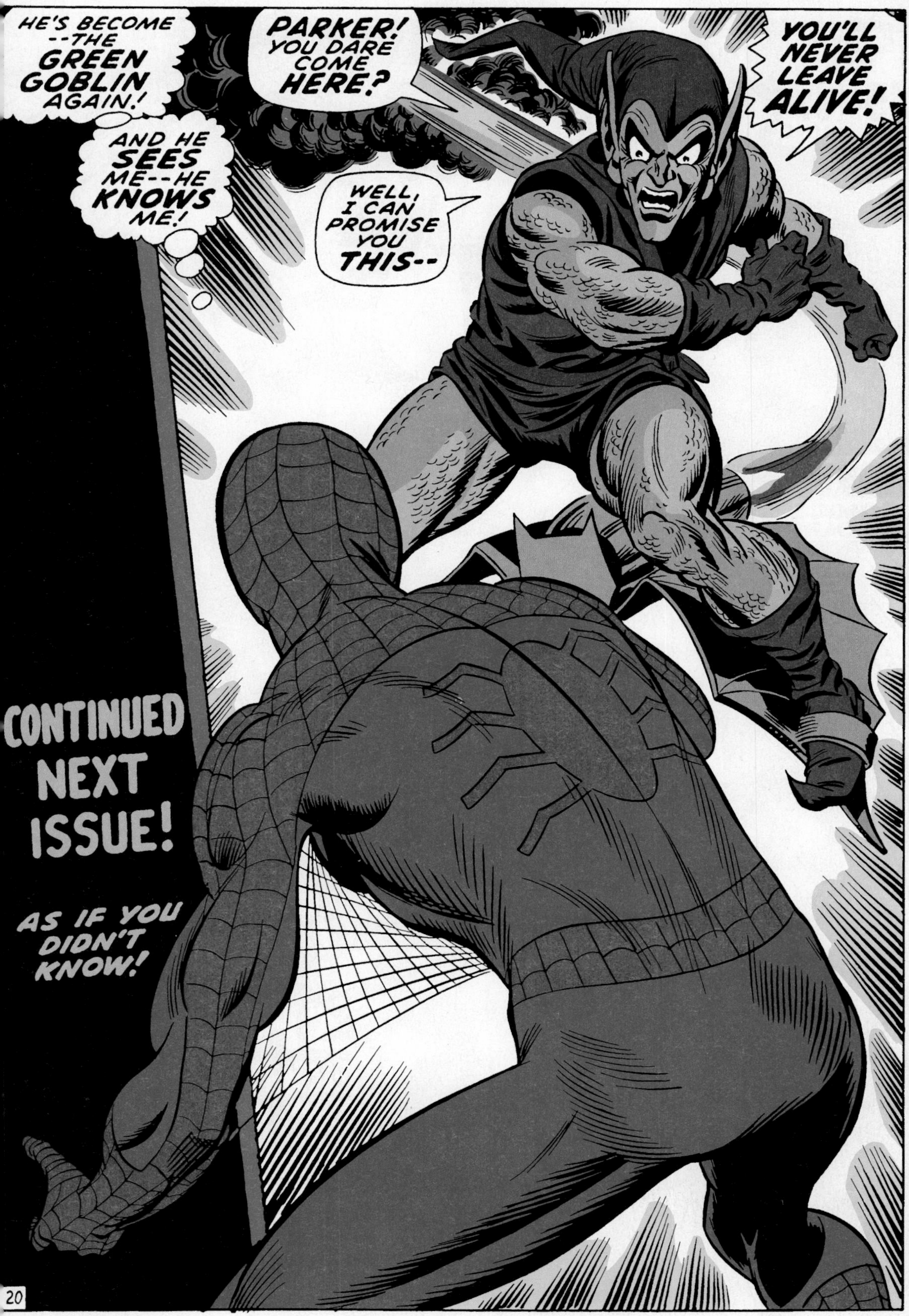
HE'S BECOME --THE GREEN GOBLIN AGAIN!
AND HE SEES ME--HE KNOWS ME!
PARKER! YOU DARE COME HERE?
WELL, I CAN PROMISE YOU THIS--
YOU'LL NEVER LEAVE ALIVE!
CONTINUED NEXT ISSUE!
AS IF YOU DIDN'T KNOW!
20

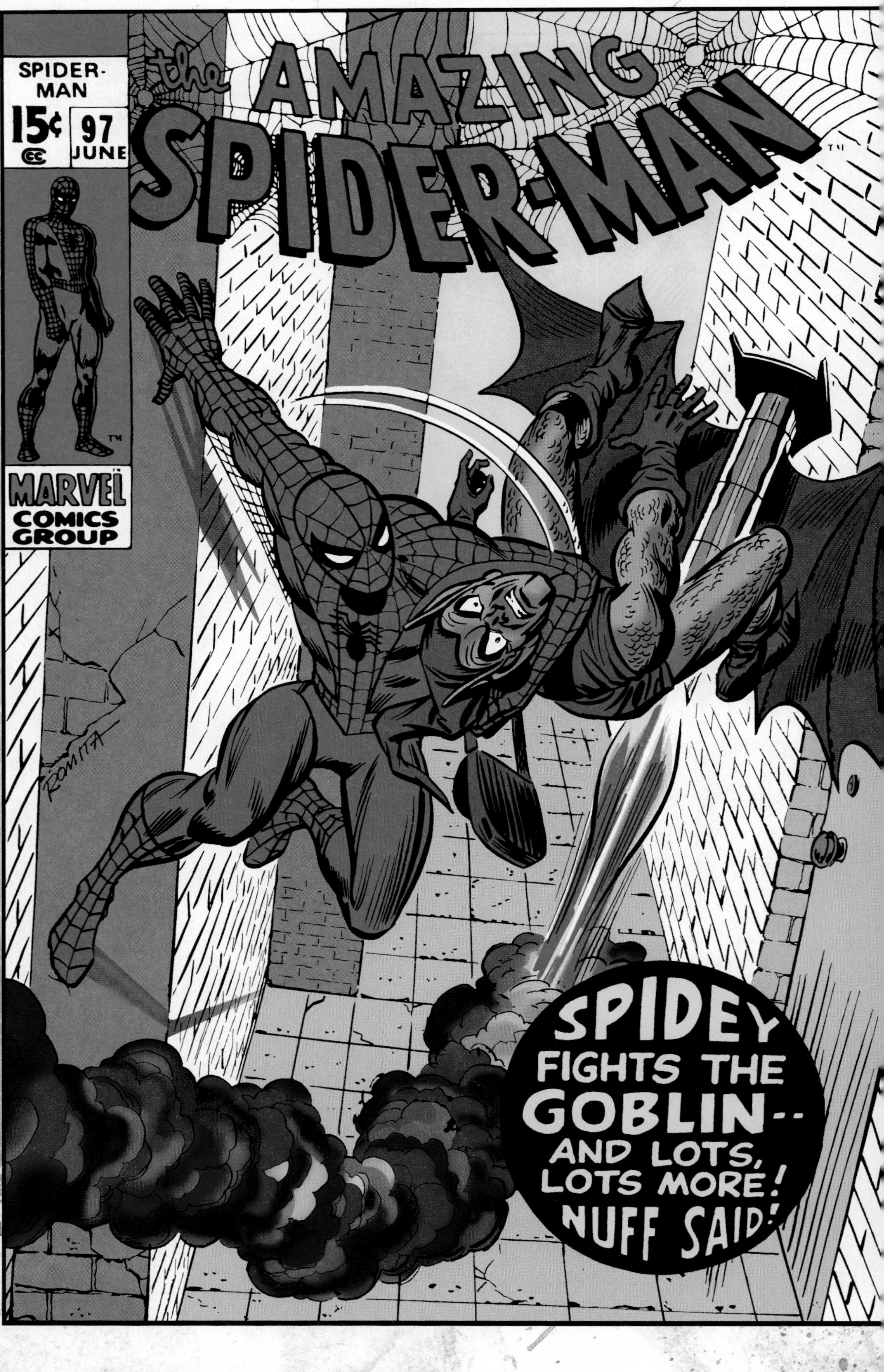
SPIDER-MAN
15¢
97
JUNE
the AMAZING SPIDER-MAN
MARVEL COMICS GROUP
ROMITA
SPIDEY FIGHTS THE GOBLIN-- AND LOTS, LOTS MORE! NUFF SAID!

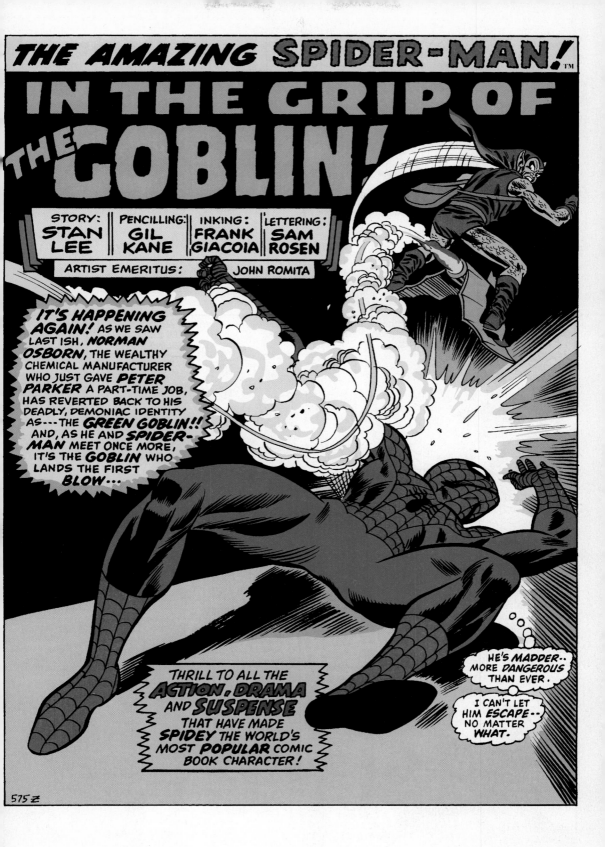

THE AMAZING SPIDER-MAN! ™

IN THE GRIP OF THE GOBLIN!

STORY: STAN LEE | PENCILLING: GIL KANE | INKING: FRANK GIACOIA | LETTERING: SAM ROSEN

ARTIST EMERITUS: JOHN ROMITA

IT'S HAPPENING AGAIN! AS WE SAW LAST ISH, *NORMAN OSBORN,* THE WEALTHY CHEMICAL MANUFACTURER WHO JUST GAVE *PETER PARKER* A PART-TIME JOB, HAS REVERTED BACK TO HIS DEADLY, DEMONIAC IDENTITY AS --- THE *GREEN GOBLIN!!* AND, AS HE AND *SPIDER-MAN* MEET ONCE MORE, IT'S THE *GOBLIN* WHO LANDS THE FIRST *BLOW...*

THRILL TO ALL THE *ACTION, DRAMA* AND *SUSPENSE* THAT HAVE MADE *SPIDEY* THE WORLD'S MOST *POPULAR* COMIC BOOK CHARACTER!

HE'S *MADDER..* MORE *DANGEROUS* THAN EVER.

I CAN'T LET HIM *ESCAPE--* NO MATTER *WHAT.*

575 z

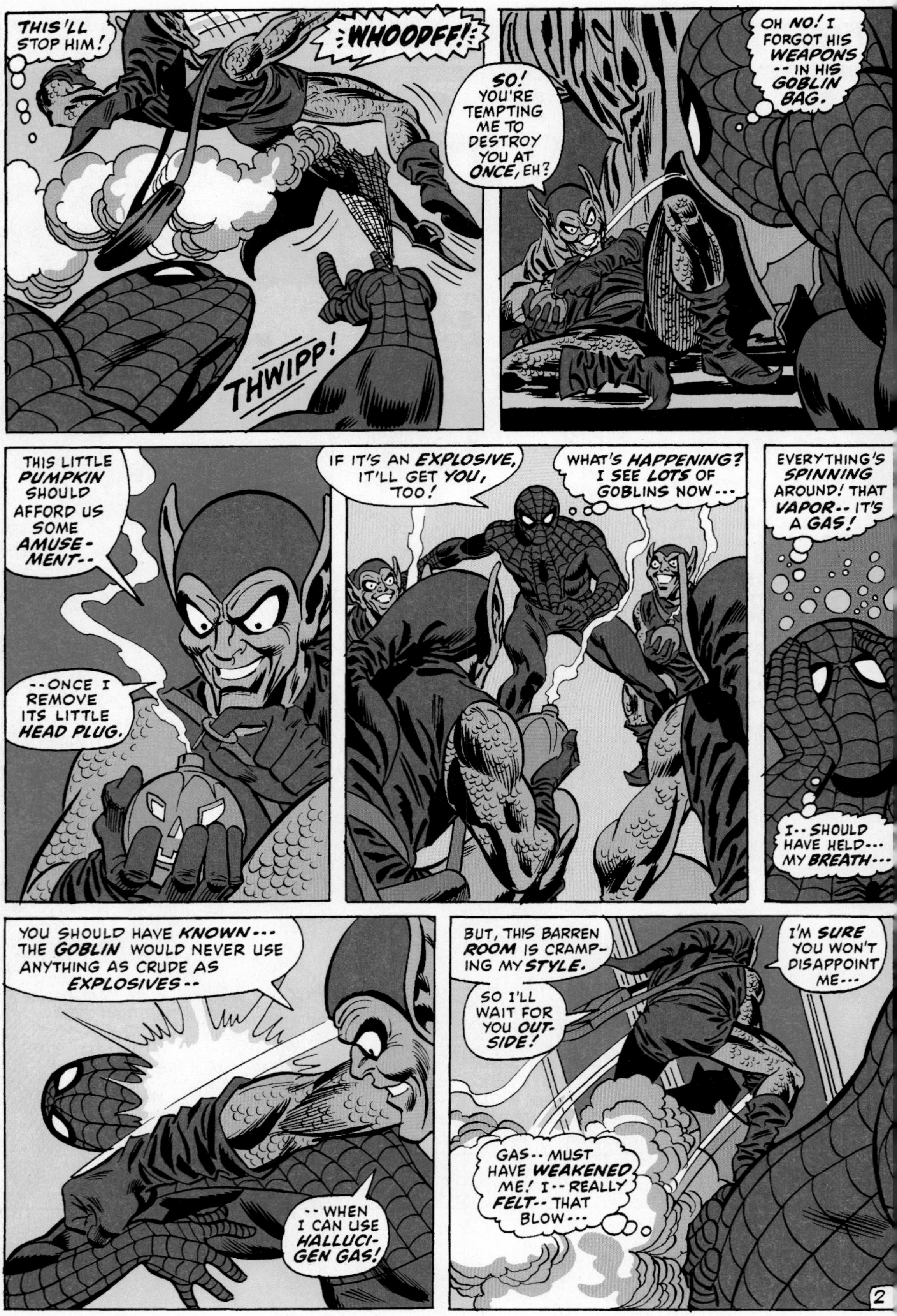
THIS'LL STOP HIM!
WHOODFF!
THWIPP!
SO! YOU'RE TEMPTING ME TO DESTROY YOU AT ONCE, EH?
OH NO! I FORGOT HIS WEAPONS -- IN HIS GOBLIN BAG.
THIS LITTLE PUMPKIN SHOULD AFFORD US SOME AMUSE-MENT--
--ONCE I REMOVE ITS LITTLE HEAD PLUG.
IF IT'S AN EXPLOSIVE, IT'LL GET YOU, TOO!
WHAT'S HAPPENING? I SEE LOTS OF GOBLINS NOW---
EVERYTHING'S SPINNING AROUND! THAT VAPOR-- IT'S A GAS!
I-- SHOULD HAVE HELD--- MY BREATH---
YOU SHOULD HAVE KNOWN--- THE GOBLIN WOULD NEVER USE ANYTHING AS CRUDE AS EXPLOSIVES--
--WHEN I CAN USE HALLUCI-GEN GAS!
BUT, THIS BARREN ROOM IS CRAMP-ING MY STYLE.
SO I'LL WAIT FOR YOU OUT-SIDE!
I'M SURE YOU WON'T DISAPPOINT ME---
GAS-- MUST HAVE WEAKENED ME! I-- REALLY FELT-- THAT BLOW---
2

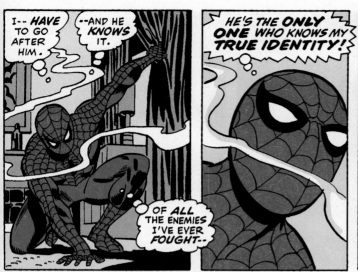

I-- HAVE TO GO AFTER HIM.

--AND HE KNOWS IT.

OF *ALL* THE ENEMIES I'VE EVER FOUGHT--

HE'S THE *ONLY* ONE WHO KNOWS MY *TRUE IDENTITY!*

MAYBE I CAN TAKE HIM BY *SURPRISE*--

--BY COMING AT HIM FROM *ABOVE*--- ALONG THE *WALL.*

THAK!

FOOL! YOU RECKONED WITHOUT MY *GOBLIN BOOMERANG.*

BUT THAT'S ONLY THE *BEGINNING.*

DON'T KEEP ME *WAITING!* THERE'S LOTS *MORE!*

HE'S-- *AWAYS* ONE JUMP *AHEAD* OF ME.

HE'S FOUGHT ME SO *OFTEN*--- IN THE PAST-- HE CAN ALMOST *ANTICIPATE* MY EVERY MOVE.

BUT, I'VE GOT TO KEEP *AFTER* HIM.

I'VE GOT TO *OUT-GUESS* HIM-- SOME-HOW!

LET'S GO, PARKER. I DON'T LIKE TO BE KEPT *WAITING.*

HE'S TAUNTING ME-- USING MY *NAME,* TO KEEP ME UP-TIGHT.

NOW I SEE HIM -- NEAR THAT *ROOF,* ABOVE.

3.

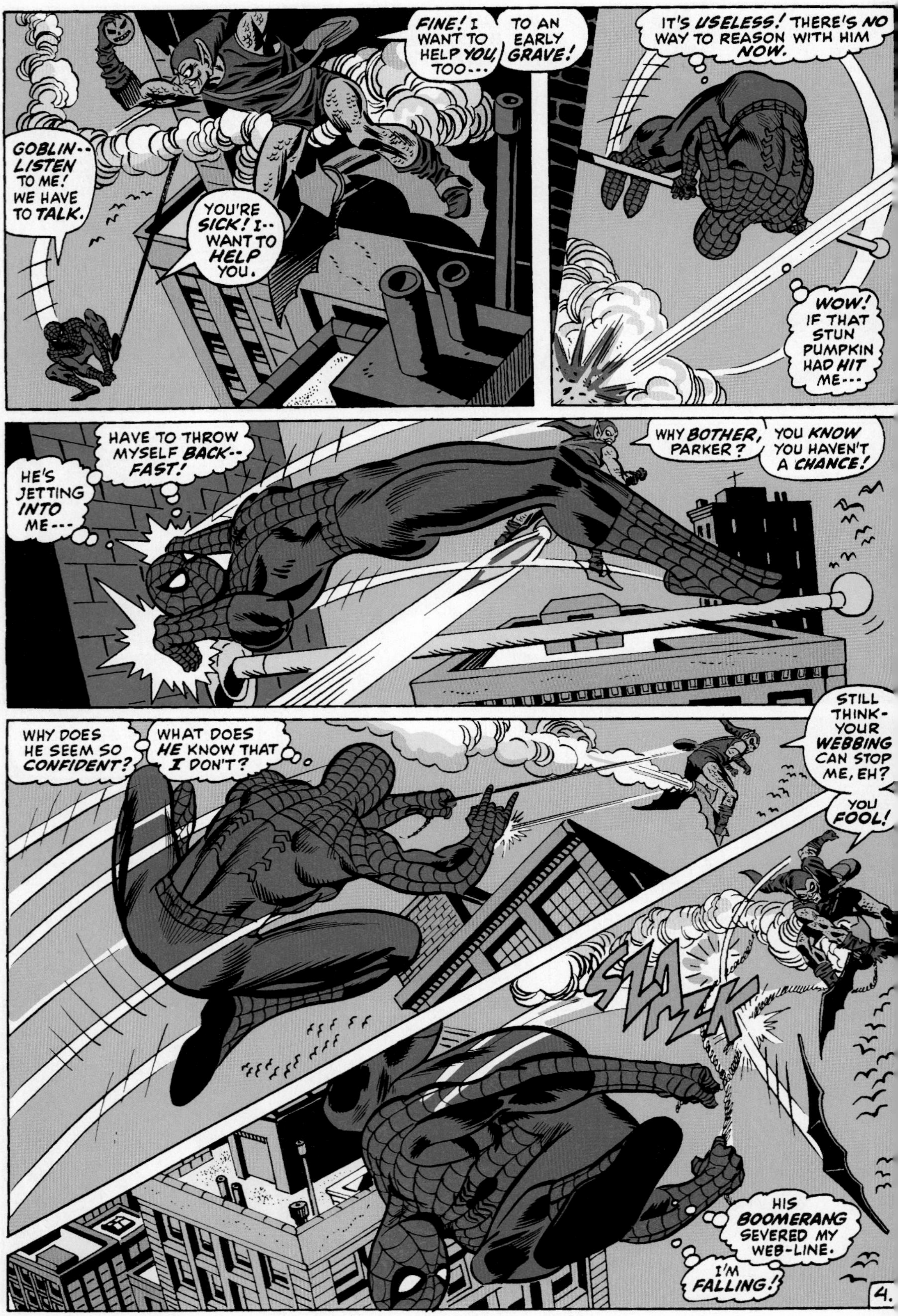
FINE! I WANT TO HELP YOU, TOO...
TO AN EARLY GRAVE!
GOBLIN-- LISTEN TO ME! WE HAVE TO TALK.
YOU'RE SICK! I-- WANT TO HELP YOU.
IT'S USELESS! THERE'S NO WAY TO REASON WITH HIM NOW.
WOW! IF THAT STUN PUMPKIN HAD HIT ME...
HAVE TO THROW MYSELF BACK-- FAST!
HE'S JETTING INTO ME...
WHY BOTHER, PARKER?
YOU KNOW YOU HAVEN'T A CHANCE!
WHY DOES HE SEEM SO CONFIDENT?
WHAT DOES HE KNOW THAT I DON'T?
STILL THINK-YOUR WEBBING CAN STOP ME, EH?
YOU FOOL!
SLAK
HIS BOOMERANG SEVERED MY WEB-LINE.
I'M FALLING!
4.

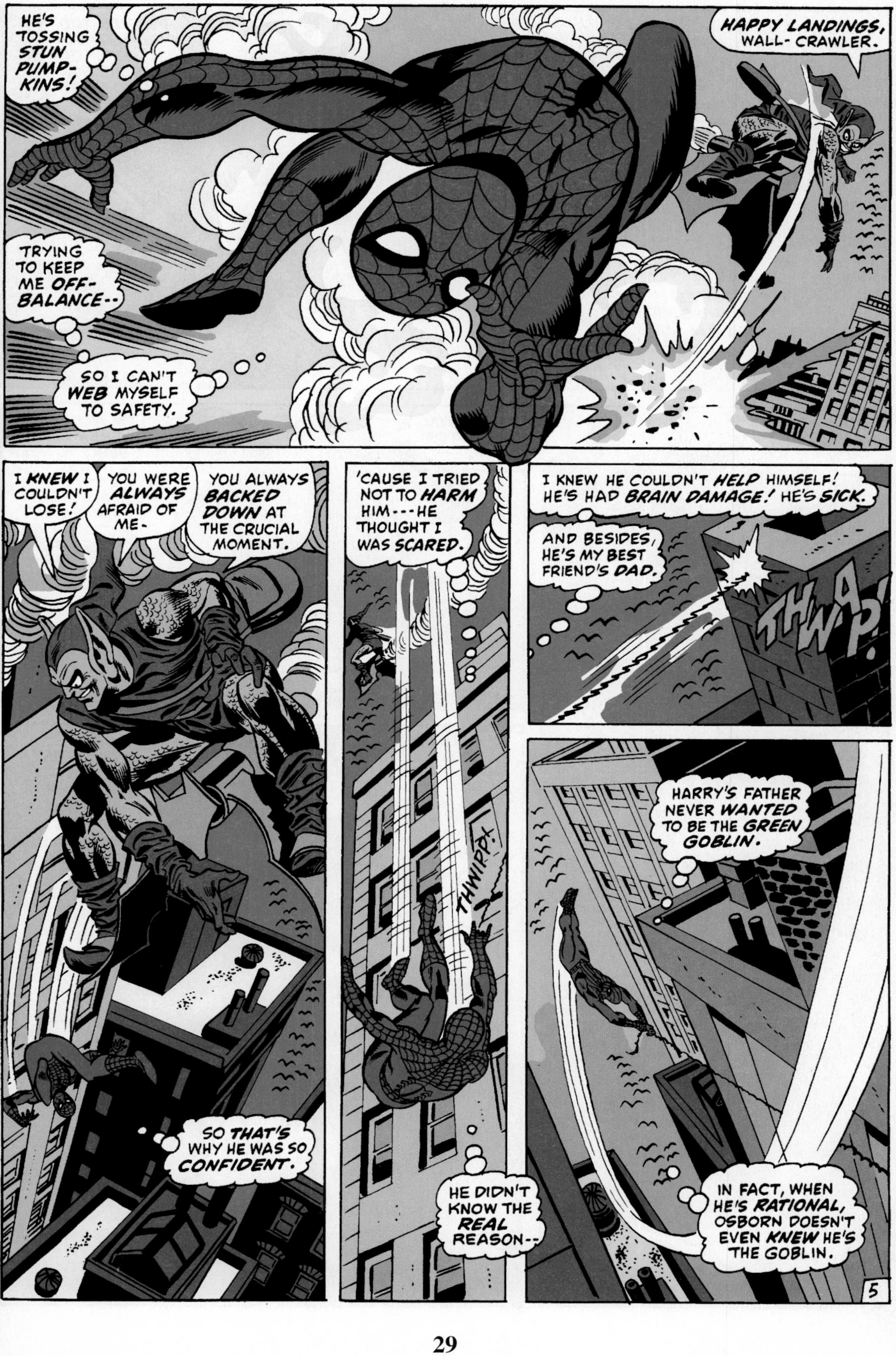
HE'S TOSSING STUN PUMPKINS!
TRYING TO KEEP ME OFF-BALANCE--
SO I CAN'T WEB MYSELF TO SAFETY.
HAPPY LANDINGS, WALL-CRAWLER.
I KNEW I COULDN'T LOSE!
YOU WERE ALWAYS AFRAID OF ME-
YOU ALWAYS BACKED DOWN AT THE CRUCIAL MOMENT.
SO THAT'S WHY HE WAS SO CONFIDENT.
'CAUSE I TRIED NOT TO HARM HIM---HE THOUGHT I WAS SCARED.
THWIPP!
HE DIDN'T KNOW THE REAL REASON--
I KNEW HE COULDN'T HELP HIMSELF! HE'S HAD BRAIN DAMAGE! HE'S SICK.
AND BESIDES, HE'S MY BEST FRIEND'S DAD.
THWAP!
HARRY'S FATHER NEVER WANTED TO BE THE GREEN GOBLIN.
IN FACT, WHEN HE'S RATIONAL, OSBORN DOESN'T EVEN KNEW HE'S THE GOBLIN.
5

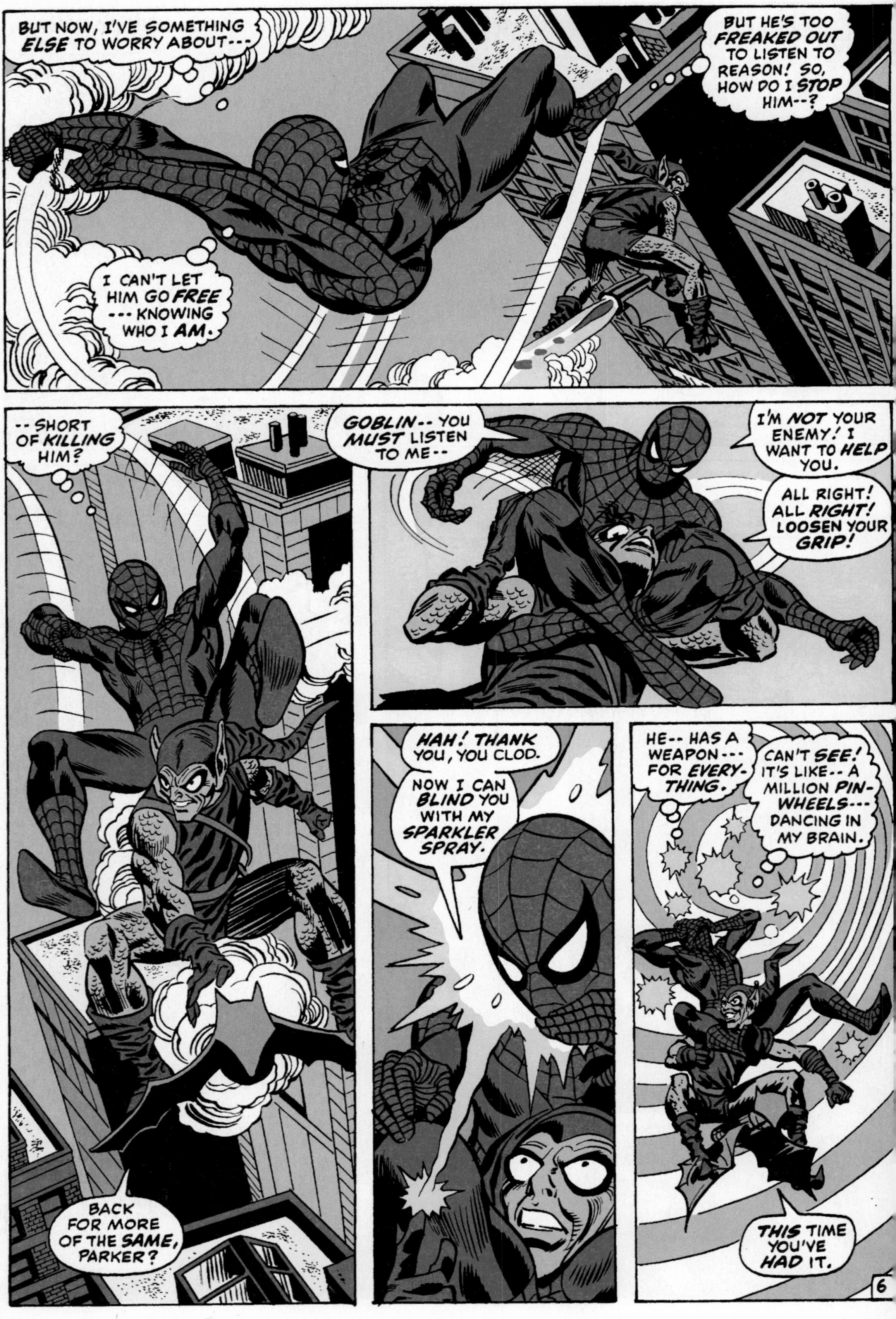
BUT NOW, I'VE SOMETHING ELSE TO WORRY ABOUT---
BUT HE'S TOO FREAKED OUT TO LISTEN TO REASON! SO, HOW DO I STOP HIM--?
I CAN'T LET HIM GO FREE --- KNOWING WHO I AM.
--SHORT OF KILLING HIM?
BACK FOR MORE OF THE SAME, PARKER?
GOBLIN-- YOU MUST LISTEN TO ME--
I'M NOT YOUR ENEMY! I WANT TO HELP YOU.
ALL RIGHT! ALL RIGHT! LOOSEN YOUR GRIP!
HAH! THANK YOU, YOU CLOD.
NOW I CAN BLIND YOU WITH MY SPARKLER SPRAY.
HE-- HAS A WEAPON--- FOR EVERY-THING.
CAN'T SEE! IT'S LIKE-- A MILLION PIN-WHEELS--- DANCING IN MY BRAIN.
THIS TIME YOU'VE HAD IT.
6

CAN'T FOCUS MY *THOUGHTS.*

WHERE *AM I?* WHAT--

I-- CAUGHT ON TO SOMETHING--

IT'S A *LEDGE!* IT STOPPED MY *FALL!*

I'LL *STAY* HERE-- TILL MY *HEAD* CLEARS.

THE DIZZINESS IS *FADING* NOW.

HE'S *GONE!* MUST HAVE FALLEN TO HIS *DEATH!* AND GOOD *RIDDANCE.*

HIS *ACCURSED* GRIP ALMOST *FINISHED* ME JUST THEN.

BUT NOW I'M FREE TO FOLLOW MY *DESTINY!*

WITH *SPIDER-MAN* BEATEN, THE GOBLIN IS *SUPREME.*

HE'S TOO *FAR* AWAY-- CAN'T REACH HIM WITH MY *WEBBING.*

AND HE'S TRAVELING TOO *FAST* FOR ME TO *CATCH* HIM.

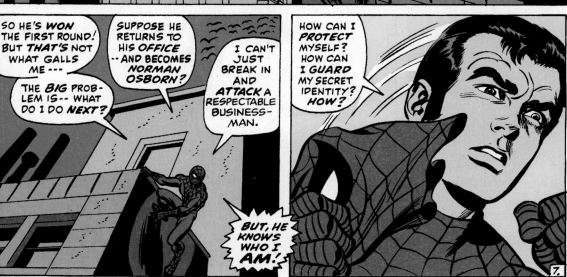

SO HE'S *WON* THE FIRST ROUND! BUT *THAT'S* NOT WHAT GALLS ME ---

THE *BIG* PROBLEM IS-- WHAT DO I DO *NEXT?*

SUPPOSE HE RETURNS TO HIS *OFFICE* -- AND BECOMES *NORMAN OSBORN?*

I CAN'T JUST BREAK IN AND *ATTACK* A RESPECTABLE BUSINESS-MAN.

HOW CAN I *PROTECT* MYSELF? HOW CAN I *GUARD* MY SECRET IDENTITY? *HOW?*

BUT, HE KNOWS WHO I *AM!*

7.

31

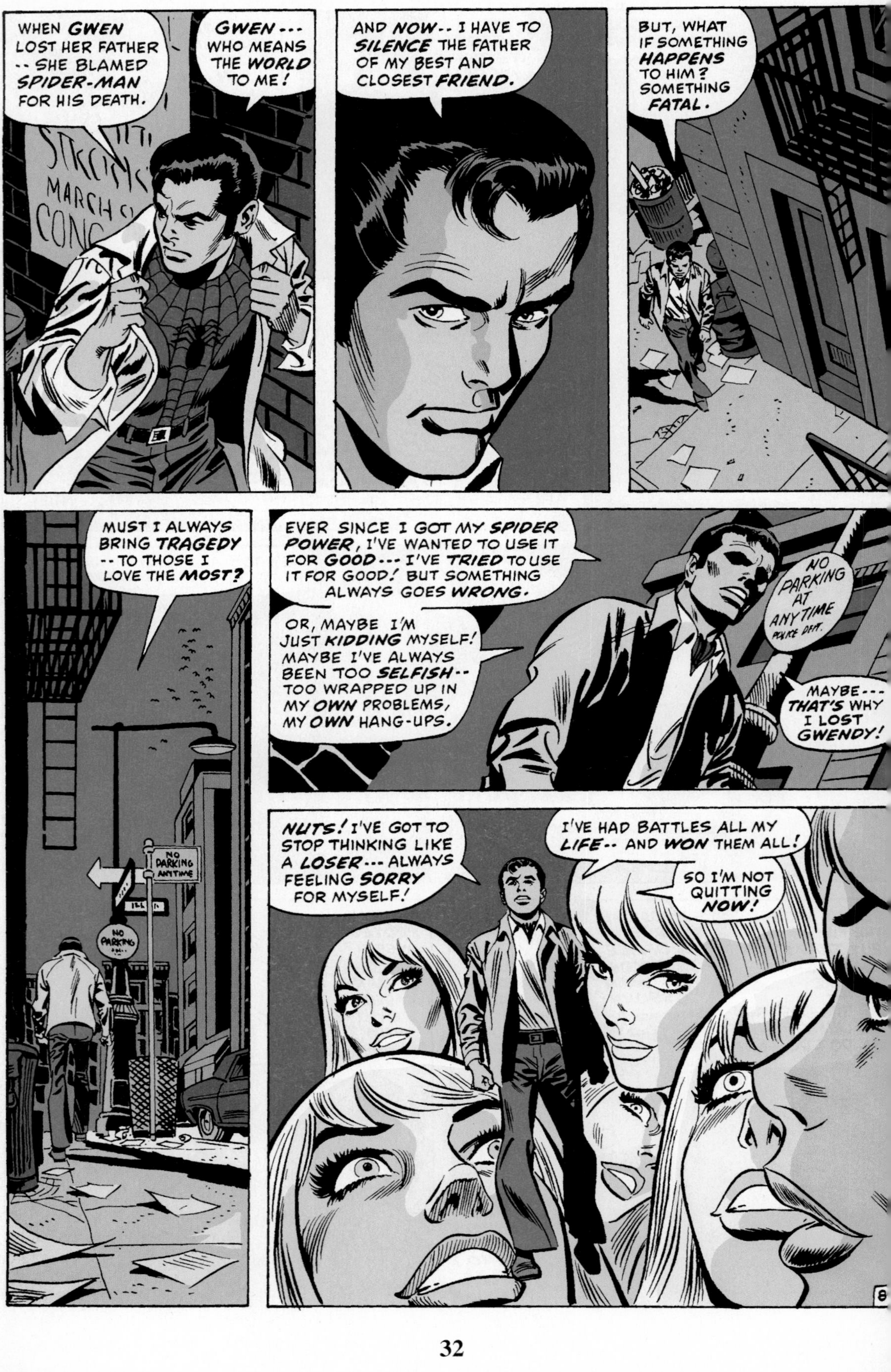

WHEN GWEN LOST HER FATHER -- SHE BLAMED SPIDER-MAN FOR HIS DEATH.
GWEN --- WHO MEANS THE WORLD TO ME!
AND NOW -- I HAVE TO SILENCE THE FATHER OF MY BEST AND CLOSEST FRIEND.
BUT, WHAT IF SOMETHING HAPPENS TO HIM? SOMETHING FATAL.
MUST I ALWAYS BRING TRAGEDY -- TO THOSE I LOVE THE MOST?
NO PARKING ANYTIME
NO PARKING
EVER SINCE I GOT MY SPIDER POWER, I'VE WANTED TO USE IT FOR GOOD --- I'VE TRIED TO USE IT FOR GOOD! BUT SOMETHING ALWAYS GOES WRONG.
OR, MAYBE I'M JUST KIDDING MYSELF! MAYBE I'VE ALWAYS BEEN TOO SELFISH -- TOO WRAPPED UP IN MY OWN PROBLEMS, MY OWN HANG-UPS.
NO PARKING AT ANYTIME POLICE DEPT.
MAYBE --- THAT'S WHY I LOST GWENDY!
NUTS! I'VE GOT TO STOP THINKING LIKE A LOSER --- ALWAYS FEELING SORRY FOR MYSELF!
I'VE HAD BATTLES ALL MY LIFE -- AND WON THEM ALL!
SO I'M NOT QUITTING NOW!
8

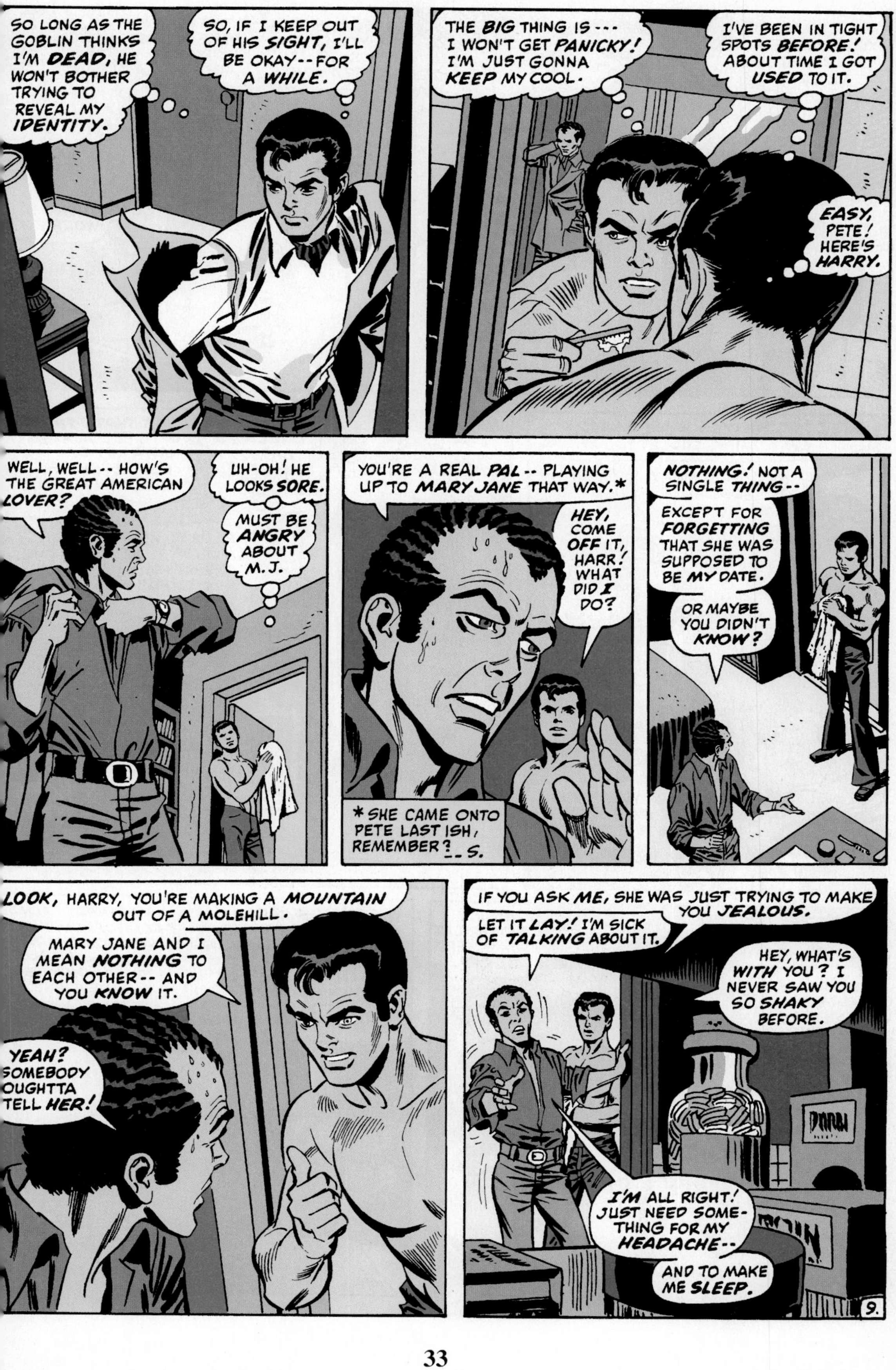
SO LONG AS THE GOBLIN THINKS I'M DEAD, HE WON'T BOTHER TRYING TO REVEAL MY IDENTITY.
SO, IF I KEEP OUT OF HIS SIGHT, I'LL BE OKAY--FOR A WHILE.
THE BIG THING IS--- I WON'T GET PANICKY! I'M JUST GONNA KEEP MY COOL.
I'VE BEEN IN TIGHT SPOTS BEFORE! ABOUT TIME I GOT USED TO IT.
EASY, PETE! HERE'S HARRY.
WELL, WELL-- HOW'S THE GREAT AMERICAN LOVER?
UH-OH! HE LOOKS SORE.
MUST BE ANGRY ABOUT M.J.
YOU'RE A REAL PAL-- PLAYING UP TO MARY JANE THAT WAY.*
HEY, COME OFF IT, HARR! WHAT DID I DO?
* SHE CAME ONTO PETE LAST ISH, REMEMBER? --S.
NOTHING! NOT A SINGLE THING--
EXCEPT FOR FORGETTING THAT SHE WAS SUPPOSED TO BE MY DATE.
OR MAYBE YOU DIDN'T KNOW?
LOOK, HARRY, YOU'RE MAKING A MOUNTAIN OUT OF A MOLEHILL.
MARY JANE AND I MEAN NOTHING TO EACH OTHER-- AND YOU KNOW IT.
YEAH? SOMEBODY OUGHTTA TELL HER!
IF YOU ASK ME, SHE WAS JUST TRYING TO MAKE YOU JEALOUS.
LET IT LAY! I'M SICK OF TALKING ABOUT IT.
HEY, WHAT'S WITH YOU? I NEVER SAW YOU SO SHAKY BEFORE.
I'M ALL RIGHT! JUST NEED SOME-THING FOR MY HEADACHE--
AND TO MAKE ME SLEEP.
9.

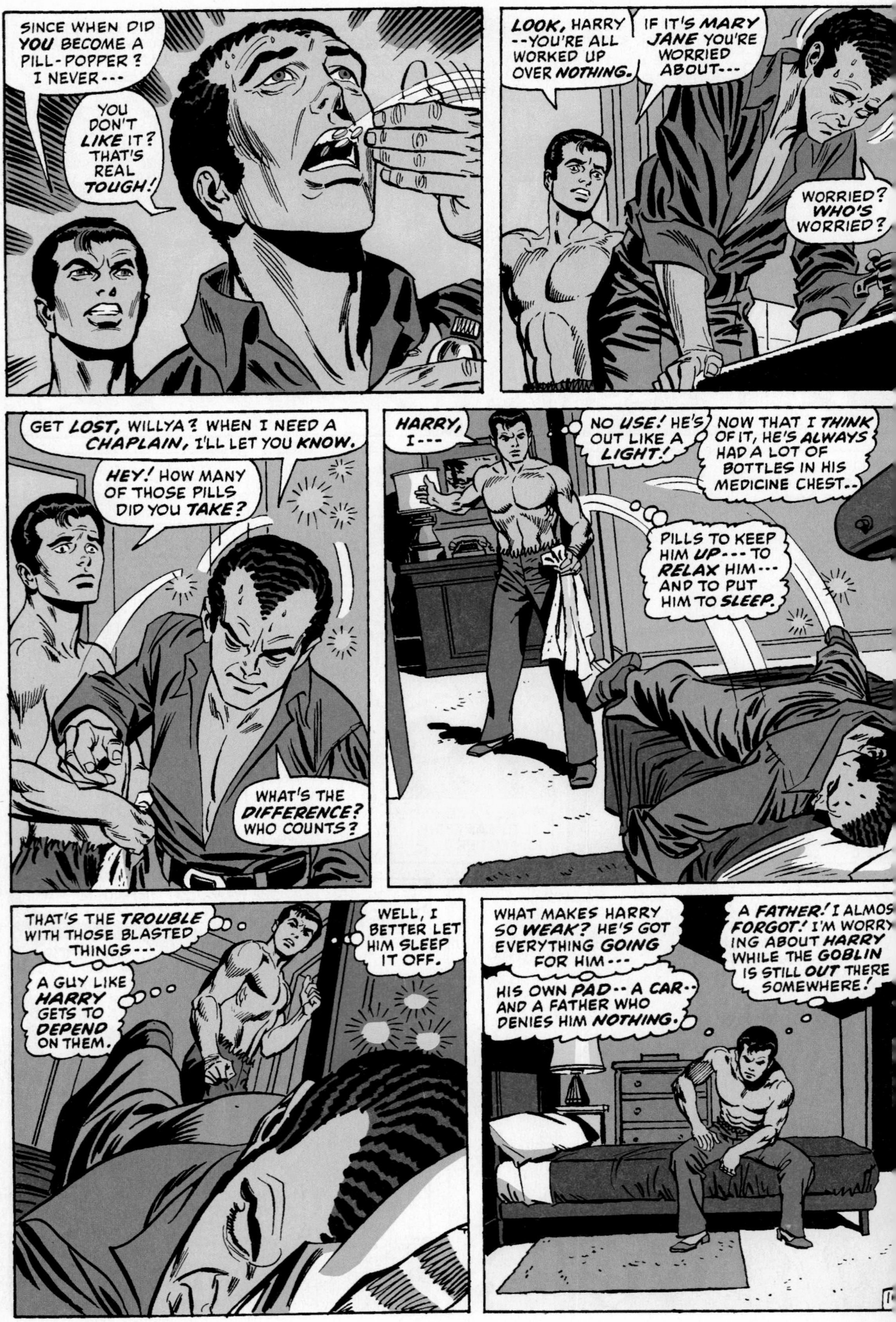
SINCE WHEN DID YOU BECOME A PILL-POPPER? I NEVER---
YOU DON'T LIKE IT? THAT'S REAL TOUGH!
LOOK, HARRY --YOU'RE ALL WORKED UP OVER NOTHING.
IF IT'S MARY JANE YOU'RE WORRIED ABOUT---
WORRIED? WHO'S WORRIED?
GET LOST, WILLYA? WHEN I NEED A CHAPLAIN, I'LL LET YOU KNOW.
HEY! HOW MANY OF THOSE PILLS DID YOU TAKE?
WHAT'S THE DIFFERENCE? WHO COUNTS?
HARRY, I---
NO USE! HE'S OUT LIKE A LIGHT!
NOW THAT I THINK OF IT, HE'S ALWAYS HAD A LOT OF BOTTLES IN HIS MEDICINE CHEST..
PILLS TO KEEP HIM UP---TO RELAX HIM---AND TO PUT HIM TO SLEEP.
THAT'S THE TROUBLE WITH THOSE BLASTED THINGS---
A GUY LIKE HARRY GETS TO DEPEND ON THEM.
WELL, I BETTER LET HIM SLEEP IT OFF.
WHAT MAKES HARRY SO WEAK? HE'S GOT EVERYTHING GOING FOR HIM---
HIS OWN PAD--A CAR--AND A FATHER WHO DENIES HIM NOTHING.
A FATHER! I ALMOS FORGOT! I'M WORRY ING ABOUT HARRY WHILE THE GOBLIN IS STILL OUT THERE SOMEWHERE!

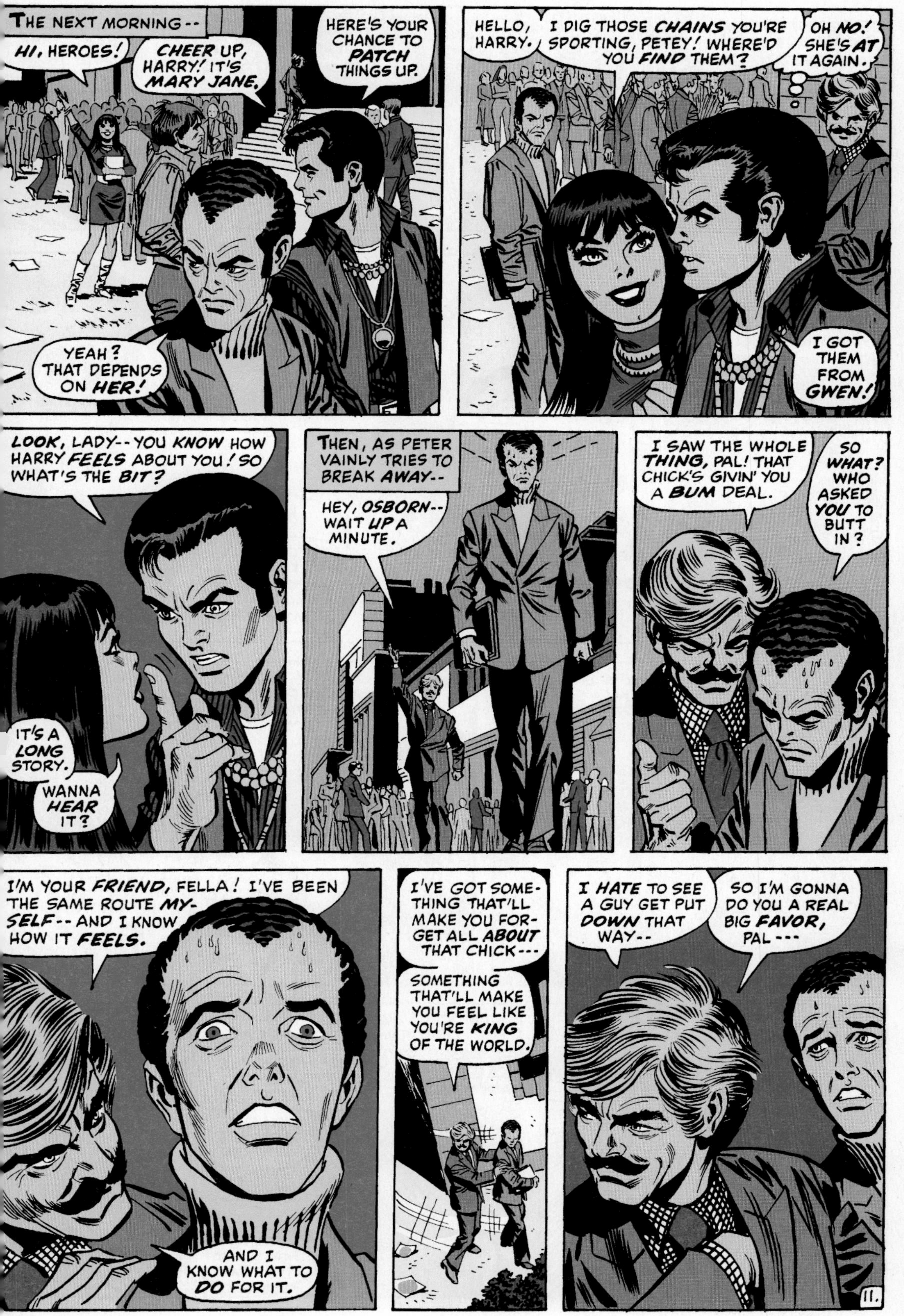
THE NEXT MORNING --
HI, HEROES!
CHEER UP, HARRY! IT'S MARY JANE.
HERE'S YOUR CHANCE TO PATCH THINGS UP.
YEAH? THAT DEPENDS ON HER!
HELLO, HARRY.
I DIG THOSE CHAINS YOU'RE SPORTING, PETEY! WHERE'D YOU FIND THEM?
OH NO! SHE'S AT IT AGAIN.
I GOT THEM FROM GWEN!
LOOK, LADY-- YOU KNOW HOW HARRY FEELS ABOUT YOU! SO WHAT'S THE BIT?
IT'S A LONG STORY.
WANNA HEAR IT?
THEN, AS PETER VAINLY TRIES TO BREAK AWAY--
HEY, OSBORN-- WAIT UP A MINUTE.
I SAW THE WHOLE THING, PAL! THAT CHICK'S GIVIN' YOU A BUM DEAL.
SO WHAT? WHO ASKED YOU TO BUTT IN?
I'M YOUR FRIEND, FELLA! I'VE BEEN THE SAME ROUTE MY-SELF-- AND I KNOW HOW IT FEELS.
AND I KNOW WHAT TO DO FOR IT.
I'VE GOT SOME-THING THAT'LL MAKE YOU FOR-GET ALL ABOUT THAT CHICK---
SOMETHING THAT'LL MAKE YOU FEEL LIKE YOU'RE KING OF THE WORLD.
I HATE TO SEE A GUY GET PUT DOWN THAT WAY--
SO I'M GONNA DO YOU A REAL BIG FAVOR, PAL ---
11.

THIS STUFF IS REAL *NEW*-- AND IT AIN'T EASY TO *COME BY*--

BUT, FOR A GUY WHO CAN *USE* 'EM, LIKE *YOU*...

LEMME *SEE*! WHAT *ARE* THOSE THINGS?

DON'T TAKE *MY* WORD FOR IT, OSBORN! JUST *TRY* A FEW-- AND *NOTHING'S* GONNA BOTHER YOU.

IT'LL BE WORTH *ANYTHING*-- TO GET HER OUT OF MY *MIND*!

12

SURE, KID --*SURE*! I *KNOW* HOW YOU FEEL.

EVERYONE'S GOT A MILLION *HANG-UPS* NOWADAYS.

THAT'S WHY THIS STUFF I GOT IS JUST WHAT THE DOCTOR *ORDERED*.

SO HOW *ABOUT* IT?

OKAY. OKAY.

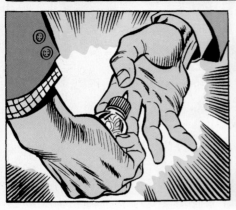

NICE DOING *BUSINESS* WITH YOU, OSBORN! SEE YOU *AGAIN*.

OH *NO*! THIS IS THE *FIRST* TIME-- AND THE *LAST*.

I'M NOT GETTING HOOKED.

YEAH-- THAT'S WHAT THEY *SAY*.

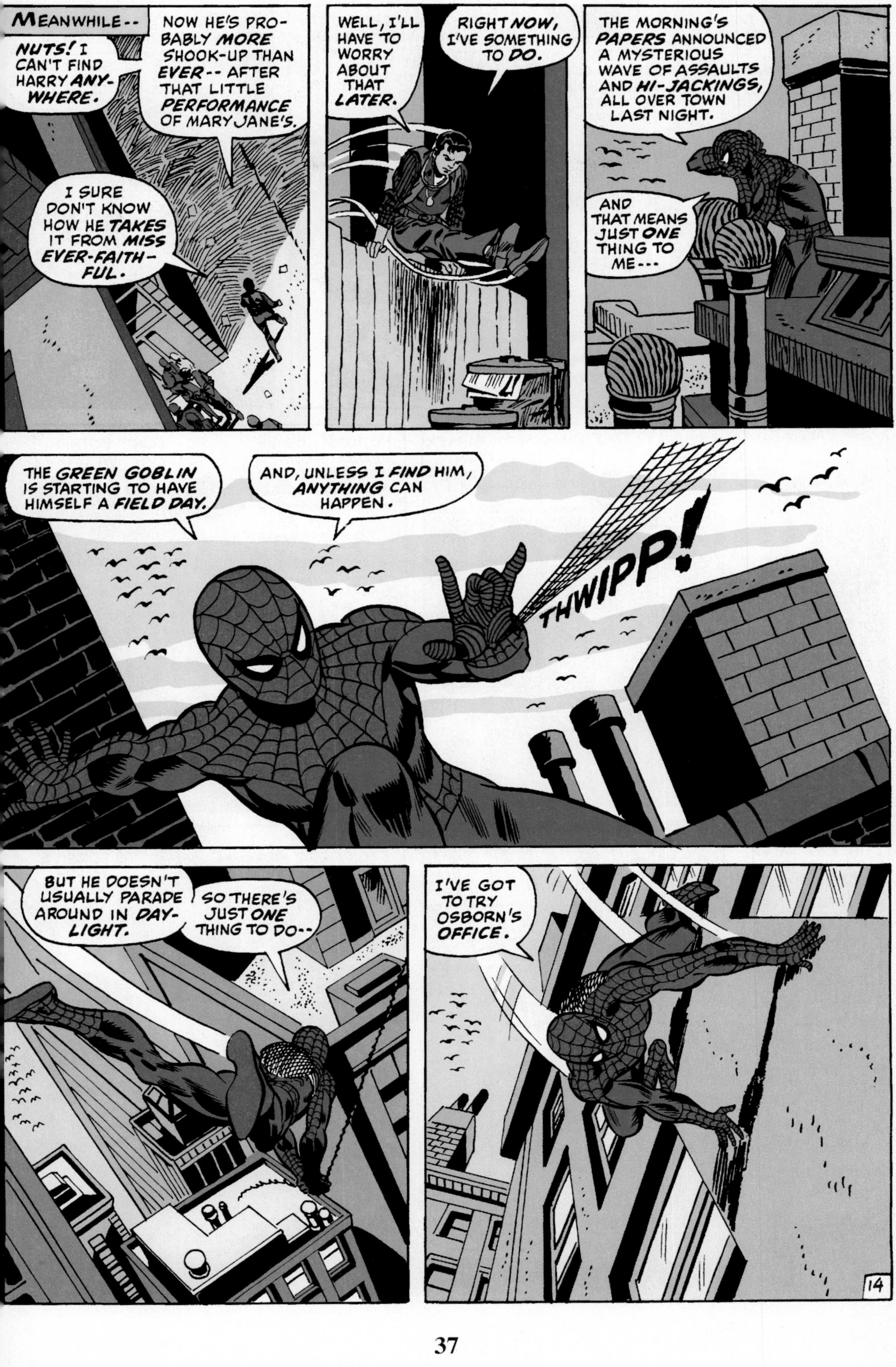
MEANWHILE--
NUTS! I CAN'T FIND HARRY ANYWHERE.
NOW HE'S PROBABLY MORE SHOOK-UP THAN EVER-- AFTER THAT LITTLE PERFORMANCE OF MARY JANE'S.
I SURE DON'T KNOW HOW HE TAKES IT FROM MISS EVER-FAITHFUL.
WELL, I'LL HAVE TO WORRY ABOUT THAT LATER.
RIGHT NOW, I'VE SOMETHING TO DO.
THE MORNING'S PAPERS ANNOUNCED A MYSTERIOUS WAVE OF ASSAULTS AND HI-JACKINGS, ALL OVER TOWN LAST NIGHT.
AND THAT MEANS JUST ONE THING TO ME---
THE GREEN GOBLIN IS STARTING TO HAVE HIMSELF A FIELD DAY.
AND, UNLESS I FIND HIM, ANYTHING CAN HAPPEN.
THWIPP!
BUT HE DOESN'T USUALLY PARADE AROUND IN DAYLIGHT.
SO THERE'S JUST ONE THING TO DO--
I'VE GOT TO TRY OSBORN'S OFFICE.
14

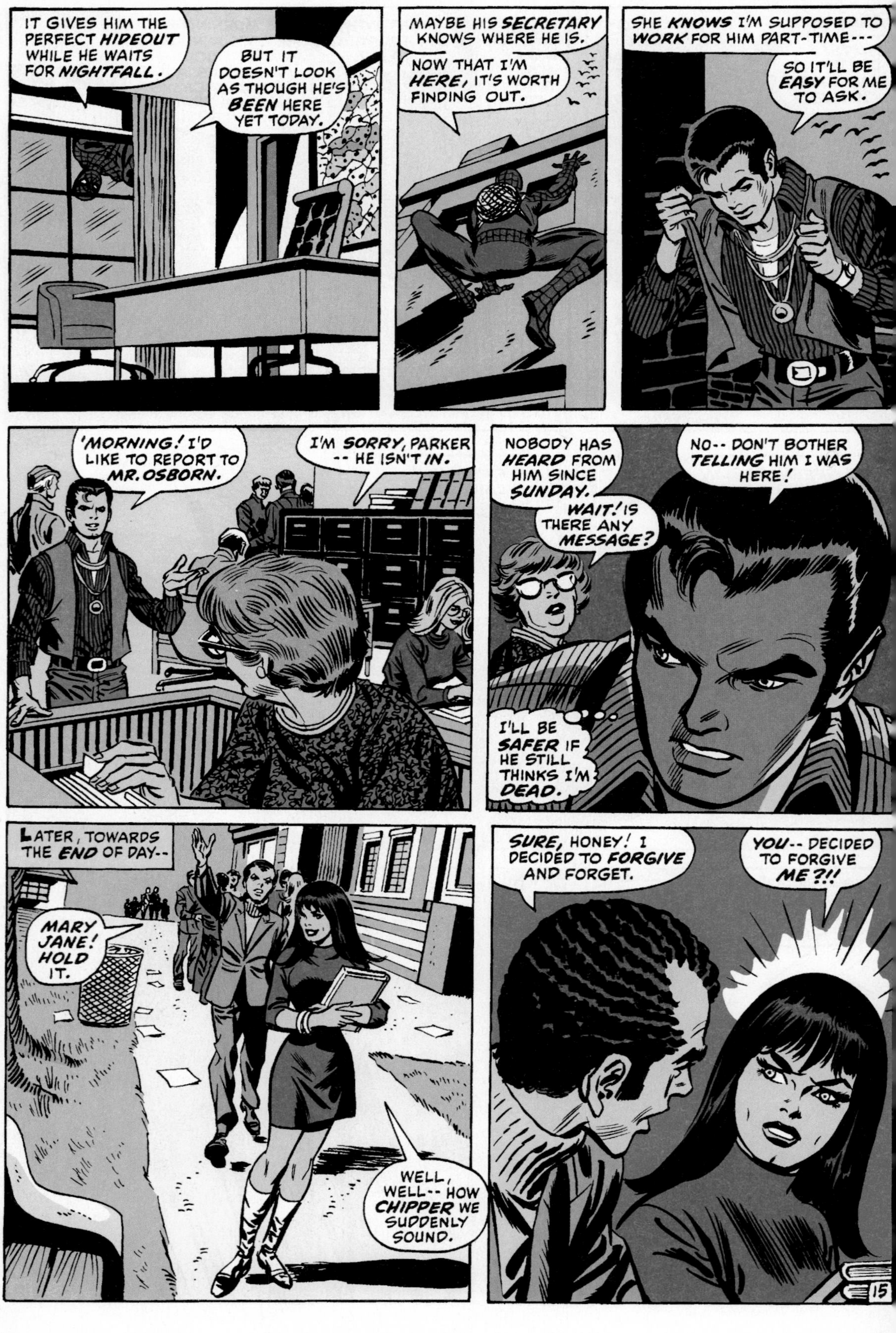
IT GIVES HIM THE PERFECT HIDEOUT WHILE HE WAITS FOR NIGHTFALL.
BUT IT DOESN'T LOOK AS THOUGH HE'S BEEN HERE YET TODAY.
MAYBE HIS SECRETARY KNOWS WHERE HE IS.
NOW THAT I'M HERE, IT'S WORTH FINDING OUT.
SHE KNOWS I'M SUPPOSED TO WORK FOR HIM PART-TIME---
SO IT'LL BE EASY FOR ME TO ASK.
'MORNING! I'D LIKE TO REPORT TO MR. OSBORN.
I'M SORRY, PARKER -- HE ISN'T IN.
NOBODY HAS HEARD FROM HIM SINCE SUNDAY.
WAIT! IS THERE ANY MESSAGE?
NO-- DON'T BOTHER TELLING HIM I WAS HERE!
I'LL BE SAFER IF HE STILL THINKS I'M DEAD.
LATER, TOWARDS THE END OF DAY--
MARY JANE! HOLD IT.
WELL, WELL-- HOW CHIPPER WE SUDDENLY SOUND.
SURE, HONEY! I DECIDED TO FORGIVE AND FORGET.
YOU-- DECIDED TO FORGIVE ME?!!
15

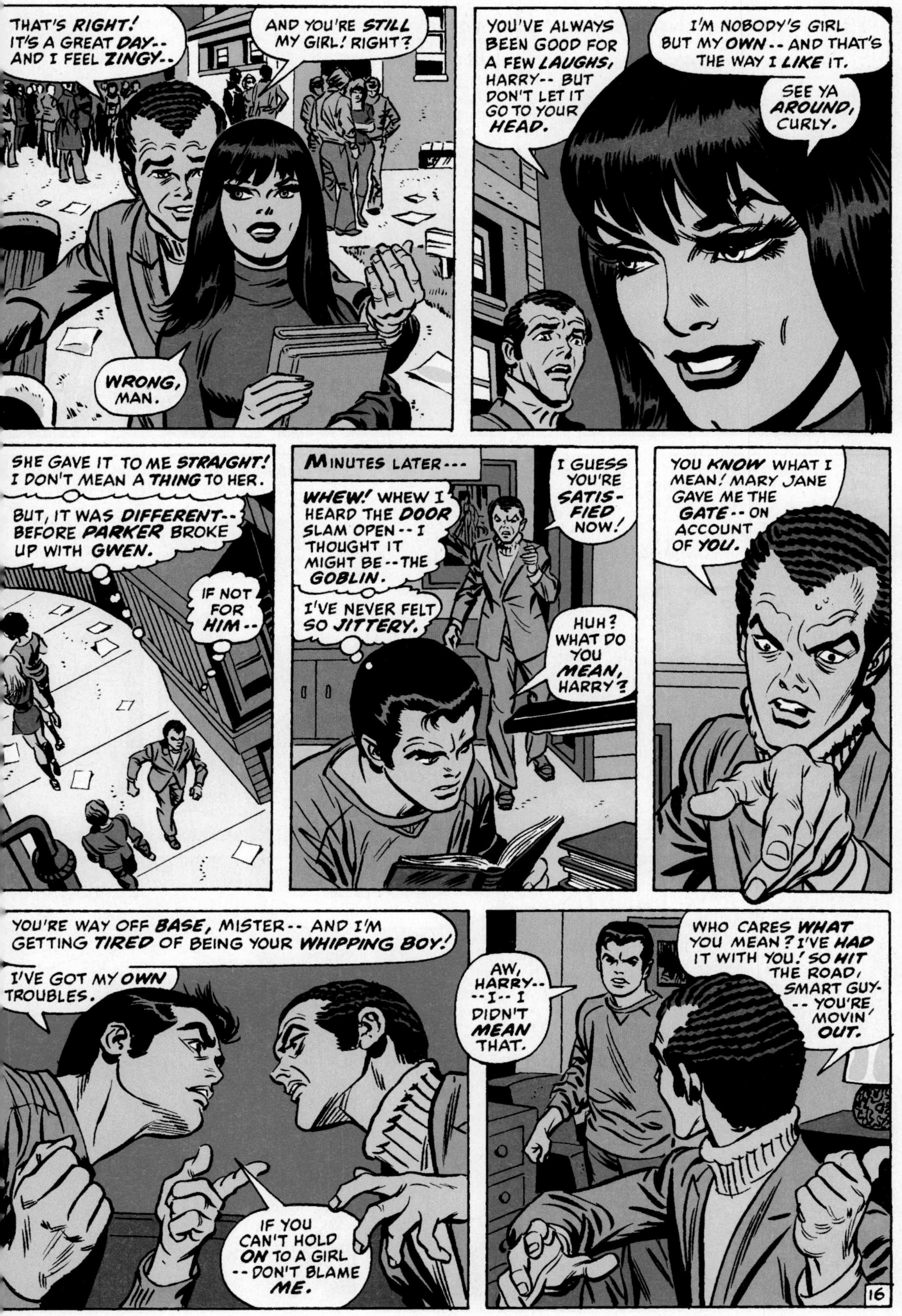
THAT'S RIGHT! IT'S A GREAT DAY.. AND I FEEL ZINGY..
AND YOU'RE STILL MY GIRL! RIGHT?
WRONG, MAN.
YOU'VE ALWAYS BEEN GOOD FOR A FEW LAUGHS, HARRY-- BUT DON'T LET IT GO TO YOUR HEAD.
I'M NOBODY'S GIRL BUT MY OWN.. AND THAT'S THE WAY I LIKE IT.
SEE YA AROUND, CURLY.
SHE GAVE IT TO ME STRAIGHT! I DON'T MEAN A THING TO HER.
BUT, IT WAS DIFFERENT-- BEFORE PARKER BROKE UP WITH GWEN.
IF NOT FOR HIM--
MINUTES LATER---
WHEW! WHEW I HEARD THE DOOR SLAM OPEN -- I THOUGHT IT MIGHT BE --THE GOBLIN.
I'VE NEVER FELT SO JITTERY.
I GUESS YOU'RE SATIS-FIED NOW!
HUH? WHAT DO YOU MEAN, HARRY?
YOU KNOW WHAT I MEAN! MARY JANE GAVE ME THE GATE -- ON ACCOUNT OF YOU.
YOU'RE WAY OFF BASE, MISTER -- AND I'M GETTING TIRED OF BEING YOUR WHIPPING BOY!
I'VE GOT MY OWN TROUBLES.
IF YOU CAN'T HOLD ON TO A GIRL -- DON'T BLAME ME.
AW, HARRY-- --I-- I DIDN'T MEAN THAT.
WHO CARES WHAT YOU MEAN? I'VE HAD IT WITH YOU! SO HIT THE ROAD, SMART GUY- -- YOU'RE MOVIN' OUT.
16

He's not *himself!* I've never *seen* him this way before! Those sudden *highs* and *lows* of his---

He's becoming *irrational*--- but he isn't *aware* of it.

No! It's *not* how I want it! It won't *help* if you move out.

That won't get her *back!*

I don't know *what* I want, Pete.

I never -- *felt* this way.

Okay, Harry-- if that's how you *want* it.

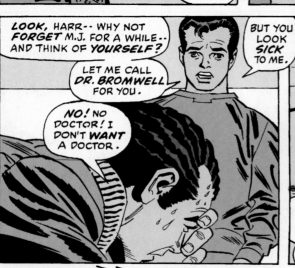

Look, Harr-- why not *forget* M.J. for a while-- and think of *yourself?*

But you look *sick* to me.

Let me call *Dr. Bromwell* for you.

No! No doctor! I don't *want* a doctor.

I'll be okay! I'm just *tired* -- been *studying* too hard -- that's all.

Then I'll take *off* for a while. Try'n get some *rest.*

He's *leaving*-- at last.

Now, as soon as I hear the *door* close--

PTHOCK

That's *it!* He's gone.

Now, where did I put that *bottle?*

Here it is.

This is all I'll need to make me feel on *top* of the world again.

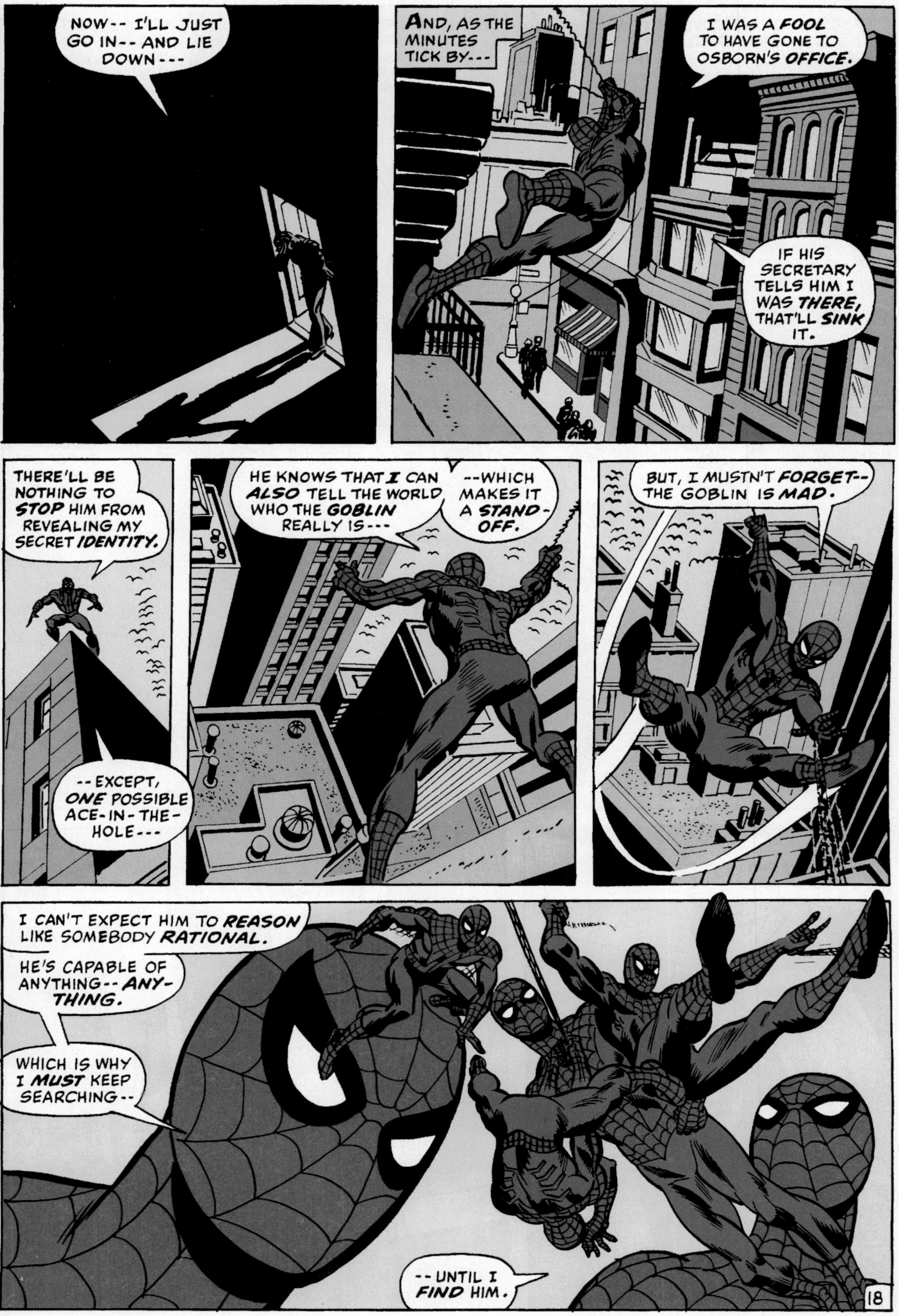
NOW-- I'LL JUST GO IN-- AND LIE DOWN---
AND, AS THE MINUTES TICK BY---
I WAS A FOOL TO HAVE GONE TO OSBORN'S OFFICE.
IF HIS SECRETARY TELLS HIM I WAS THERE, THAT'LL SINK IT.
THERE'LL BE NOTHING TO STOP HIM FROM REVEALING MY SECRET IDENTITY.
--EXCEPT, ONE POSSIBLE ACE-IN-THE-HOLE---
HE KNOWS THAT I CAN ALSO TELL THE WORLD WHO THE GOBLIN REALLY IS---
--WHICH MAKES IT A STAND-OFF.
BUT, I MUSTN'T FORGET-- THE GOBLIN IS MAD.
I CAN'T EXPECT HIM TO REASON LIKE SOMEBODY RATIONAL.
HE'S CAPABLE OF ANYTHING-- ANY-THING.
WHICH IS WHY I MUST KEEP SEARCHING--
--UNTIL I FIND HIM.
18

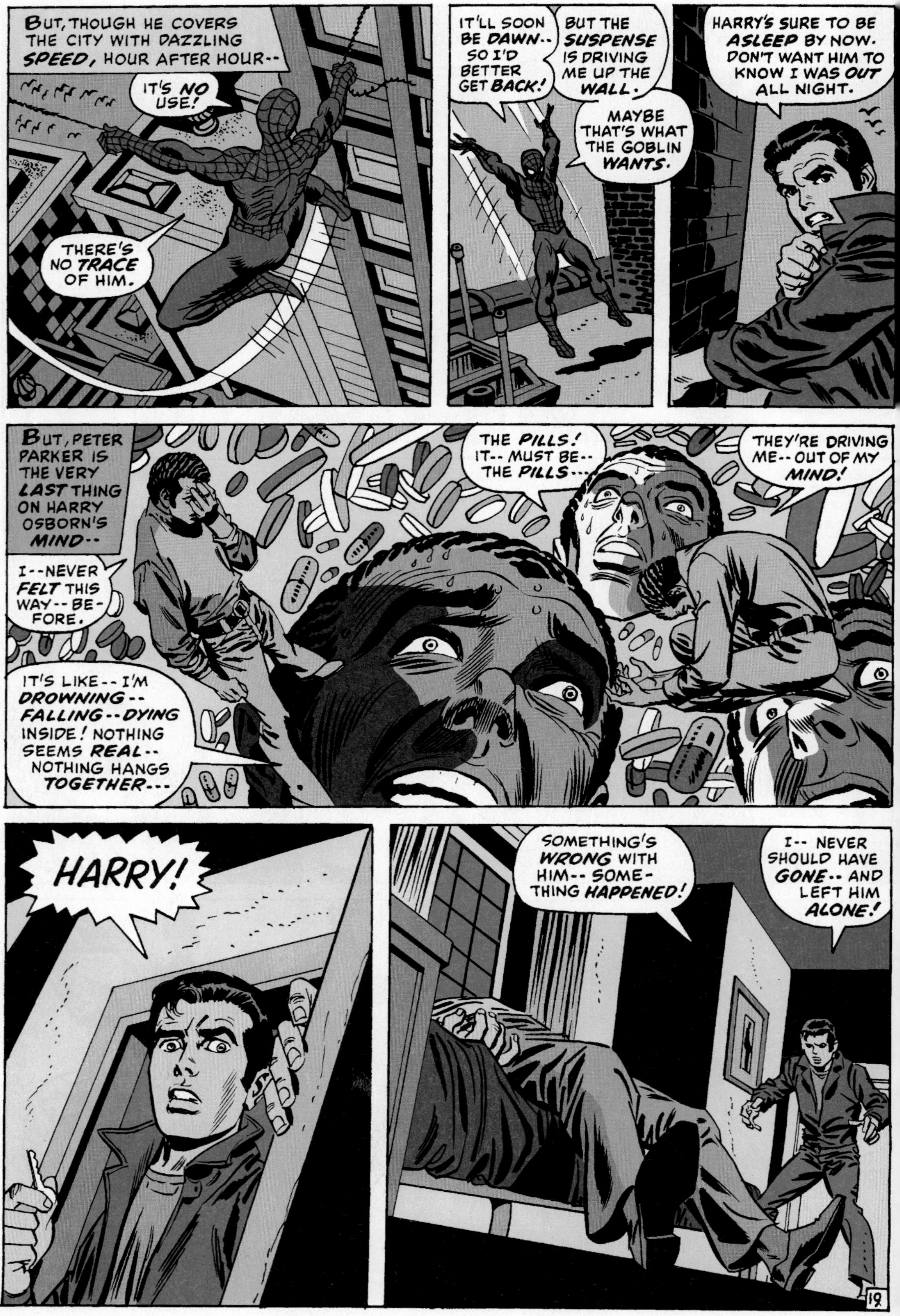
BUT, THOUGH HE COVERS THE CITY WITH DAZZLING SPEED, HOUR AFTER HOUR--
IT'S NO USE!
THERE'S NO TRACE OF HIM.
IT'LL SOON BE DAWN-- SO I'D BETTER GET BACK!
BUT THE SUSPENSE IS DRIVING ME UP THE WALL.
MAYBE THAT'S WHAT THE GOBLIN WANTS.
HARRY'S SURE TO BE ASLEEP BY NOW. DON'T WANT HIM TO KNOW I WAS OUT ALL NIGHT.
BUT, PETER PARKER IS THE VERY LAST THING ON HARRY OSBORN'S MIND--
I--NEVER FELT THIS WAY--BE-FORE.
IT'S LIKE-- I'M DROWNING-- FALLING--DYING INSIDE! NOTHING SEEMS REAL-- NOTHING HANGS TOGETHER---
THE PILLS! IT-- MUST BE-- THE PILLS---
THEY'RE DRIVING ME-- OUT OF MY MIND!
HARRY!
SOMETHING'S WRONG WITH HIM-- SOME-THING HAPPENED!
I-- NEVER SHOULD HAVE GONE-- AND LEFT HIM ALONE!
19

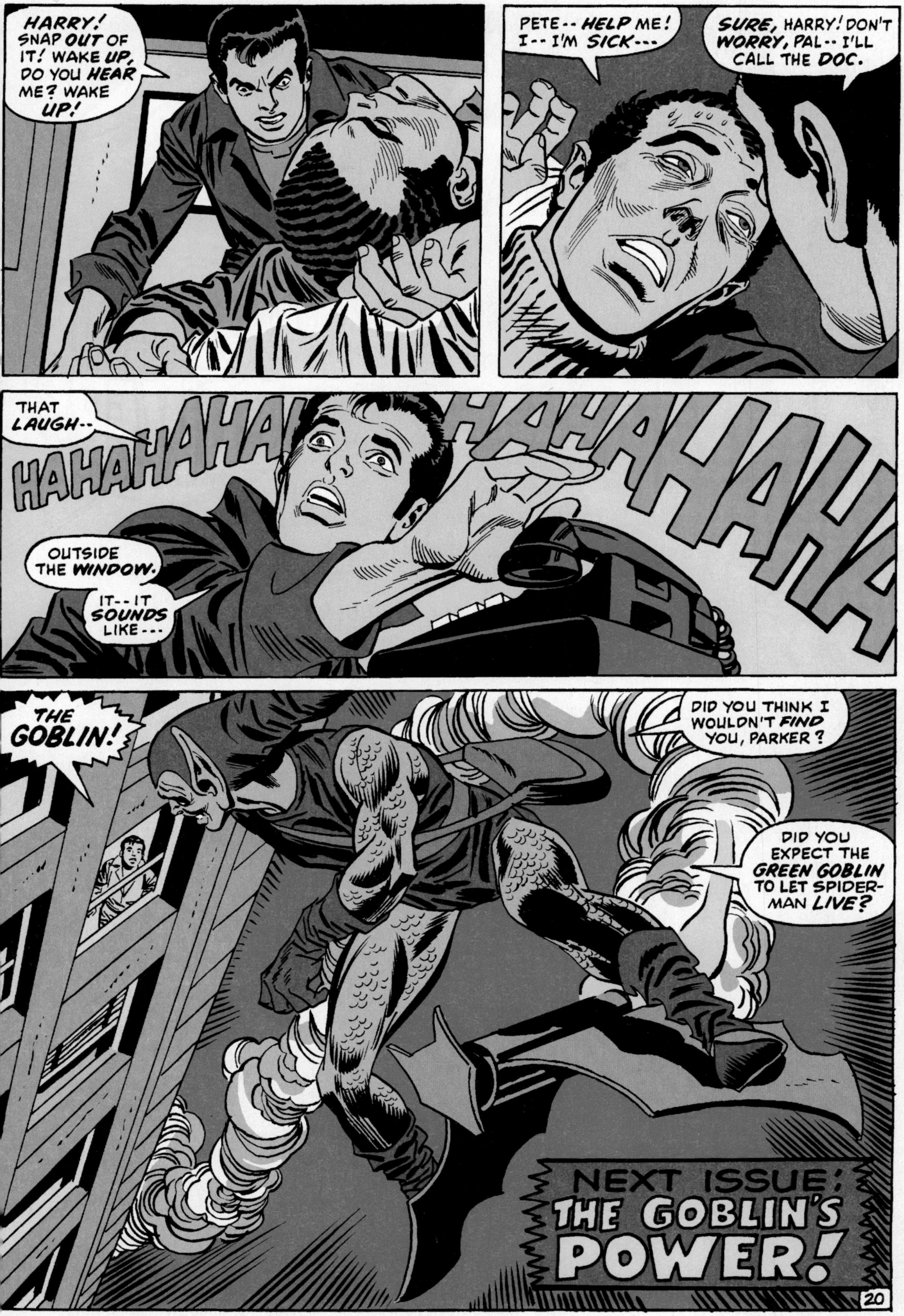
HARRY! SNAP OUT OF IT! WAKE UP, DO YOU HEAR ME? WAKE UP!
PETE-- HELP ME! I-- I'M SICK---
SURE, HARRY! DON'T WORRY, PAL-- I'LL CALL THE DOC.
THAT LAUGH--
HAHAHAHAHAHAHAHAHAHAHA
OUTSIDE THE WINDOW.
IT-- IT SOUNDS LIKE---
THE GOBLIN!
DID YOU THINK I WOULDN'T FIND YOU, PARKER?
DID YOU EXPECT THE GREEN GOBLIN TO LET SPIDER-MAN LIVE?
NEXT ISSUE: THE GOBLIN'S POWER!
20

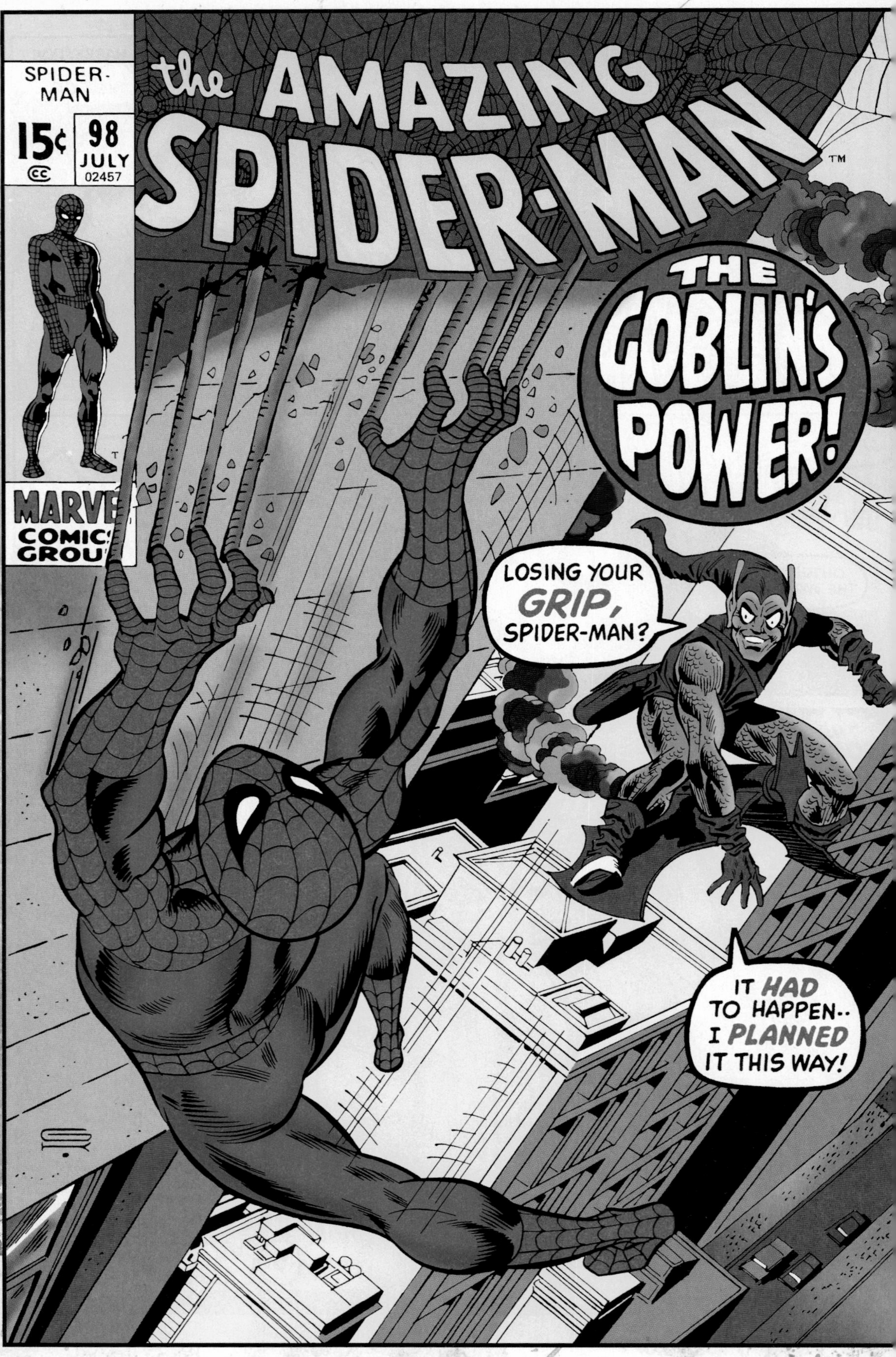

SPIDER-MAN
15¢
98
JULY
02457
the AMAZING
SPIDER-MAN
TM
MARVEL COMICS GROUP
THE GOBLIN'S POWER!
LOSING YOUR GRIP, SPIDER-MAN?
IT HAD TO HAPPEN.. I PLANNED IT THIS WAY!

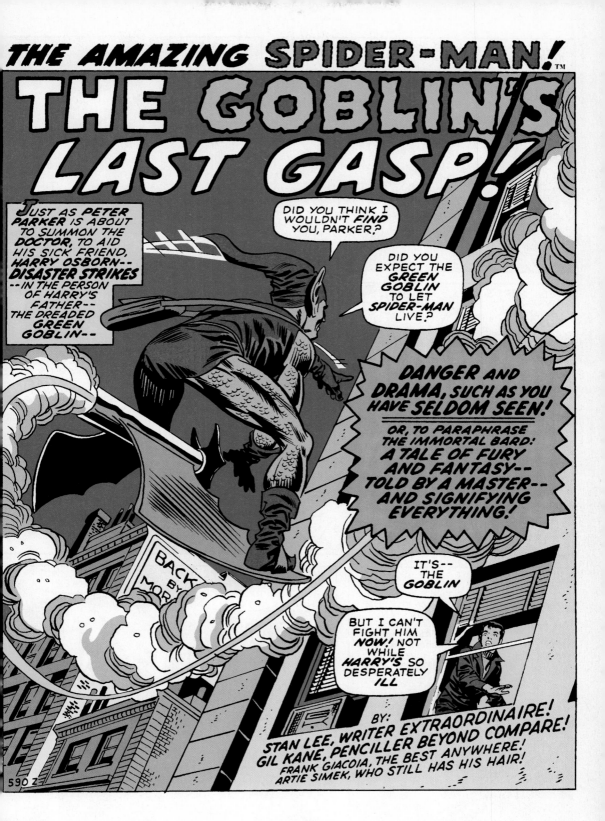

THE AMAZING SPIDER-MAN! ™

THE GOBLIN'S LAST GASP!

JUST AS PETER PARKER IS ABOUT TO SUMMON THE DOCTOR, TO AID HIS SICK FRIEND, HARRY OSBORN-- DISASTER STRIKES --IN THE PERSON OF HARRY'S FATHER-- THE DREADED GREEN GOBLIN--

DID YOU THINK I WOULDN'T FIND YOU, PARKER?

DID YOU EXPECT THE GREEN GOBLIN TO LET SPIDER-MAN LIVE?

DANGER AND DRAMA, SUCH AS YOU HAVE SELDOM SEEN!

OR, TO PARAPHRASE THE IMMORTAL BARD: A TALE OF FURY AND FANTASY-- TOLD BY A MASTER-- AND SIGNIFYING EVERYTHING!

IT'S-- THE GOBLIN

BUT I CAN'T FIGHT HIM NOW! NOT WHILE HARRY'S SO DESPERATELY ILL

BY: STAN LEE, WRITER EXTRAORDINAIRE! GIL KANE, PENCILLER BEYOND COMPARE! FRANK GIACOIA, THE BEST ANYWHERE! ARTIE SIMEK, WHO STILL HAS HIS HAIR!

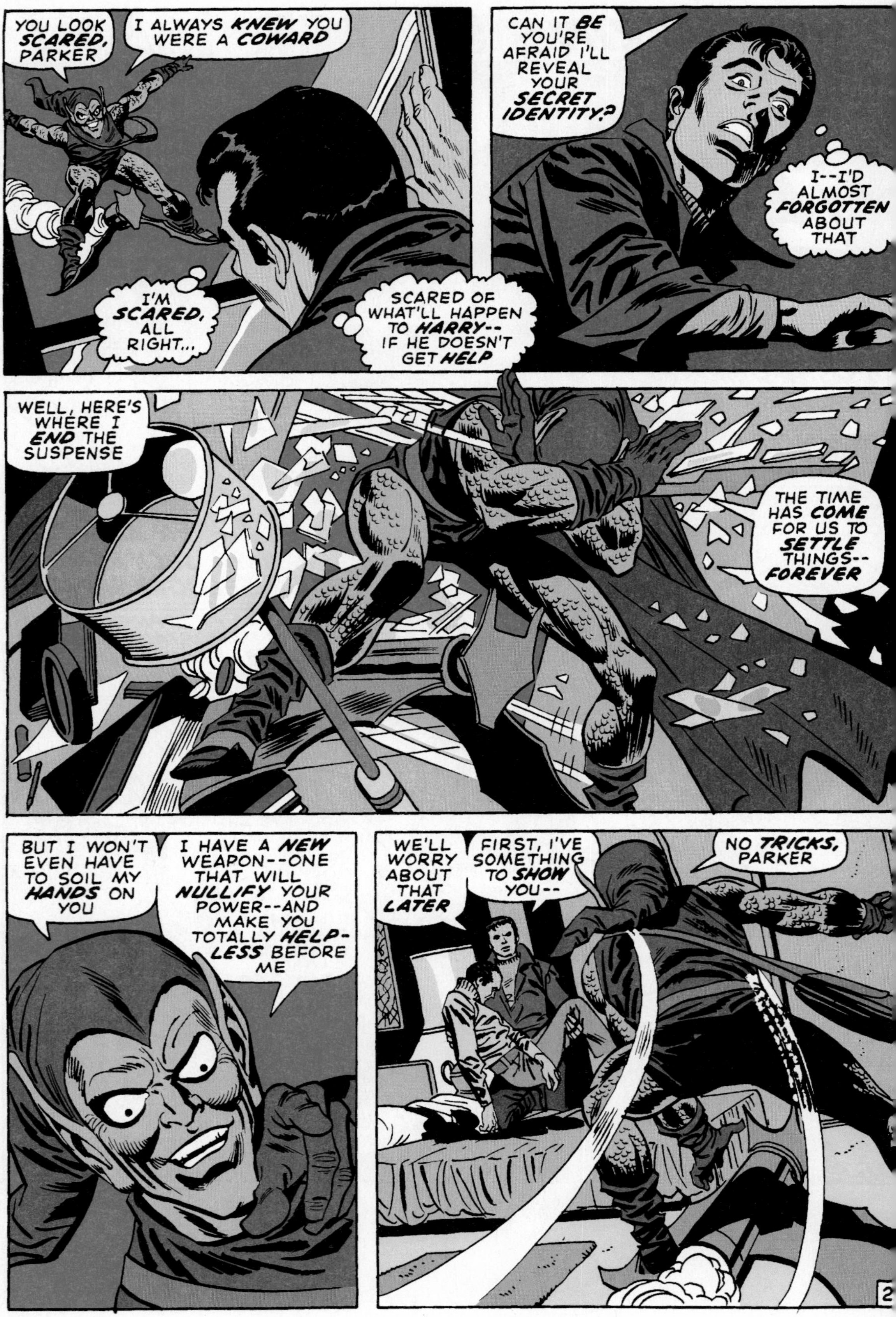
YOU LOOK SCARED, PARKER
I ALWAYS KNEW YOU WERE A COWARD
I'M SCARED, ALL RIGHT...
SCARED OF WHAT'LL HAPPEN TO HARRY-- IF HE DOESN'T GET HELP
CAN IT BE YOU'RE AFRAID I'LL REVEAL YOUR SECRET IDENTITY?
I--I'D ALMOST FORGOTTEN ABOUT THAT
WELL, HERE'S WHERE I END THE SUSPENSE
THE TIME HAS COME FOR US TO SETTLE THINGS-- FOREVER
BUT I WON'T EVEN HAVE TO SOIL MY HANDS ON YOU
I HAVE A NEW WEAPON--ONE THAT WILL NULLIFY YOUR POWER--AND MAKE YOU TOTALLY HELP-LESS BEFORE ME
WE'LL WORRY ABOUT THAT LATER
FIRST, I'VE SOMETHING TO SHOW YOU--
NO TRICKS, PARKER
2

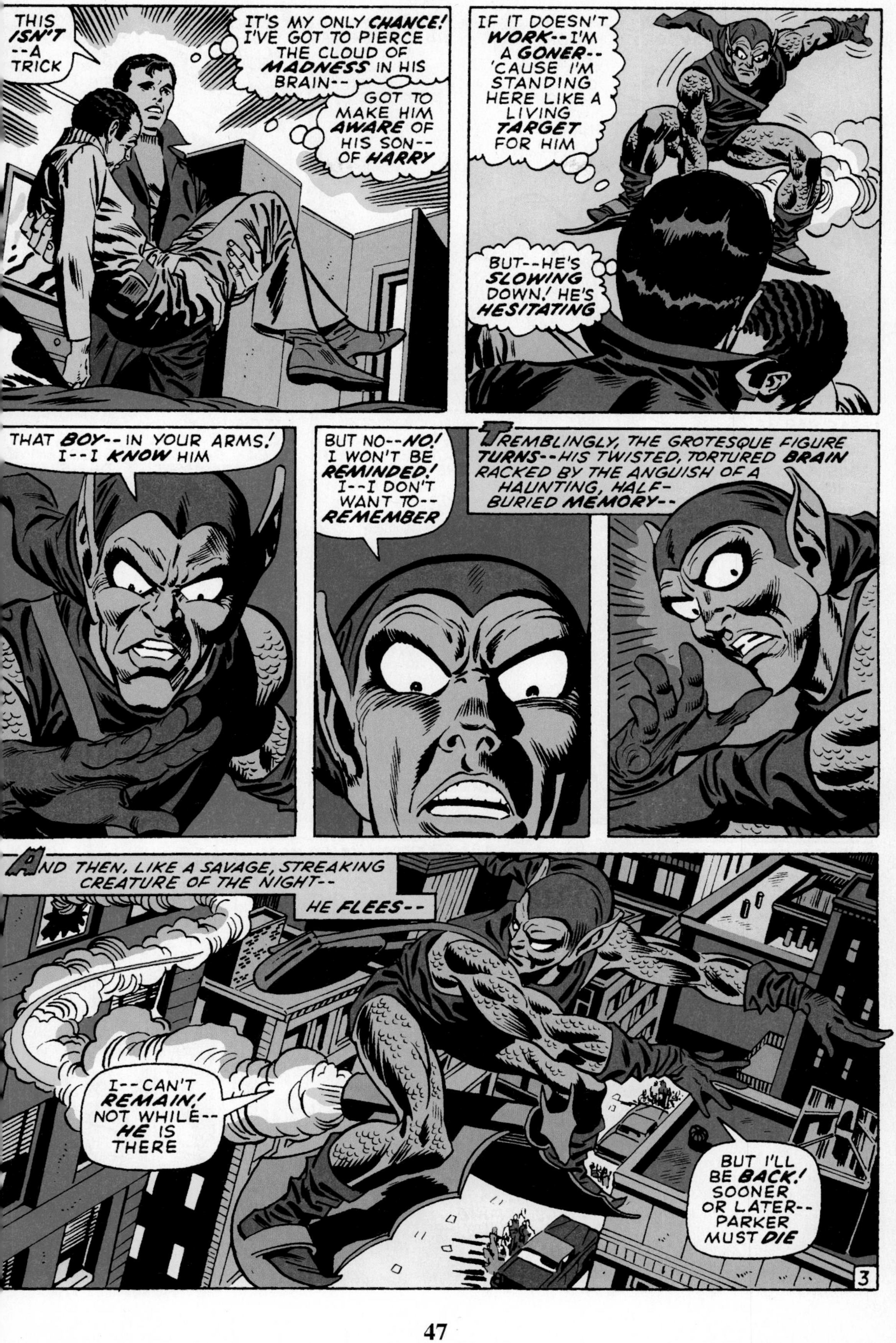
THIS ISN'T --A TRICK
IT'S MY ONLY CHANCE! I'VE GOT TO PIERCE THE CLOUD OF MADNESS IN HIS BRAIN--
GOT TO MAKE HIM AWARE OF HIS SON-- OF HARRY
IF IT DOESN'T WORK--I'M A GONER-- 'CAUSE I'M STANDING HERE LIKE A LIVING TARGET FOR HIM
BUT--HE'S SLOWING DOWN! HE'S HESITATING
THAT BOY--IN YOUR ARMS! I--I KNOW HIM
BUT NO--NO! I WON'T BE REMINDED! I--I DON'T WANT TO--REMEMBER
TREMBLINGLY, THE GROTESQUE FIGURE TURNS--HIS TWISTED, TORTURED BRAIN RACKED BY THE ANGUISH OF A HAUNTING, HALF-BURIED MEMORY--
AND THEN, LIKE A SAVAGE, STREAKING CREATURE OF THE NIGHT--
HE FLEES--
I--CAN'T REMAIN! NOT WHILE-- HE IS THERE
BUT I'LL BE BACK! SOONER OR LATER-- PARKER MUST DIE
3

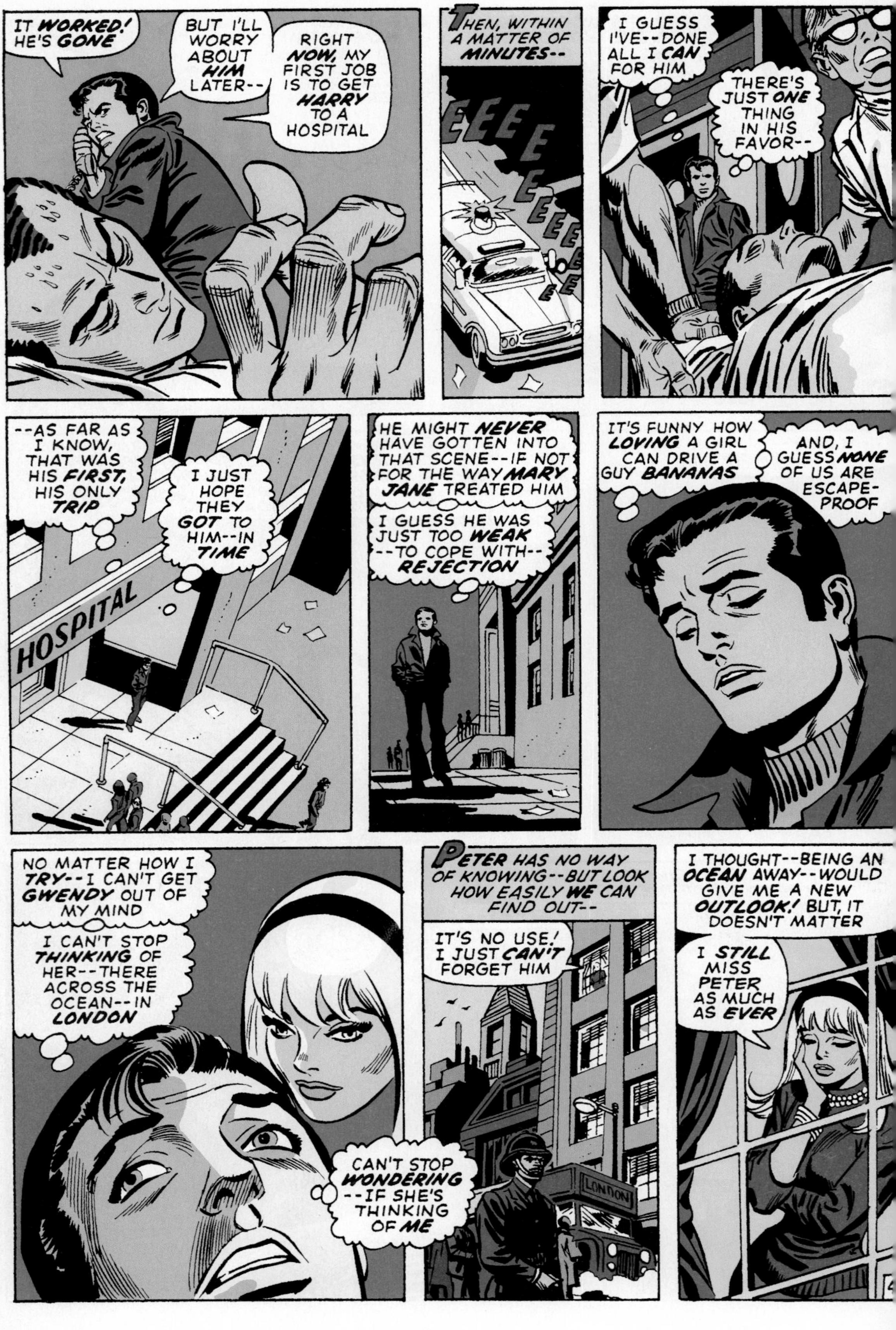
IT WORKED! HE'S GONE
BUT I'LL WORRY ABOUT HIM LATER--
RIGHT NOW, MY FIRST JOB IS TO GET HARRY TO A HOSPITAL
THEN, WITHIN A MATTER OF MINUTES--
EEEEEEEEEEEE
I GUESS I'VE--DONE ALL I CAN FOR HIM
THERE'S JUST ONE THING IN HIS FAVOR--
--AS FAR AS I KNOW, THAT WAS HIS FIRST, HIS ONLY TRIP
I JUST HOPE THEY GOT TO HIM--IN TIME
HOSPITAL
HE MIGHT NEVER HAVE GOTTEN INTO THAT SCENE--IF NOT FOR THE WAY MARY JANE TREATED HIM
I GUESS HE WAS JUST TOO WEAK --TO COPE WITH-- REJECTION
IT'S FUNNY HOW LOVING A GIRL CAN DRIVE A GUY BANANAS
AND, I GUESS NONE OF US ARE ESCAPE-PROOF
NO MATTER HOW I TRY--I CAN'T GET GWENDY OUT OF MY MIND
I CAN'T STOP THINKING OF HER--THERE ACROSS THE OCEAN--IN LONDON
CAN'T STOP WONDERING --IF SHE'S THINKING OF ME
PETER HAS NO WAY OF KNOWING--BUT LOOK HOW EASILY WE CAN FIND OUT--
IT'S NO USE! I JUST CAN'T FORGET HIM
LONDON
I THOUGHT--BEING AN OCEAN AWAY--WOULD GIVE ME A NEW OUTLOOK! BUT, IT DOESN'T MATTER
I STILL MISS PETER AS MUCH AS EVER

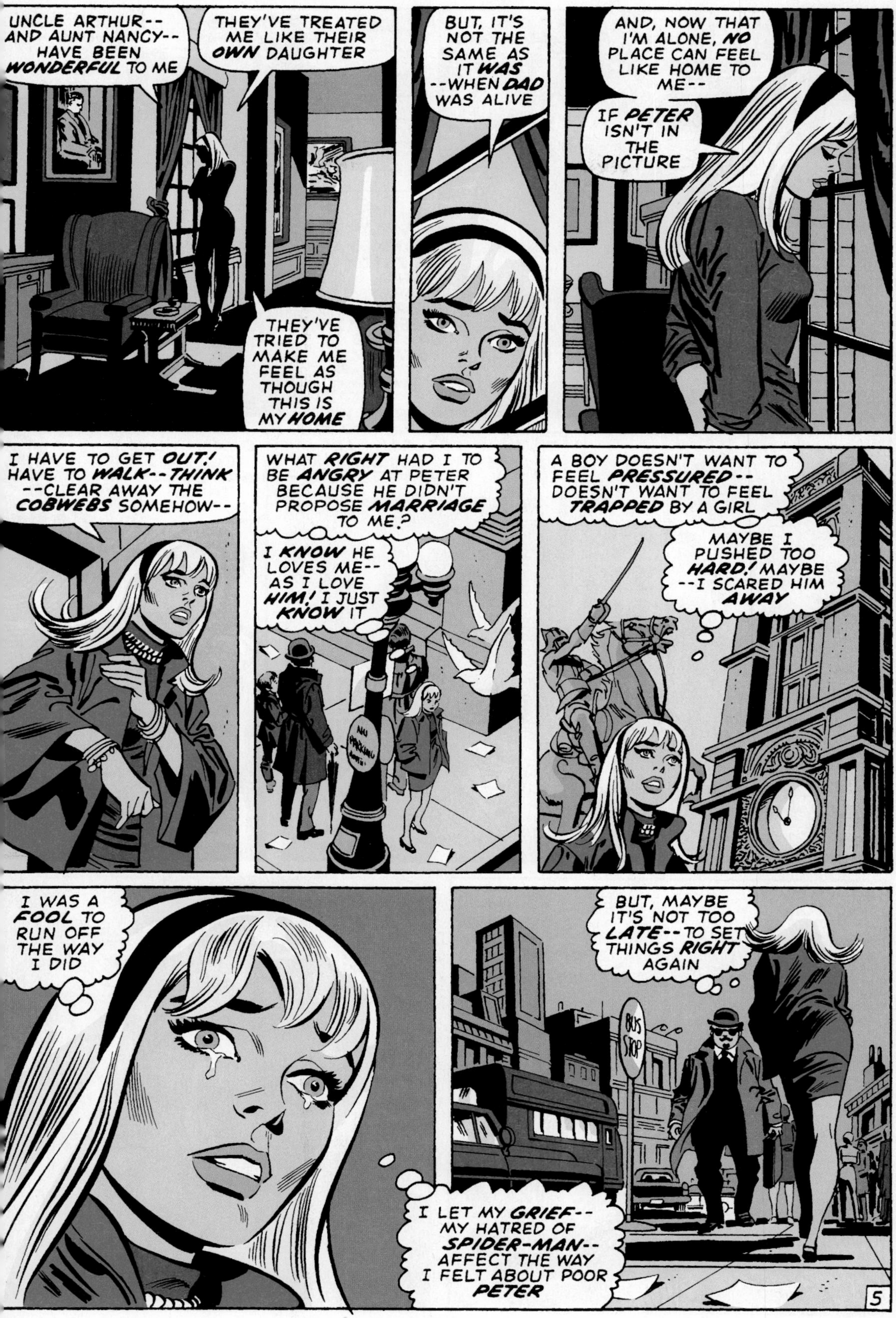
UNCLE ARTHUR-- AND AUNT NANCY-- HAVE BEEN WONDERFUL TO ME
THEY'VE TREATED ME LIKE THEIR OWN DAUGHTER
THEY'VE TRIED TO MAKE ME FEEL AS THOUGH THIS IS MY HOME
BUT, IT'S NOT THE SAME AS IT WAS --WHEN DAD WAS ALIVE
AND, NOW THAT I'M ALONE, NO PLACE CAN FEEL LIKE HOME TO ME--
IF PETER ISN'T IN THE PICTURE
I HAVE TO GET OUT! HAVE TO WALK--THINK --CLEAR AWAY THE COBWEBS SOMEHOW--
WHAT RIGHT HAD I TO BE ANGRY AT PETER BECAUSE HE DIDN'T PROPOSE MARRIAGE TO ME?
I KNOW HE LOVES ME-- AS I LOVE HIM! I JUST KNOW IT
A BOY DOESN'T WANT TO FEEL PRESSURED-- DOESN'T WANT TO FEEL TRAPPED BY A GIRL
MAYBE I PUSHED TOO HARD! MAYBE --I SCARED HIM AWAY
I WAS A FOOL TO RUN OFF THE WAY I DID
BUT, MAYBE IT'S NOT TOO LATE--TO SET THINGS RIGHT AGAIN
BUS STOP
I LET MY GRIEF-- MY HATRED OF SPIDER-MAN-- AFFECT THE WAY I FELT ABOUT POOR PETER
5

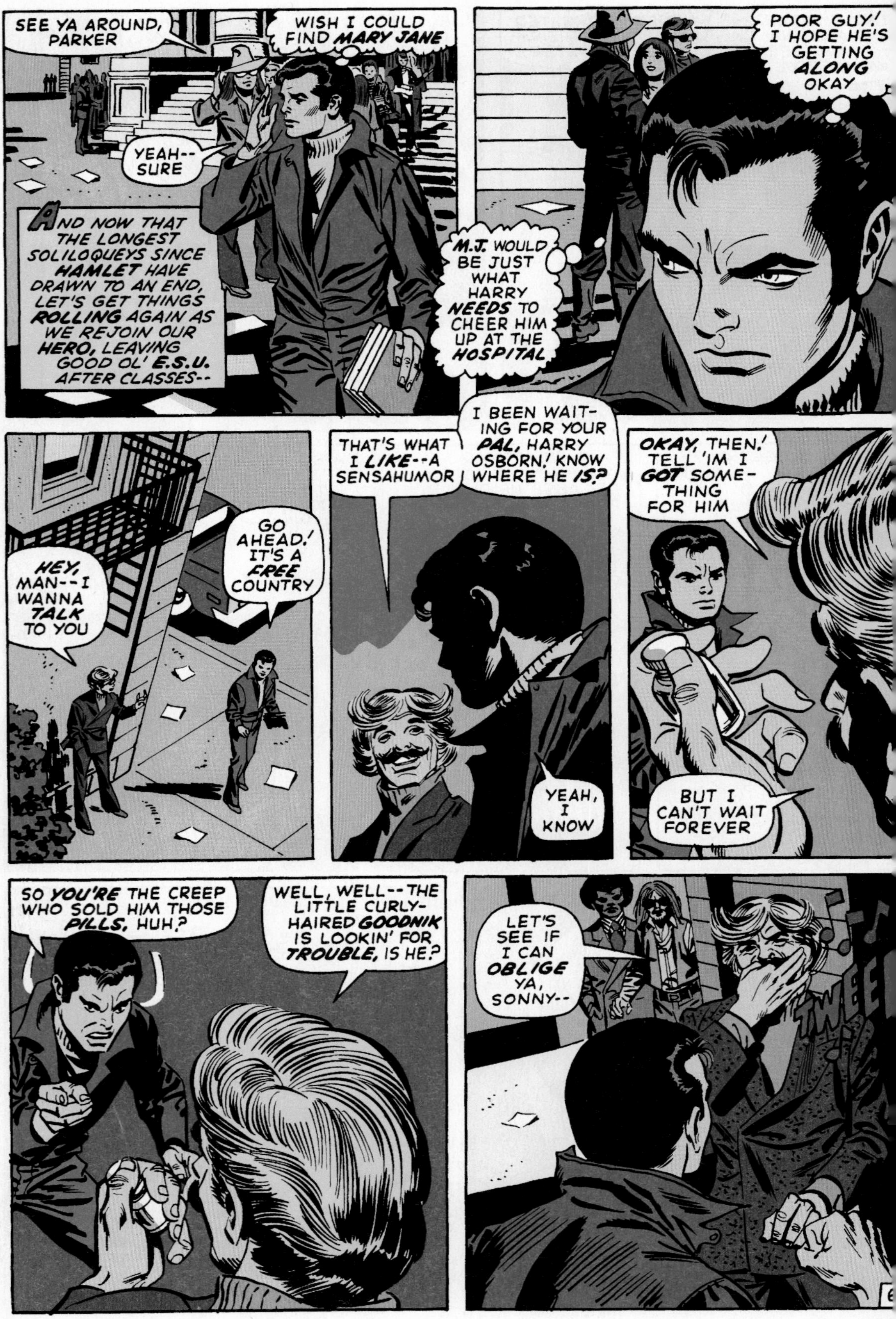
SEE YA AROUND, PARKER
WISH I COULD FIND MARY JANE
YEAH-- SURE
AND NOW THAT THE LONGEST SOLILOQUEYS SINCE HAMLET HAVE DRAWN TO AN END, LET'S GET THINGS ROLLING AGAIN AS WE REJOIN OUR HERO, LEAVING GOOD OL' E.S.U. AFTER CLASSES--
POOR GUY! I HOPE HE'S GETTING ALONG OKAY
M.J. WOULD BE JUST WHAT HARRY NEEDS TO CHEER HIM UP AT THE HOSPITAL
HEY, MAN--I WANNA TALK TO YOU
GO AHEAD! IT'S A FREE COUNTRY
THAT'S WHAT I LIKE--A SENSAHUMOR
I BEEN WAITING FOR YOUR PAL, HARRY OSBORN! KNOW WHERE HE IS?
YEAH, I KNOW
OKAY, THEN! TELL 'IM I GOT SOMETHING FOR HIM
BUT I CAN'T WAIT FOREVER
SO YOU'RE THE CREEP WHO SOLD HIM THOSE PILLS, HUH?
WELL, WELL--THE LITTLE CURLY-HAIRED GOODNIK IS LOOKIN' FOR TROUBLE, IS HE?
LET'S SEE IF I CAN OBLIGE YA, SONNY--
TWEE

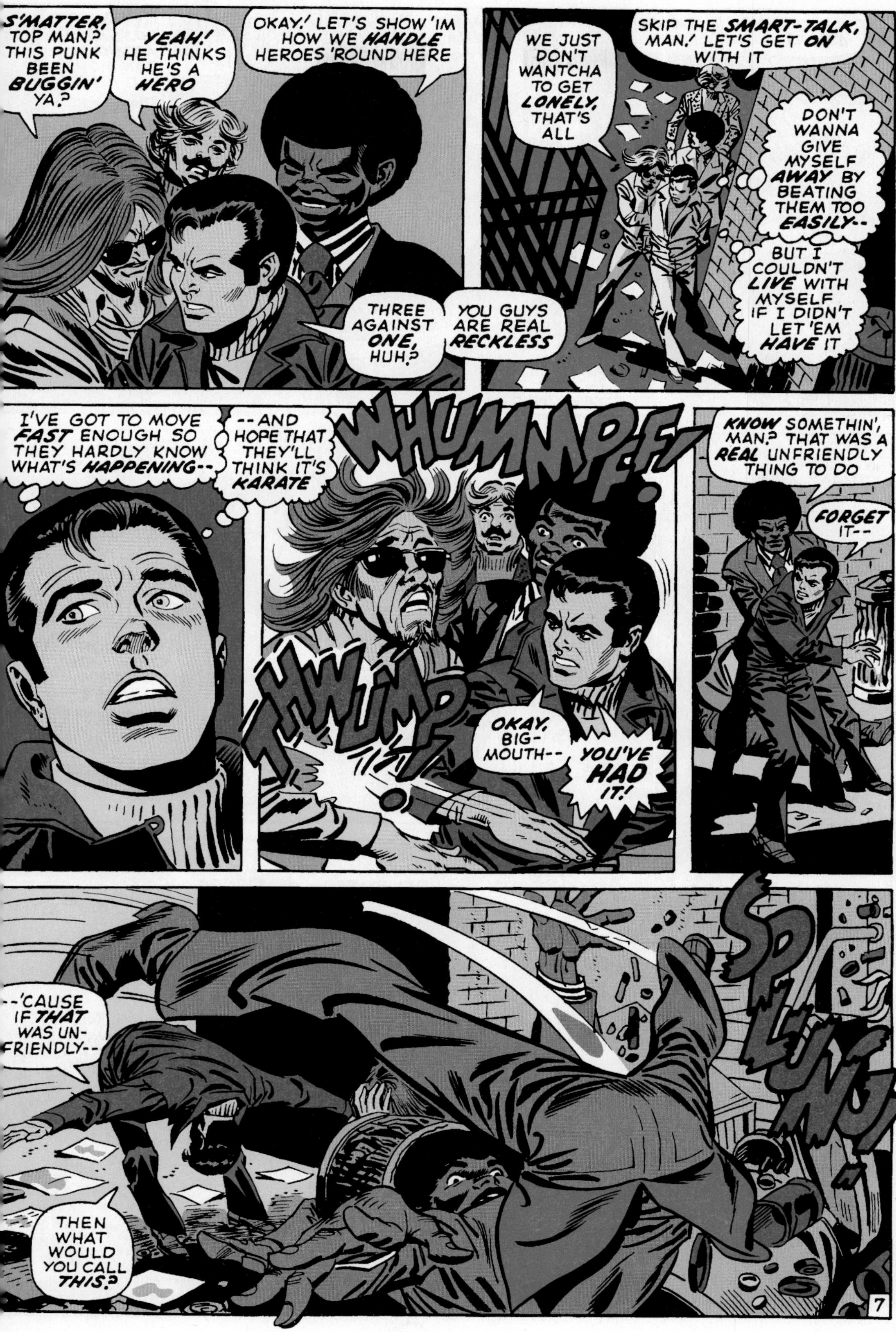
S'MATTER, TOP MAN? THIS PUNK BEEN BUGGIN' YA?
YEAH! HE THINKS HE'S A HERO
OKAY! LET'S SHOW 'IM HOW WE HANDLE HEROES 'ROUND HERE
THREE AGAINST ONE, HUH?
YOU GUYS ARE REAL RECKLESS
WE JUST DON'T WANTCHA TO GET LONELY, THAT'S ALL
SKIP THE SMART-TALK, MAN! LET'S GET ON WITH IT
DON'T WANNA GIVE MYSELF AWAY BY BEATING THEM TOO EASILY--
BUT I COULDN'T LIVE WITH MYSELF IF I DIDN'T LET 'EM HAVE IT
I'VE GOT TO MOVE FAST ENOUGH SO THEY HARDLY KNOW WHAT'S HAPPENING--
--AND HOPE THAT THEY'LL THINK IT'S KARATE
WHUMMPFF!
THWUMP
OKAY, BIG-MOUTH--
YOU'VE HAD IT!
KNOW SOMETHIN', MAN? THAT WAS A REAL UNFRIENDLY THING TO DO
FORGET IT--
--'CAUSE IF THAT WAS UN-FRIENDLY--
THEN WHAT WOULD YOU CALL THIS?
SPLUNG!
7

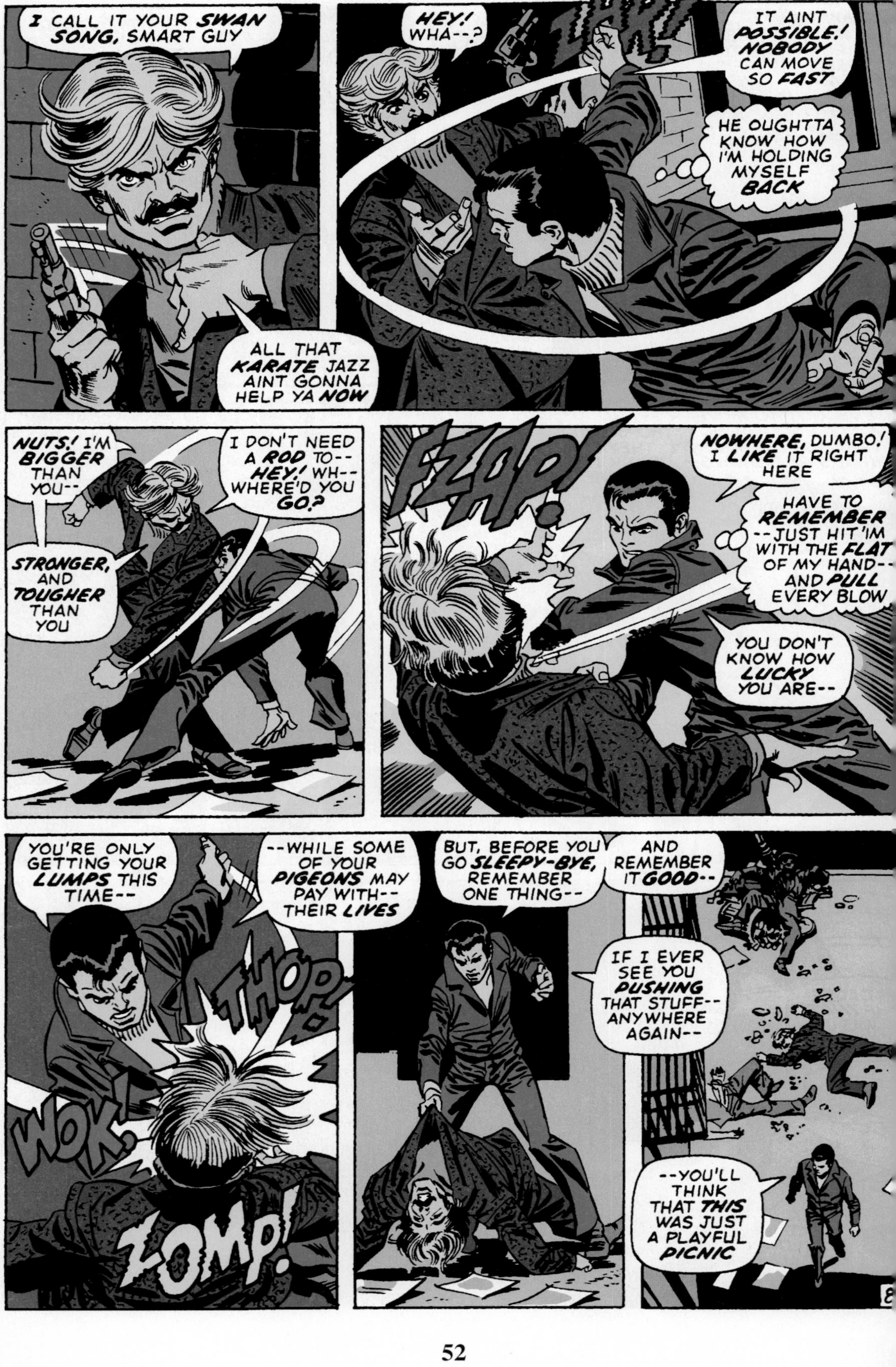

I CALL IT YOUR SWAN SONG, SMART GUY
ALL THAT KARATE JAZZ AINT GONNA HELP YA NOW
HEY! WHA--?
ZAK!
IT AINT POSSIBLE! NOBODY CAN MOVE SO FAST
HE OUGHTTA KNOW HOW I'M HOLDING MYSELF BACK
NUTS! I'M BIGGER THAN YOU--
STRONGER, AND TOUGHER THAN YOU
I DON'T NEED A ROD TO-- HEY! WH-- WHERE'D YOU GO?
FZAP!
NOWHERE, DUMBO! I LIKE IT RIGHT HERE
HAVE TO REMEMBER --JUST HIT 'IM WITH THE FLAT OF MY HAND-- AND PULL EVERY BLOW
YOU DON'T KNOW HOW LUCKY YOU ARE--
YOU'RE ONLY GETTING YOUR LUMPS THIS TIME--
--WHILE SOME OF YOUR PIGEONS MAY PAY WITH-- THEIR LIVES
THOP!
WOK!
ZOMP!
BUT, BEFORE YOU GO SLEEPY-BYE, REMEMBER ONE THING--
AND REMEMBER IT GOOD--
IF I EVER SEE YOU PUSHING THAT STUFF-- ANYWHERE AGAIN--
--YOU'LL THINK THAT THIS WAS JUST A PLAYFUL PICNIC
8

EVEN THOUGH I *TRIED* TO HOLD MYSELF BACK--THEY *STILL* MAY GET SUSPICIOUS

BUT *LET* 'EM! NONE OF THEM CAN *PROVE* ANYTHING

AND I WOULDN'T HAVE *MISSED* THAT LITTLE SESSION NO MATTER *WHAT*

BUT, AS *PETER PARKER* WALKS BY, LOST IN HIS OWN PRIVATE THOUGHTS--

ROBBIE! THIS IS *JAMESON!* I WANNA *SEE* YOU

I'LL BE RIGHT *IN*, J.J.

YEAH? THAT'S REAL *NICE* OF YOU, MISTER-- CONSIDERING I'M THE *BOSS* AROUND HERE

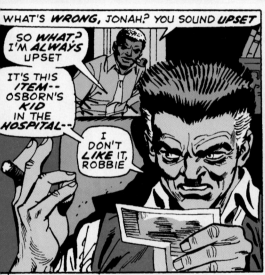

WHAT'S *WRONG*, JONAH? YOU SOUND *UPSET*

SO *WHAT?* I'M *ALWAYS* UPSET

IT'S THIS *ITEM*-- OSBORN'S *KID* IN THE *HOSPITAL*--

I DON'T *LIKE* IT, ROBBIE

NOBODY LIKES IT! DRUGS ARE A *BAD* SCENE

YEAH? I'LL TELL YOU A *WORSE* ONE--

THAT KID'S *FATHER* IS ONE OF OUR BIGGEST *ADVERTISERS!* HE'S NOT GONNA *LIKE* US PRINTING THIS STORY

I'M GONNA PRETEND I DIDN'T HEAR YOU *SAY* THAT, JONAH

YOU NEVER SQUASHED A STORY *BEFORE* BECAUSE IT MIGHT LOSE YOU SOME *ADS*

SIMMER DOWN! I'M NOT DOING IT *NOW*, EITHER

I JUST WANNA *TALK*, THAT'S ALL

HOW WILL YOU *RUN* THE STORY? WHAT *ANGLE* WILL YOU USE?

I'VE GOT IT ALL FIGURED *OUT*--

I'M SHOWING THAT DRUGS AREN'T JUST A *GHETTO* HANGUP! THEY HIT THE *RICH* --SAME AS THE POOR

IT'S *EVERYONE'S* PROBLEM! WE'VE *ALL* GOT TO FACE IT

WELL, DON'T JUST *STAND* THERE, MAN! I WANT IT IN THE *NEXT* EDITION

9.

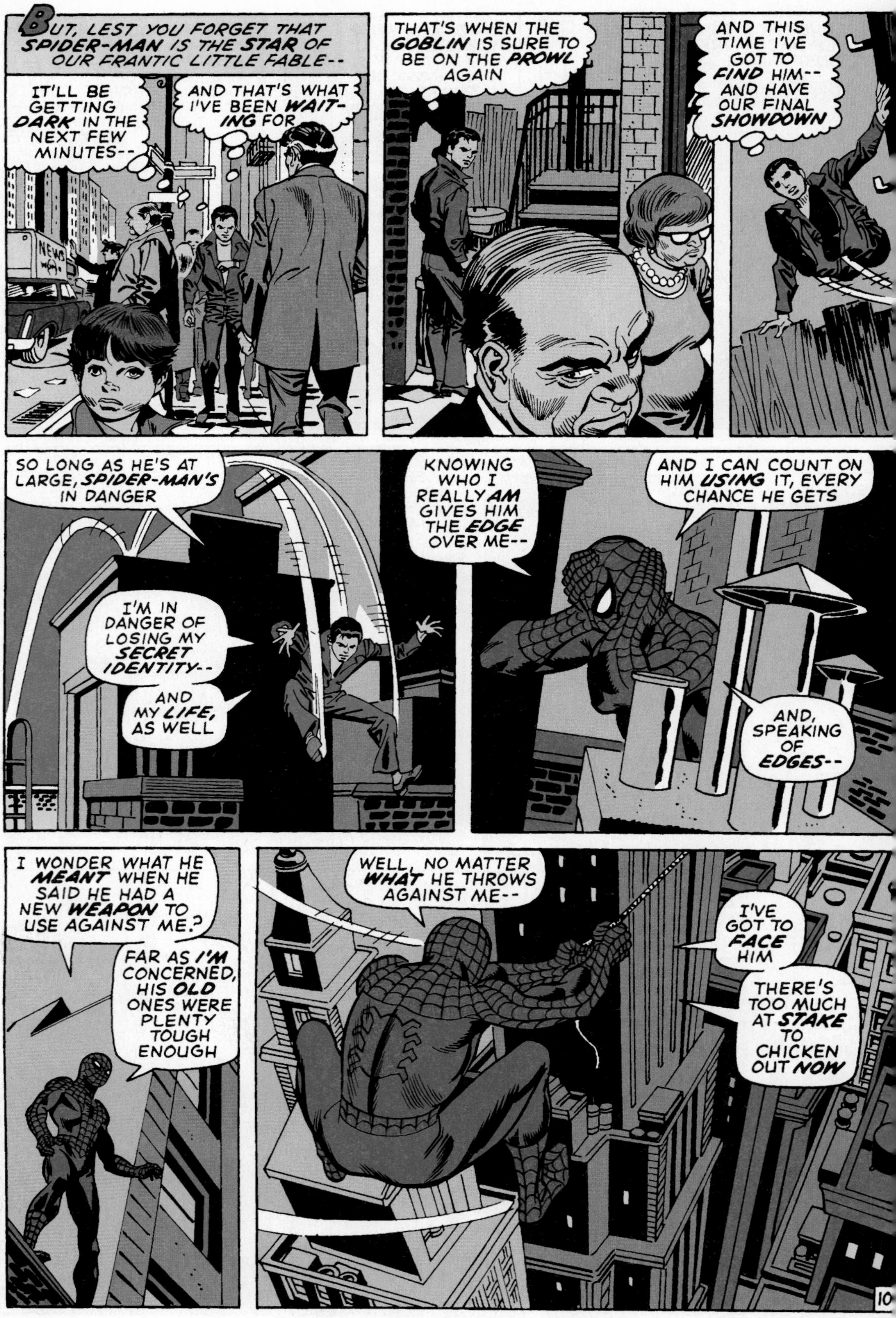
BUT, LEST YOU FORGET THAT SPIDER-MAN IS THE STAR OF OUR FRANTIC LITTLE FABLE--
IT'LL BE GETTING DARK IN THE NEXT FEW MINUTES--
AND THAT'S WHAT I'VE BEEN WAITING FOR
THAT'S WHEN THE GOBLIN IS SURE TO BE ON THE PROWL AGAIN
AND THIS TIME I'VE GOT TO FIND HIM-- AND HAVE OUR FINAL SHOWDOWN
SO LONG AS HE'S AT LARGE, SPIDER-MAN'S IN DANGER
I'M IN DANGER OF LOSING MY SECRET IDENTITY--
AND MY LIFE, AS WELL
KNOWING WHO I REALLY AM GIVES HIM THE EDGE OVER ME--
AND I CAN COUNT ON HIM USING IT, EVERY CHANCE HE GETS
AND, SPEAKING OF EDGES--
I WONDER WHAT HE MEANT WHEN HE SAID HE HAD A NEW WEAPON TO USE AGAINST ME?
FAR AS I'M CONCERNED, HIS OLD ONES WERE PLENTY TOUGH ENOUGH
WELL, NO MATTER WHAT HE THROWS AGAINST ME--
I'VE GOT TO FACE HIM
THERE'S TOO MUCH AT STAKE TO CHICKEN OUT NOW
10

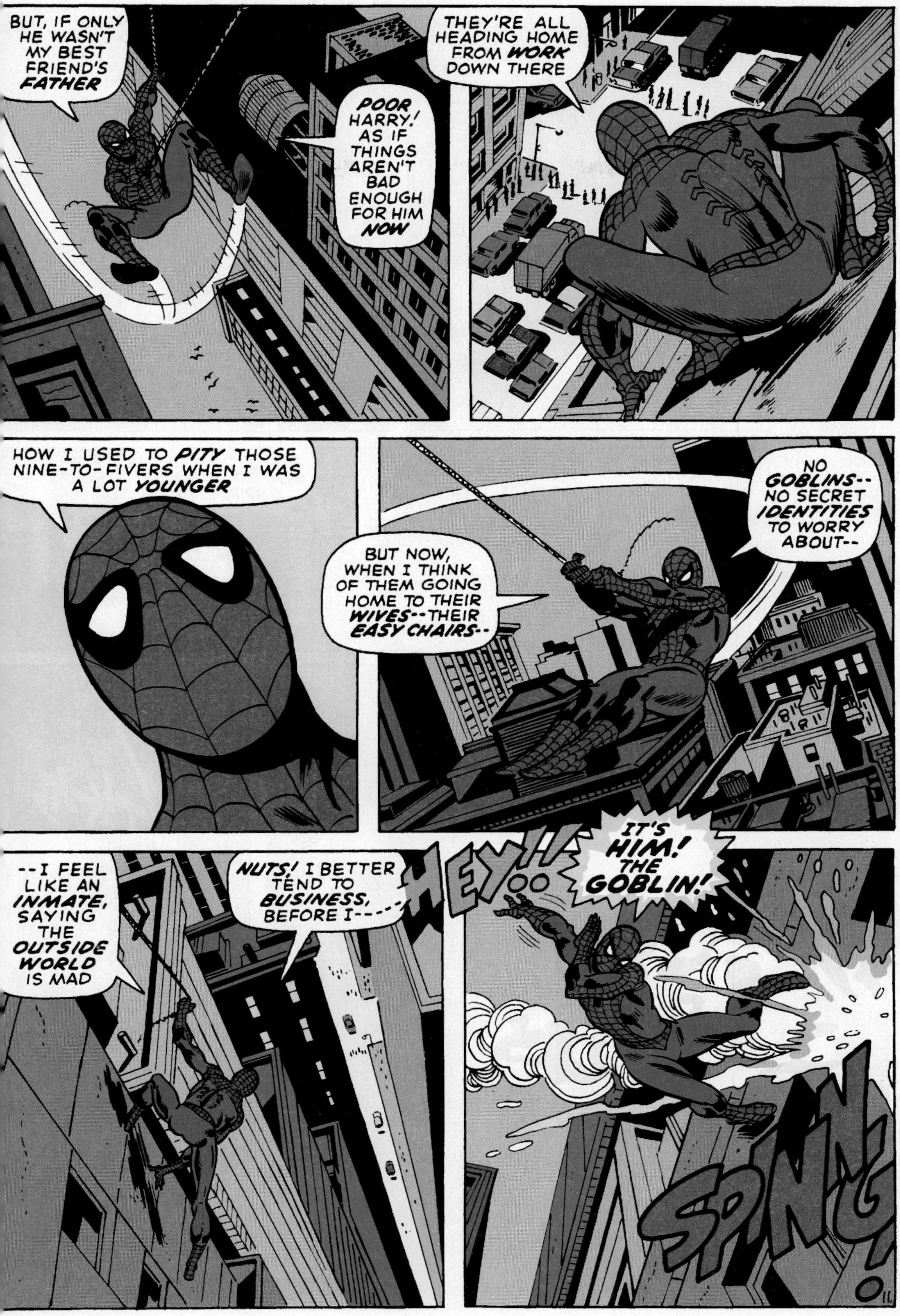
BUT, IF ONLY HE WASN'T MY BEST FRIEND'S FATHER
POOR HARRY! AS IF THINGS AREN'T BAD ENOUGH FOR HIM NOW
THEY'RE ALL HEADING HOME FROM WORK DOWN THERE
HOW I USED TO PITY THOSE NINE-TO-FIVERS WHEN I WAS A LOT YOUNGER
BUT NOW, WHEN I THINK OF THEM GOING HOME TO THEIR WIVES--THEIR EASY CHAIRS--
NO GOBLINS--NO SECRET IDENTITIES TO WORRY ABOUT--
--I FEEL LIKE AN INMATE, SAYING THE OUTSIDE WORLD IS MAD
NUTS! I BETTER TEND TO BUSINESS, BEFORE I----
HEY!!
IT'S HIM! THE GOBLIN!
SPANG!

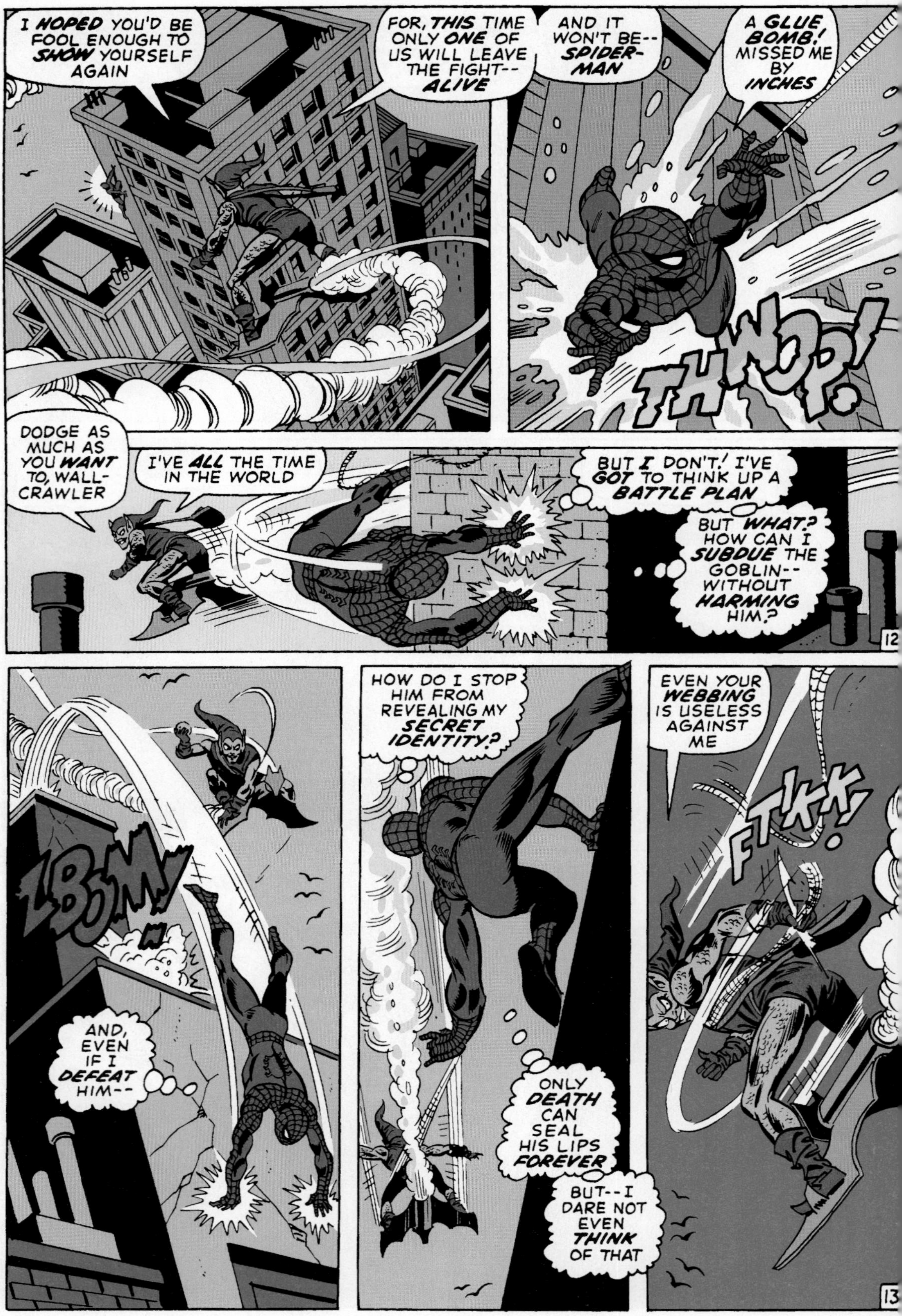
I HOPED YOU'D BE FOOL ENOUGH TO SHOW YOURSELF AGAIN
FOR, THIS TIME ONLY ONE OF US WILL LEAVE THE FIGHT-- ALIVE
AND IT WON'T BE-- SPIDER-MAN
A GLUE BOMB! MISSED ME BY INCHES
THWOP!
DODGE AS MUCH AS YOU WANT TO, WALL-CRAWLER
I'VE ALL THE TIME IN THE WORLD
BUT I DON'T! I'VE GOT TO THINK UP A BATTLE PLAN
BUT WHAT? HOW CAN I SUBDUE THE GOBLIN-- WITHOUT HARMING HIM?
12
LBOOM
AND, EVEN IF I DEFEAT HIM--
HOW DO I STOP HIM FROM REVEALING MY SECRET IDENTITY?
ONLY DEATH CAN SEAL HIS LIPS FOREVER
BUT--I DARE NOT EVEN THINK OF THAT
EVEN YOUR WEBBING IS USELESS AGAINST ME
FTIKK!
13

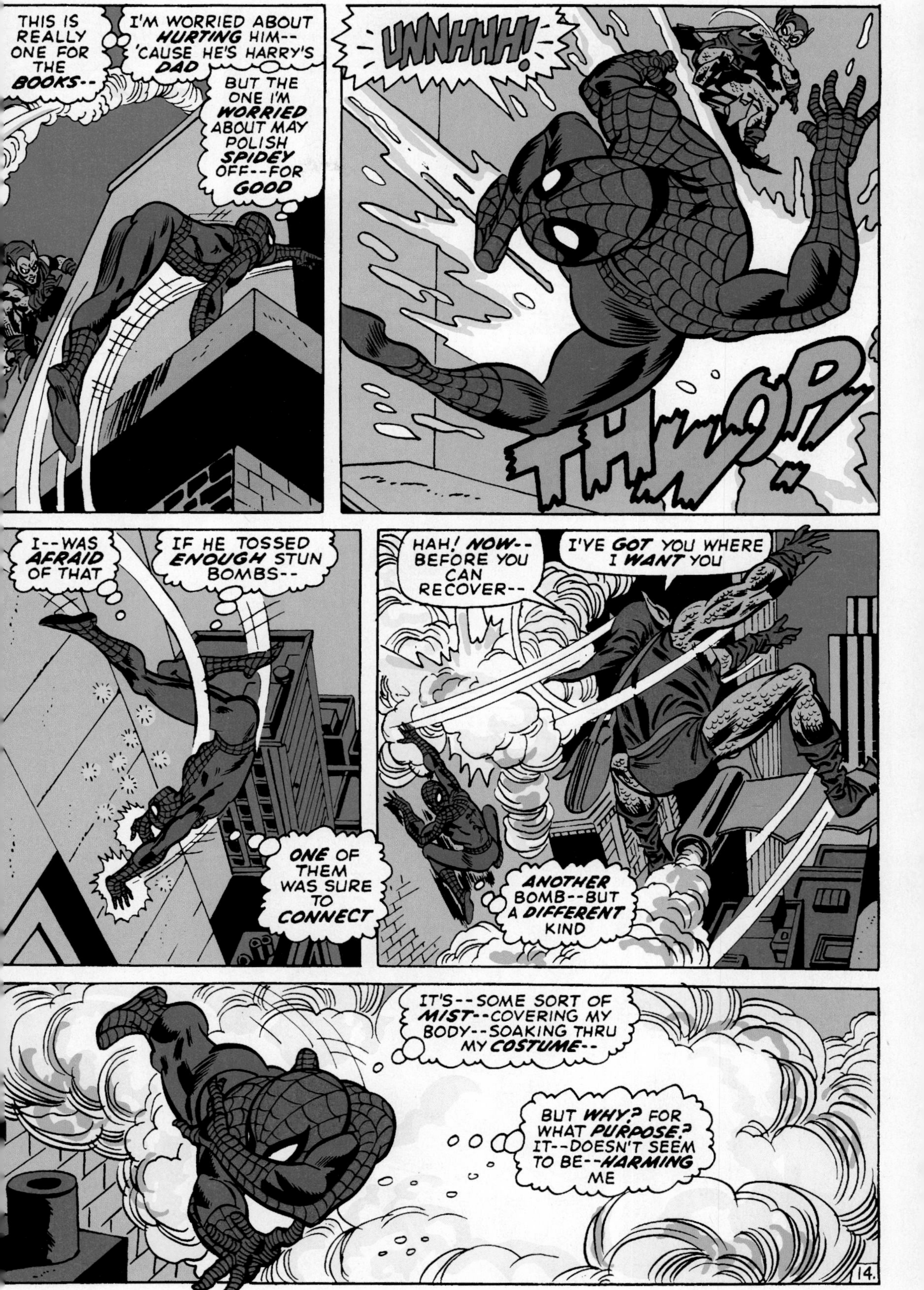

THIS IS REALLY ONE FOR THE BOOKS--
I'M WORRIED ABOUT HURTING HIM-- 'CAUSE HE'S HARRY'S DAD
BUT THE ONE I'M WORRIED ABOUT MAY POLISH SPIDEY OFF--FOR GOOD
UNNHHH!
THWOP!
I--WAS AFRAID OF THAT
IF HE TOSSED ENOUGH STUN BOMBS--
ONE OF THEM WAS SURE TO CONNECT
HAH! NOW-- BEFORE YOU CAN RECOVER--
I'VE GOT YOU WHERE I WANT YOU
ANOTHER BOMB--BUT A DIFFERENT KIND
IT'S--SOME SORT OF MIST--COVERING MY BODY--SOAKING THRU MY COSTUME--
BUT WHY? FOR WHAT PURPOSE? IT--DOESN'T SEEM TO BE--HARMING ME
14.

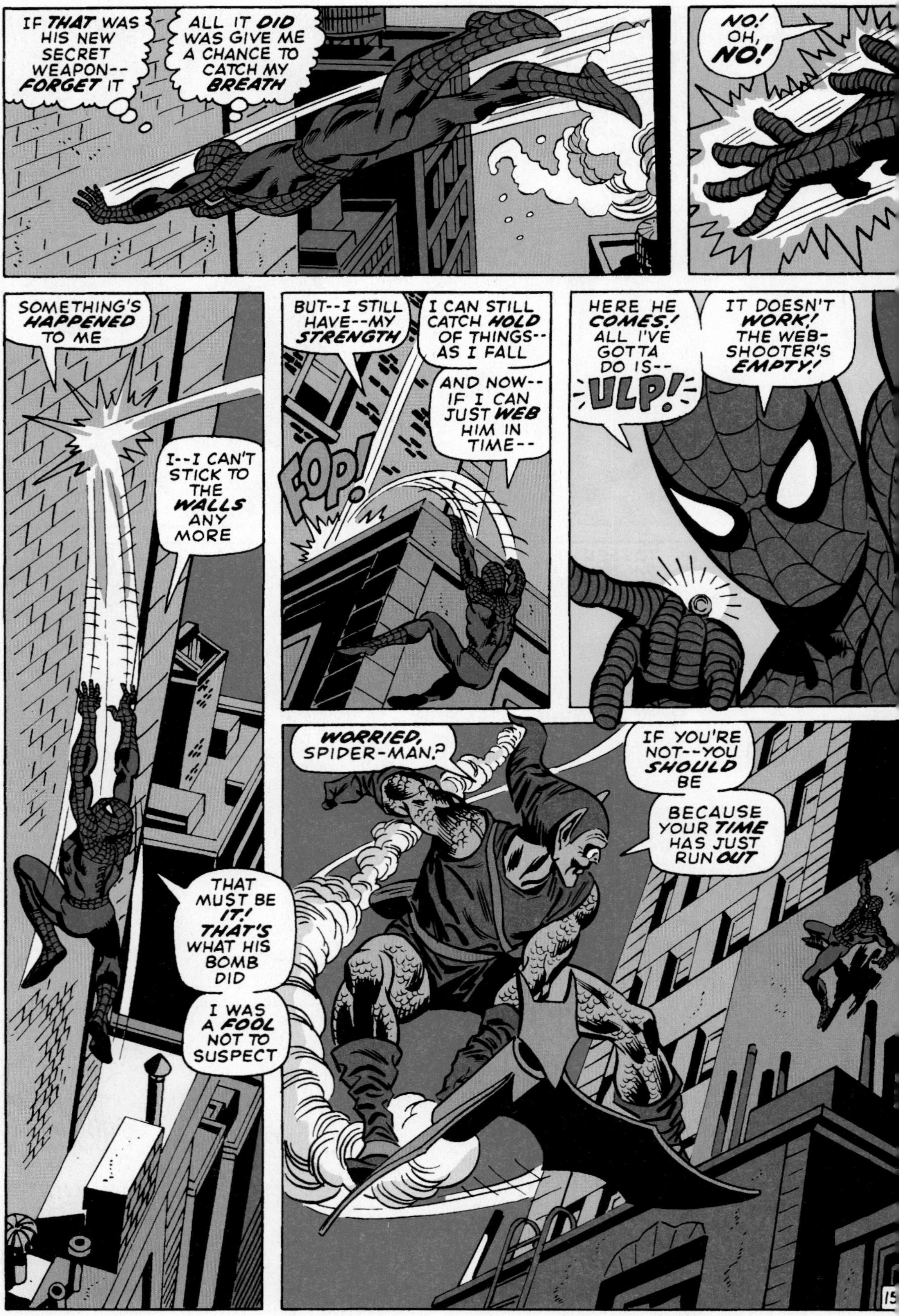
IF THAT WAS HIS NEW SECRET WEAPON-- FORGET IT
ALL IT DID WAS GIVE ME A CHANCE TO CATCH MY BREATH
NO! OH, NO!
SOMETHING'S HAPPENED TO ME
I--I CAN'T STICK TO THE WALLS ANY MORE
THAT MUST BE IT! THAT'S WHAT HIS BOMB DID
I WAS A FOOL NOT TO SUSPECT
BUT--I STILL HAVE--MY STRENGTH
I CAN STILL CATCH HOLD OF THINGS--AS I FALL
AND NOW--IF I CAN JUST WEB HIM IN TIME--
FOP!
HERE HE COMES! ALL I'VE GOTTA DO IS--
ULP!
IT DOESN'T WORK! THE WEB-SHOOTER'S EMPTY!
WORRIED, SPIDER-MAN?
IF YOU'RE NOT--YOU SHOULD BE
BECAUSE YOUR TIME HAS JUST RUN OUT
15

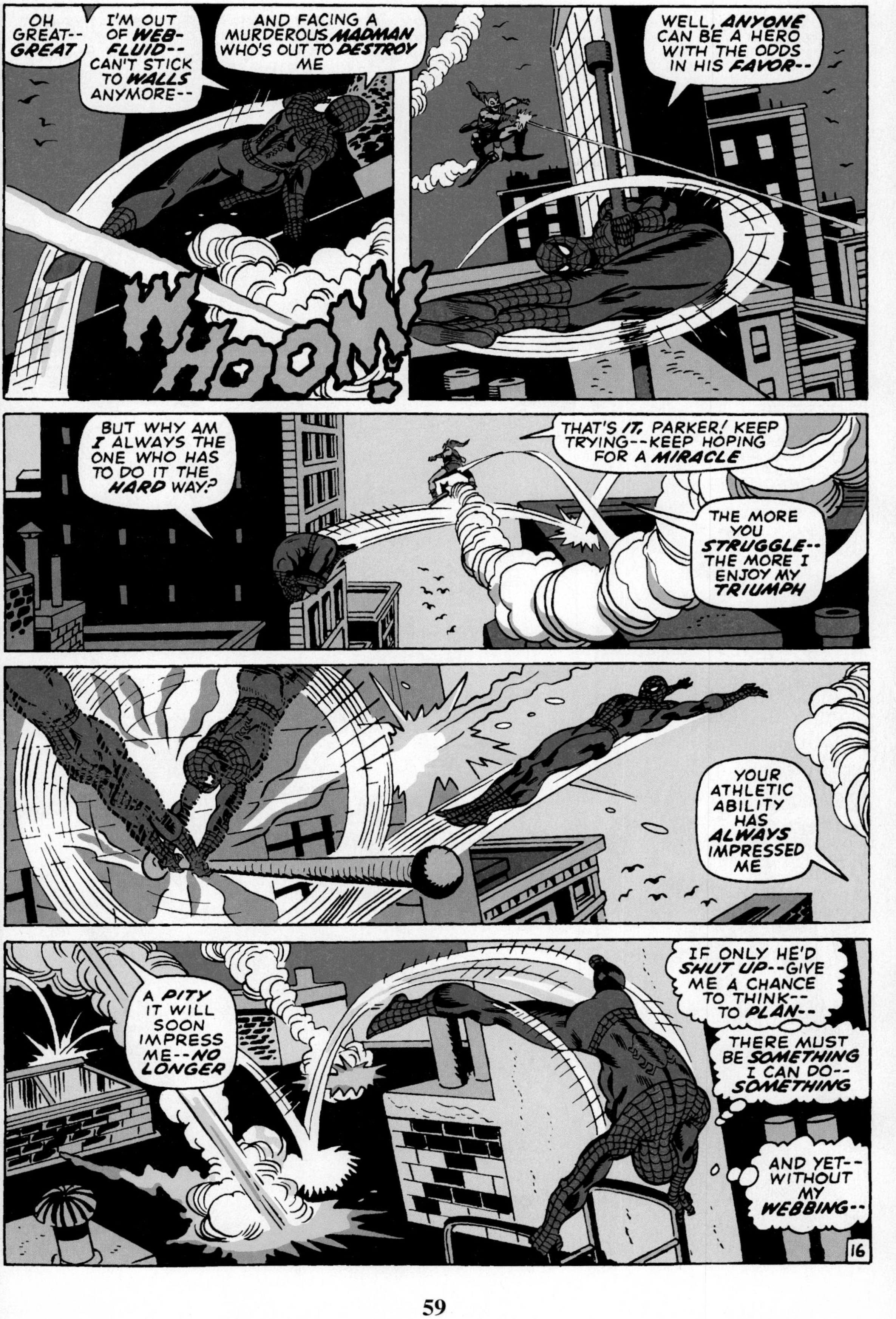

OH GREAT-- GREAT
I'M OUT OF WEB-FLUID-- CAN'T STICK TO WALLS ANYMORE--
AND FACING A MURDEROUS MADMAN WHO'S OUT TO DESTROY ME
WHOOM!
WELL, ANYONE CAN BE A HERO WITH THE ODDS IN HIS FAVOR--
BUT WHY AM I ALWAYS THE ONE WHO HAS TO DO IT THE HARD WAY?
THAT'S IT, PARKER! KEEP TRYING--KEEP HOPING FOR A MIRACLE
THE MORE YOU STRUGGLE-- THE MORE I ENJOY MY TRIUMPH
YOUR ATHLETIC ABILITY HAS ALWAYS IMPRESSED ME
A PITY IT WILL SOON IMPRESS ME--NO LONGER
IF ONLY HE'D SHUT UP--GIVE ME A CHANCE TO THINK-- TO PLAN--
THERE MUST BE SOMETHING I CAN DO-- SOMETHING
AND YET-- WITHOUT MY WEBBING--
16

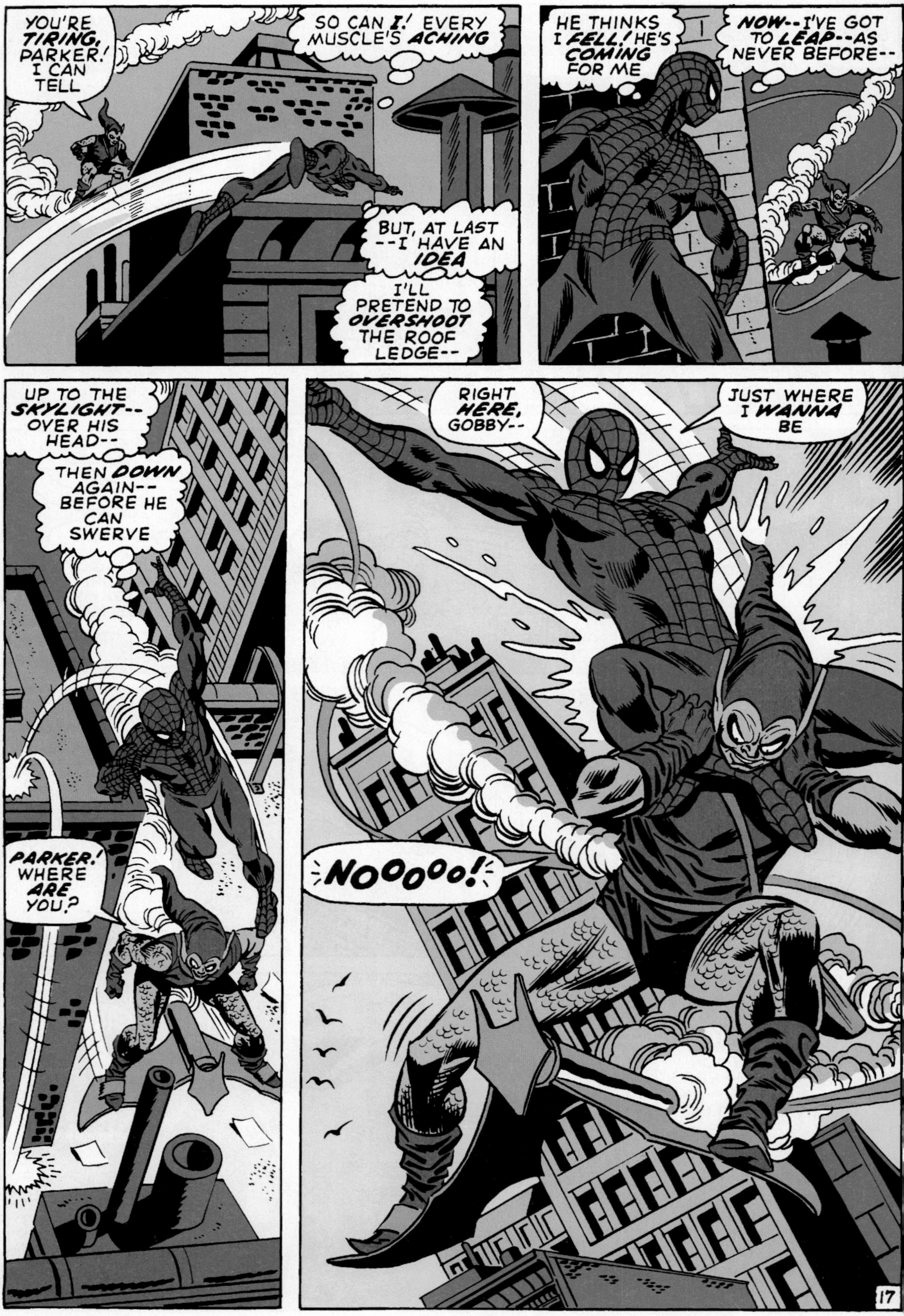
YOU'RE TIRING, PARKER! I CAN TELL
SO CAN I! EVERY MUSCLE'S ACHING
BUT, AT LAST --I HAVE AN IDEA
I'LL PRETEND TO OVERSHOOT THE ROOF LEDGE--
HE THINKS I FELL! HE'S COMING FOR ME
NOW--I'VE GOT TO LEAP--AS NEVER BEFORE--
UP TO THE SKYLIGHT-- OVER HIS HEAD--
THEN DOWN AGAIN-- BEFORE HE CAN SWERVE
PARKER! WHERE ARE YOU?
RIGHT HERE, GOBBY--
JUST WHERE I WANNA BE
NOOOOO!
17

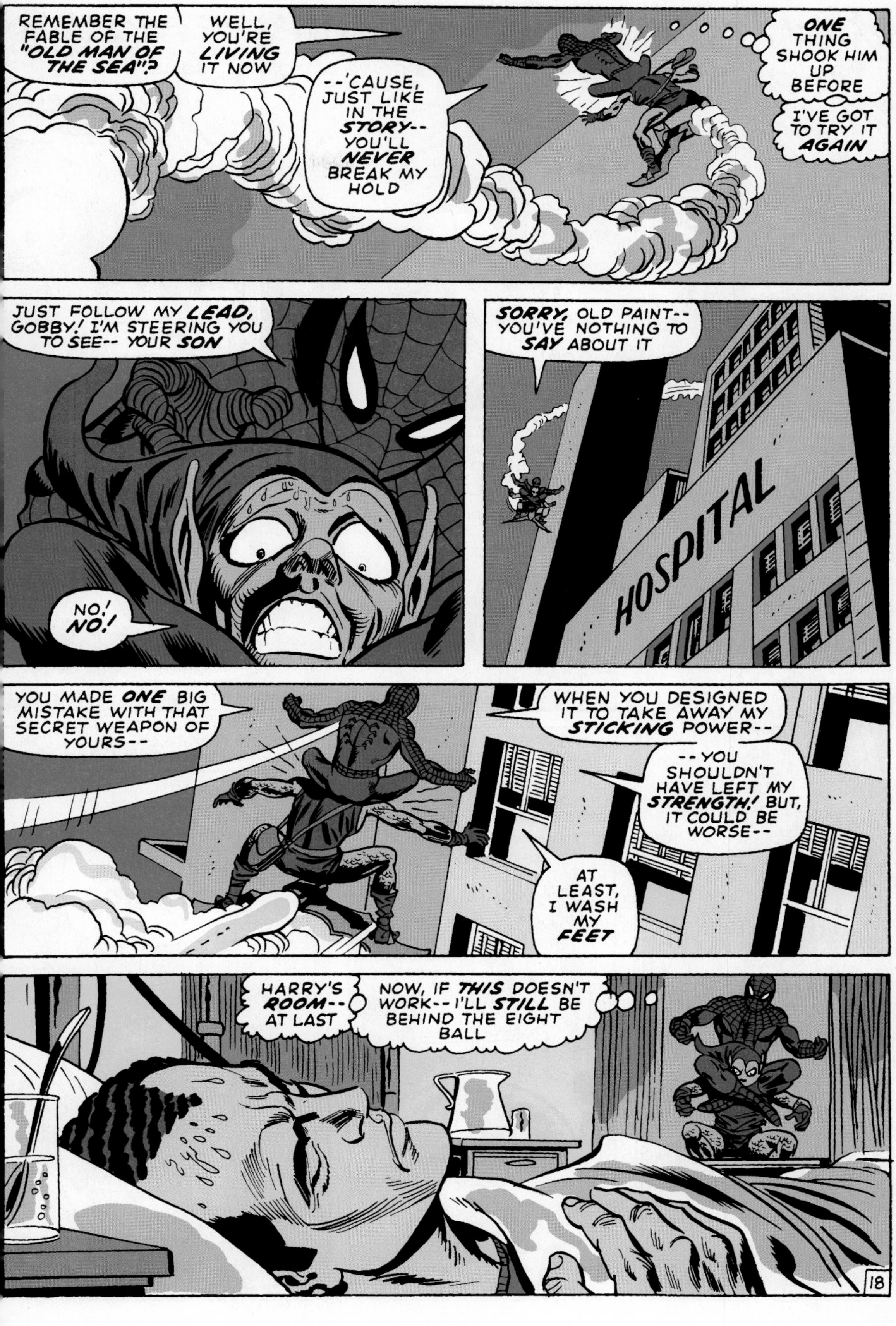

REMEMBER THE FABLE OF THE "OLD MAN OF THE SEA"?
WELL, YOU'RE LIVING IT NOW
--'CAUSE, JUST LIKE IN THE STORY-- YOU'LL NEVER BREAK MY HOLD
ONE THING SHOOK HIM UP BEFORE
I'VE GOT TO TRY IT AGAIN
JUST FOLLOW MY LEAD, GOBBY! I'M STEERING YOU TO SEE-- YOUR SON
NO! NO!
SORRY, OLD PAINT-- YOU'VE NOTHING TO SAY ABOUT IT
HOSPITAL
YOU MADE ONE BIG MISTAKE WITH THAT SECRET WEAPON OF YOURS--
WHEN YOU DESIGNED IT TO TAKE AWAY MY STICKING POWER--
--YOU SHOULDN'T HAVE LEFT MY STRENGTH! BUT, IT COULD BE WORSE--
AT LEAST, I WASH MY FEET
HARRY'S ROOM-- AT LAST
NOW, IF THIS DOESN'T WORK-- I'LL STILL BE BEHIND THE EIGHT BALL
18

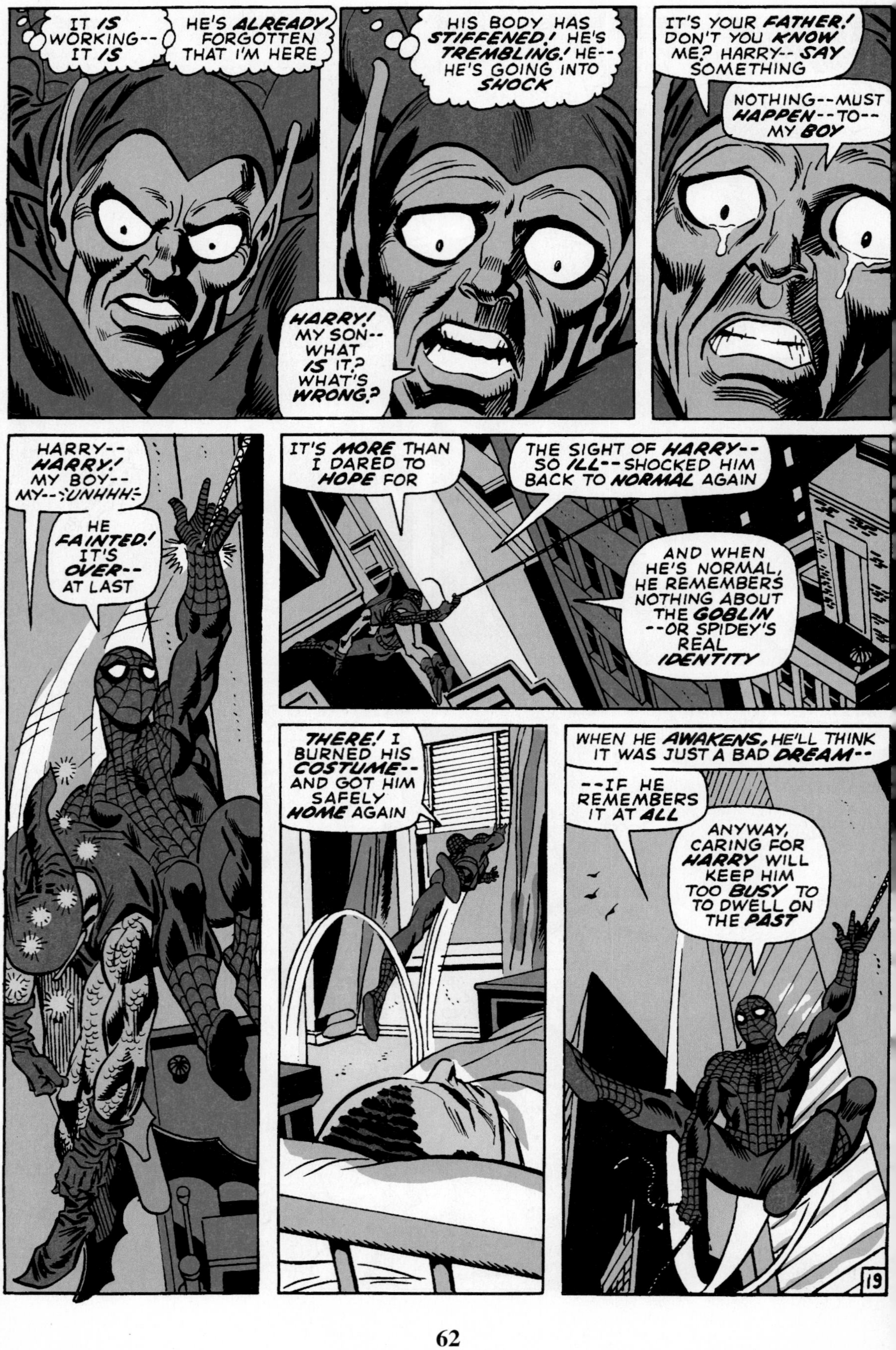
IT IS WORKING-- IT IS
HE'S ALREADY FORGOTTEN THAT I'M HERE
HIS BODY HAS STIFFENED! HE'S TREMBLING! HE-- HE'S GOING INTO SHOCK
HARRY! MY SON-- WHAT IS IT? WHAT'S WRONG?
IT'S YOUR FATHER! DON'T YOU KNOW ME? HARRY-- SAY SOMETHING
NOTHING--MUST HAPPEN--TO-- MY BOY
HARRY-- HARRY! MY BOY-- MY--UNHHH
HE FAINTED! IT'S OVER-- AT LAST
IT'S MORE THAN I DARED TO HOPE FOR
THE SIGHT OF HARRY-- SO ILL--SHOCKED HIM BACK TO NORMAL AGAIN
AND WHEN HE'S NORMAL, HE REMEMBERS NOTHING ABOUT THE GOBLIN --OR SPIDEY'S REAL IDENTITY
THERE! I BURNED HIS COSTUME-- AND GOT HIM SAFELY HOME AGAIN
WHEN HE AWAKENS, HE'LL THINK IT WAS JUST A BAD DREAM--
--IF HE REMEMBERS IT AT ALL
ANYWAY, CARING FOR HARRY WILL KEEP HIM TOO BUSY TO TO DWELL ON THE PAST
19

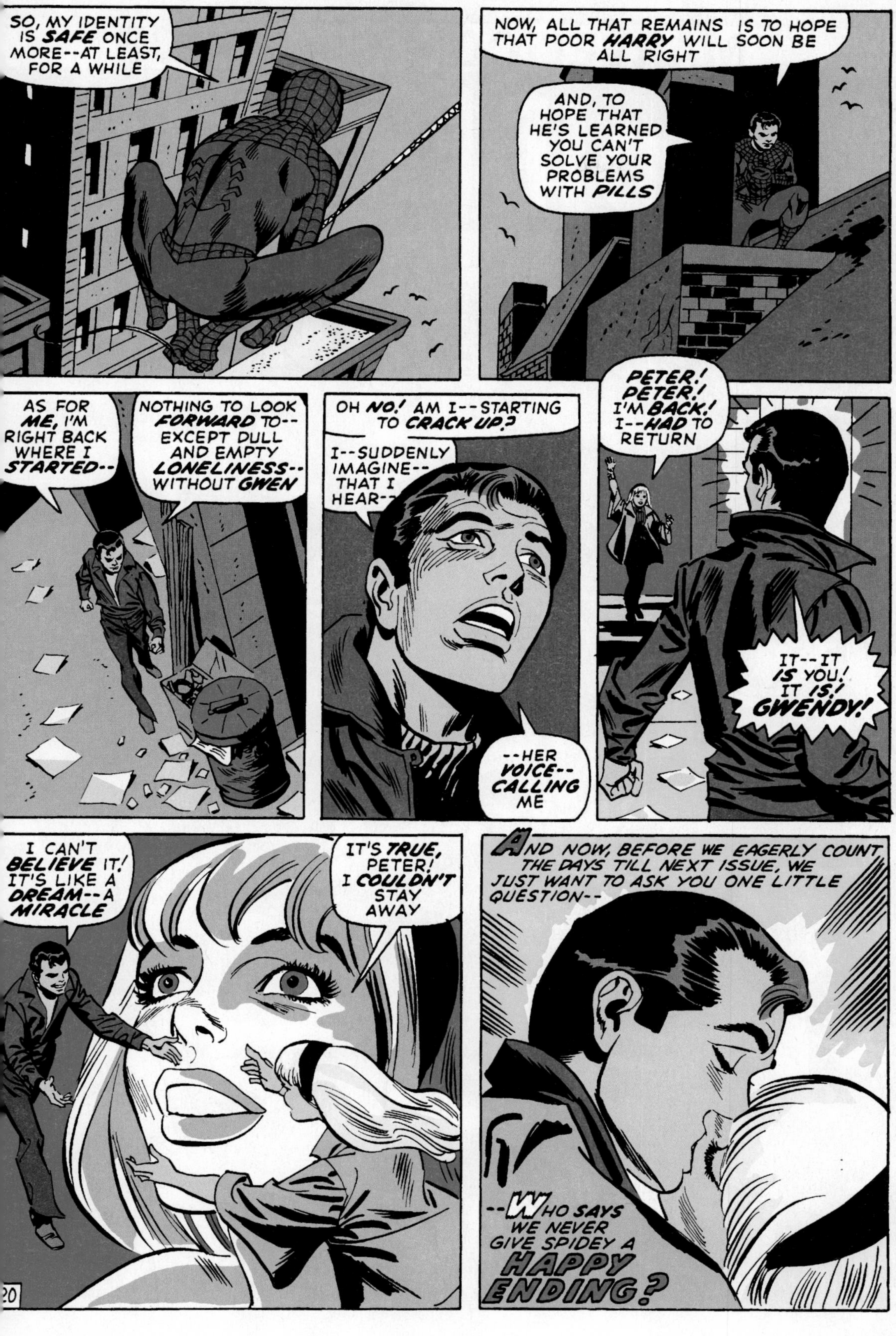
SO, MY IDENTITY IS SAFE ONCE MORE--AT LEAST, FOR A WHILE
NOW, ALL THAT REMAINS IS TO HOPE THAT POOR HARRY WILL SOON BE ALL RIGHT
AND, TO HOPE THAT HE'S LEARNED YOU CAN'T SOLVE YOUR PROBLEMS WITH PILLS
AS FOR ME, I'M RIGHT BACK WHERE I STARTED--
NOTHING TO LOOK FORWARD TO--EXCEPT DULL AND EMPTY LONELINESS--WITHOUT GWEN
OH NO! AM I--STARTING TO CRACK UP?
I--SUDDENLY IMAGINE--THAT I HEAR--
--HER VOICE--CALLING ME
PETER! PETER! I'M BACK! I--HAD TO RETURN
IT--IT IS YOU! IT IS! GWENDY!
I CAN'T BELIEVE IT! IT'S LIKE A DREAM--A MIRACLE
IT'S TRUE, PETER! I COULDN'T STAY AWAY
AND NOW, BEFORE WE EAGERLY COUNT THE DAYS TILL NEXT ISSUE, WE JUST WANT TO ASK YOU ONE LITTLE QUESTION--
--WHO SAYS WE NEVER GIVE SPIDEY A HAPPY ENDING?
20

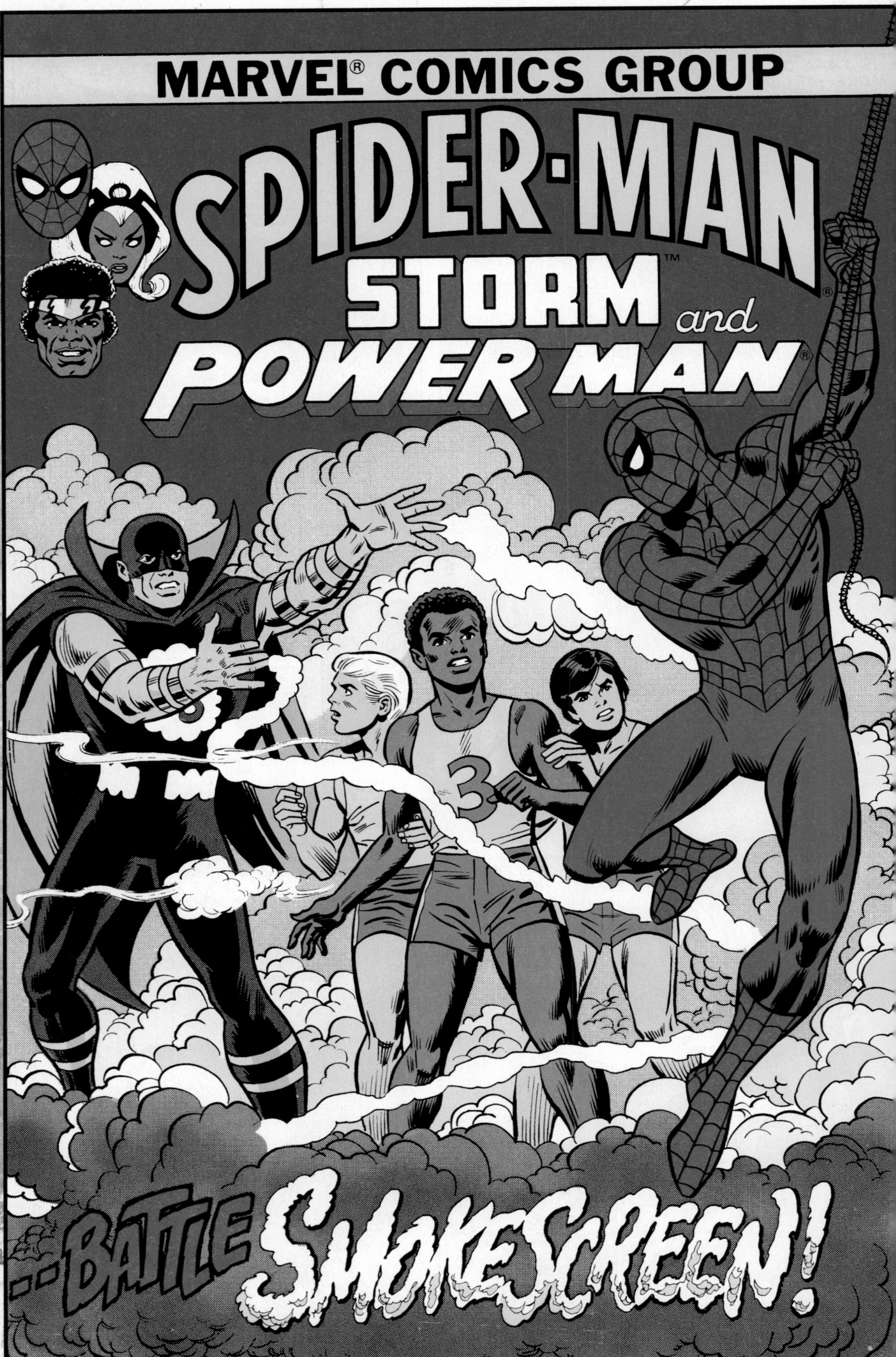

MARVEL® COMICS GROUP
SPIDER-MAN™
STORM®
and
POWER MAN®
--BATTLE SMOKESCREEN!

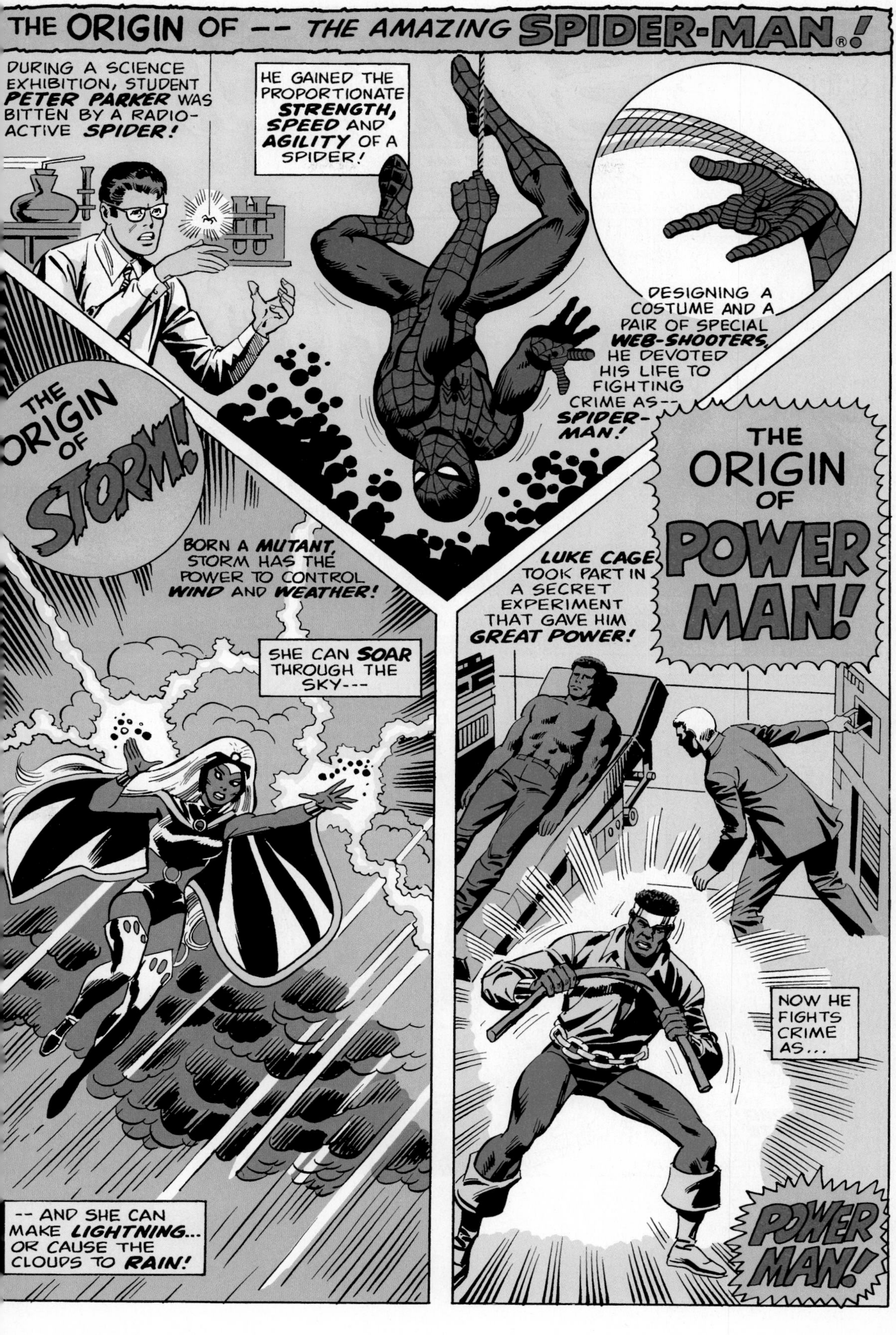
THE ORIGIN OF -- THE AMAZING SPIDER-MAN®!
DURING A SCIENCE EXHIBITION, STUDENT PETER PARKER WAS BITTEN BY A RADIO-ACTIVE SPIDER!
HE GAINED THE PROPORTIONATE STRENGTH, SPEED AND AGILITY OF A SPIDER!
DESIGNING A COSTUME AND A PAIR OF SPECIAL WEB-SHOOTERS, HE DEVOTED HIS LIFE TO FIGHTING CRIME AS-- SPIDER-MAN!
THE ORIGIN OF STORM!
BORN A MUTANT, STORM HAS THE POWER TO CONTROL WIND AND WEATHER!
SHE CAN SOAR THROUGH THE SKY---
-- AND SHE CAN MAKE LIGHTNING... OR CAUSE THE CLOUDS TO RAIN!
THE ORIGIN OF POWER MAN!
LUKE CAGE TOOK PART IN A SECRET EXPERIMENT THAT GAVE HIM GREAT POWER!
NOW HE FIGHTS CRIME AS...
POWER MAN!

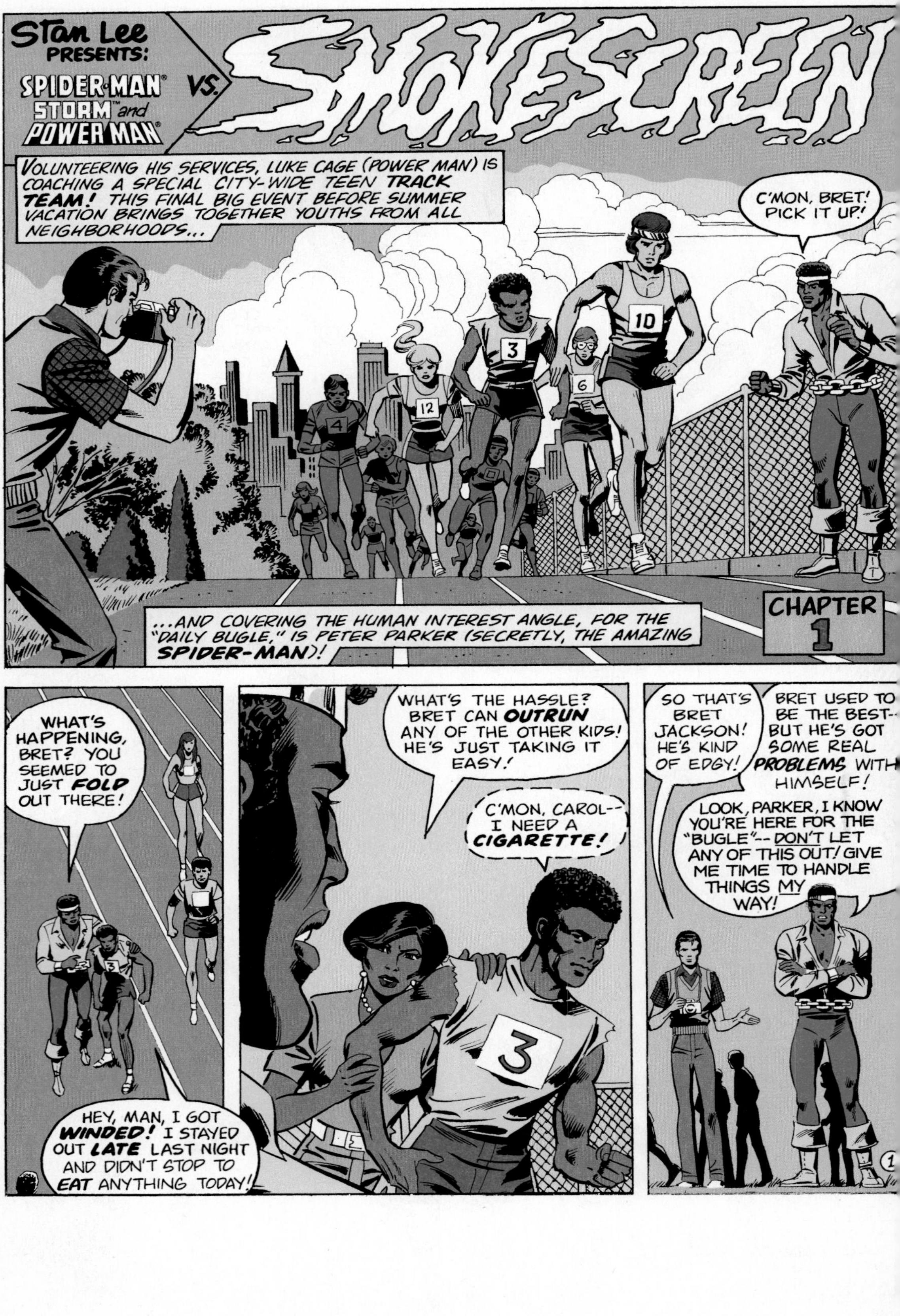

Stan Lee PRESENTS:
SPIDER-MAN® STORM™ and POWER MAN®
VS.
SMOKESCREEN
VOLUNTEERING HIS SERVICES, LUKE CAGE (POWER MAN) IS COACHING A SPECIAL CITY-WIDE TEEN TRACK TEAM! THIS FINAL BIG EVENT BEFORE SUMMER VACATION BRINGS TOGETHER YOUTHS FROM ALL NEIGHBORHOODS...
C'MON, BRET! PICK IT UP!
...AND COVERING THE HUMAN INTEREST ANGLE, FOR THE "DAILY BUGLE," IS PETER PARKER (SECRETLY, THE AMAZING SPIDER-MAN)!
CHAPTER 1
WHAT'S HAPPENING, BRET? YOU SEEMED TO JUST FOLD OUT THERE!
HEY, MAN, I GOT WINDED! I STAYED OUT LATE LAST NIGHT AND DIDN'T STOP TO EAT ANYTHING TODAY!
WHAT'S THE HASSLE? BRET CAN OUTRUN ANY OF THE OTHER KIDS! HE'S JUST TAKING IT EASY!
C'MON, CAROL-- I NEED A CIGARETTE!
SO THAT'S BRET JACKSON! HE'S KIND OF EDGY!
BRET USED TO BE THE BEST-- BUT HE'S GOT SOME REAL PROBLEMS WITH HIMSELF!
LOOK, PARKER, I KNOW YOU'RE HERE FOR THE "BUGLE"-- DON'T LET ANY OF THIS OUT! GIVE ME TIME TO HANDLE THINGS MY WAY!

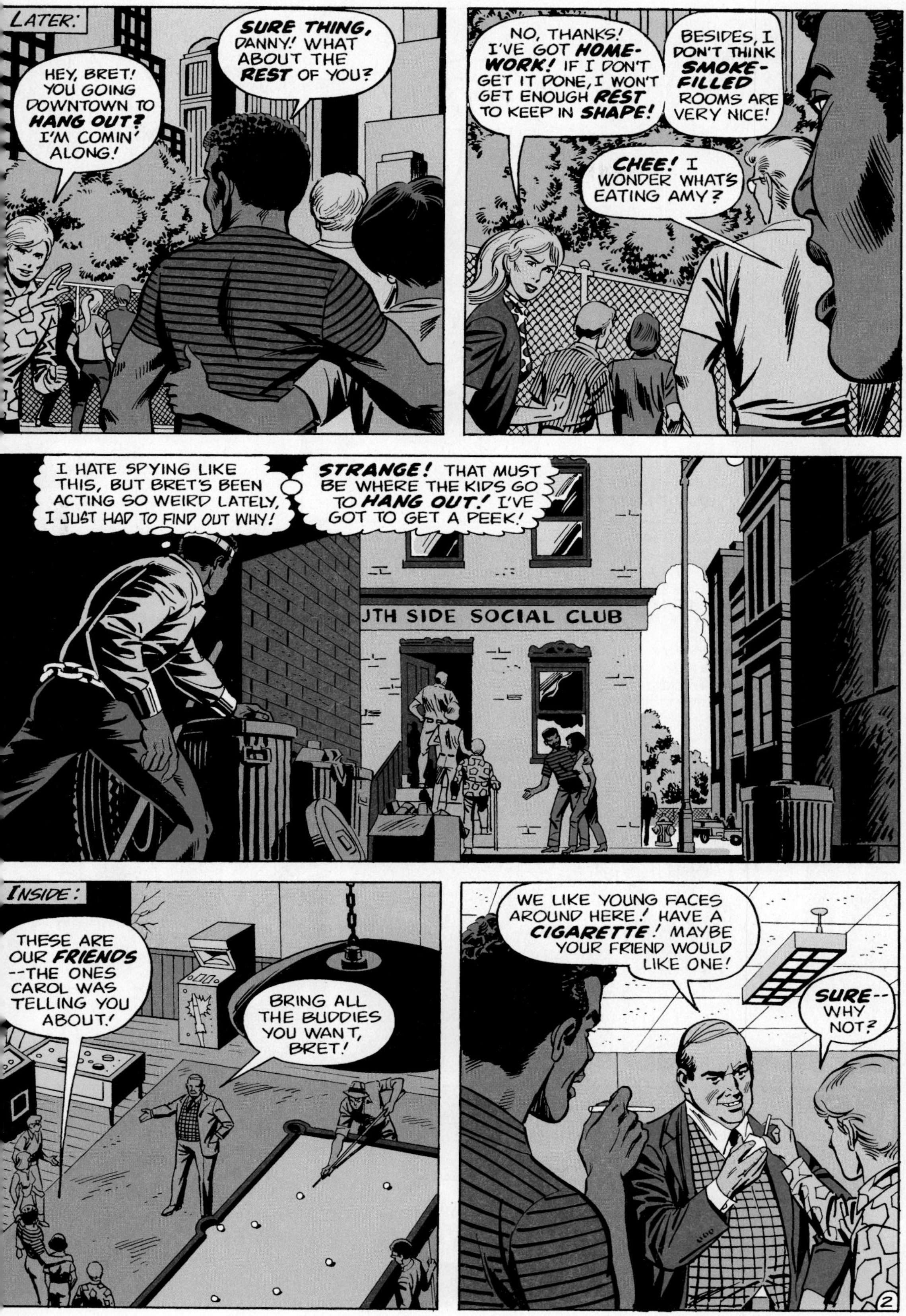
LATER:
HEY, BRET! YOU GOING DOWNTOWN TO HANG OUT? I'M COMIN' ALONG!
SURE THING, DANNY! WHAT ABOUT THE REST OF YOU?
NO, THANKS! I'VE GOT HOME-WORK! IF I DON'T GET IT DONE, I WON'T GET ENOUGH REST TO KEEP IN SHAPE!
BESIDES, I DON'T THINK SMOKE-FILLED ROOMS ARE VERY NICE!
CHEE! I WONDER WHAT'S EATING AMY?
I HATE SPYING LIKE THIS, BUT BRET'S BEEN ACTING SO WEIRD LATELY, I JUST HAD TO FIND OUT WHY!
STRANGE! THAT MUST BE WHERE THE KIDS GO TO HANG OUT! I'VE GOT TO GET A PEEK!
JTH SIDE SOCIAL CLUB
INSIDE:
THESE ARE OUR FRIENDS --THE ONES CAROL WAS TELLING YOU ABOUT!
BRING ALL THE BUDDIES YOU WANT, BRET!
WE LIKE YOUNG FACES AROUND HERE! HAVE A CIGARETTE! MAYBE YOUR FRIEND WOULD LIKE ONE!
SURE-- WHY NOT?
2

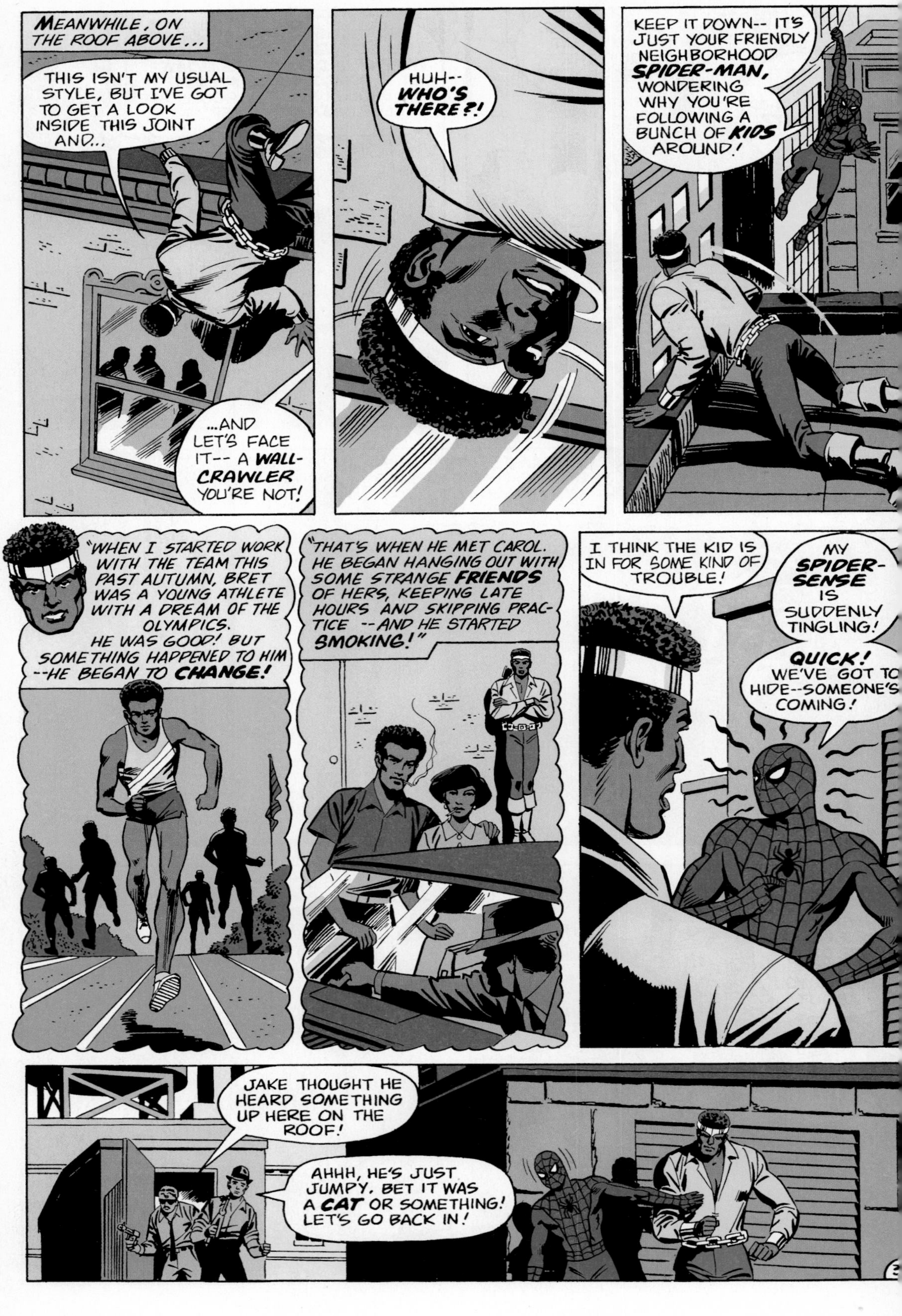
MEANWHILE, ON THE ROOF ABOVE...
THIS ISN'T MY USUAL STYLE, BUT I'VE GOT TO GET A LOOK INSIDE THIS JOINT AND...
...AND LET'S FACE IT-- A WALL-CRAWLER YOU'RE NOT!
HUH-- WHO'S THERE?!
KEEP IT DOWN-- IT'S JUST YOUR FRIENDLY NEIGHBORHOOD SPIDER-MAN, WONDERING WHY YOU'RE FOLLOWING A BUNCH OF KIDS AROUND!
"WHEN I STARTED WORK WITH THE TEAM THIS PAST AUTUMN, BRET WAS A YOUNG ATHLETE WITH A DREAM OF THE OLYMPICS. HE WAS GOOD! BUT SOMETHING HAPPENED TO HIM --HE BEGAN TO CHANGE!
"THAT'S WHEN HE MET CAROL. HE BEGAN HANGING OUT WITH SOME STRANGE FRIENDS OF HERS, KEEPING LATE HOURS AND SKIPPING PRACTICE --AND HE STARTED SMOKING!"
I THINK THE KID IS IN FOR SOME KIND OF TROUBLE!
MY SPIDER-SENSE IS SUDDENLY TINGLING!
QUICK! WE'VE GOT TO HIDE--SOMEONE'S COMING!
JAKE THOUGHT HE HEARD SOMETHING UP HERE ON THE ROOF!
AHHH, HE'S JUST JUMPY. BET IT WAS A CAT OR SOMETHING! LET'S GO BACK IN!

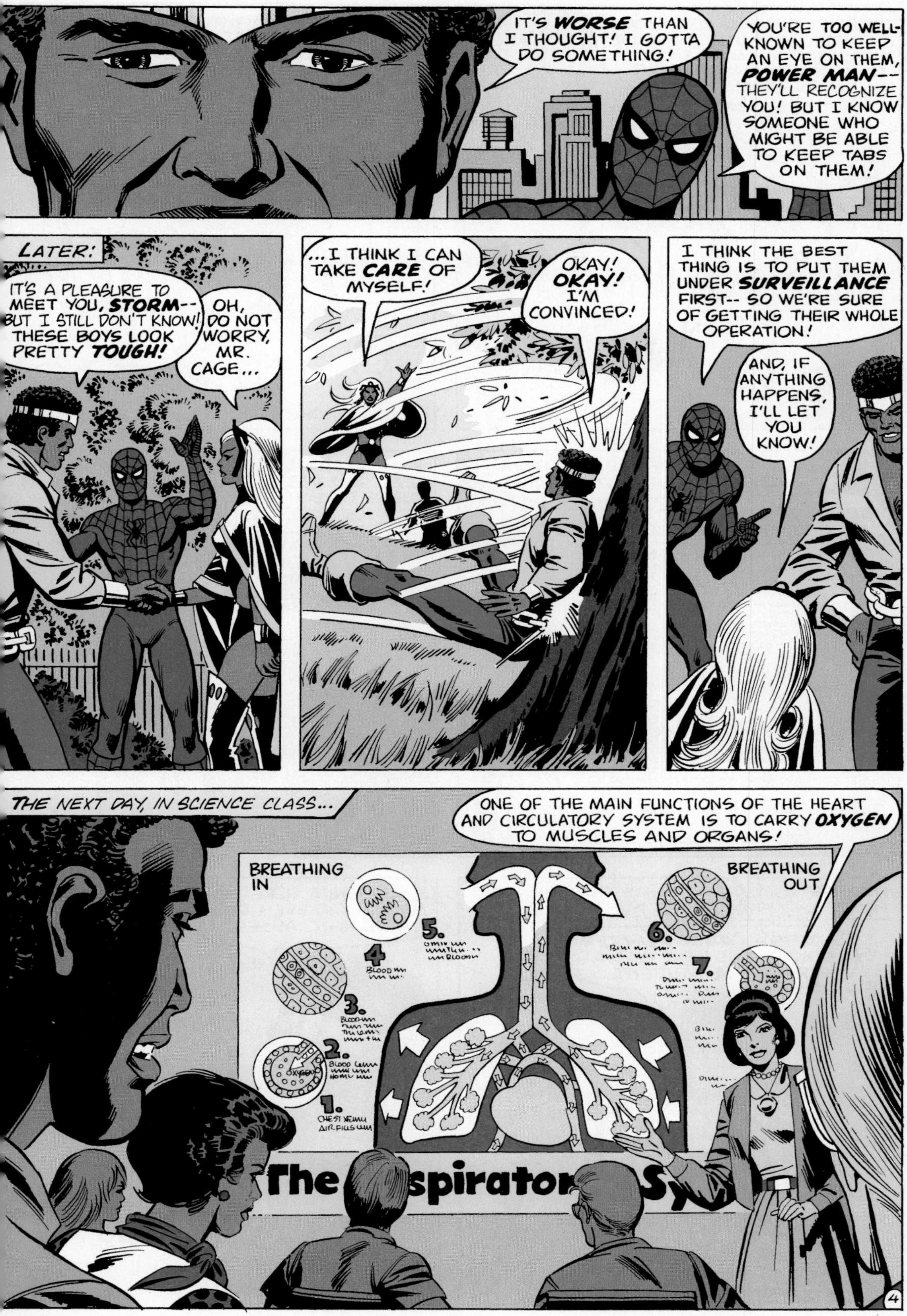

IT'S WORSE THAN I THOUGHT! I GOTTA DO SOMETHING!
YOU'RE TOO WELL-KNOWN TO KEEP AN EYE ON THEM, POWER MAN-- THEY'LL RECOGNIZE YOU! BUT I KNOW SOMEONE WHO MIGHT BE ABLE TO KEEP TABS ON THEM!
LATER:
IT'S A PLEASURE TO MEET YOU, STORM-- BUT I STILL DON'T KNOW! THESE BOYS LOOK PRETTY TOUGH!
OH, DO NOT WORRY, MR. CAGE...
...I THINK I CAN TAKE CARE OF MYSELF!
OKAY! OKAY! I'M CONVINCED!
I THINK THE BEST THING IS TO PUT THEM UNDER SURVEILLANCE FIRST-- SO WE'RE SURE OF GETTING THEIR WHOLE OPERATION!
AND, IF ANYTHING HAPPENS, I'LL LET YOU KNOW!
THE NEXT DAY, IN SCIENCE CLASS...
ONE OF THE MAIN FUNCTIONS OF THE HEART AND CIRCULATORY SYSTEM IS TO CARRY OXYGEN TO MUSCLES AND ORGANS!
BREATHING IN
BREATHING OUT
1.
2.
3.
4
5.
6.
7.
OXYGEN
4

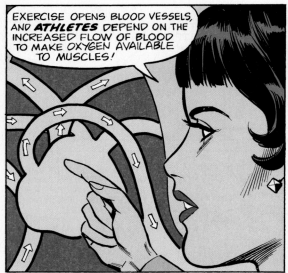

EXERCISE OPENS BLOOD VESSELS, AND **ATHLETES** DEPEND ON THE INCREASED FLOW OF BLOOD TO MAKE OXYGEN AVAILABLE TO MUSCLES!

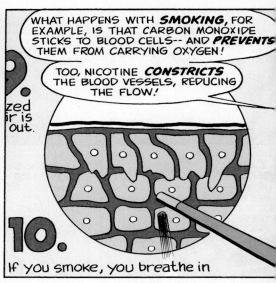

WHAT HAPPENS WITH **SMOKING**, FOR EXAMPLE, IS THAT CARBON MONOXIDE STICKS TO BLOOD CELLS-- AND **PREVENTS** THEM FROM CARRYING OXYGEN!

TOO, NICOTINE **CONSTRICTS** THE BLOOD VESSELS, REDUCING THE FLOW!

zed ir is out.

10.

If you smoke, you breathe in

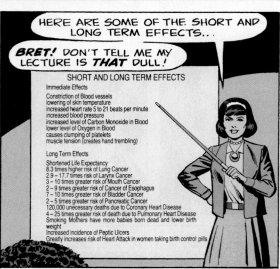

HERE ARE SOME OF THE SHORT AND LONG TERM EFFECTS...

BRET! DON'T TELL ME MY LECTURE IS **THAT** DULL!

SHORT AND LONG TERM EFFECTS

Immediate Effects
Constriction of Blood vessels
lowering of skin temperature
increased heart rate 5 to 21 beats per minute
increased blood pressure
increased level of Carbon Monoxide in Blood
lower level of Oxygen in Blood
causes clumping of platelets
muscle tension (creates hand trembling)

Long Term Effects
Shortened Life Expectancy
8.3 times higher risk of Lung Cancer
2.9 – 17.7 times risk of Larynx Cancer
3 – 10 times greater risk of Mouth Cancer
2 – 9 times greater risk of Cancer of Esophagus
7 – 10 times greater risk of Bladder Cancer
2 – 5 times greater risk of Pancreatic Cancer
120,000 unecessary deaths due to Coronary Heart Disease
4 – 25 times greater risk of death due to Pulmonary Heart Disease
Smoking Mothers have more babies born dead and lower birth weight
Increased incidence of Peptic Ulcers
Greatly increases risk of Heart Attack in women taking birth control pills

NO! I MEAN-- I DON'T **FEEL** TOO WELL! I GUESS I STAYED OUT A LITTLE **LATE** LAST NIGHT!

BRET--YOUR GRADES HAVE REALLY BEEN **SLIPPING!**

YOU'D BETTER GIVE SOME THOUGHT TO THE WAY YOUR DECISIONS ARE AFFECTING YOUR LIFE!

MEANWHILE, IN THE PRINCIPAL'S OFFICE...

IS THAT THE RIGHT FILE?

SURE IS-- **CAROL HUNTER!** LOOK AT THIS! SHE WAS A STRAIGHT **A** STUDENT...

...SUDDENLY, HERE SHE IS MAKING Cs, EVEN Ds, AND MISSING CLASSES!

HAVE YOU LOOKED AT BRET'S RECORD? IT'S BEGINNING TO LOOK THE SAME!

WE MIGHT HAVE TO PULL HIM **OFF** THE TRACK TEAM!

HUNTER, CAROL

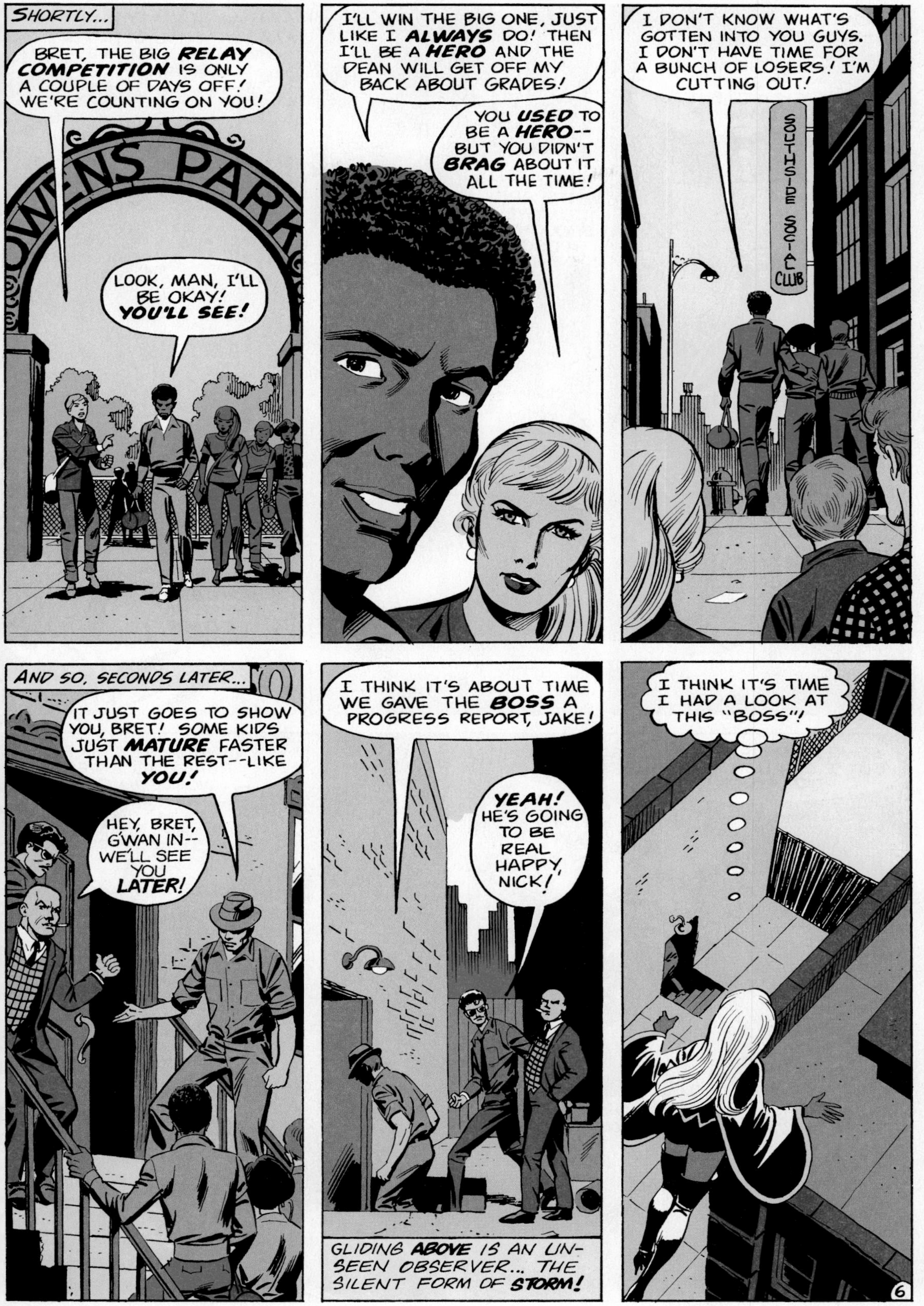
SHORTLY...
BRET, THE BIG RELAY COMPETITION IS ONLY A COUPLE OF DAYS OFF! WE'RE COUNTING ON YOU!
OWENS PARK
LOOK, MAN, I'LL BE OKAY! YOU'LL SEE!
I'LL WIN THE BIG ONE, JUST LIKE I ALWAYS DO! THEN I'LL BE A HERO AND THE DEAN WILL GET OFF MY BACK ABOUT GRADES!
YOU USED TO BE A HERO-- BUT YOU DIDN'T BRAG ABOUT IT ALL THE TIME!
I DON'T KNOW WHAT'S GOTTEN INTO YOU GUYS. I DON'T HAVE TIME FOR A BUNCH OF LOSERS! I'M CUTTING OUT!
SOUTHSIDE SOCIAL CLUB
AND SO, SECONDS LATER...
IT JUST GOES TO SHOW YOU, BRET! SOME KIDS JUST MATURE FASTER THAN THE REST--LIKE YOU!
HEY, BRET, G'WAN IN-- WE'LL SEE YOU LATER!
I THINK IT'S ABOUT TIME WE GAVE THE BOSS A PROGRESS REPORT, JAKE!
YEAH! HE'S GOING TO BE REAL HAPPY, NICK!
GLIDING ABOVE IS AN UNSEEN OBSERVER... THE SILENT FORM OF STORM!
I THINK IT'S TIME I HAD A LOOK AT THIS "BOSS"!
6

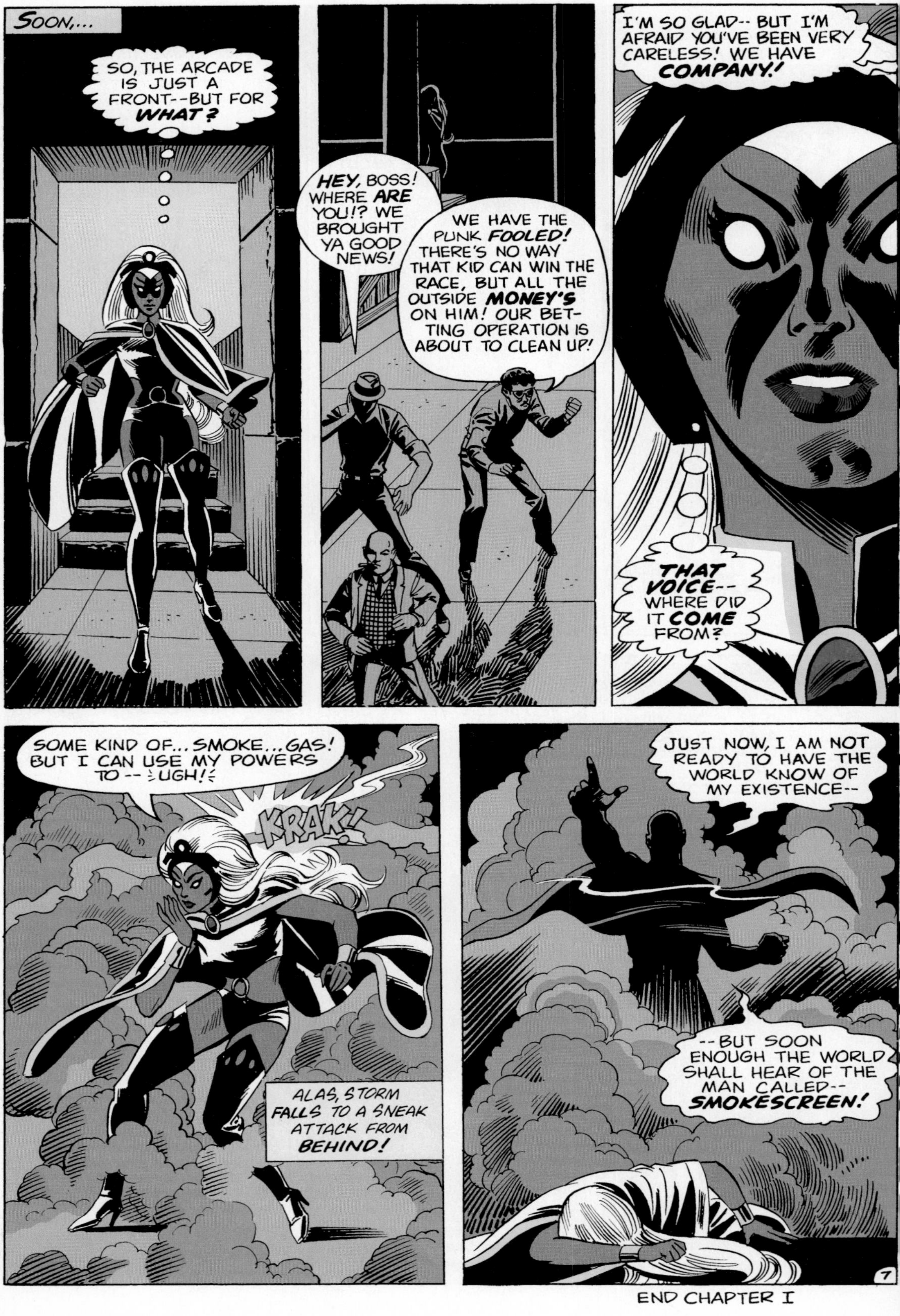
SOON,...
SO, THE ARCADE IS JUST A FRONT--BUT FOR WHAT?
HEY, BOSS! WHERE ARE YOU!? WE BROUGHT YA GOOD NEWS!
WE HAVE THE PUNK FOOLED! THERE'S NO WAY THAT KID CAN WIN THE RACE, BUT ALL THE OUTSIDE MONEY'S ON HIM! OUR BETTING OPERATION IS ABOUT TO CLEAN UP!
I'M SO GLAD-- BUT I'M AFRAID YOU'VE BEEN VERY CARELESS! WE HAVE COMPANY!
THAT VOICE-- WHERE DID IT COME FROM?
SOME KIND OF... SMOKE... GAS! BUT I CAN USE MY POWERS TO-- UGH!
KRAK!
ALAS, STORM FALLS TO A SNEAK ATTACK FROM BEHIND!
JUST NOW, I AM NOT READY TO HAVE THE WORLD KNOW OF MY EXISTENCE--
--BUT SOON ENOUGH THE WORLD SHALL HEAR OF THE MAN CALLED-- SMOKESCREEN!
7

END CHAPTER I

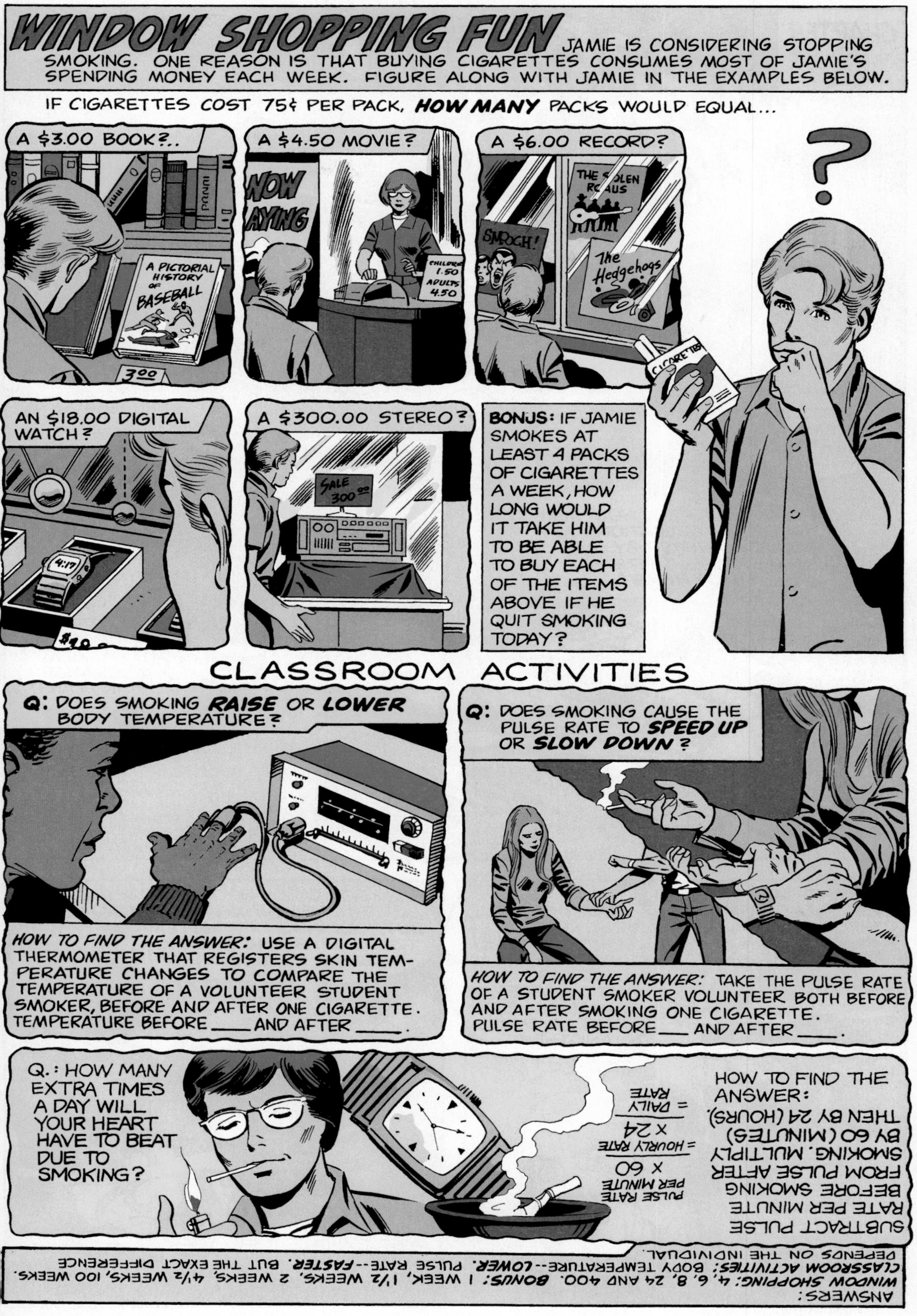
WINDOW SHOPPING FUN
JAMIE IS CONSIDERING STOPPING SMOKING. ONE REASON IS THAT BUYING CIGARETTES CONSUMES MOST OF JAMIE'S SPENDING MONEY EACH WEEK. FIGURE ALONG WITH JAMIE IN THE EXAMPLES BELOW.
IF CIGARETTES COST 75¢ PER PACK, HOW MANY PACKS WOULD EQUAL...
A $3.00 BOOK?..
A PICTORIAL HISTORY OF BASEBALL
3.00
A $4.50 MOVIE?
NOW PLAYING
CHILDREN 1.50 ADULTS 4.50
A $6.00 RECORD?
The Hedgehogs
SMOOCH!
CIGARETTES
AN $18.00 DIGITAL WATCH?
4:19
A $300.00 STEREO?
SALE 300.00
BONUS: IF JAMIE SMOKES AT LEAST 4 PACKS OF CIGARETTES A WEEK, HOW LONG WOULD IT TAKE HIM TO BE ABLE TO BUY EACH OF THE ITEMS ABOVE IF HE QUIT SMOKING TODAY?
CLASSROOM ACTIVITIES
Q: DOES SMOKING RAISE OR LOWER BODY TEMPERATURE?
HOW TO FIND THE ANSWER: USE A DIGITAL THERMOMETER THAT REGISTERS SKIN TEMPERATURE CHANGES TO COMPARE THE TEMPERATURE OF A VOLUNTEER STUDENT SMOKER, BEFORE AND AFTER ONE CIGARETTE. TEMPERATURE BEFORE ____ AND AFTER ____.
Q: DOES SMOKING CAUSE THE PULSE RATE TO SPEED UP OR SLOW DOWN?
HOW TO FIND THE ANSWER: TAKE THE PULSE RATE OF A STUDENT SMOKER VOLUNTEER BOTH BEFORE AND AFTER SMOKING ONE CIGARETTE. PULSE RATE BEFORE ____ AND AFTER ____.
Q.: HOW MANY EXTRA TIMES A DAY WILL YOUR HEART HAVE TO BEAT DUE TO SMOKING?
HOW TO FIND THE ANSWER: SUBTRACT PULSE RATE PER MINUTE BEFORE SMOKING FROM PULSE AFTER SMOKING. MULTIPLY BY 60 (MINUTES) THEN BY 24 (HOURS).
PULSE RATE PER MINUTE x 60 = HOURLY RATE x 24 = DAILY RATE
ANSWERS: WINDOW SHOPPING: 4, 6, 8, 24 AND 400. BONUS: 1 WEEK, 1 1/2 WEEKS, 2 WEEKS, 4 1/2 WEEKS, 100 WEEKS. CLASSROOM ACTIVITIES: BODY TEMPERATURE--LOWER. PULSE RATE--FASTER. BUT THE EXACT DIFFERENCE DEPENDS ON THE INDIVIDUAL.

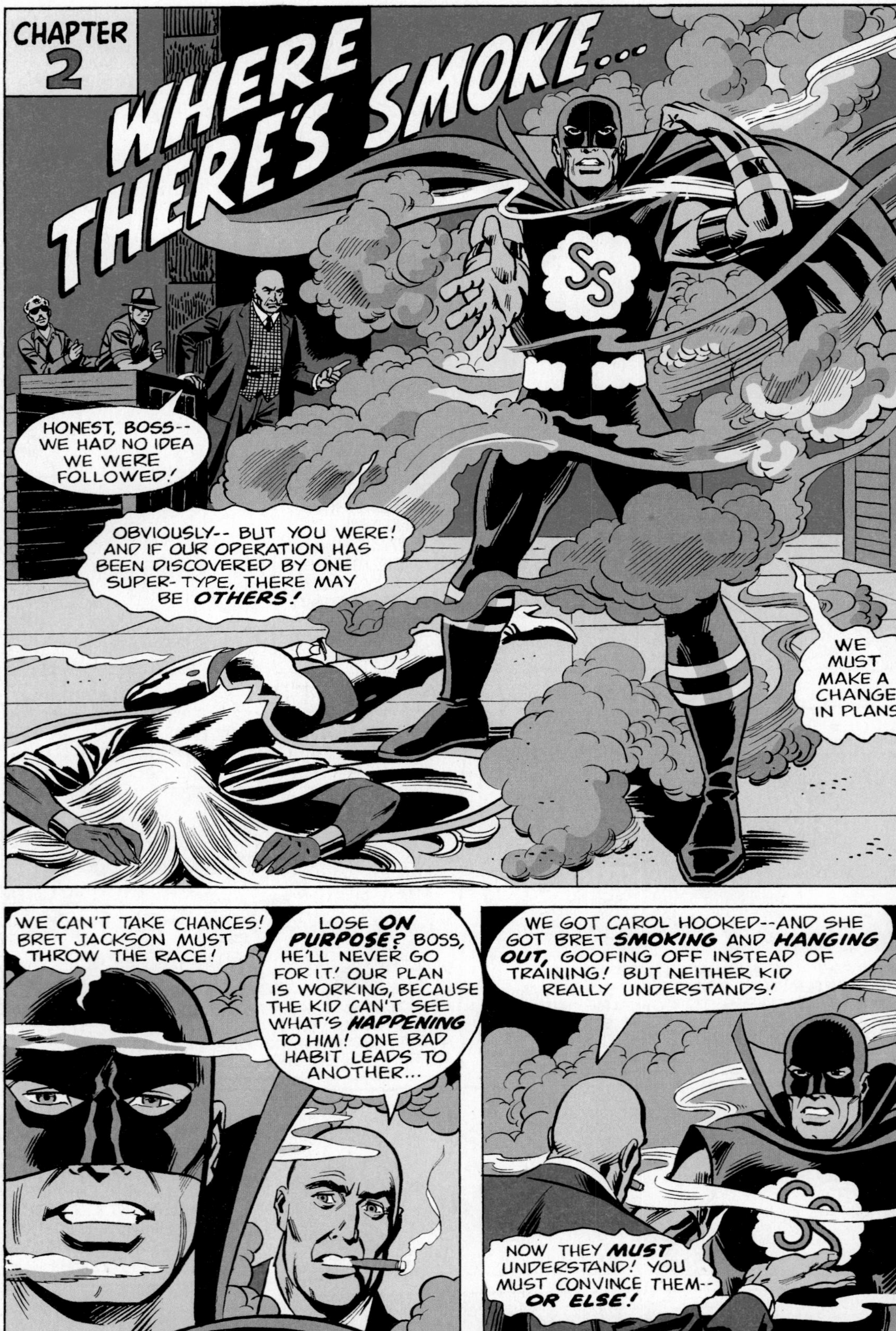
CHAPTER 2
WHERE THERE'S SMOKE...
HONEST, BOSS-- WE HAD NO IDEA WE WERE FOLLOWED!
OBVIOUSLY-- BUT YOU WERE! AND IF OUR OPERATION HAS BEEN DISCOVERED BY ONE SUPER-TYPE, THERE MAY BE OTHERS!
WE MUST MAKE A CHANGE IN PLANS!
WE CAN'T TAKE CHANCES! BRET JACKSON MUST THROW THE RACE!
LOSE ON PURPOSE? BOSS, HE'LL NEVER GO FOR IT! OUR PLAN IS WORKING, BECAUSE THE KID CAN'T SEE WHAT'S HAPPENING TO HIM! ONE BAD HABIT LEADS TO ANOTHER...
WE GOT CAROL HOOKED--AND SHE GOT BRET SMOKING AND HANGING OUT, GOOFING OFF INSTEAD OF TRAINING! BUT NEITHER KID REALLY UNDERSTANDS!
NOW THEY MUST UNDERSTAND! YOU MUST CONVINCE THEM-- OR ELSE!
8

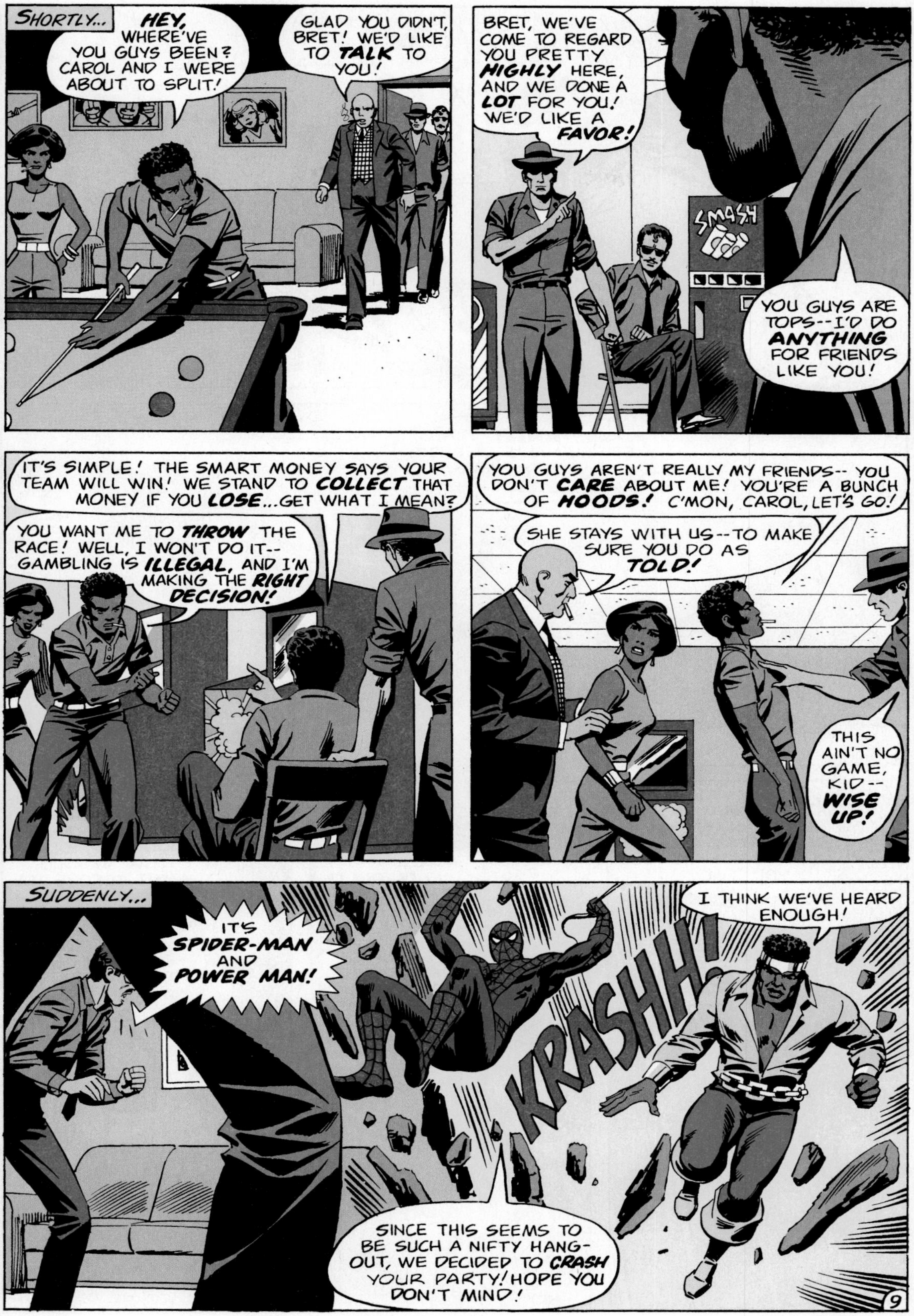

SHORTLY...
HEY, WHERE'VE YOU GUYS BEEN? CAROL AND I WERE ABOUT TO SPLIT!
GLAD YOU DIDN'T, BRET! WE'D LIKE TO TALK TO YOU!
BRET, WE'VE COME TO REGARD YOU PRETTY HIGHLY HERE, AND WE DONE A LOT FOR YOU! WE'D LIKE A FAVOR!
SMASH
YOU GUYS ARE TOPS--I'D DO ANYTHING FOR FRIENDS LIKE YOU!
IT'S SIMPLE! THE SMART MONEY SAYS YOUR TEAM WILL WIN! WE STAND TO COLLECT THAT MONEY IF YOU LOSE...GET WHAT I MEAN?
YOU WANT ME TO THROW THE RACE! WELL, I WON'T DO IT--GAMBLING IS ILLEGAL, AND I'M MAKING THE RIGHT DECISION!
YOU GUYS AREN'T REALLY MY FRIENDS-- YOU DON'T CARE ABOUT ME! YOU'RE A BUNCH OF HOODS! C'MON, CAROL, LET'S GO!
SHE STAYS WITH US--TO MAKE SURE YOU DO AS TOLD!
THIS AIN'T NO GAME, KID-- WISE UP!
SUDDENLY...
IT'S SPIDER-MAN AND POWER MAN!
I THINK WE'VE HEARD ENOUGH!
KRASHH!
SINCE THIS SEEMS TO BE SUCH A NIFTY HANG-OUT, WE DECIDED TO CRASH YOUR PARTY! HOPE YOU DON'T MIND!
9

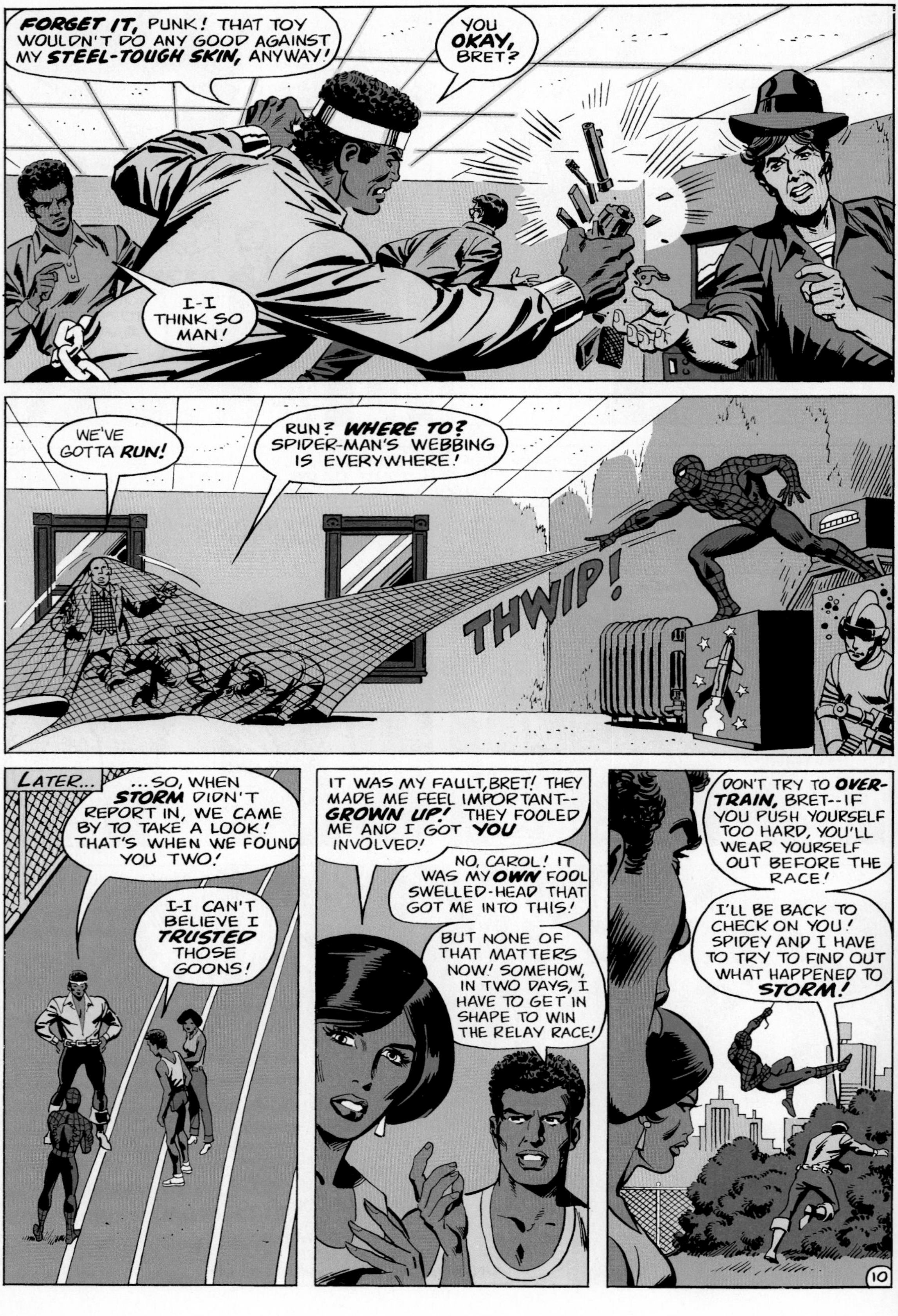
FORGET IT, PUNK! THAT TOY WOULDN'T DO ANY GOOD AGAINST MY STEEL-TOUGH SKIN, ANYWAY!
YOU OKAY, BRET?
I-I THINK SO MAN!
WE'VE GOTTA RUN!
RUN? WHERE TO? SPIDER-MAN'S WEBBING IS EVERYWHERE!
THWIP!
LATER...
...SO, WHEN STORM DIDN'T REPORT IN, WE CAME BY TO TAKE A LOOK! THAT'S WHEN WE FOUND YOU TWO!
I-I CAN'T BELIEVE I TRUSTED THOSE GOONS!
IT WAS MY FAULT, BRET! THEY MADE ME FEEL IMPORTANT-- GROWN UP! THEY FOOLED ME AND I GOT YOU INVOLVED!
NO, CAROL! IT WAS MY OWN FOOL SWELLED-HEAD THAT GOT ME INTO THIS!
BUT NONE OF THAT MATTERS NOW! SOMEHOW, IN TWO DAYS, I HAVE TO GET IN SHAPE TO WIN THE RELAY RACE!
DON'T TRY TO OVER-TRAIN, BRET--IF YOU PUSH YOURSELF TOO HARD, YOU'LL WEAR YOURSELF OUT BEFORE THE RACE!
I'LL BE BACK TO CHECK ON YOU! SPIDEY AND I HAVE TO TRY TO FIND OUT WHAT HAPPENED TO STORM!
10

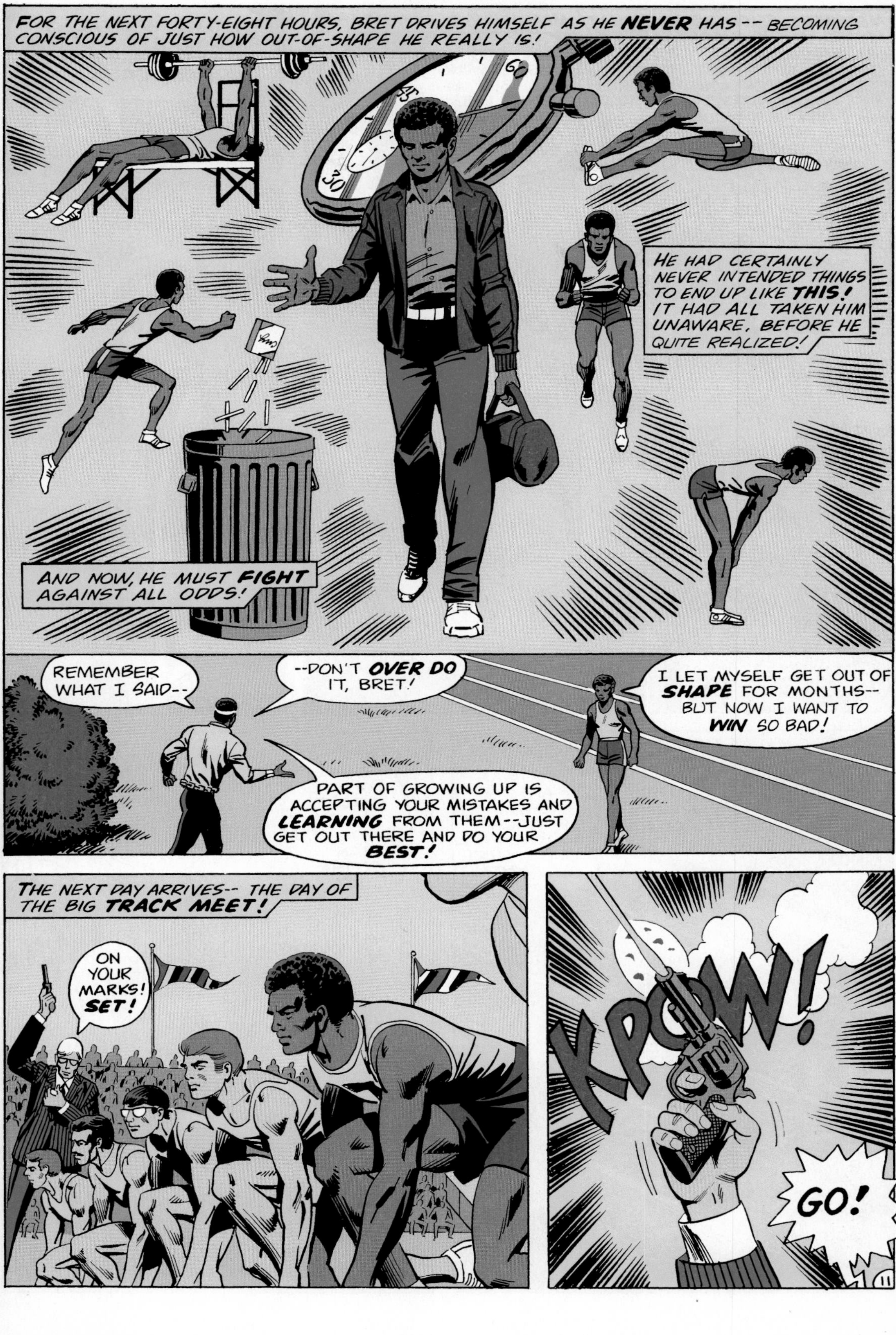
FOR THE NEXT FORTY-EIGHT HOURS, BRET DRIVES HIMSELF AS HE NEVER HAS -- BECOMING CONSCIOUS OF JUST HOW OUT-OF-SHAPE HE REALLY IS!
HE HAD CERTAINLY NEVER INTENDED THINGS TO END UP LIKE THIS! IT HAD ALL TAKEN HIM UNAWARE, BEFORE HE QUITE REALIZED!
AND NOW, HE MUST FIGHT AGAINST ALL ODDS!
REMEMBER WHAT I SAID--
--DON'T OVER DO IT, BRET!
I LET MYSELF GET OUT OF SHAPE FOR MONTHS-- BUT NOW I WANT TO WIN SO BAD!
PART OF GROWING UP IS ACCEPTING YOUR MISTAKES AND LEARNING FROM THEM--JUST GET OUT THERE AND DO YOUR BEST!
THE NEXT DAY ARRIVES-- THE DAY OF THE BIG TRACK MEET!
ON YOUR MARKS! SET!
KPOW!
GO!
11

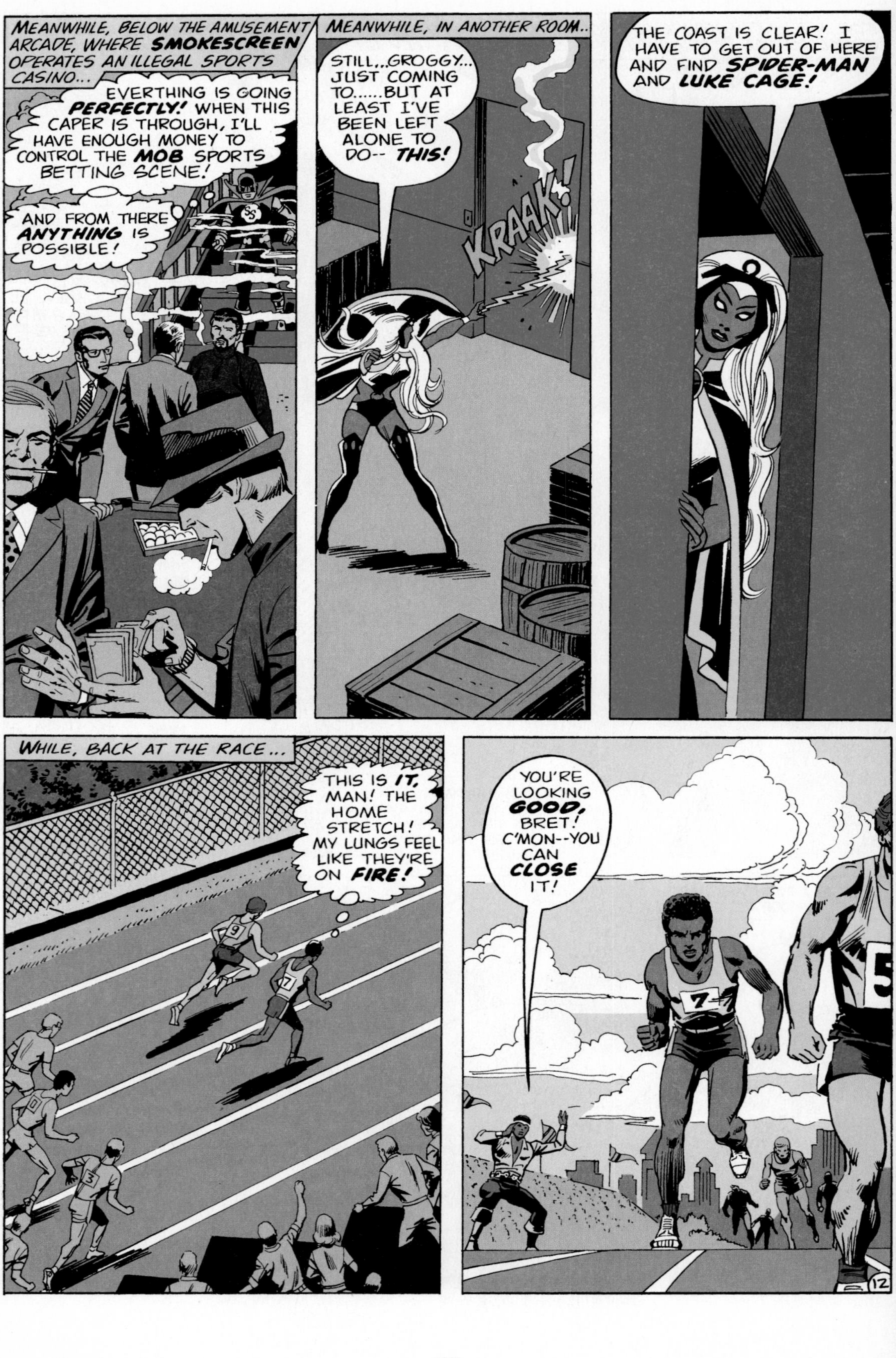
MEANWHILE, BELOW THE AMUSEMENT ARCADE, WHERE SMOKESCREEN OPERATES AN ILLEGAL SPORTS CASINO...
EVERTHING IS GOING PERFECTLY! WHEN THIS CAPER IS THROUGH, I'LL HAVE ENOUGH MONEY TO CONTROL THE MOB SPORTS BETTING SCENE!
AND FROM THERE ANYTHING IS POSSIBLE!
MEANWHILE, IN ANOTHER ROOM...
STILL,..GROGGY... JUST COMING TO......BUT AT LEAST I'VE BEEN LEFT ALONE TO DO-- THIS!
KRAAK!
THE COAST IS CLEAR! I HAVE TO GET OUT OF HERE AND FIND SPIDER-MAN AND LUKE CAGE!
WHILE, BACK AT THE RACE...
THIS IS IT, MAN! THE HOME STRETCH! MY LUNGS FEEL LIKE THEY'RE ON FIRE!
YOU'RE LOOKING GOOD, BRET! C'MON--YOU CAN CLOSE IT!
12

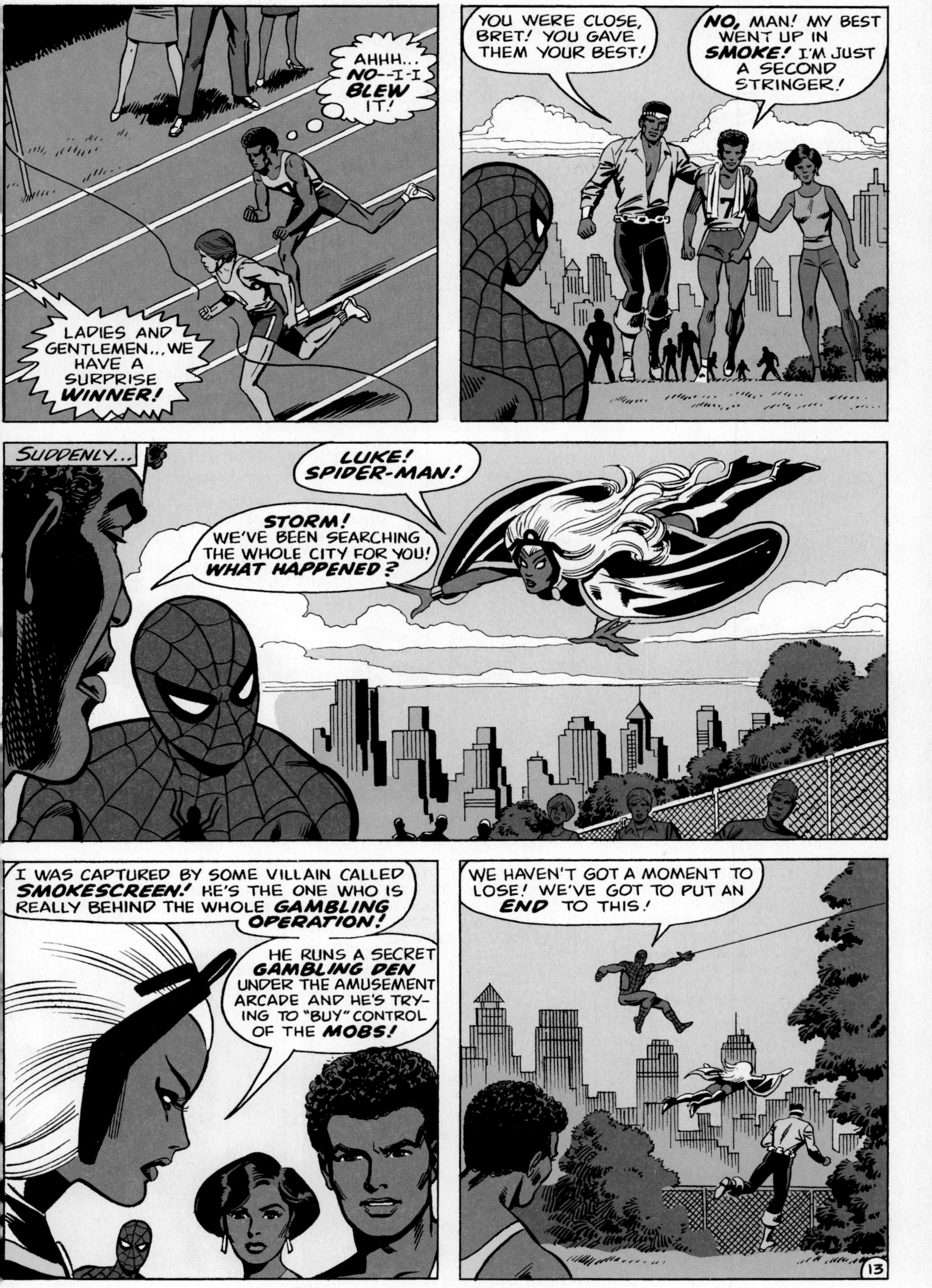
AHHH... NO--I-I BLEW IT!
LADIES AND GENTLEMEN..., WE HAVE A SURPRISE WINNER!
YOU WERE CLOSE, BRET! YOU GAVE THEM YOUR BEST!
NO, MAN! MY BEST WENT UP IN SMOKE! I'M JUST A SECOND STRINGER!
SUDDENLY...
LUKE! SPIDER-MAN!
STORM! WE'VE BEEN SEARCHING THE WHOLE CITY FOR YOU! WHAT HAPPENED?
I WAS CAPTURED BY SOME VILLAIN CALLED SMOKESCREEN! HE'S THE ONE WHO IS REALLY BEHIND THE WHOLE GAMBLING OPERATION!
HE RUNS A SECRET GAMBLING DEN UNDER THE AMUSEMENT ARCADE AND HE'S TRYING TO "BUY" CONTROL OF THE MOBS!
WE HAVEN'T GOT A MOMENT TO LOSE! WE'VE GOT TO PUT AN END TO THIS!
13

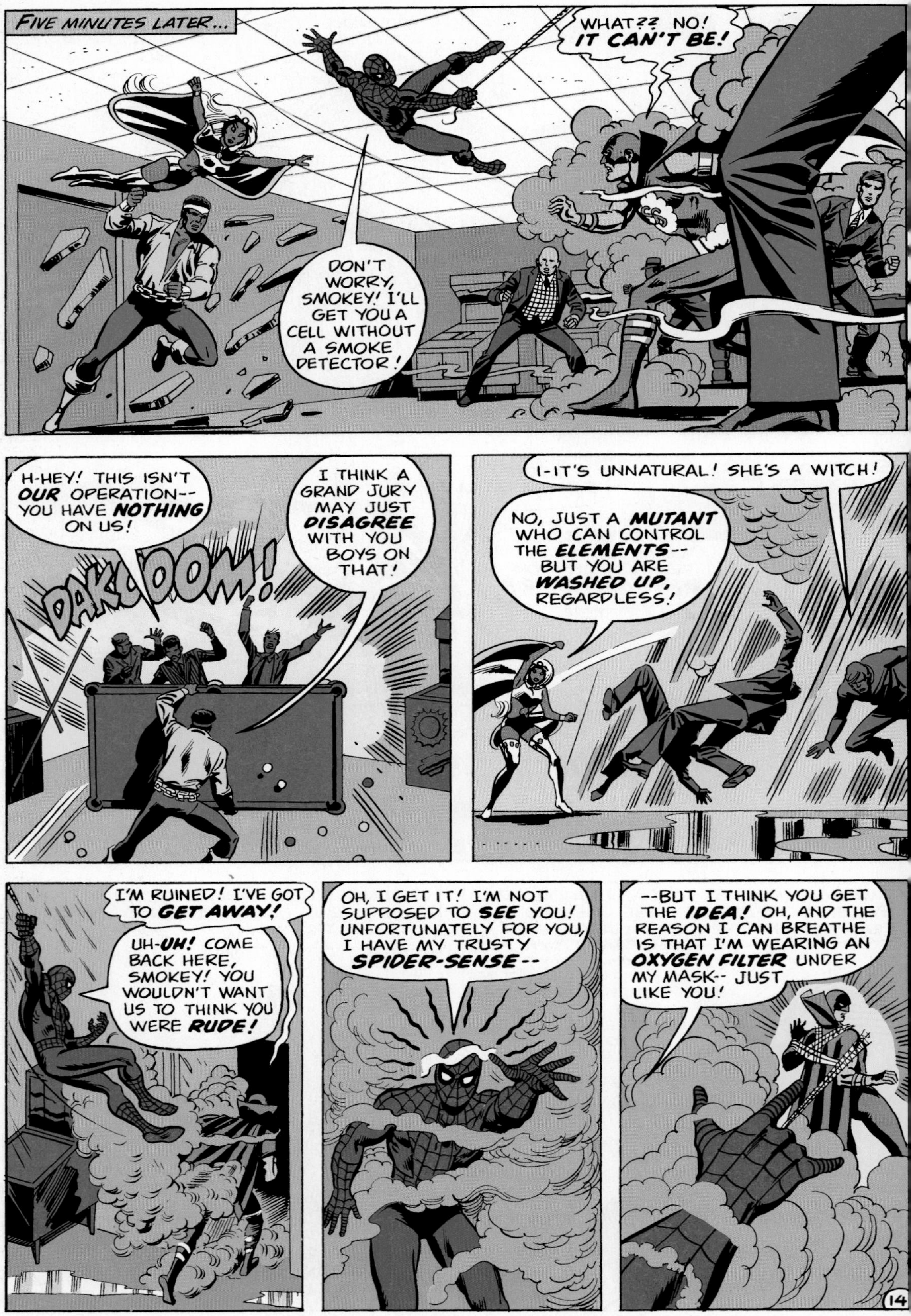
FIVE MINUTES LATER...
WHAT?? NO! IT CAN'T BE!
DON'T WORRY, SMOKEY! I'LL GET YOU A CELL WITHOUT A SMOKE DETECTOR!
H-HEY! THIS ISN'T OUR OPERATION-- YOU HAVE NOTHING ON US!
I THINK A GRAND JURY MAY JUST DISAGREE WITH YOU BOYS ON THAT!
DAKOOOM!
I-IT'S UNNATURAL! SHE'S A WITCH!
NO, JUST A MUTANT WHO CAN CONTROL THE ELEMENTS-- BUT YOU ARE WASHED UP, REGARDLESS!
I'M RUINED! I'VE GOT TO GET AWAY!
UH-UH! COME BACK HERE, SMOKEY! YOU WOULDN'T WANT US TO THINK YOU WERE RUDE!
OH, I GET IT! I'M NOT SUPPOSED TO SEE YOU! UNFORTUNATELY FOR YOU, I HAVE MY TRUSTY SPIDER-SENSE--
--BUT I THINK YOU GET THE IDEA! OH, AND THE REASON I CAN BREATHE IS THAT I'M WEARING AN OXYGEN FILTER UNDER MY MASK-- JUST LIKE YOU!
14

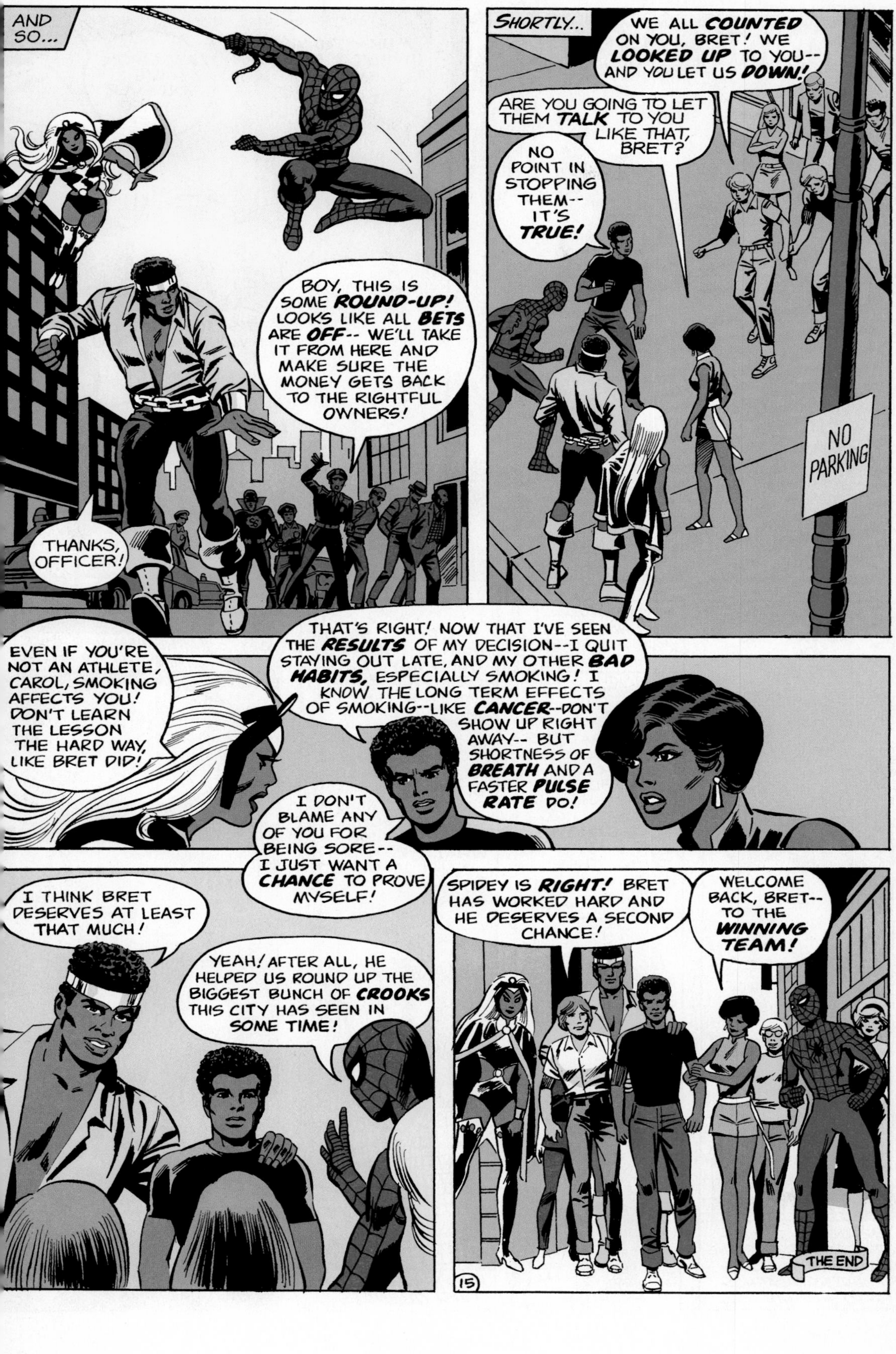
AND SO...
BOY, THIS IS SOME ROUND-UP! LOOKS LIKE ALL BETS ARE OFF-- WE'LL TAKE IT FROM HERE AND MAKE SURE THE MONEY GETS BACK TO THE RIGHTFUL OWNERS!
THANKS, OFFICER!
SHORTLY...
WE ALL COUNTED ON YOU, BRET! WE LOOKED UP TO YOU-- AND YOU LET US DOWN!
ARE YOU GOING TO LET THEM TALK TO YOU LIKE THAT, BRET?
NO POINT IN STOPPING THEM-- IT'S TRUE!
NO PARKING
EVEN IF YOU'RE NOT AN ATHLETE, CAROL, SMOKING AFFECTS YOU! DON'T LEARN THE LESSON THE HARD WAY, LIKE BRET DID!
THAT'S RIGHT! NOW THAT I'VE SEEN THE RESULTS OF MY DECISION--I QUIT STAYING OUT LATE, AND MY OTHER BAD HABITS, ESPECIALLY SMOKING! I KNOW THE LONG TERM EFFECTS OF SMOKING--LIKE CANCER--DON'T SHOW UP RIGHT AWAY-- BUT SHORTNESS OF BREATH AND A FASTER PULSE RATE DO!
I DON'T BLAME ANY OF YOU FOR BEING SORE-- I JUST WANT A CHANCE TO PROVE MYSELF!
I THINK BRET DESERVES AT LEAST THAT MUCH!
YEAH! AFTER ALL, HE HELPED US ROUND UP THE BIGGEST BUNCH OF CROOKS THIS CITY HAS SEEN IN SOME TIME!
SPIDEY IS RIGHT! BRET HAS WORKED HARD AND HE DESERVES A SECOND CHANCE!
WELCOME BACK, BRET-- TO THE WINNING TEAM!
15
THE END

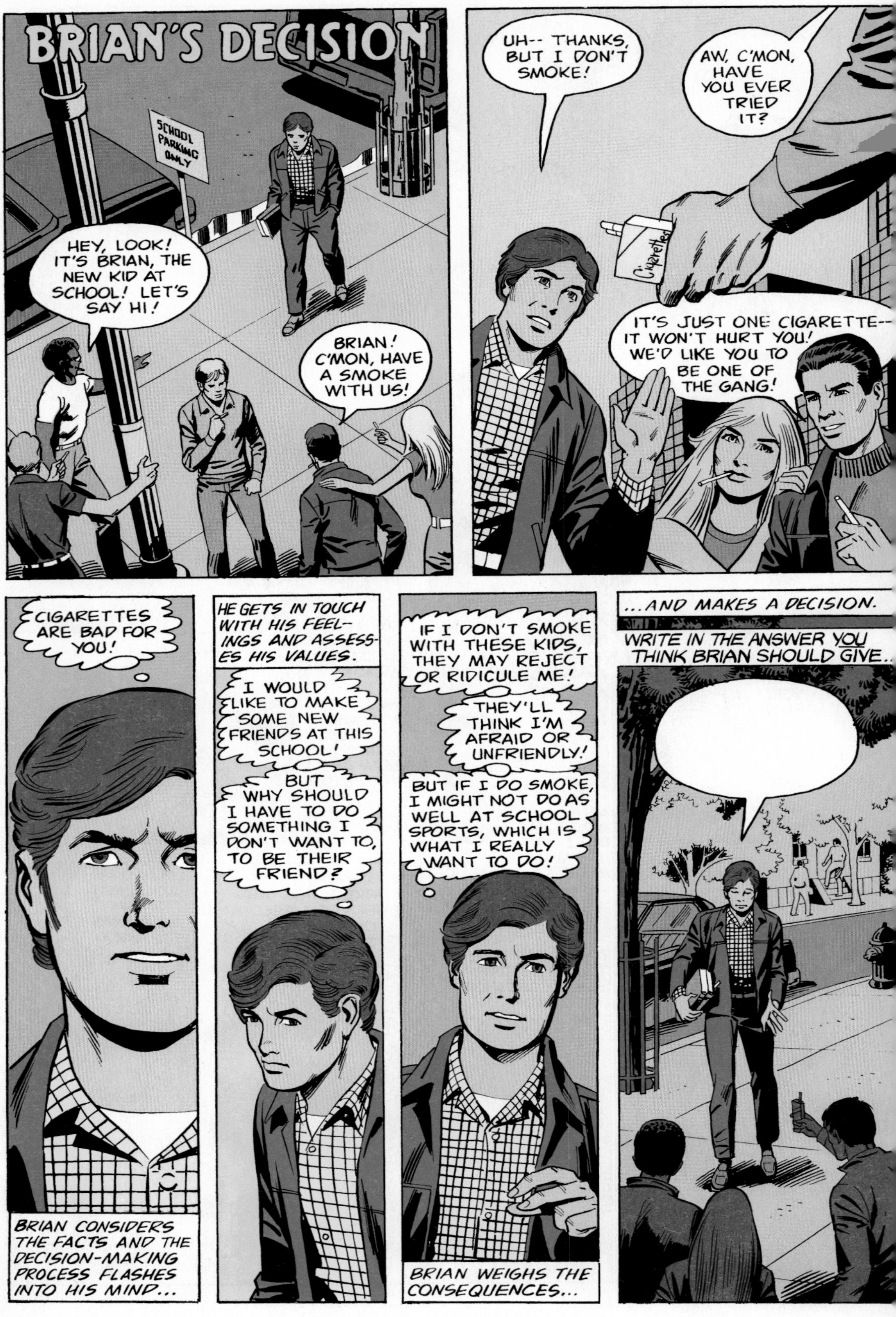
BRIAN'S DECISION
SCHOOL PARKING ONLY
HEY, LOOK! IT'S BRIAN, THE NEW KID AT SCHOOL! LET'S SAY HI!
BRIAN! C'MON, HAVE A SMOKE WITH US!
UH-- THANKS, BUT I DON'T SMOKE!
AW, C'MON, HAVE YOU EVER TRIED IT?
Cigarettes
IT'S JUST ONE CIGARETTE-- IT WON'T HURT YOU! WE'D LIKE YOU TO BE ONE OF THE GANG!
CIGARETTES ARE BAD FOR YOU!
BRIAN CONSIDERS THE FACTS AND THE DECISION-MAKING PROCESS FLASHES INTO HIS MIND...
HE GETS IN TOUCH WITH HIS FEELINGS AND ASSESSES HIS VALUES.
I WOULD LIKE TO MAKE SOME NEW FRIENDS AT THIS SCHOOL!
BUT WHY SHOULD I HAVE TO DO SOMETHING I DON'T WANT TO, TO BE THEIR FRIEND?
IF I DON'T SMOKE WITH THESE KIDS, THEY MAY REJECT OR RIDICULE ME!
THEY'LL THINK I'M AFRAID OR UNFRIENDLY!
BUT IF I DO SMOKE, I MIGHT NOT DO AS WELL AT SCHOOL SPORTS, WHICH IS WHAT I REALLY WANT TO DO!
BRIAN WEIGHS THE CONSEQUENCES...
...AND MAKES A DECISION.
WRITE IN THE ANSWER YOU THINK BRIAN SHOULD GIVE...

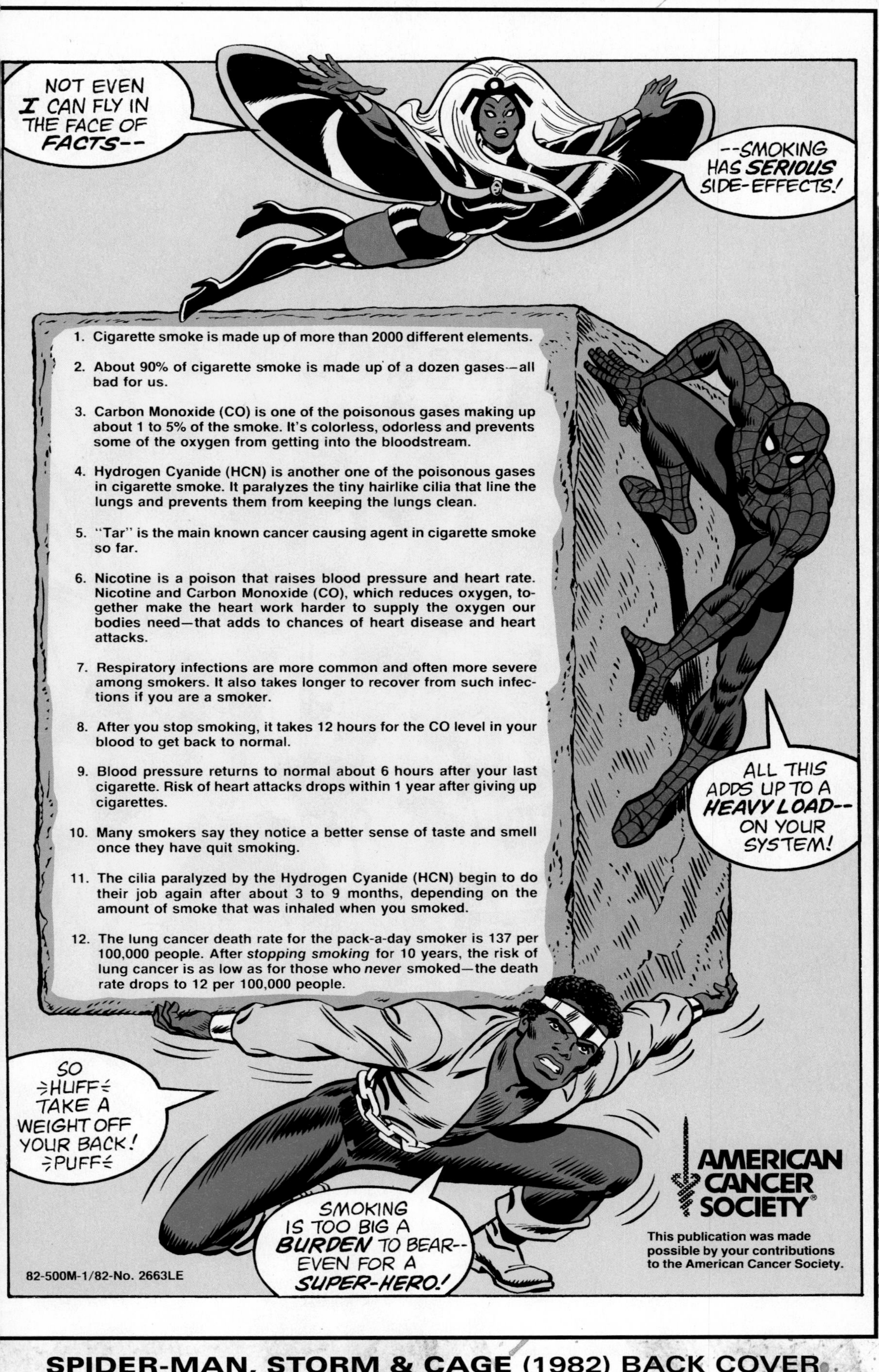
NOT EVEN I CAN FLY IN THE FACE OF FACTS--
--SMOKING HAS SERIOUS SIDE-EFFECTS!
1. Cigarette smoke is made up of more than 2000 different elements.
2. About 90% of cigarette smoke is made up of a dozen gases—all bad for us.
3. Carbon Monoxide (CO) is one of the poisonous gases making up about 1 to 5% of the smoke. It's colorless, odorless and prevents some of the oxygen from getting into the bloodstream.
4. Hydrogen Cyanide (HCN) is another one of the poisonous gases in cigarette smoke. It paralyzes the tiny hairlike cilia that line the lungs and prevents them from keeping the lungs clean.
5. "Tar" is the main known cancer causing agent in cigarette smoke so far.
6. Nicotine is a poison that raises blood pressure and heart rate. Nicotine and Carbon Monoxide (CO), which reduces oxygen, together make the heart work harder to supply the oxygen our bodies need—that adds to chances of heart disease and heart attacks.
7. Respiratory infections are more common and often more severe among smokers. It also takes longer to recover from such infections if you are a smoker.
8. After you stop smoking, it takes 12 hours for the CO level in your blood to get back to normal.
9. Blood pressure returns to normal about 6 hours after your last cigarette. Risk of heart attacks drops within 1 year after giving up cigarettes.
10. Many smokers say they notice a better sense of taste and smell once they have quit smoking.
11. The cilia paralyzed by the Hydrogen Cyanide (HCN) begin to do their job again after about 3 to 9 months, depending on the amount of smoke that was inhaled when you smoked.
12. The lung cancer death rate for the pack-a-day smoker is 137 per 100,000 people. After stopping smoking for 10 years, the risk of lung cancer is as low as for those who never smoked—the death rate drops to 12 per 100,000 people.
ALL THIS ADDS UP TO A HEAVY LOAD-- ON YOUR SYSTEM!
SO ⋗HUFF⋖ TAKE A WEIGHT OFF YOUR BACK! ⋗PUFF⋖
SMOKING IS TOO BIG A BURDEN TO BEAR-- EVEN FOR A SUPER-HERO!
AMERICAN CANCER SOCIETY®
This publication was made possible by your contributions to the American Cancer Society.
82-500M-1/82-No. 2663LE

SPIDER-MAN, STORM & CAGE (1982) BACK COVER

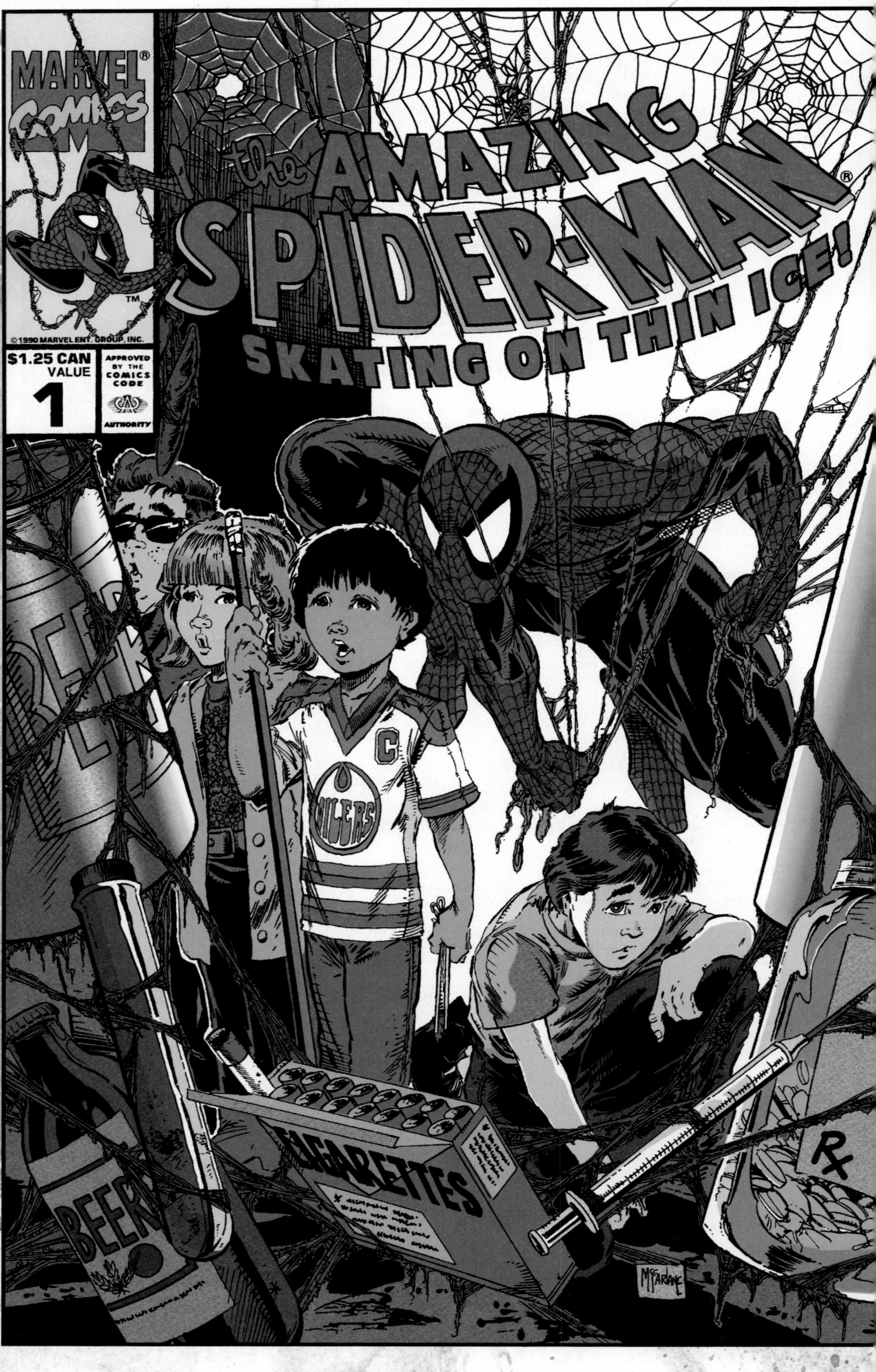
MARVEL® COMICS
the AMAZING SPIDER-MAN®
SKATING ON THIN ICE!
TM
©1990 MARVEL ENT. GROUP, INC.
$1.25 CAN VALUE
1
APPROVED BY THE COMICS CODE AUTHORITY
C
OILERS
CIGARETTES
BEER
Rx
McFARLANE

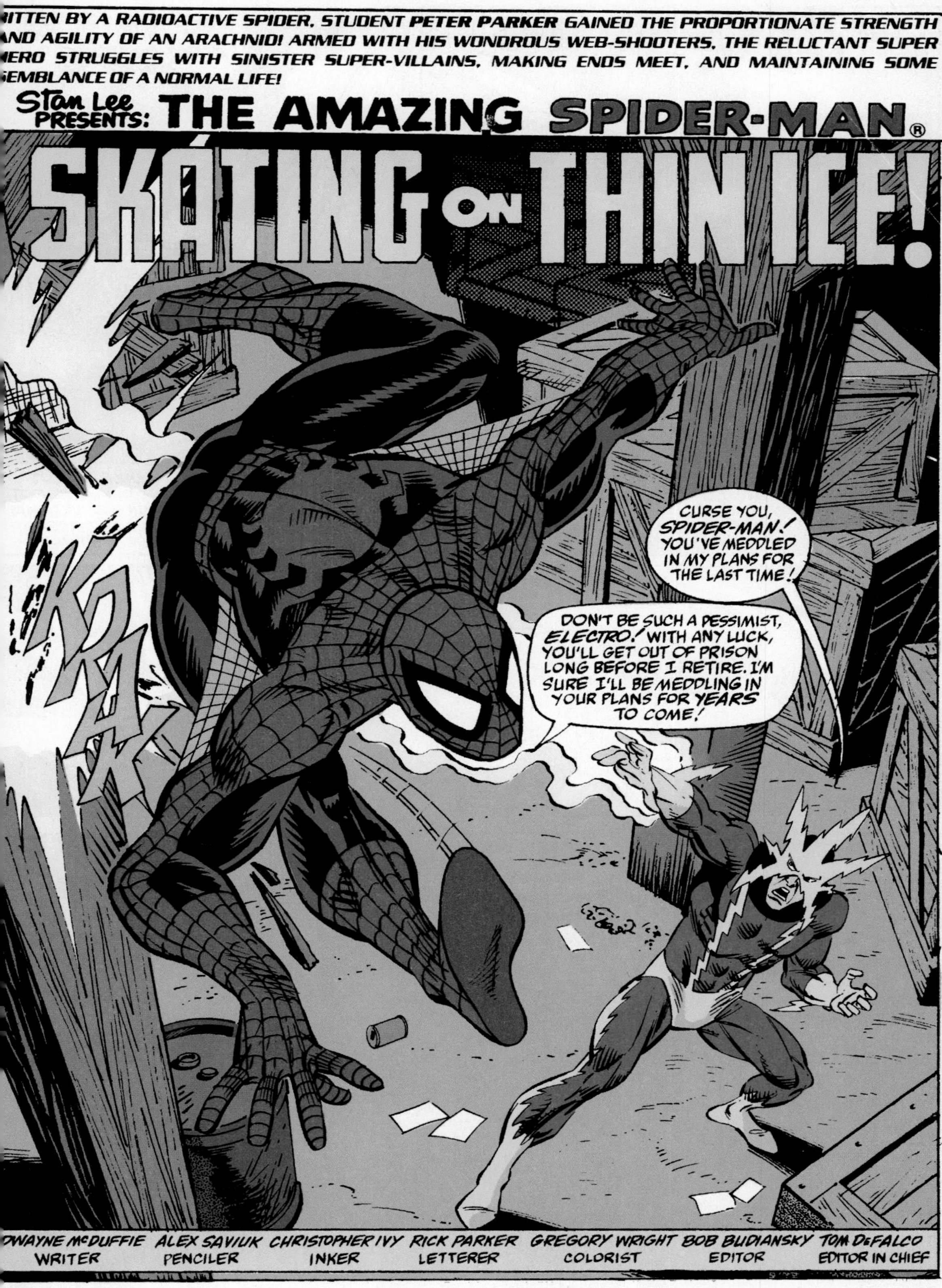

ITTEN BY A RADIOACTIVE SPIDER, STUDENT PETER PARKER GAINED THE PROPORTIONATE STRENGTH AND AGILITY OF AN ARACHNID! ARMED WITH HIS WONDROUS WEB-SHOOTERS, THE RELUCTANT SUPER HERO STRUGGLES WITH SINISTER SUPER-VILLAINS, MAKING ENDS MEET, AND MAINTAINING SOME SEMBLANCE OF A NORMAL LIFE!
Stan Lee PRESENTS: THE AMAZING SPIDER-MAN®
SKATING ON THIN ICE!
KRAKK
CURSE YOU, SPIDER-MAN! YOU'VE MEDDLED IN MY PLANS FOR THE LAST TIME!
DON'T BE SUCH A PESSIMIST, ELECTRO! WITH ANY LUCK, YOU'LL GET OUT OF PRISON LONG BEFORE I RETIRE. I'M SURE I'LL BE MEDDLING IN YOUR PLANS FOR YEARS TO COME!
DWAYNE McDUFFIE WRITER
ALEX SAVIUK PENCILER
CHRISTOPHER IVY INKER
RICK PARKER LETTERER
GREGORY WRIGHT COLORIST
BOB BUDIANSKY EDITOR
TOM DeFALCO EDITOR IN CHIEF

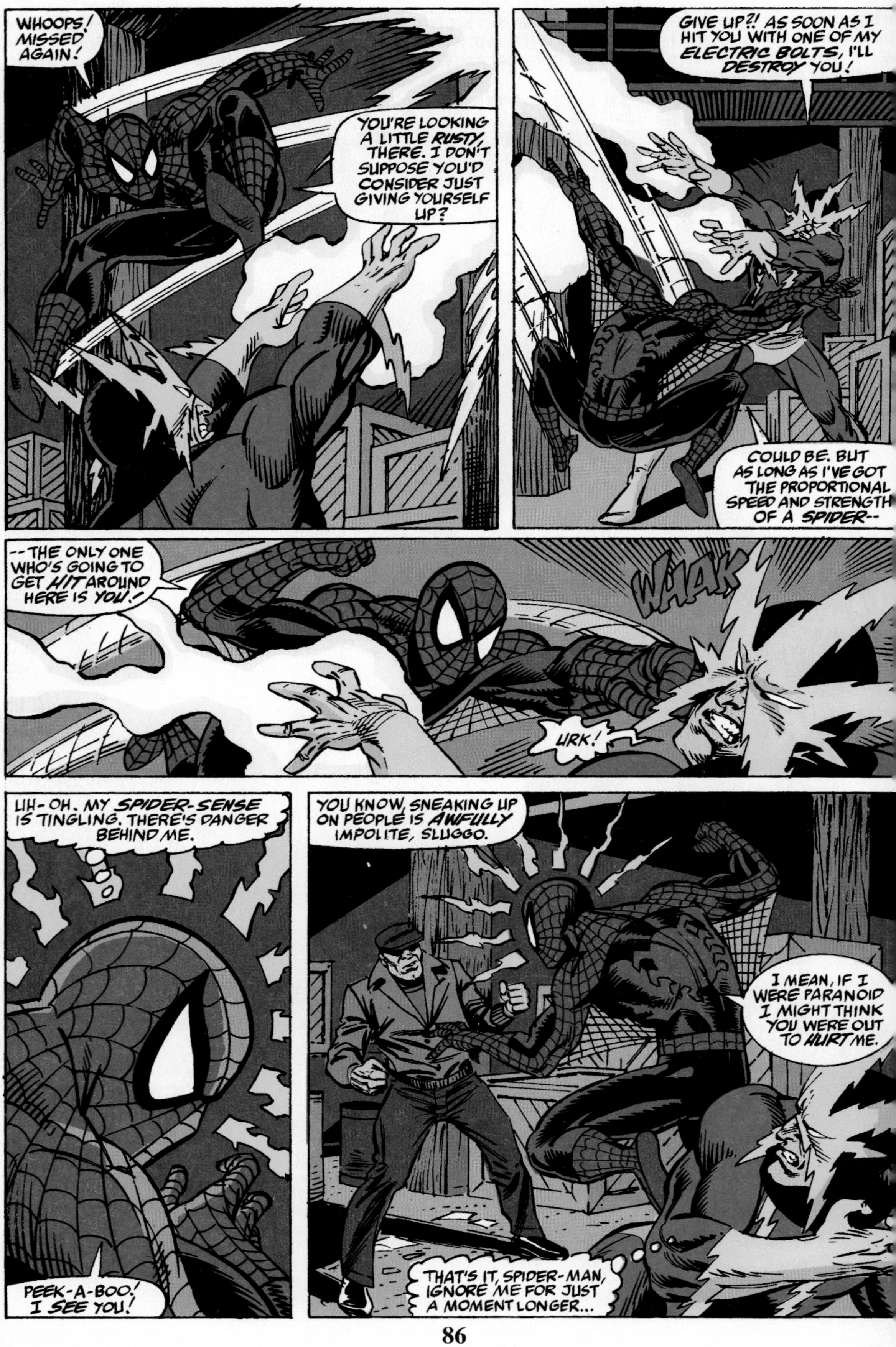
WHOOPS! MISSED AGAIN!
YOU'RE LOOKING A LITTLE RUSTY, THERE. I DON'T SUPPOSE YOU'D CONSIDER JUST GIVING YOURSELF UP?
GIVE UP?! AS SOON AS I HIT YOU WITH ONE OF MY ELECTRIC BOLTS, I'LL DESTROY YOU!
COULD BE. BUT AS LONG AS I'VE GOT THE PROPORTIONAL SPEED AND STRENGTH OF A SPIDER--
--THE ONLY ONE WHO'S GOING TO GET HIT AROUND HERE IS YOU!
WHAK
URK!
UH-OH. MY SPIDER-SENSE IS TINGLING. THERE'S DANGER BEHIND ME.
PEEK-A-BOO! I SEE YOU!
YOU KNOW, SNEAKING UP ON PEOPLE IS AWFULLY IMPOLITE, SLUGGO.
I MEAN, IF I WERE PARANOID I MIGHT THINK YOU WERE OUT TO HURT ME.
THAT'S IT, SPIDER-MAN, IGNORE ME FOR JUST A MOMENT LONGER...

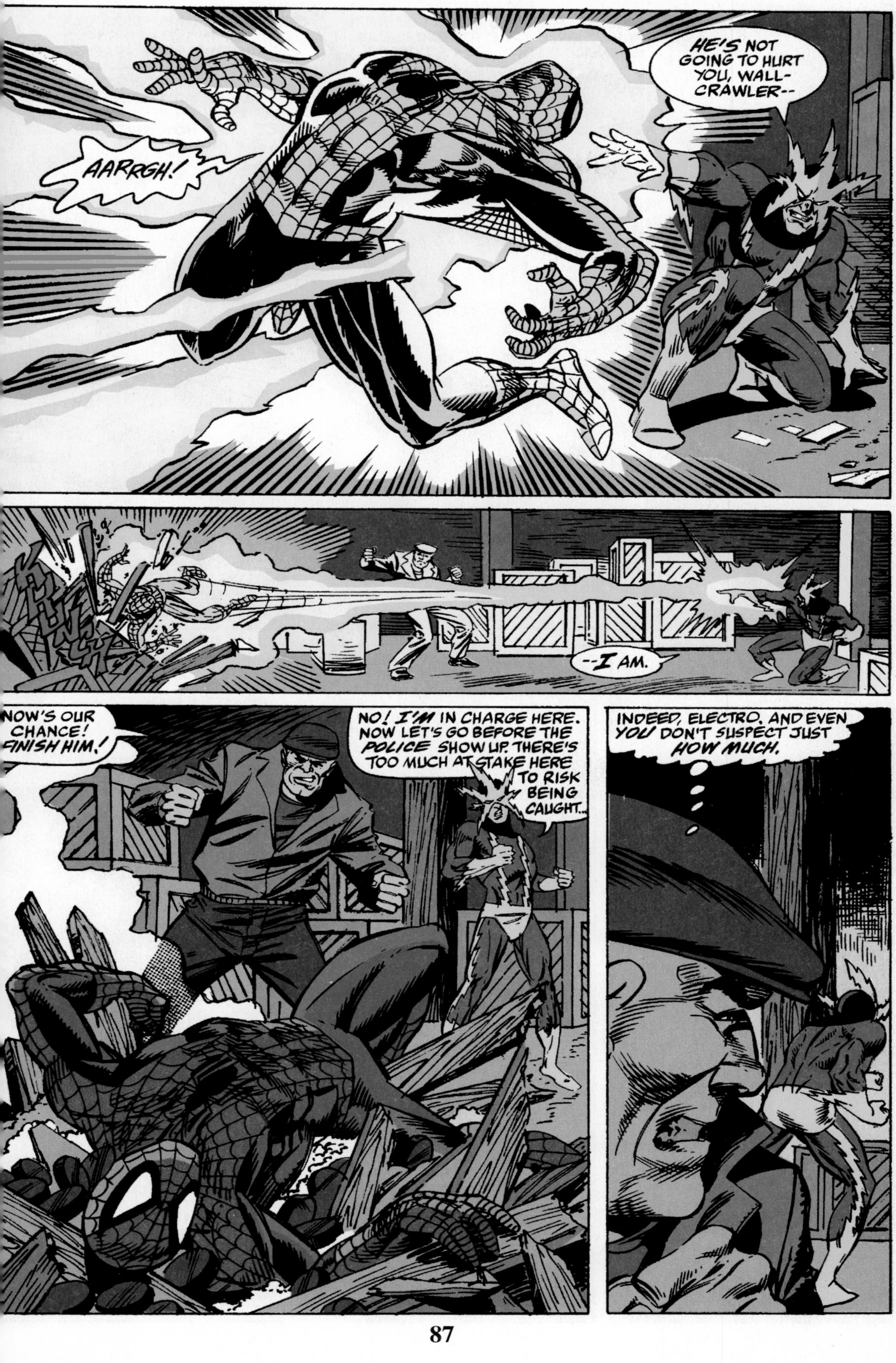
AARRGH!
HE'S NOT GOING TO HURT YOU, WALL-CRAWLER--
--I AM.
NOW'S OUR CHANCE! FINISH HIM!
NO! I'M IN CHARGE HERE. NOW LET'S GO BEFORE THE POLICE SHOW UP. THERE'S TOO MUCH AT STAKE HERE TO RISK BEING CAUGHT...
INDEED, ELECTRO, AND EVEN YOU DON'T SUSPECT JUST HOW MUCH.

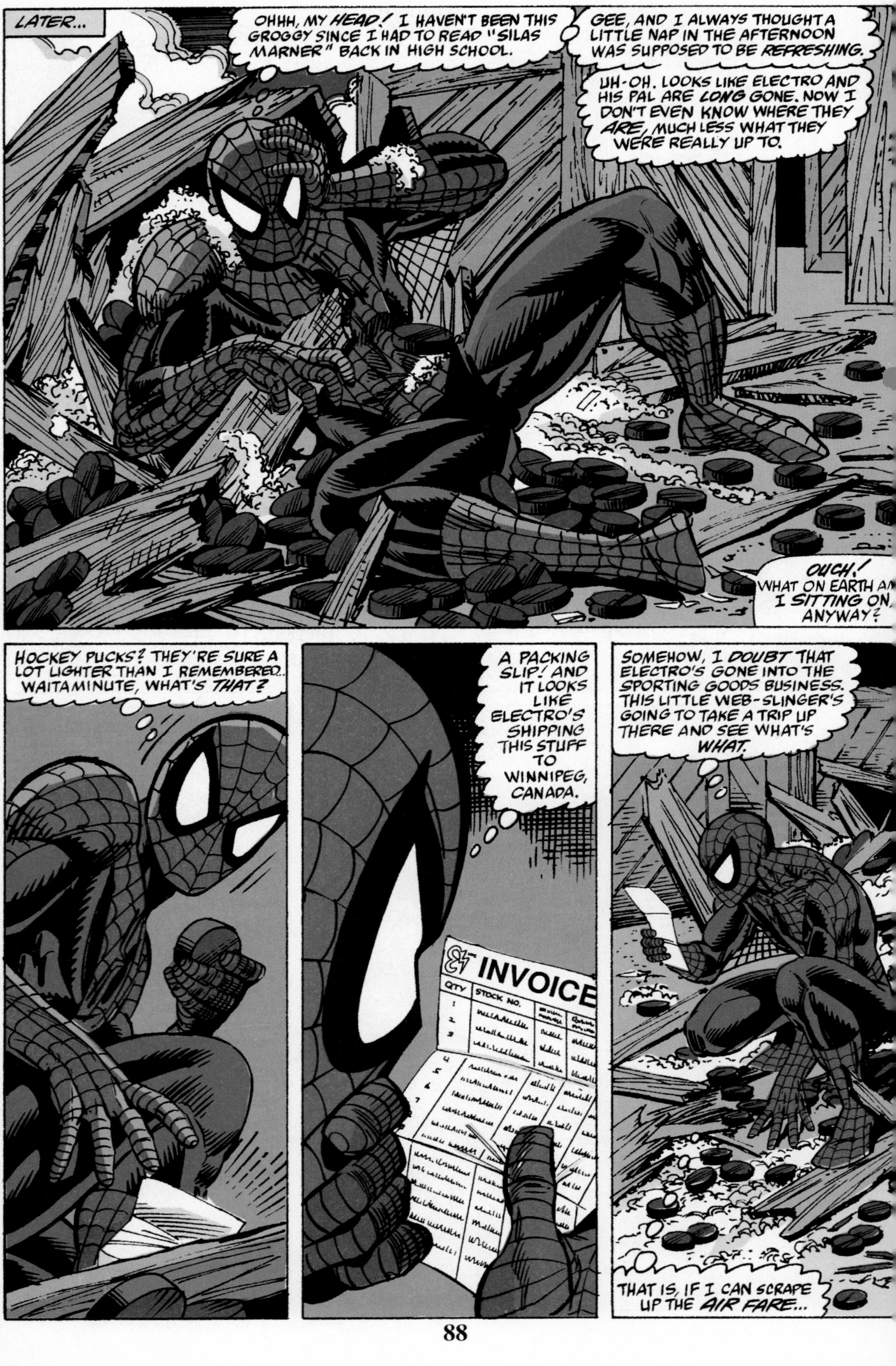
LATER...
OHHH, MY HEAD! I HAVEN'T BEEN THIS GROGGY SINCE I HAD TO READ "SILAS MARNER" BACK IN HIGH SCHOOL.
GEE, AND I ALWAYS THOUGHT A LITTLE NAP IN THE AFTERNOON WAS SUPPOSED TO BE REFRESHING.
UH-OH. LOOKS LIKE ELECTRO AND HIS PAL ARE LONG GONE. NOW I DON'T EVEN KNOW WHERE THEY ARE, MUCH LESS WHAT THEY WERE REALLY UP TO.
OUCH! WHAT ON EARTH AM I SITTING ON, ANYWAY?
HOCKEY PUCKS? THEY'RE SURE A LOT LIGHTER THAN I REMEMBERED... WAITAMINUTE, WHAT'S THAT?
A PACKING SLIP! AND IT LOOKS LIKE ELECTRO'S SHIPPING THIS STUFF TO WINNIPEG, CANADA.
INVOICE
QTY
STOCK NO.
SOMEHOW, I DOUBT THAT ELECTRO'S GONE INTO THE SPORTING GOODS BUSINESS. THIS LITTLE WEB-SLINGER'S GOING TO TAKE A TRIP UP THERE AND SEE WHAT'S WHAT.
THAT IS, IF I CAN SCRAPE UP THE AIR FARE...

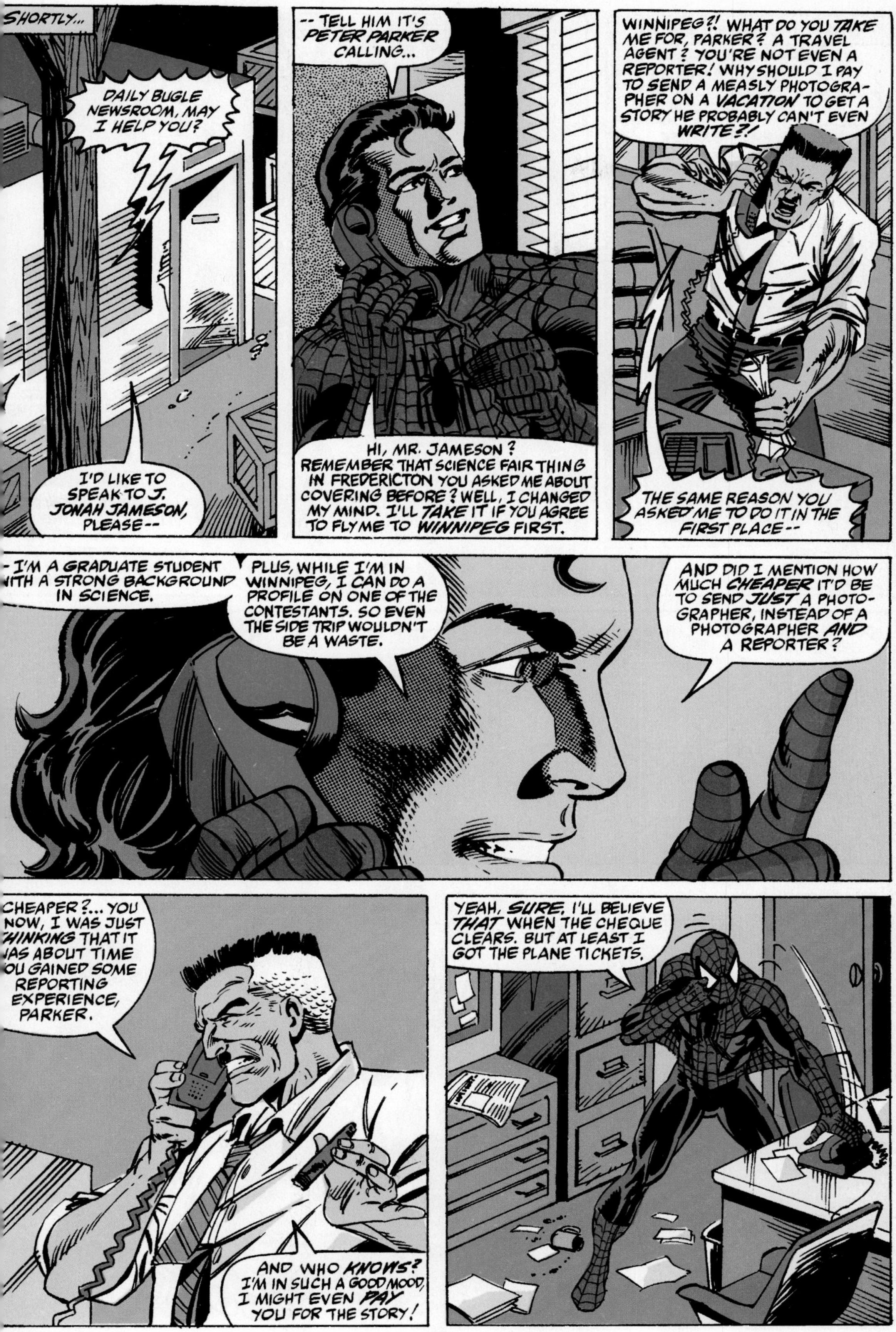
SHORTLY...
DAILY BUGLE NEWSROOM, MAY I HELP YOU?
I'D LIKE TO SPEAK TO J. JONAH JAMESON, PLEASE--
-- TELL HIM IT'S PETER PARKER CALLING...
HI, MR. JAMESON? REMEMBER THAT SCIENCE FAIR THING IN FREDERICTON YOU ASKED ME ABOUT COVERING BEFORE? WELL, I CHANGED MY MIND. I'LL TAKE IT IF YOU AGREE TO FLY ME TO WINNIPEG FIRST.
WINNIPEG?! WHAT DO YOU TAKE ME FOR, PARKER? A TRAVEL AGENT? YOU'RE NOT EVEN A REPORTER! WHY SHOULD I PAY TO SEND A MEASLY PHOTOGRAPHER ON A VACATION TO GET A STORY HE PROBABLY CAN'T EVEN WRITE?!
THE SAME REASON YOU ASKED ME TO DO IT IN THE FIRST PLACE--
-- I'M A GRADUATE STUDENT WITH A STRONG BACKGROUND IN SCIENCE.
PLUS, WHILE I'M IN WINNIPEG, I CAN DO A PROFILE ON ONE OF THE CONTESTANTS. SO EVEN THE SIDE TRIP WOULDN'T BE A WASTE.
AND DID I MENTION HOW MUCH CHEAPER IT'D BE TO SEND JUST A PHOTOGRAPHER, INSTEAD OF A PHOTOGRAPHER AND A REPORTER?
CHEAPER?... YOU KNOW, I WAS JUST THINKING THAT IT WAS ABOUT TIME YOU GAINED SOME REPORTING EXPERIENCE, PARKER.
AND WHO KNOWS? I'M IN SUCH A GOOD MOOD, I MIGHT EVEN PAY YOU FOR THE STORY!
YEAH, SURE. I'LL BELIEVE THAT WHEN THE CHEQUE CLEARS. BUT AT LEAST I GOT THE PLANE TICKETS.

THE NEXT DAY, IN WINNIPEG...

WASN'T TOO HARD TO FIGURE OUT WHO I SHOULD DO A STORY ON. THIS KID IS REALLY BRIGHT!

THIS IS THE ADDRESS HER MOTHER GAVE ME, SOME KIND OF COMMUNITY CENTER...

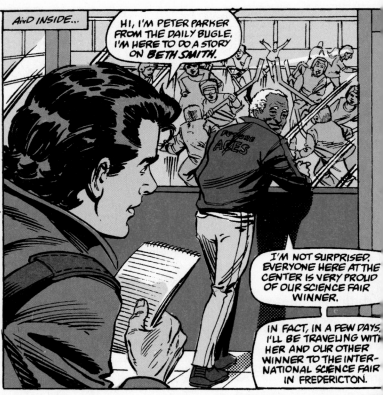

AND INSIDE...

HI, I'M PETER PARKER FROM THE DAILY BUGLE. I'M HERE TO DO A STORY ON BETH SMITH.

I'M NOT SURPRISED. EVERYONE HERE AT THE CENTER IS VERY PROUD OF OUR SCIENCE FAIR WINNER.

IN FACT, IN A FEW DAYS, I'LL BE TRAVELING WITH HER AND OUR OTHER WINNER TO THE INTERNATIONAL SCIENCE FAIR IN FREDERICTON.

DO YOU RUN THIS CENTER, MR...?

CARNEGIE. CALL ME HERB. AND NO, I DON'T. I JUST LIKE WORKING WITH YOUNG PEOPLE, AND I KNOW A BIT ABOUT HOCKEY.

THAT'S BETH OVER THERE, SHE--

WHUMP

--AH, SHE'S NOT *QUITE* AS GOOD AN ATHLETE AS SHE IS A SCIENTIST, JUST YET. SHE NEVER STOPS TRYING THOUGH. AND SHE'LL GET THERE.

HAT'S REALLY WHAT ALL THIS IS BOUT-- LEARNING HOW TO WORK OGETHER. LEARNING RESPECT OR EACH OTHER, AND FOR OURSELVES.

WHO'S THE GUY WITH THE PUCK NOW? HE'S REALLY GOOD!

OH, ALAN? YES, HE HAS A LOT OF POTENTIAL. THERE'S NO TELLING HOW FAR HE COULD GO.

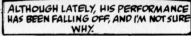

ALTHOUGH LATELY, HIS PERFORMANCE HAS BEEN FALLING OFF, AND I'M NOT SURE WHY.

HAT REALLY TROUBLES ME. E'S A TEAM LEADER, AND HIS LACKING OFF IS BEGINNING O AFFECT THE OTHER KIDS.

EXCUSE ME, PETER. I WANT TO WRAP UP PRACTICE.

91

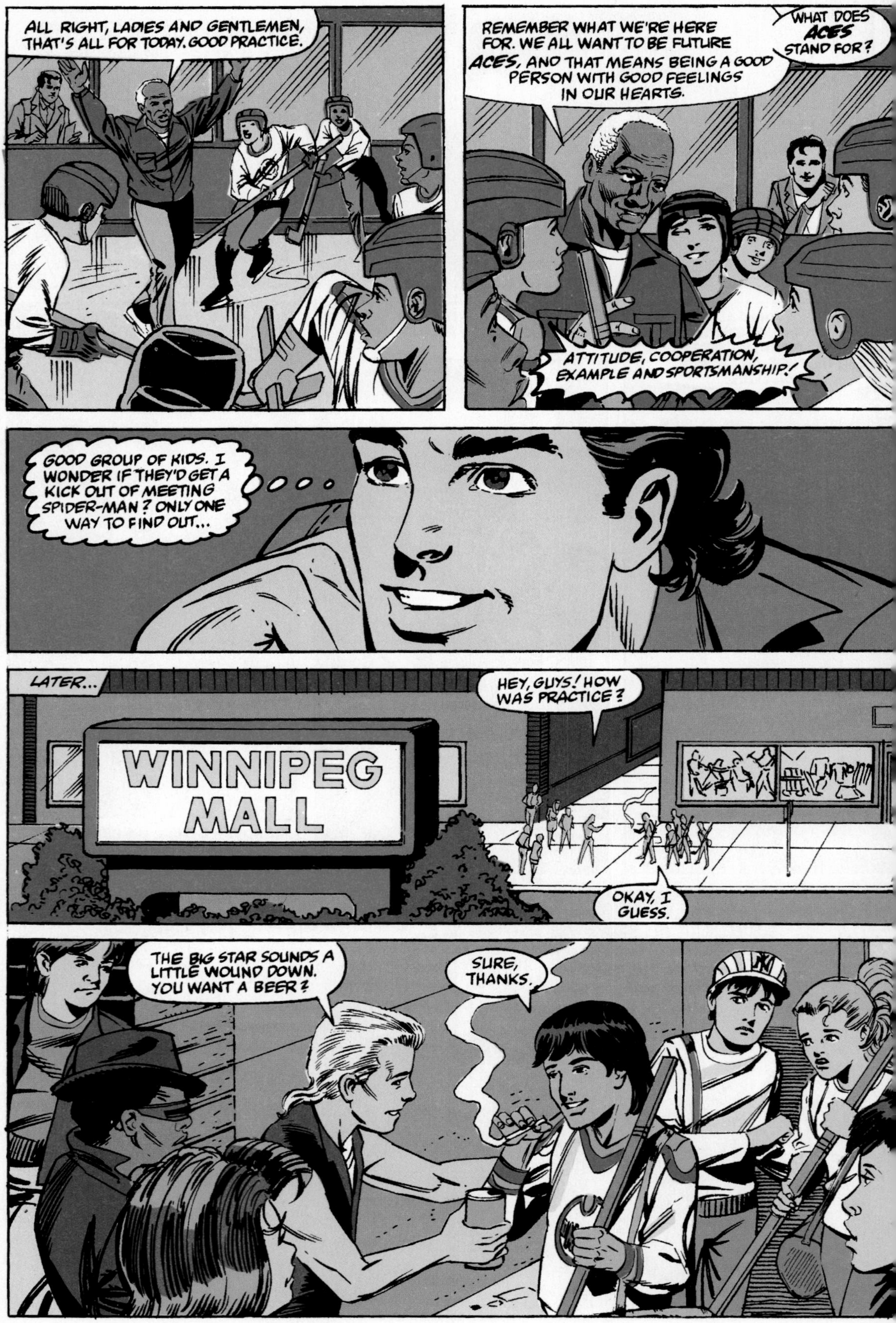
ALL RIGHT, LADIES AND GENTLEMEN, THAT'S ALL FOR TODAY. GOOD PRACTICE.
REMEMBER WHAT WE'RE HERE FOR. WE ALL WANT TO BE FUTURE ACES, AND THAT MEANS BEING A GOOD PERSON WITH GOOD FEELINGS IN OUR HEARTS.
WHAT DOES ACES STAND FOR?
ATTITUDE, COOPERATION, EXAMPLE AND SPORTSMANSHIP!
GOOD GROUP OF KIDS. I WONDER IF THEY'D GET A KICK OUT OF MEETING SPIDER-MAN? ONLY ONE WAY TO FIND OUT...
LATER...
WINNIPEG MALL
HEY, GUYS! HOW WAS PRACTICE?
OKAY, I GUESS.
THE BIG STAR SOUNDS A LITTLE WOUND DOWN. YOU WANT A BEER?
SURE, THANKS.

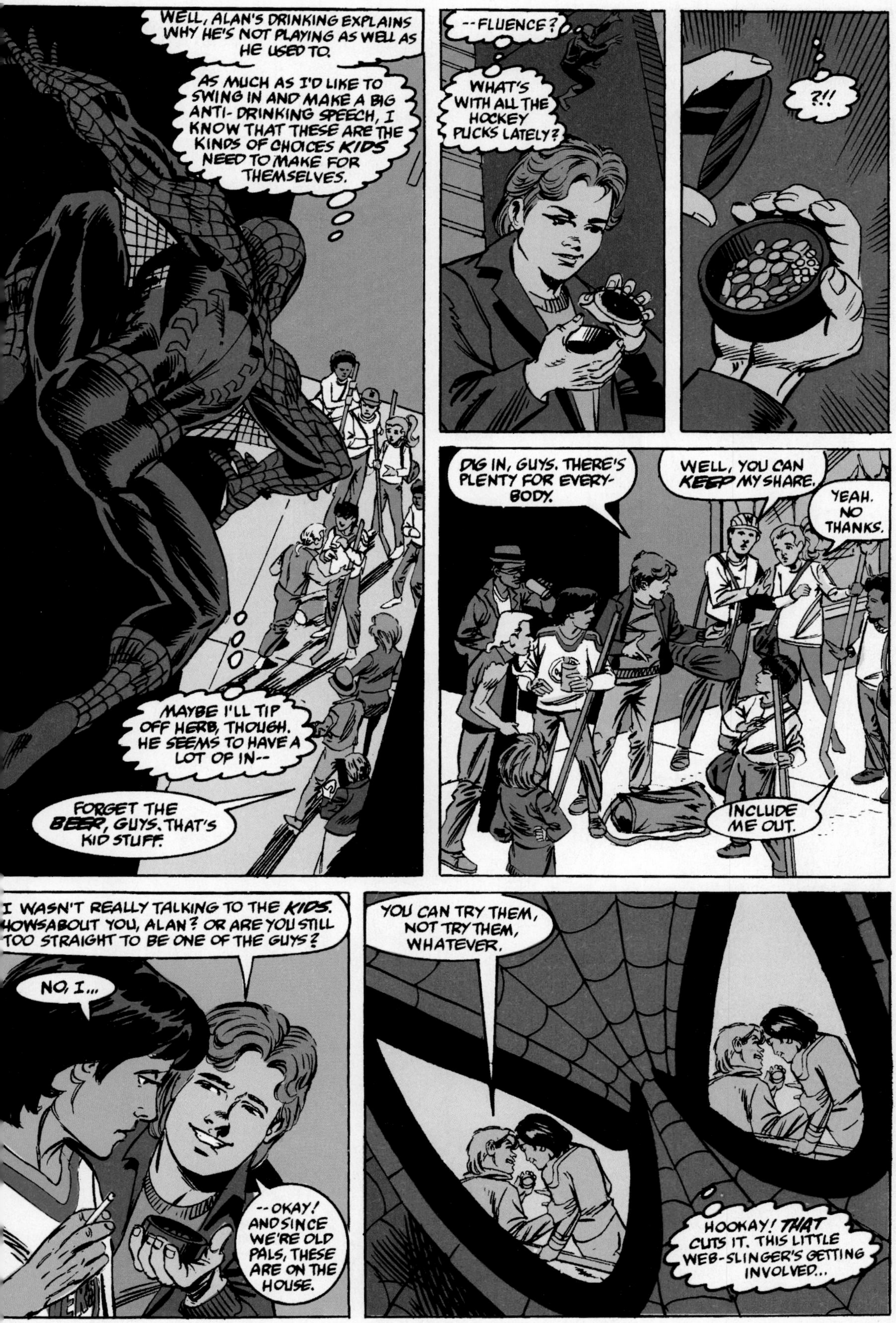
WELL, ALAN'S DRINKING EXPLAINS WHY HE'S NOT PLAYING AS WELL AS HE USED TO.
AS MUCH AS I'D LIKE TO SWING IN AND MAKE A BIG ANTI-DRINKING SPEECH, I KNOW THAT THESE ARE THE KINDS OF CHOICES KIDS NEED TO MAKE FOR THEMSELVES.
MAYBE I'LL TIP OFF HERB, THOUGH. HE SEEMS TO HAVE A LOT OF IN--
FORGET THE BEER, GUYS. THAT'S KID STUFF.
--FLUENCE?
WHAT'S WITH ALL THE HOCKEY PUCKS LATELY?
?!!
DIG IN, GUYS. THERE'S PLENTY FOR EVERY-BODY.
WELL, YOU CAN KEEP MY SHARE.
YEAH. NO THANKS.
INCLUDE ME OUT.
I WASN'T REALLY TALKING TO THE KIDS. HOWSABOUT YOU, ALAN? OR ARE YOU STILL TOO STRAIGHT TO BE ONE OF THE GUYS?
NO, I...
--OKAY! AND SINCE WE'RE OLD PALS, THESE ARE ON THE HOUSE.
YOU CAN TRY THEM, NOT TRY THEM, WHATEVER.
HOOKAY! THAT CUTS IT. THIS LITTLE WEB-SLINGER'S GETTING INVOLVED...

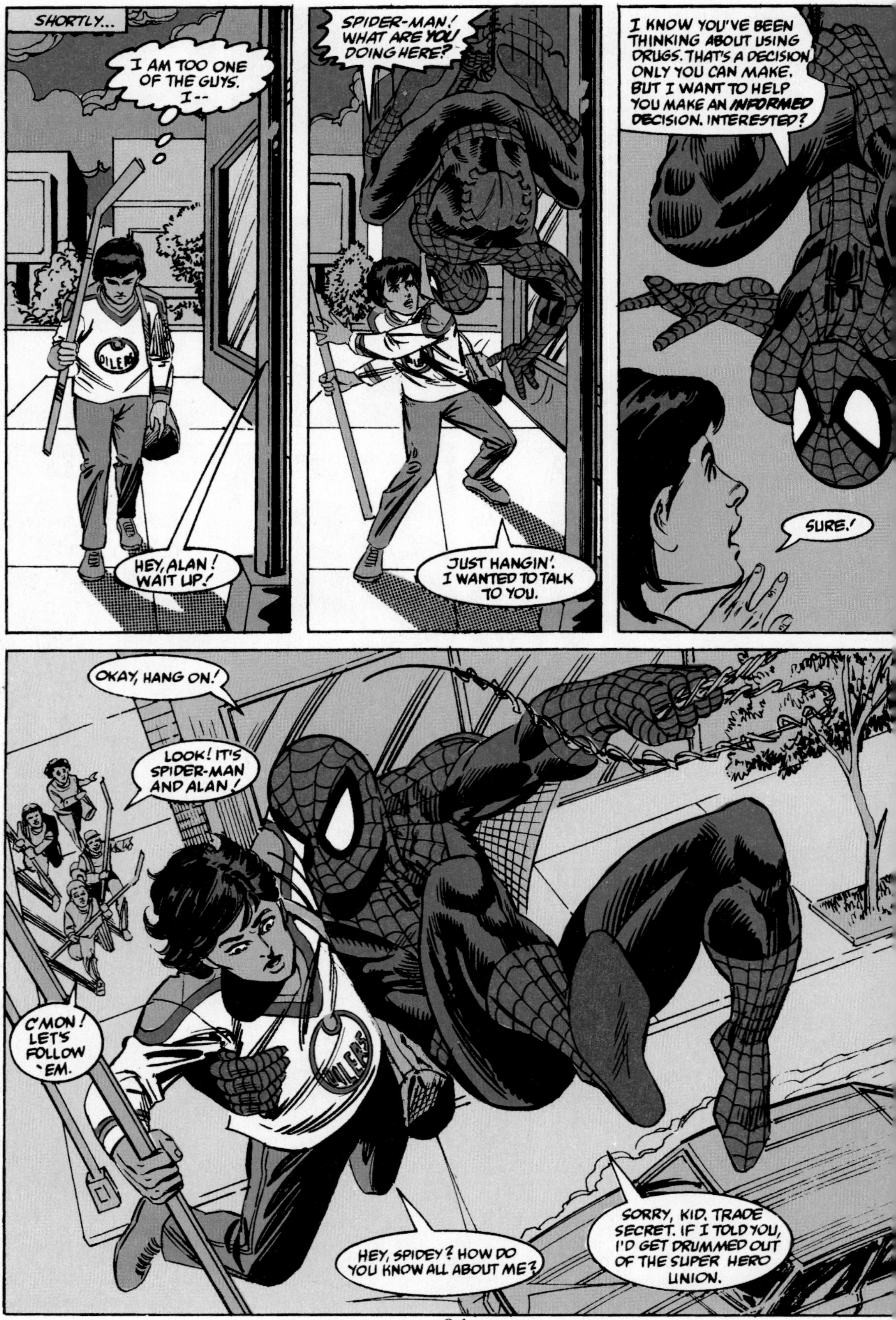
SHORTLY...
I AM TOO ONE OF THE GUYS. I--
HEY, ALAN! WAIT UP!
SPIDER-MAN! WHAT ARE YOU DOING HERE?
JUST HANGIN'. I WANTED TO TALK TO YOU.
I KNOW YOU'VE BEEN THINKING ABOUT USING DRUGS. THAT'S A DECISION ONLY YOU CAN MAKE. BUT I WANT TO HELP YOU MAKE AN INFORMED DECISION. INTERESTED?
SURE!
OKAY, HANG ON!
LOOK! IT'S SPIDER-MAN AND ALAN!
C'MON! LET'S FOLLOW 'EM.
HEY, SPIDEY? HOW DO YOU KNOW ALL ABOUT ME?
SORRY, KID. TRADE SECRET. IF I TOLD YOU, I'D GET DRUMMED OUT OF THE SUPER HERO UNION.

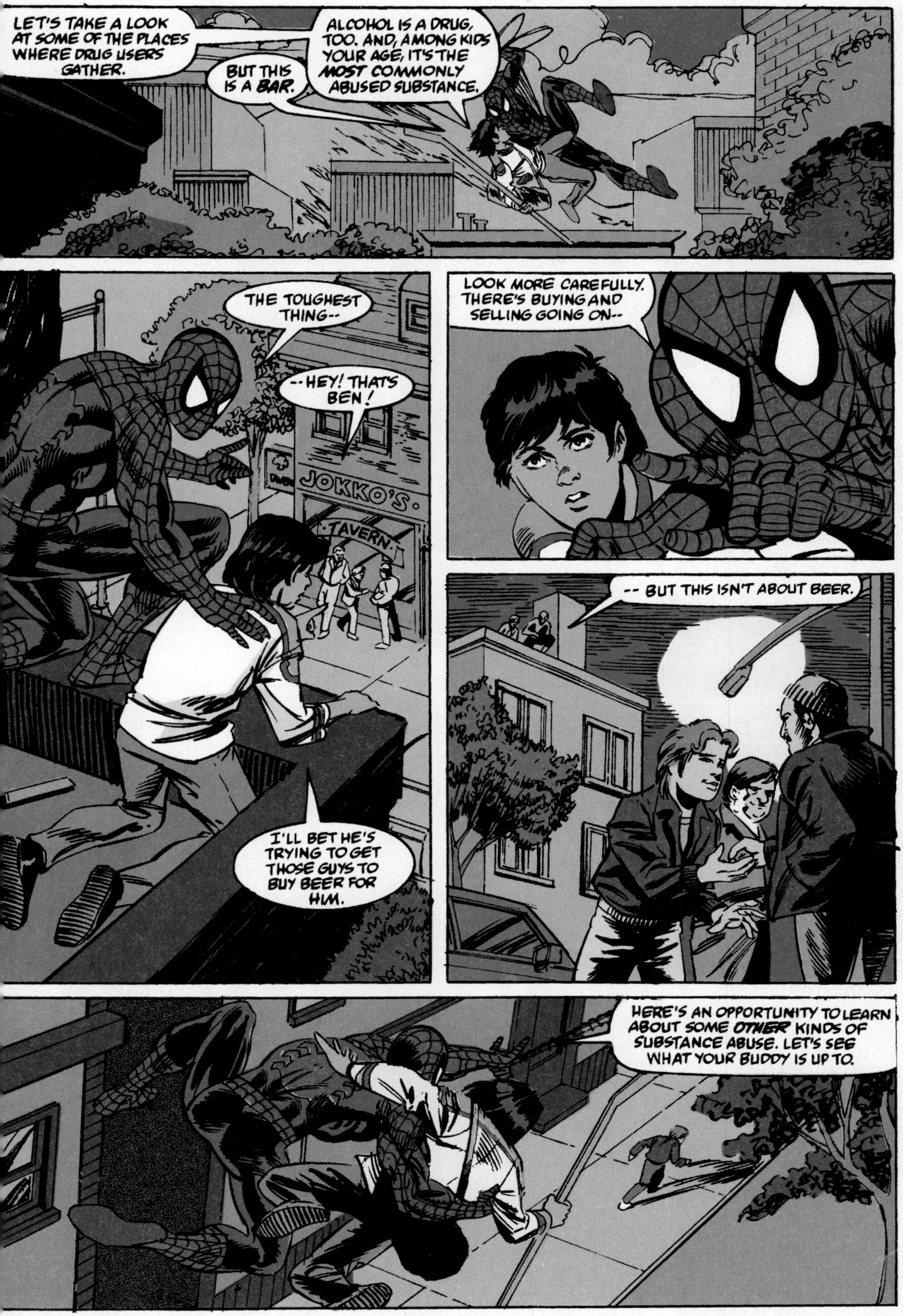

LET'S TAKE A LOOK AT SOME OF THE PLACES WHERE DRUG USERS GATHER.
BUT THIS IS A BAR.
ALCOHOL IS A DRUG, TOO. AND, AMONG KIDS YOUR AGE, IT'S THE MOST COMMONLY ABUSED SUBSTANCE.
THE TOUGHEST THING--
--HEY! THAT'S BEN!
JOKKO'S
TAVERN
I'LL BET HE'S TRYING TO GET THOSE GUYS TO BUY BEER FOR HIM.
LOOK MORE CAREFULLY. THERE'S BUYING AND SELLING GOING ON--
-- BUT THIS ISN'T ABOUT BEER.
HERE'S AN OPPORTUNITY TO LEARN ABOUT SOME OTHER KINDS OF SUBSTANCE ABUSE. LET'S SEE WHAT YOUR BUDDY IS UP TO.

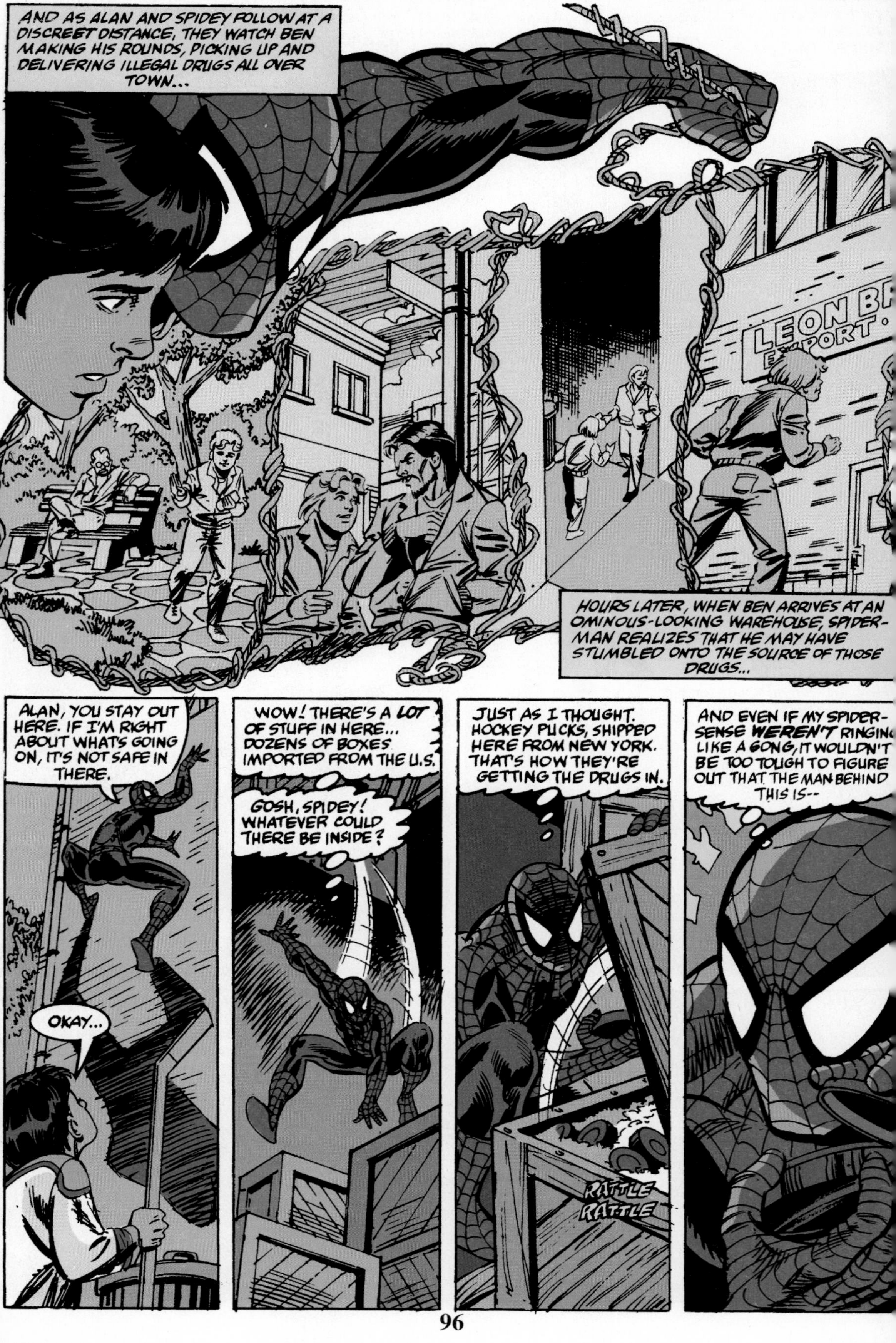
AND AS ALAN AND SPIDEY FOLLOW AT A DISCREET DISTANCE, THEY WATCH BEN MAKING HIS ROUNDS, PICKING UP AND DELIVERING ILLEGAL DRUGS ALL OVER TOWN...
HOURS LATER, WHEN BEN ARRIVES AT AN OMINOUS-LOOKING WAREHOUSE, SPIDER-MAN REALIZES THAT HE MAY HAVE STUMBLED ONTO THE SOURCE OF THOSE DRUGS...
ALAN, YOU STAY OUT HERE. IF I'M RIGHT ABOUT WHAT'S GOING ON, IT'S NOT SAFE IN THERE.
OKAY...
WOW! THERE'S A LOT OF STUFF IN HERE... DOZENS OF BOXES IMPORTED FROM THE U.S.
GOSH, SPIDEY! WHATEVER COULD THERE BE INSIDE?
JUST AS I THOUGHT. HOCKEY PUCKS, SHIPPED HERE FROM NEW YORK. THAT'S HOW THEY'RE GETTING THE DRUGS IN.
RATTLE RATTLE
AND EVEN IF MY SPIDER-SENSE WEREN'T RINGING LIKE A GONG, IT WOULDN'T BE TOO TOUGH TO FIGURE OUT THAT THE MAN BEHIND THIS IS--

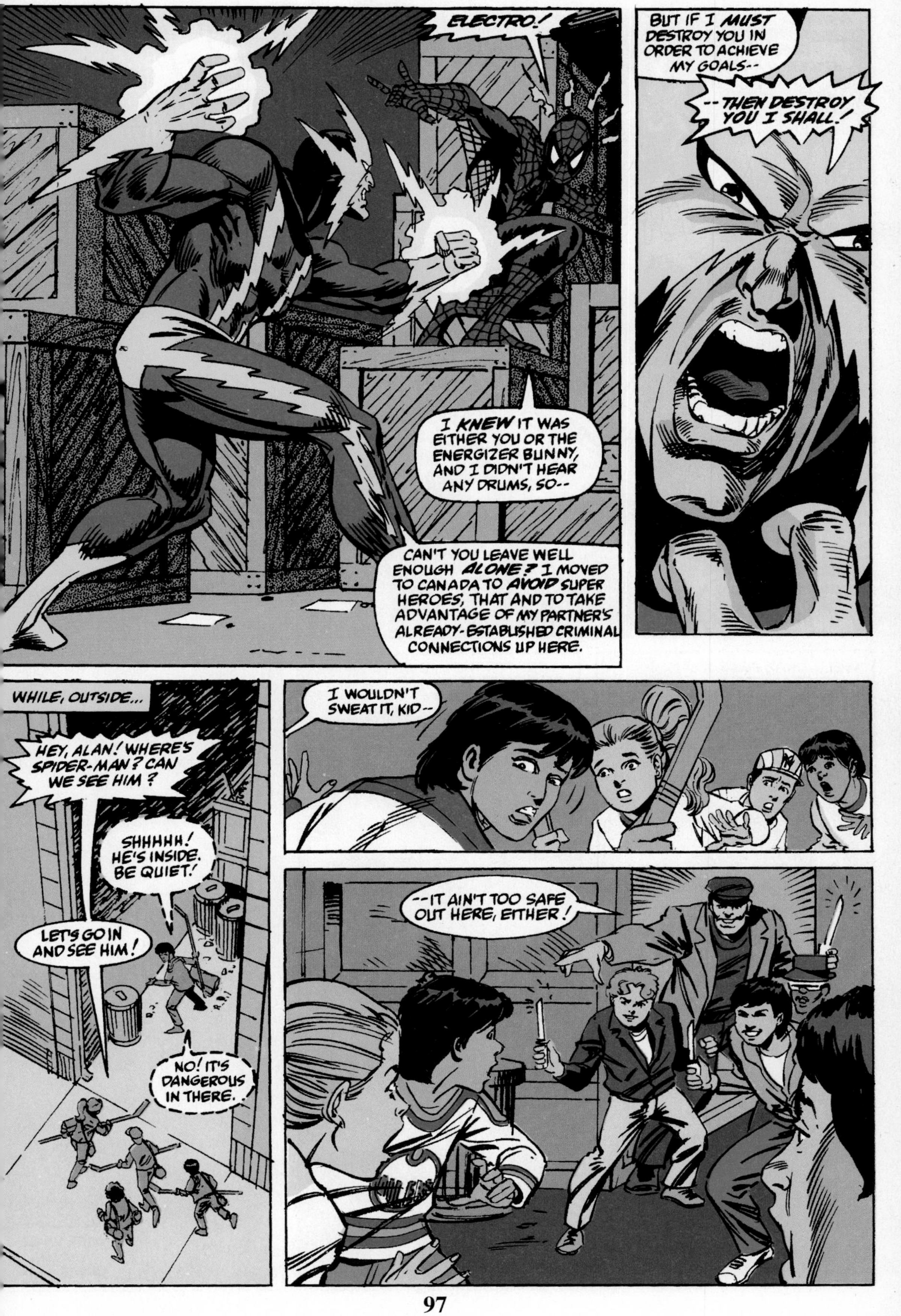
ELECTRO!
I KNEW IT WAS EITHER YOU OR THE ENERGIZER BUNNY, AND I DIDN'T HEAR ANY DRUMS, SO--
CAN'T YOU LEAVE WELL ENOUGH ALONE? I MOVED TO CANADA TO AVOID SUPER HEROES; THAT AND TO TAKE ADVANTAGE OF MY PARTNER'S ALREADY-ESTABLISHED CRIMINAL CONNECTIONS UP HERE.
BUT IF I MUST DESTROY YOU IN ORDER TO ACHIEVE MY GOALS--
--THEN DESTROY YOU I SHALL!
WHILE, OUTSIDE...
HEY, ALAN! WHERE'S SPIDER-MAN? CAN WE SEE HIM?
SHHHHH! HE'S INSIDE. BE QUIET!
LET'S GO IN AND SEE HIM!
NO! IT'S DANGEROUS IN THERE.
I WOULDN'T SWEAT IT, KID--
--IT AIN'T TOO SAFE OUT HERE, EITHER!

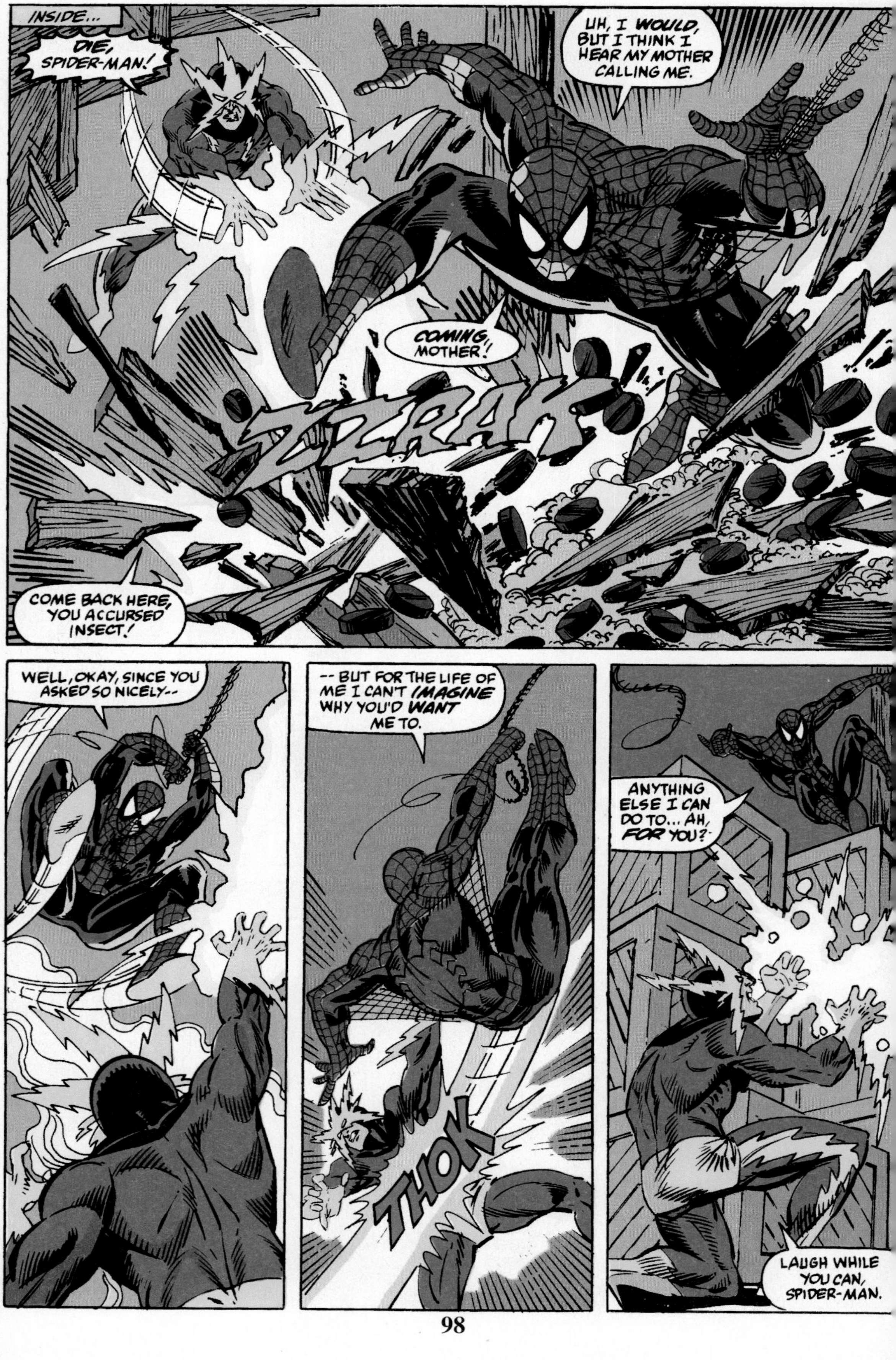
INSIDE...
DIE, SPIDER-MAN!
UH, I WOULD, BUT I THINK I HEAR MY MOTHER CALLING ME.
COMING, MOTHER!
SKRAK
COME BACK HERE, YOU ACCURSED INSECT!
WELL, OKAY, SINCE YOU ASKED SO NICELY--
-- BUT FOR THE LIFE OF ME I CAN'T IMAGINE WHY YOU'D WANT ME TO.
THOK
ANYTHING ELSE I CAN DO TO... AH, FOR YOU?
LAUGH WHILE YOU CAN, SPIDER-MAN.

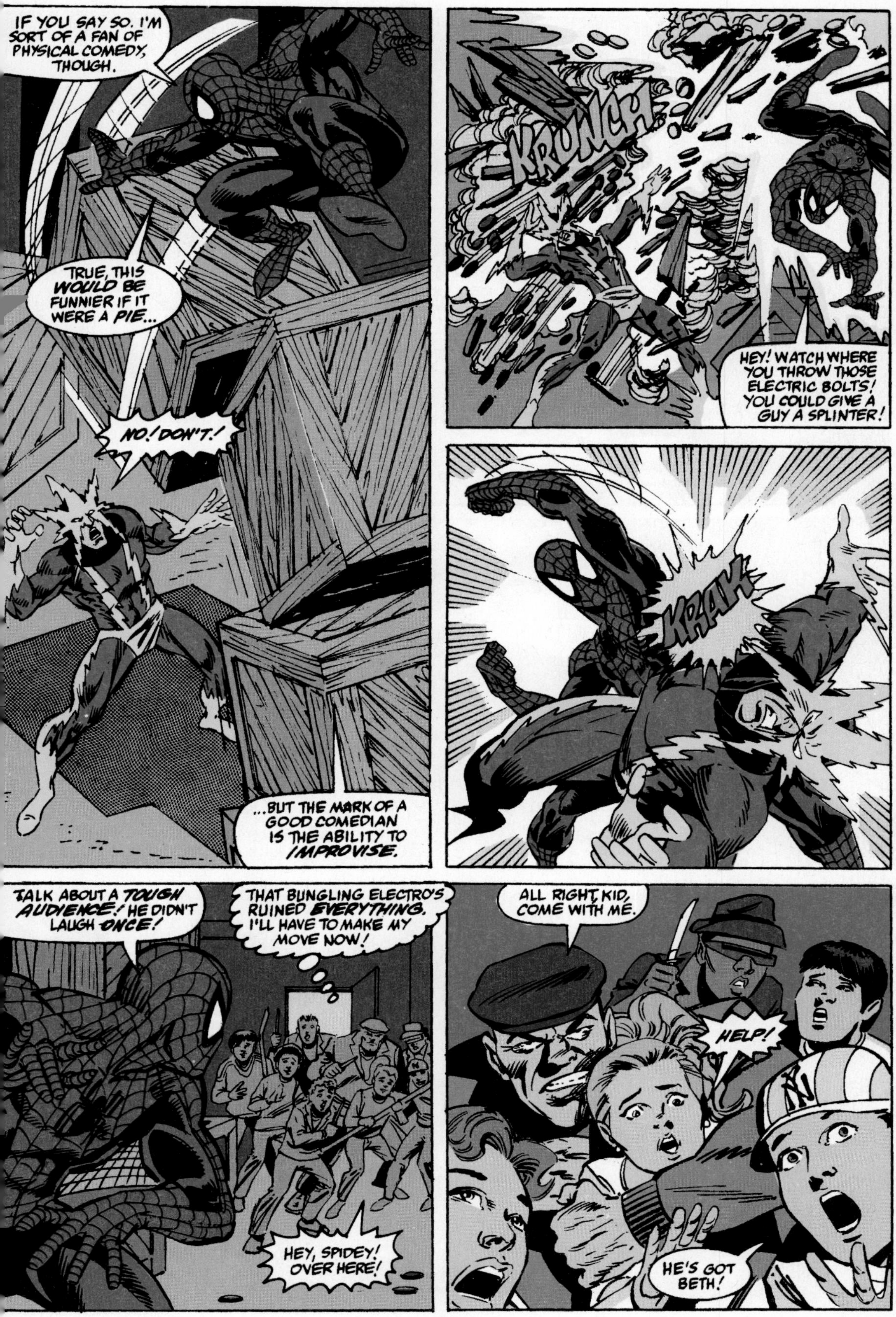
IF YOU SAY SO. I'M SORT OF A FAN OF PHYSICAL COMEDY, THOUGH.
TRUE, THIS WOULD BE FUNNIER IF IT WERE A PIE...
NO! DON'T!
...BUT THE MARK OF A GOOD COMEDIAN IS THE ABILITY TO IMPROVISE.
KRUNCH
HEY! WATCH WHERE YOU THROW THOSE ELECTRIC BOLTS! YOU COULD GIVE A GUY A SPLINTER!
KRAK
TALK ABOUT A TOUGH AUDIENCE! HE DIDN'T LAUGH ONCE!
THAT BUNGLING ELECTRO'S RUINED EVERYTHING. I'LL HAVE TO MAKE MY MOVE NOW!
HEY, SPIDEY! OVER HERE!
ALL RIGHT, KID, COME WITH ME.
HELP!
HE'S GOT BETH!

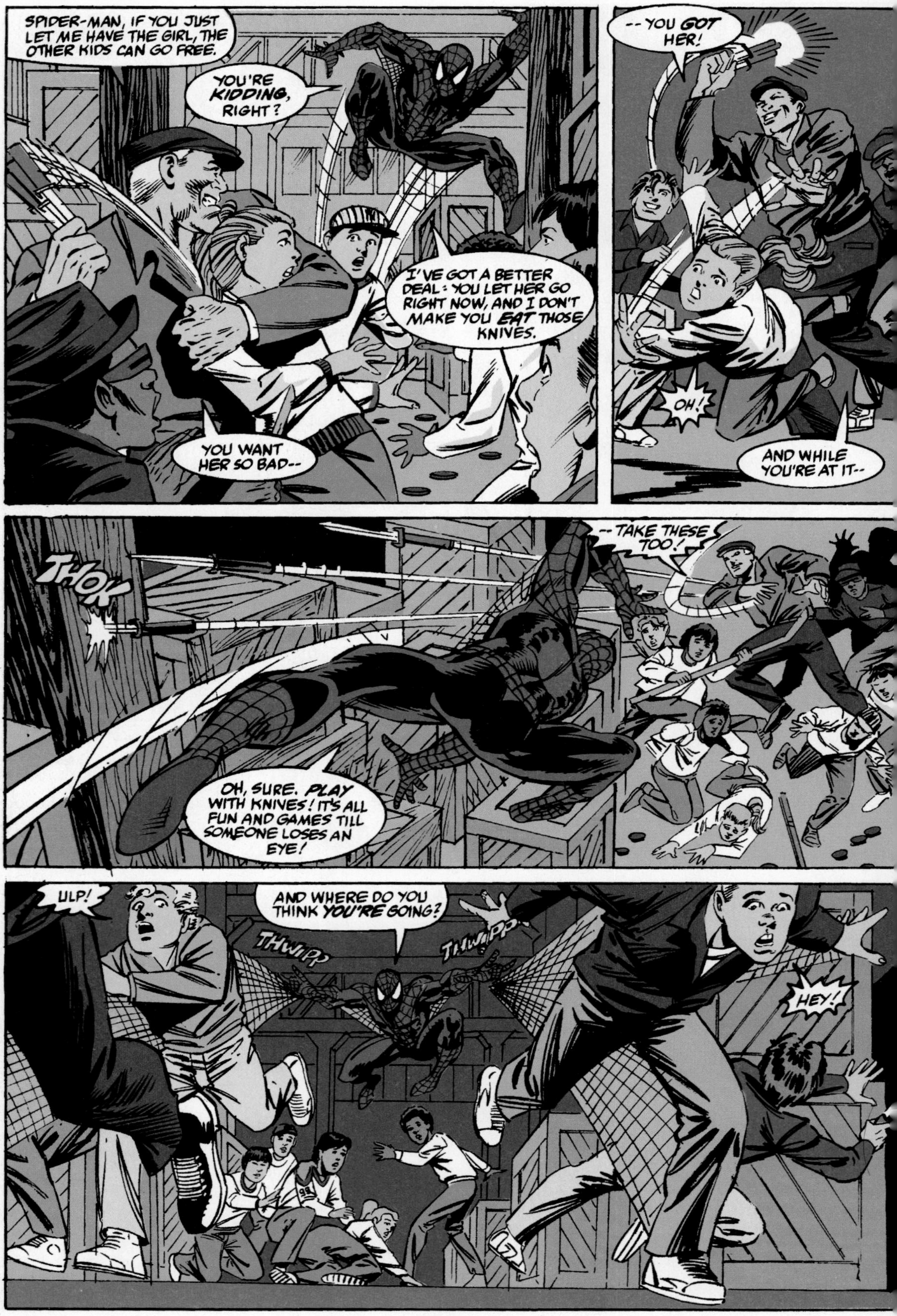
SPIDER-MAN, IF YOU JUST LET ME HAVE THE GIRL, THE OTHER KIDS CAN GO FREE.
YOU'RE KIDDING, RIGHT?
I'VE GOT A BETTER DEAL: YOU LET HER GO RIGHT NOW, AND I DON'T MAKE YOU EAT THOSE KNIVES.
YOU WANT HER SO BAD--
--YOU GOT HER!
OH!
AND WHILE YOU'RE AT IT--
--TAKE THESE TOO!
THOK
OH, SURE. PLAY WITH KNIVES! IT'S ALL FUN AND GAMES TILL SOMEONE LOSES AN EYE!
ULP!
AND WHERE DO YOU THINK YOU'RE GOING?
THWIPP
THWIPP
HEY!

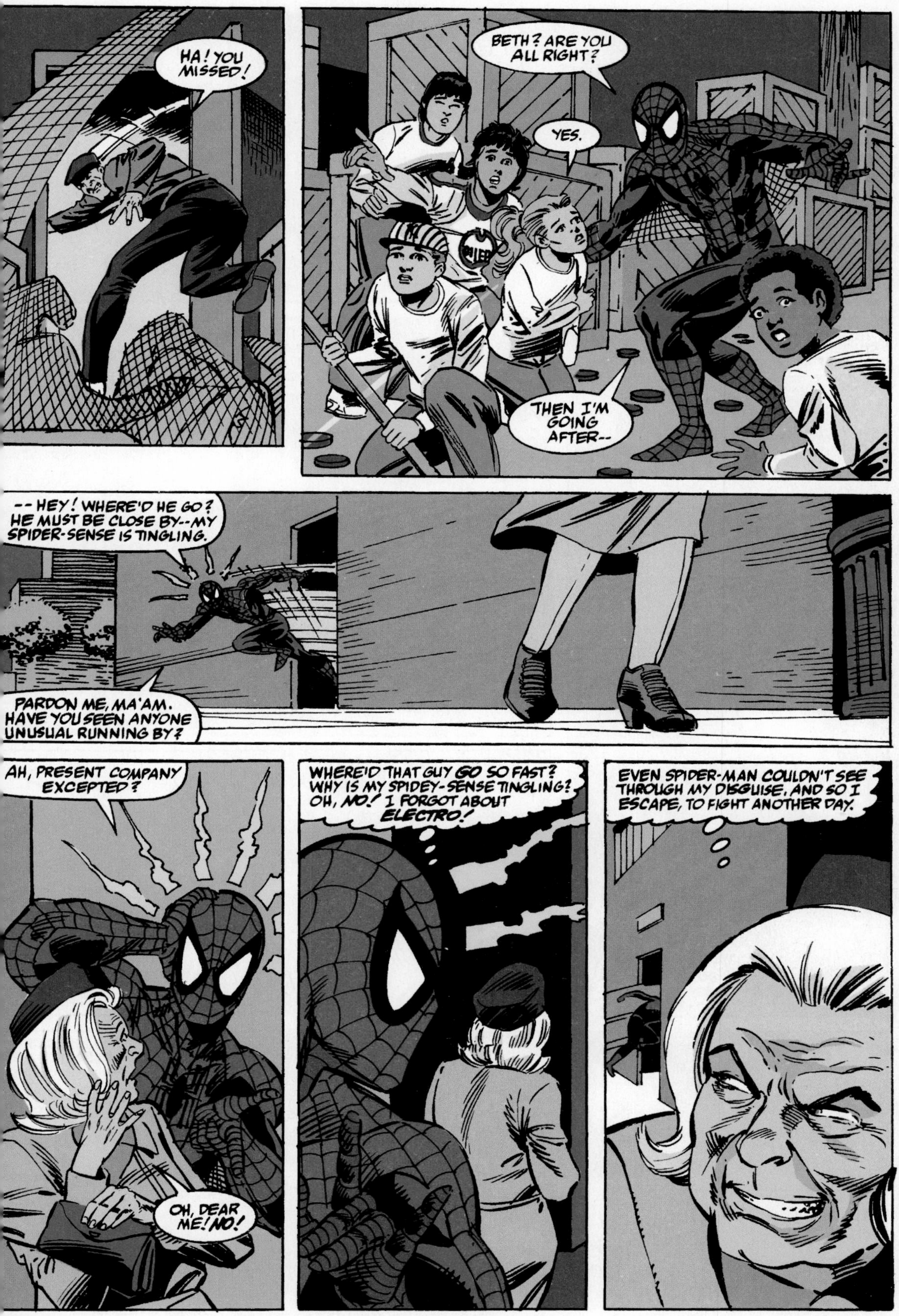

HA! YOU MISSED!
BETH? ARE YOU ALL RIGHT?
YES.
THEN I'M GOING AFTER--
--HEY! WHERE'D HE GO? HE MUST BE CLOSE BY--MY SPIDER-SENSE IS TINGLING.
PARDON ME, MA'AM. HAVE YOU SEEN ANYONE UNUSUAL RUNNING BY?
AH, PRESENT COMPANY EXCEPTED?
OH, DEAR ME! NO!
WHERE'D THAT GUY GO SO FAST? WHY IS MY SPIDEY-SENSE TINGLING? OH, NO! I FORGOT ABOUT ELECTRO!
EVEN SPIDER-MAN COULDN'T SEE THROUGH MY DISGUISE. AND SO I ESCAPE, TO FIGHT ANOTHER DAY.

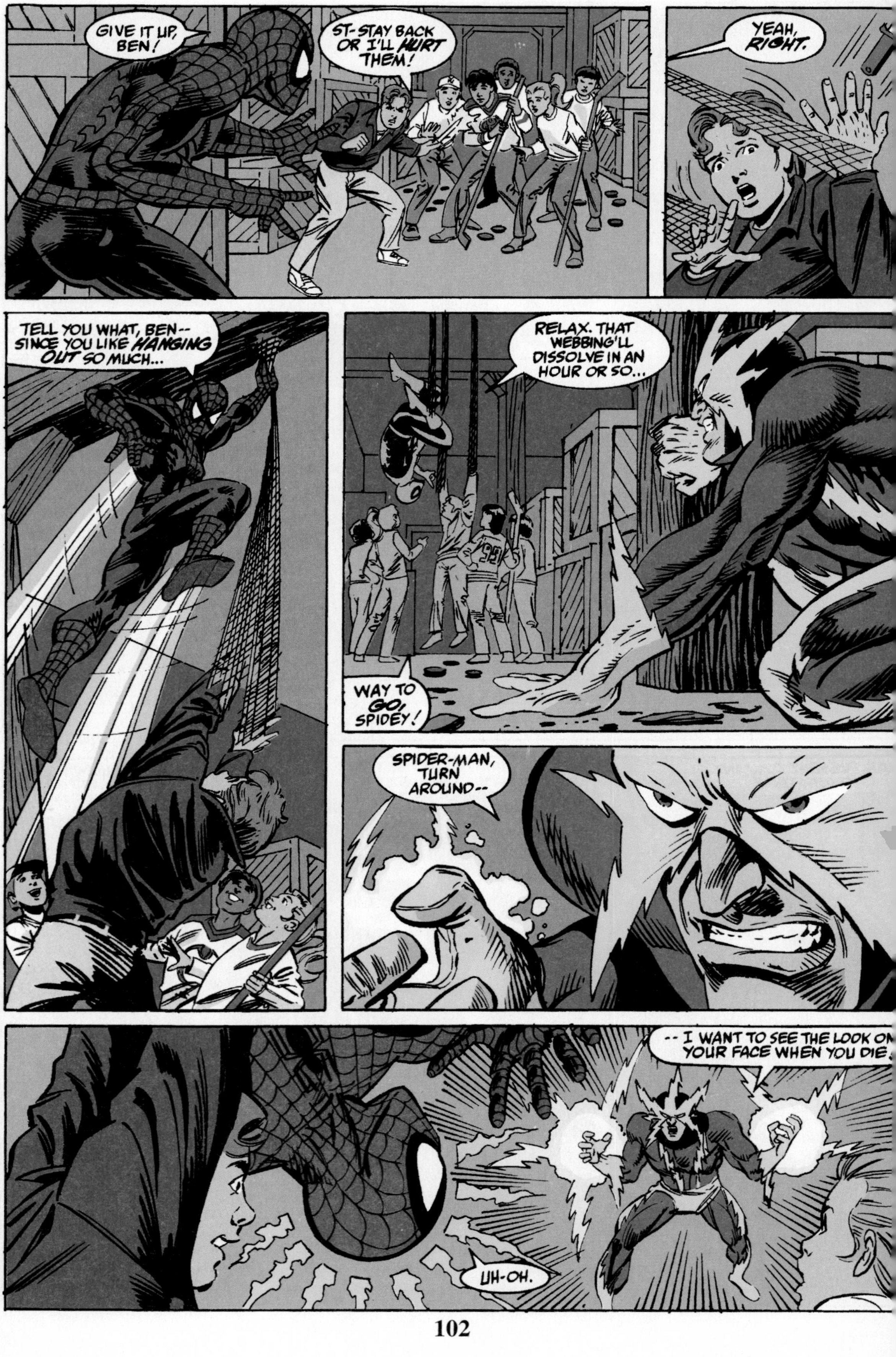
GIVE IT UP, BEN!
ST-STAY BACK OR I'LL HURT THEM!
YEAH, RIGHT.
TELL YOU WHAT, BEN-- SINCE YOU LIKE HANGING OUT SO MUCH...
RELAX. THAT WEBBING'LL DISSOLVE IN AN HOUR OR SO...
WAY TO GO, SPIDEY!
SPIDER-MAN, TURN AROUND--
-- I WANT TO SEE THE LOOK ON YOUR FACE WHEN YOU DIE.
UH-OH.

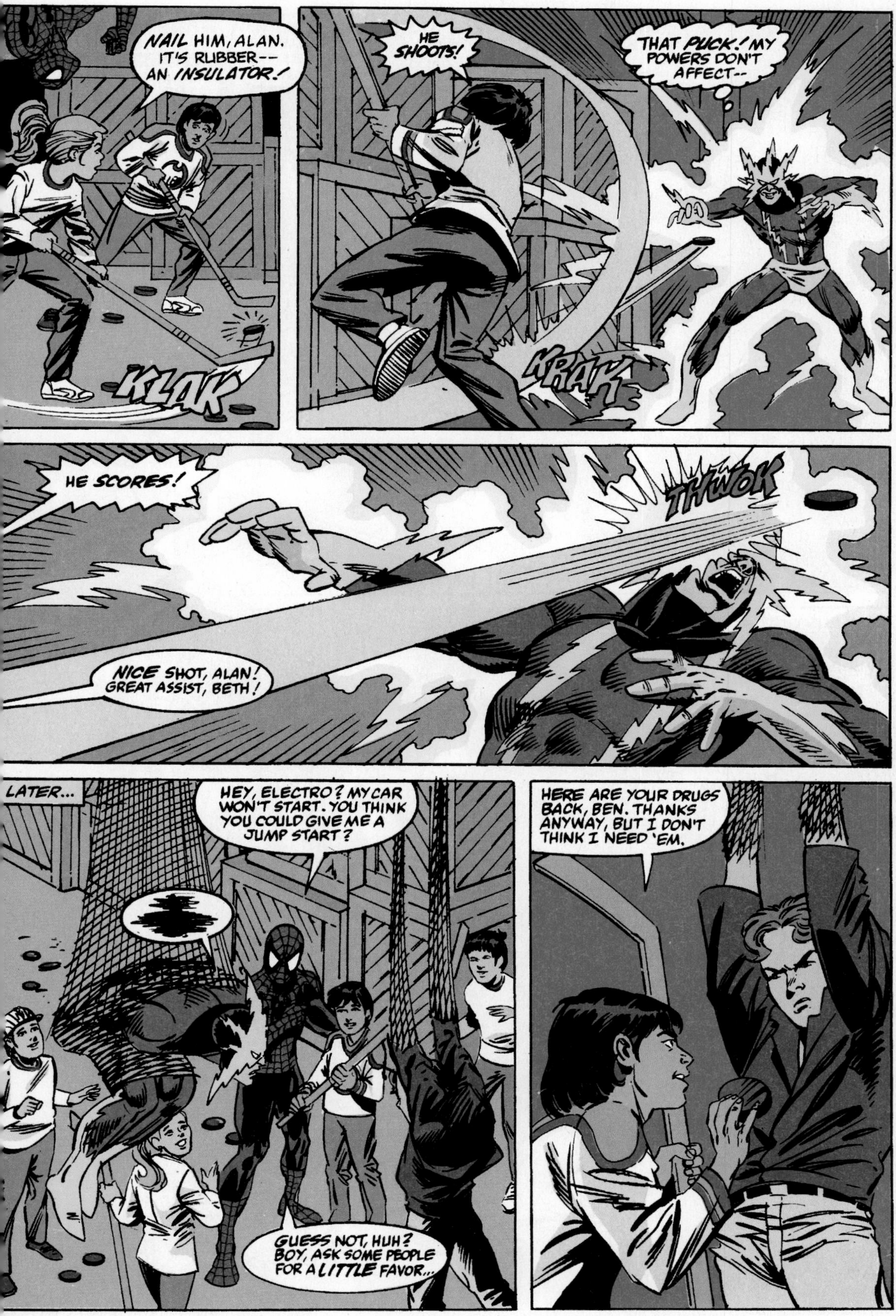
NAIL HIM, ALAN. IT'S RUBBER-- AN INSULATOR!
KLAK
HE SHOOTS!
KRAK
THAT PUCK! MY POWERS DON'T AFFECT--
HE SCORES!
THWOK
NICE SHOT, ALAN! GREAT ASSIST, BETH!
LATER...
HEY, ELECTRO? MY CAR WON'T START. YOU THINK YOU COULD GIVE ME A JUMP START?
GUESS NOT, HUH? BOY, ASK SOME PEOPLE FOR A LITTLE FAVOR...
HERE ARE YOUR DRUGS BACK, BEN. THANKS ANYWAY, BUT I DON'T THINK I NEED 'EM.

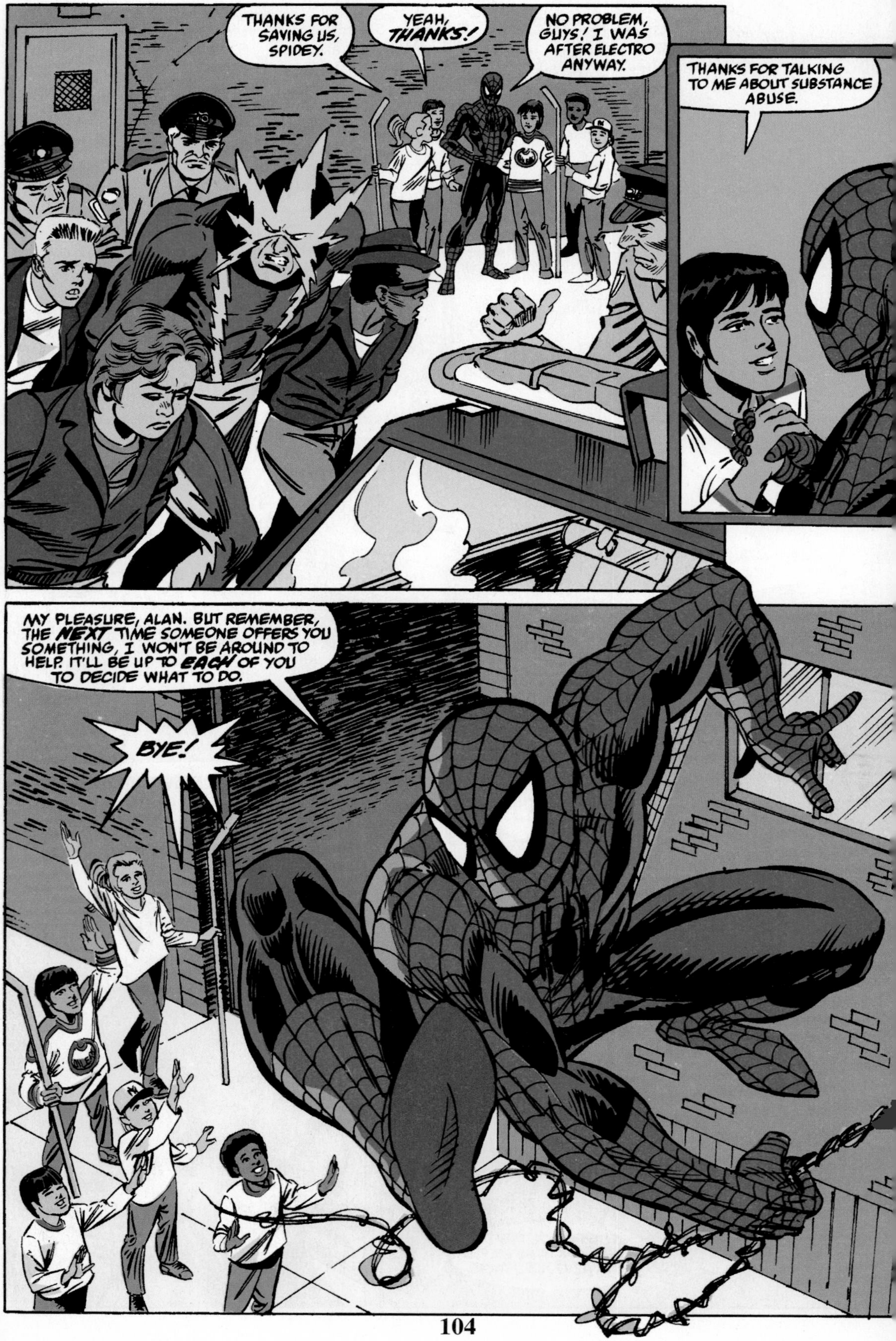
THANKS FOR SAVING US, SPIDEY.
YEAH, THANKS!
NO PROBLEM, GUYS! I WAS AFTER ELECTRO ANYWAY.
THANKS FOR TALKING TO ME ABOUT SUBSTANCE ABUSE.
MY PLEASURE, ALAN. BUT REMEMBER, THE NEXT TIME SOMEONE OFFERS YOU SOMETHING, I WON'T BE AROUND TO HELP. IT'LL BE UP TO EACH OF YOU TO DECIDE WHAT TO DO.
BYE!

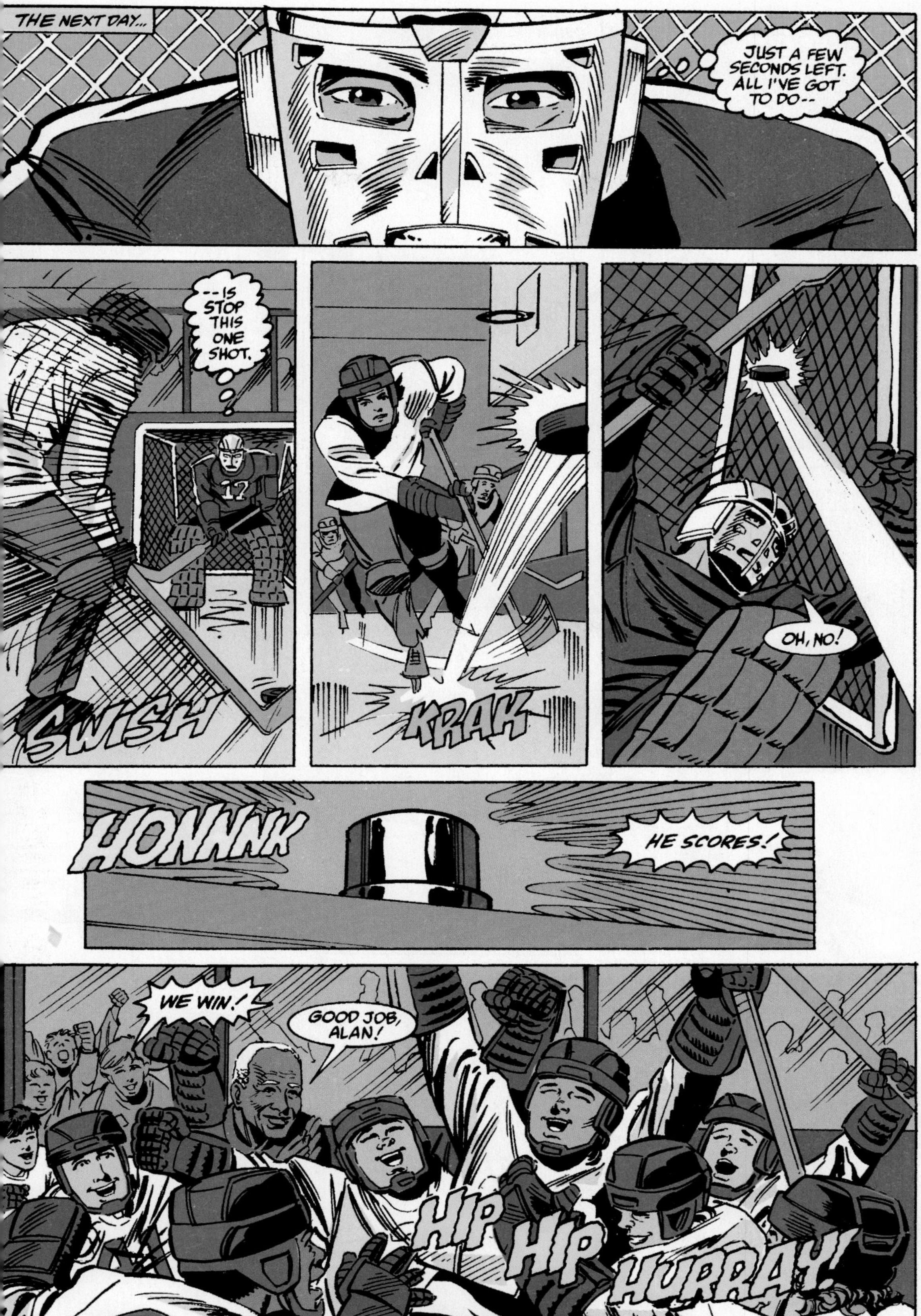
THE NEXT DAY...
JUST A FEW SECONDS LEFT. ALL I'VE GOT TO DO--
--IS STOP THIS ONE SHOT.
SWISH
KRAK
OH, NO!
HONNNK
HE SCORES!
WE WIN!
GOOD JOB, ALAN!
HIP HIP HURRAY!

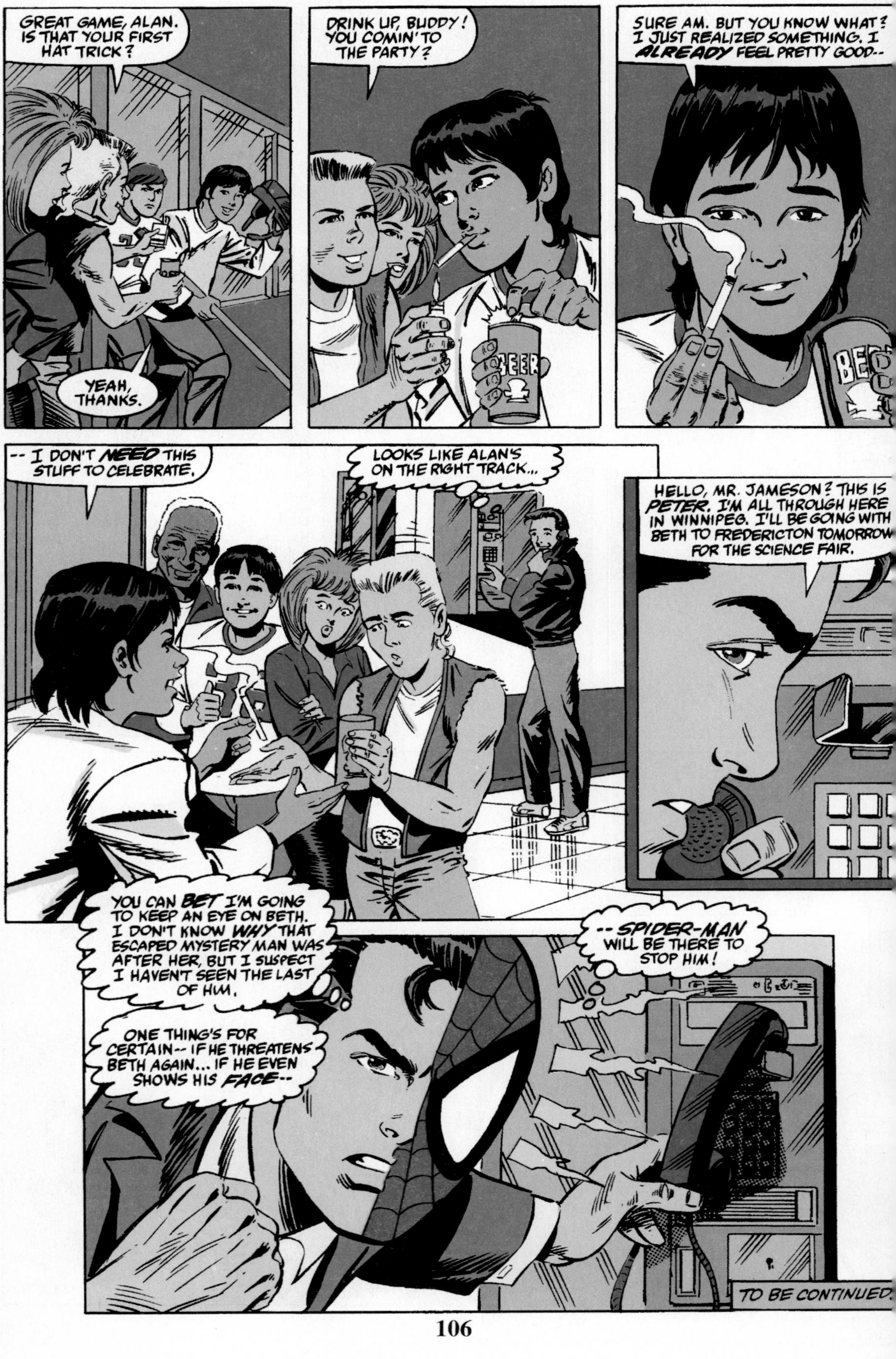
GREAT GAME, ALAN. IS THAT YOUR FIRST HAT TRICK?
YEAH, THANKS.
DRINK UP, BUDDY! YOU COMIN' TO THE PARTY?
BEER
SURE AM. BUT YOU KNOW WHAT? I JUST REALIZED SOMETHING. I ALREADY FEEL PRETTY GOOD--
-- I DON'T NEED THIS STUFF TO CELEBRATE.
LOOKS LIKE ALAN'S ON THE RIGHT TRACK...
HELLO, MR. JAMESON? THIS IS PETER. I'M ALL THROUGH HERE IN WINNIPEG. I'LL BE GOING WITH BETH TO FREDERICTON TOMORROW FOR THE SCIENCE FAIR.
YOU CAN BET I'M GOING TO KEEP AN EYE ON BETH. I DON'T KNOW WHY THAT ESCAPED MYSTERY MAN WAS AFTER HER, BUT I SUSPECT I HAVEN'T SEEN THE LAST OF HIM.
ONE THING'S FOR CERTAIN-- IF HE THREATENS BETH AGAIN... IF HE EVEN SHOWS HIS FACE--
-- SPIDER-MAN WILL BE THERE TO STOP HIM!
TO BE CONTINUED.

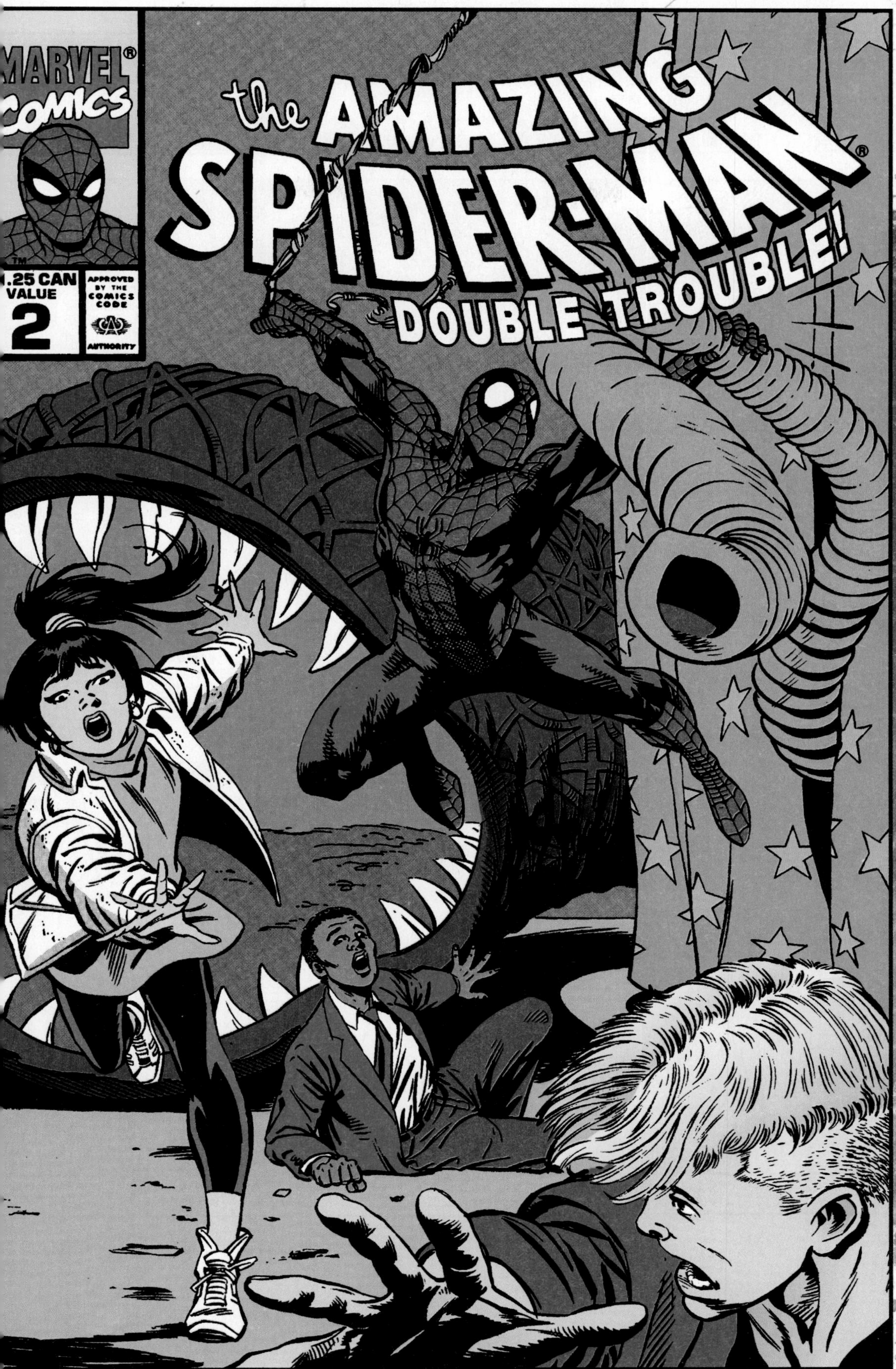
MARVEL COMICS
the AMAZING SPIDER-MAN
DOUBLE TROUBLE!
.25 CAN VALUE
2
APPROVED BY THE COMICS CODE AUTHORITY

BITTEN BY A RADIOACTIVE SPIDER, STUDENT **PETER PARKER** GAINED THE PROPORTIONATE STRENGT AND AGILITY OF AN ARACHNID! ARMED WITH HIS WONDROUS WEB-SHOOTERS, THE RELUCTANT SUPE HERO STRUGGLES WITH SINISTER SUPER-VILLAINS, MAKING ENDS MEET, AND MAINTAINING SOM SEMBLANCE OF A NORMAL LIFE!

Stan Lee PRESENTS: THE AMAZING SPIDER-MAN®

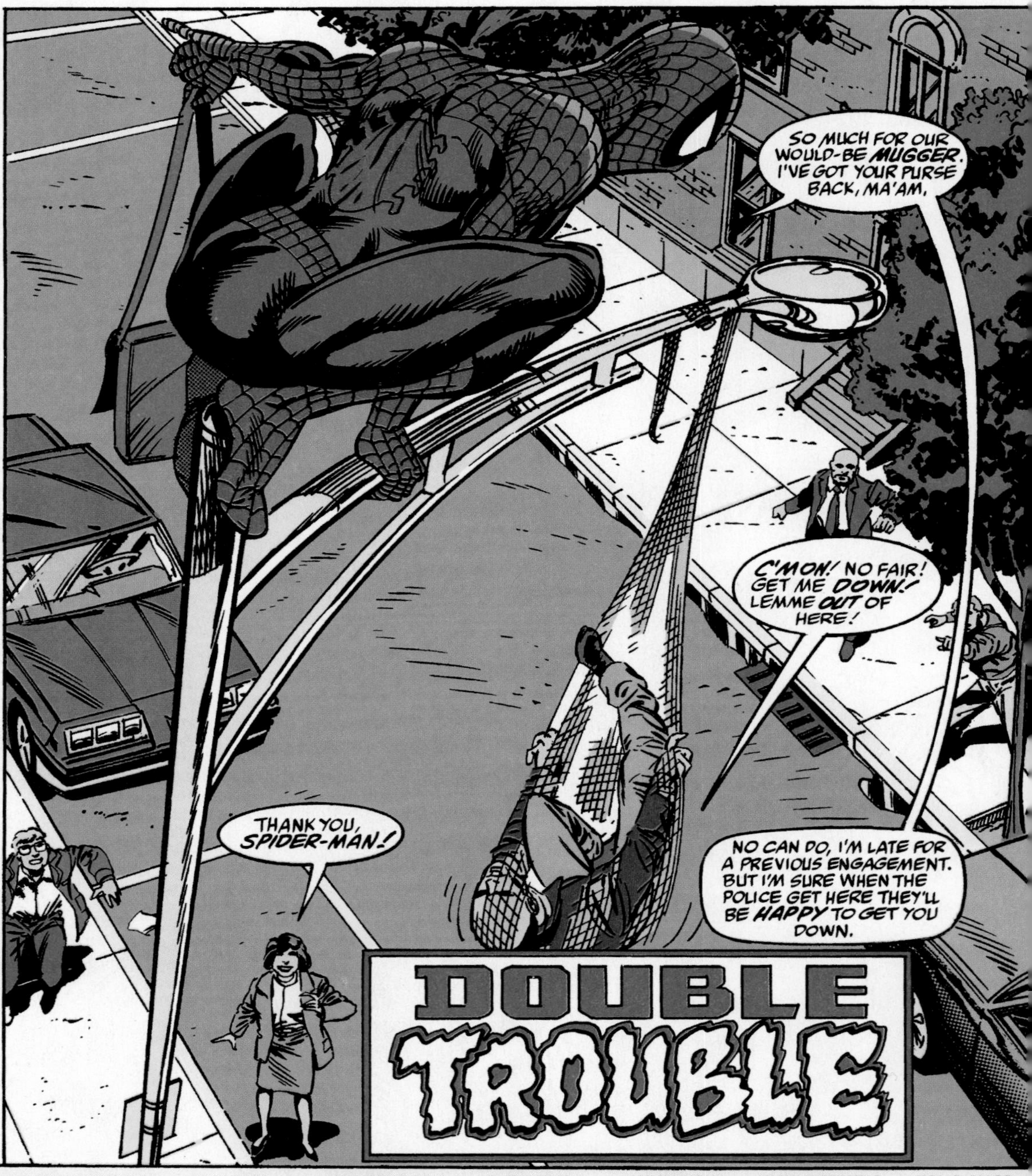
SO MUCH FOR OUR WOULD-BE *MUGGER*. I'VE GOT YOUR PURSE BACK, MA'AM.
C'MON! NO FAIR! GET ME *DOWN!* LEMME *OUT* OF HERE!
THANK YOU, SPIDER-MAN!
NO CAN DO, I'M LATE FOR A PREVIOUS ENGAGEMENT. BUT I'M SURE WHEN THE POLICE GET HERE THEY'LL BE *HAPPY* TO GET YOU DOWN.
DOUBLE TROUBLE

DWAYNE McDUFFIE	HERB TRIMPE	CHRISTOPHER IVY	RICK PARKER	GREG WRIGHT	GLENN HERDLING	TOM DeFALCO
Writer	Penciler	Inker	Letterer	Colorist	Reprint Editor	Editor-in-Chief

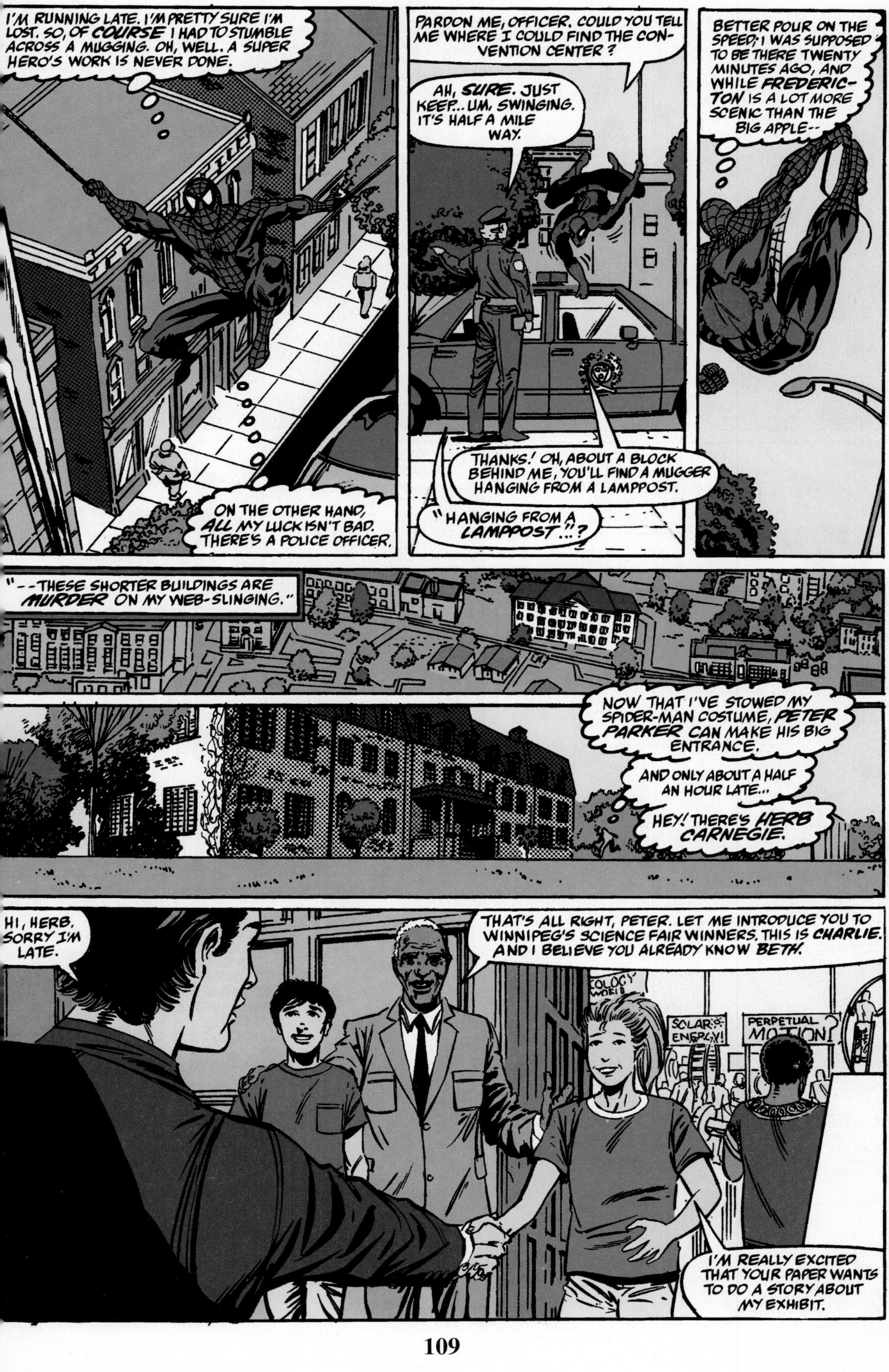
I'M RUNNING LATE. I'M PRETTY SURE I'M LOST. SO, OF COURSE I HAD TO STUMBLE ACROSS A MUGGING. OH, WELL. A SUPER HERO'S WORK IS NEVER DONE.
ON THE OTHER HAND, ALL MY LUCK ISN'T BAD. THERE'S A POLICE OFFICER.
PARDON ME, OFFICER. COULD YOU TELL ME WHERE I COULD FIND THE CONVENTION CENTER?
AH, SURE. JUST KEEP... UM, SWINGING. IT'S HALF A MILE WAY.
THANKS! OH, ABOUT A BLOCK BEHIND ME, YOU'LL FIND A MUGGER HANGING FROM A LAMPPOST.
"HANGING FROM A LAMPPOST..."?
BETTER POUR ON THE SPEED; I WAS SUPPOSED TO BE THERE TWENTY MINUTES AGO, AND WHILE FREDERICTON IS A LOT MORE SCENIC THAN THE BIG APPLE--
"--THESE SHORTER BUILDINGS ARE MURDER ON MY WEB-SLINGING."
NOW THAT I'VE STOWED MY SPIDER-MAN COSTUME, PETER PARKER CAN MAKE HIS BIG ENTRANCE.
AND ONLY ABOUT A HALF AN HOUR LATE...
HEY! THERE'S HERB CARNEGIE.
HI, HERB. SORRY I'M LATE.
THAT'S ALL RIGHT, PETER. LET ME INTRODUCE YOU TO WINNIPEG'S SCIENCE FAIR WINNERS. THIS IS CHARLIE. AND I BELIEVE YOU ALREADY KNOW BETH.
SOLAR ENERGY!
PERPETUAL MOTION?
I'M REALLY EXCITED THAT YOUR PAPER WANTS TO DO A STORY ABOUT MY EXHIBIT.

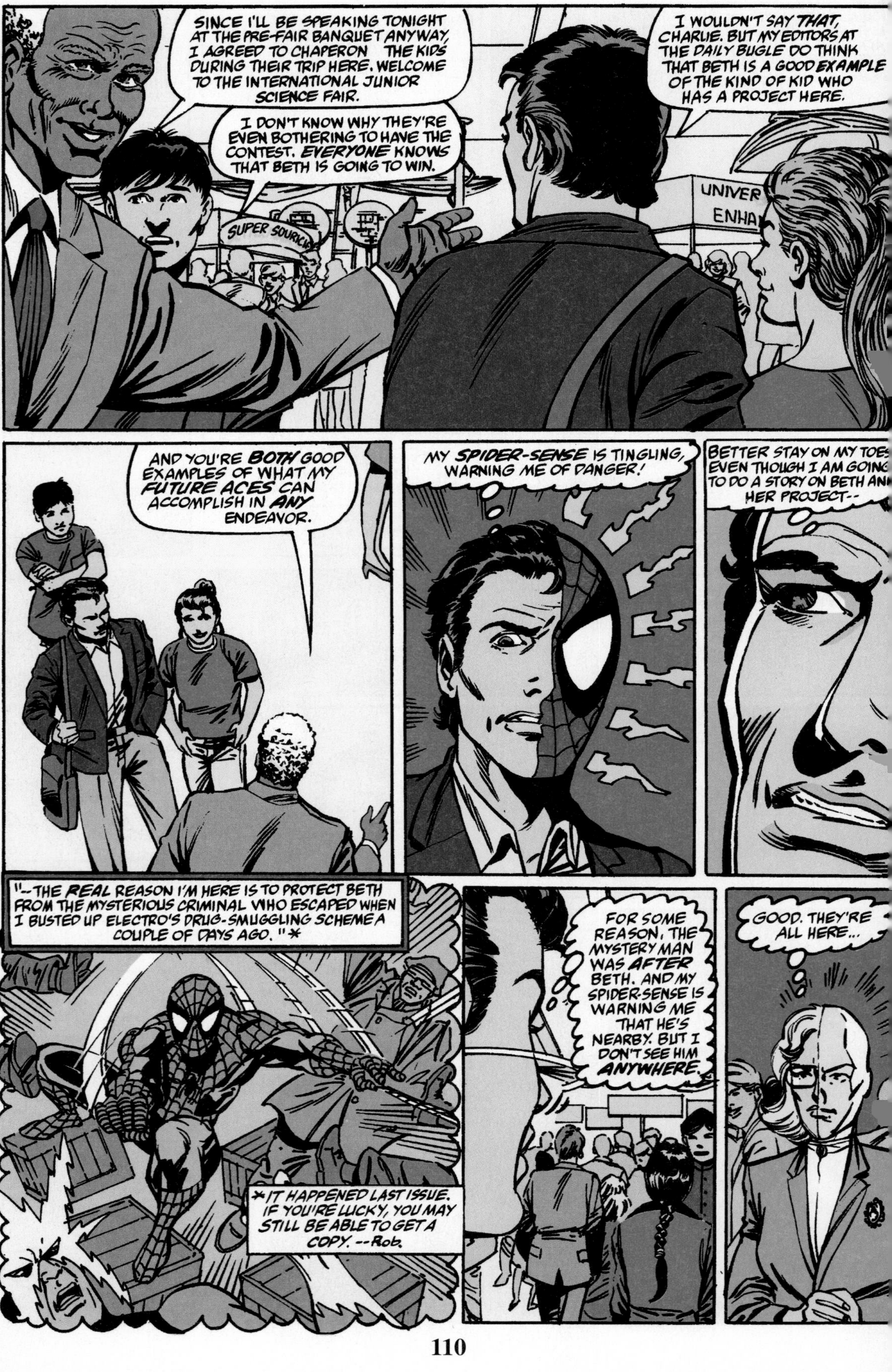
SINCE I'LL BE SPEAKING TONIGHT AT THE PRE-FAIR BANQUET ANYWAY, I AGREED TO CHAPERON THE KIDS DURING THEIR TRIP HERE. WELCOME TO THE INTERNATIONAL JUNIOR SCIENCE FAIR.
I DON'T KNOW WHY THEY'RE EVEN BOTHERING TO HAVE THE CONTEST. EVERYONE KNOWS THAT BETH IS GOING TO WIN.
SUPER SOURCIN
I WOULDN'T SAY THAT, CHARLIE. BUT MY EDITORS AT THE DAILY BUGLE DO THINK THAT BETH IS A GOOD EXAMPLE OF THE KIND OF KID WHO HAS A PROJECT HERE.
UNIVER
ENHA
AND YOU'RE BOTH GOOD EXAMPLES OF WHAT MY FUTURE ACES CAN ACCOMPLISH IN ANY ENDEAVOR.
MY SPIDER-SENSE IS TINGLING, WARNING ME OF DANGER!
BETTER STAY ON MY TOES EVEN THOUGH I AM GOING TO DO A STORY ON BETH AN HER PROJECT--
"--THE REAL REASON I'M HERE IS TO PROTECT BETH FROM THE MYSTERIOUS CRIMINAL WHO ESCAPED WHEN I BUSTED UP ELECTRO'S DRUG-SMUGGLING SCHEME A COUPLE OF DAYS AGO." *
*IT HAPPENED LAST ISSUE. IF YOU'RE LUCKY, YOU MAY STILL BE ABLE TO GET A COPY. --Rob.
FOR SOME REASON, THE MYSTERY MAN WAS AFTER BETH. AND MY SPIDER-SENSE IS WARNING ME THAT HE'S NEARBY. BUT I DON'T SEE HIM ANYWHERE.
GOOD. THEY'RE ALL HERE...

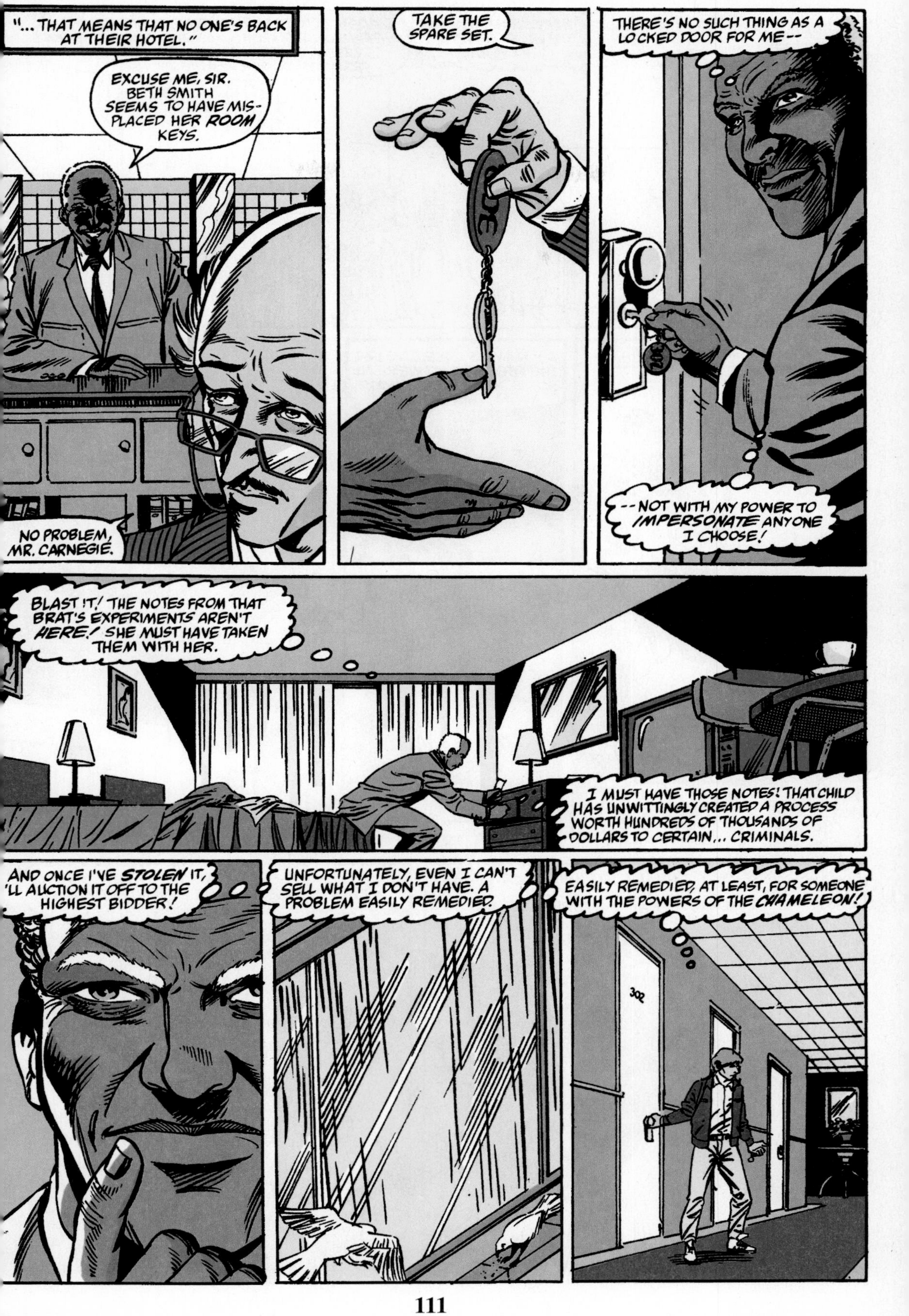
"... THAT MEANS THAT NO ONE'S BACK AT THEIR HOTEL."
EXCUSE ME, SIR. BETH SMITH SEEMS TO HAVE MIS-PLACED HER ROOM KEYS.
NO PROBLEM, MR. CARNEGIE.
TAKE THE SPARE SET.
THERE'S NO SUCH THING AS A LOCKED DOOR FOR ME--
--NOT WITH MY POWER TO IMPERSONATE ANYONE I CHOOSE!
BLAST IT! THE NOTES FROM THAT BRAT'S EXPERIMENTS AREN'T HERE! SHE MUST HAVE TAKEN THEM WITH HER.
I MUST HAVE THOSE NOTES! THAT CHILD HAS UNWITTINGLY CREATED A PROCESS WORTH HUNDREDS OF THOUSANDS OF DOLLARS TO CERTAIN... CRIMINALS.
AND ONCE I'VE STOLEN IT, I'LL AUCTION IT OFF TO THE HIGHEST BIDDER!
UNFORTUNATELY, EVEN I CAN'T SELL WHAT I DON'T HAVE. A PROBLEM EASILY REMEDIED.
EASILY REMEDIED, AT LEAST, FOR SOMEONE WITH THE POWERS OF THE CHAMELEON!
302

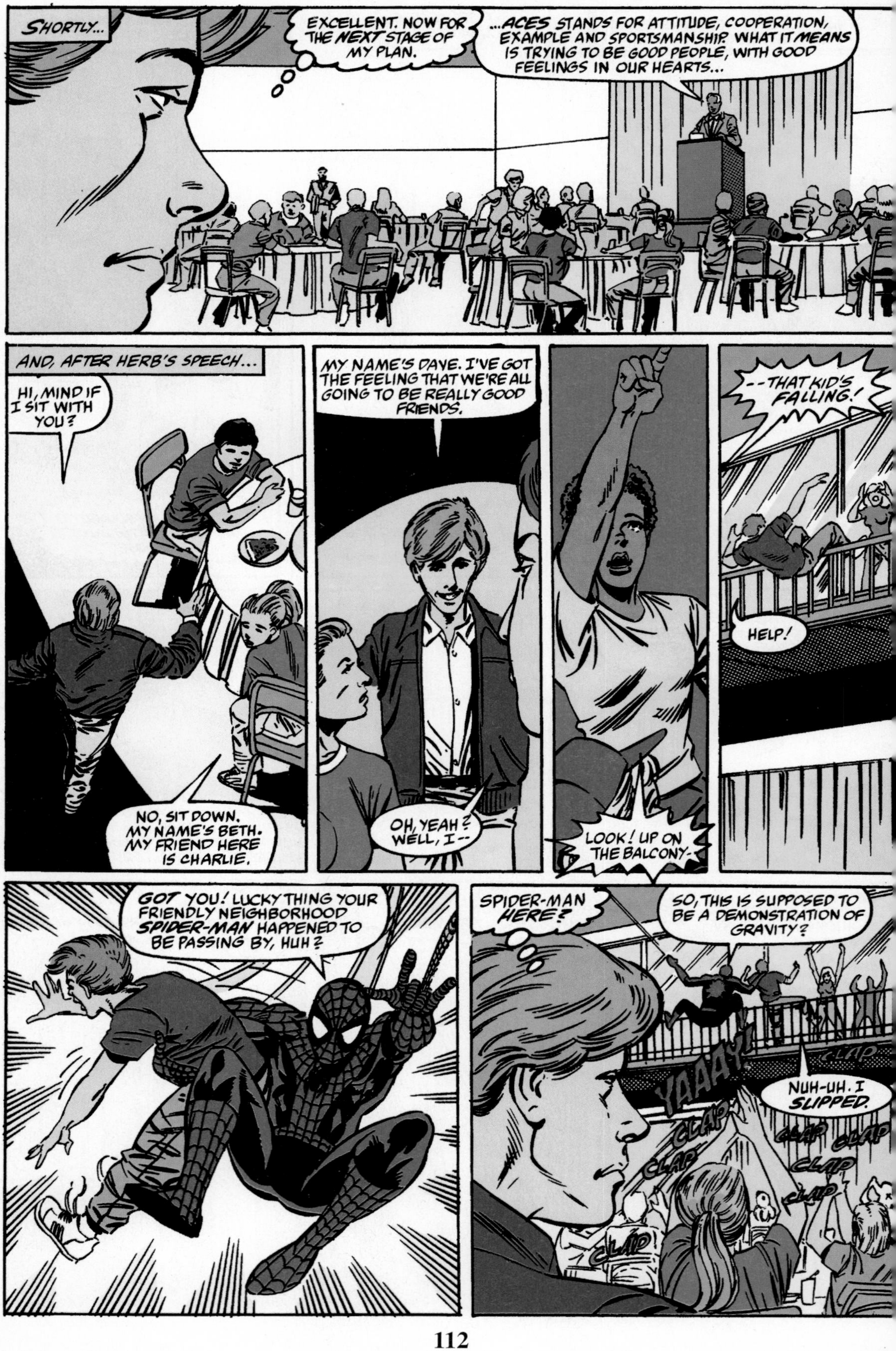
SHORTLY...
EXCELLENT. NOW FOR THE NEXT STAGE OF MY PLAN.
...ACES STANDS FOR ATTITUDE, COOPERATION, EXAMPLE AND SPORTSMANSHIP. WHAT IT MEANS IS TRYING TO BE GOOD PEOPLE, WITH GOOD FEELINGS IN OUR HEARTS...
AND, AFTER HERB'S SPEECH...
HI, MIND IF I SIT WITH YOU?
NO, SIT DOWN. MY NAME'S BETH. MY FRIEND HERE IS CHARLIE.
MY NAME'S DAVE. I'VE GOT THE FEELING THAT WE'RE ALL GOING TO BE REALLY GOOD FRIENDS.
OH, YEAH? WELL, I--
LOOK! UP ON THE BALCONY-
--THAT KID'S FALLING!
HELP!
GOT YOU! LUCKY THING YOUR FRIENDLY NEIGHBORHOOD SPIDER-MAN HAPPENED TO BE PASSING BY, HUH?
SPIDER-MAN HERE?
SO, THIS IS SUPPOSED TO BE A DEMONSTRATION OF GRAVITY?
NUH-UH. I SLIPPED.
YAAAY!
CLAP
CLAP
CLAP
CLAP
CLAP
CLAP
CLAP
CLAP

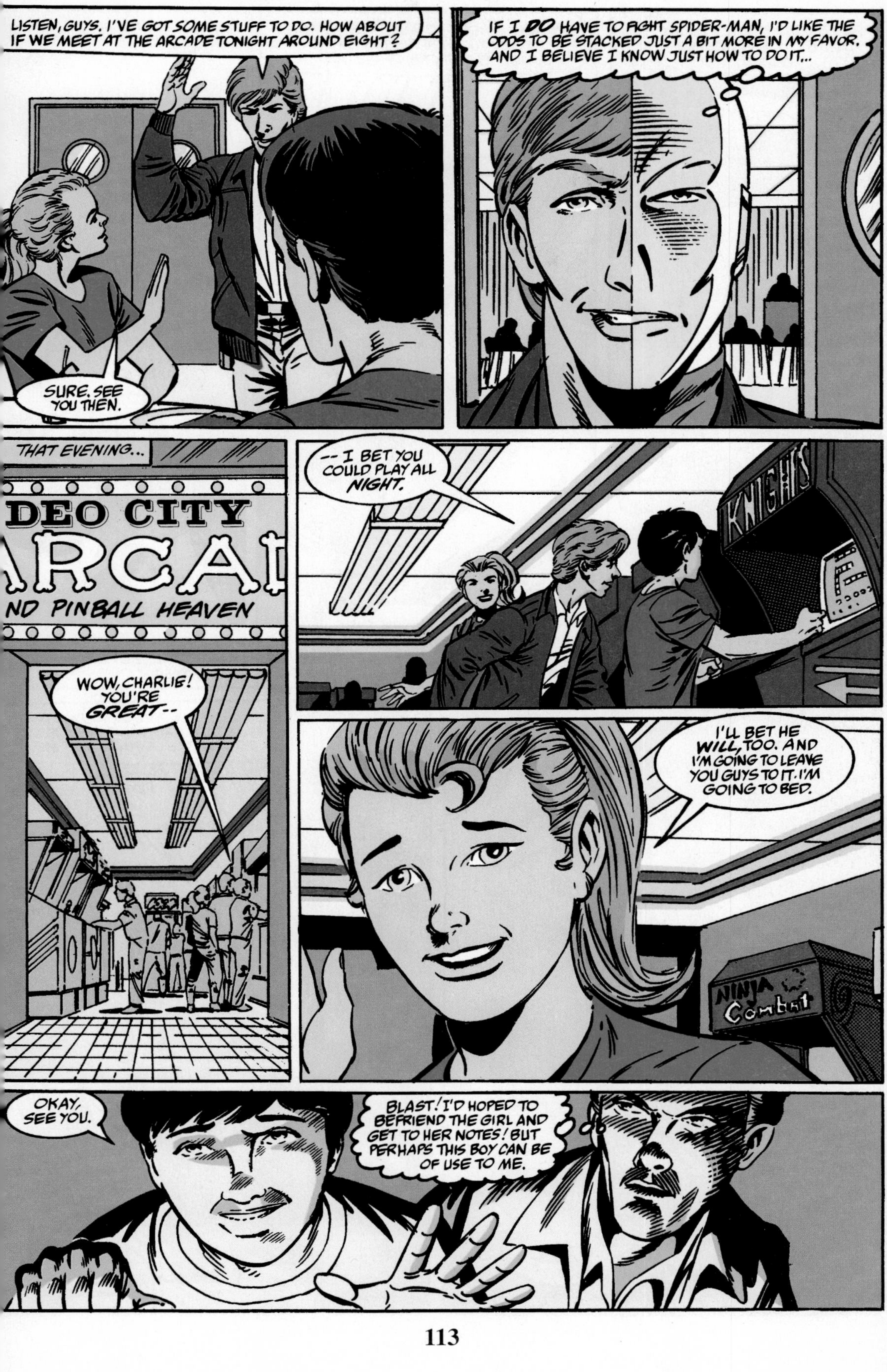
LISTEN, GUYS, I'VE GOT SOME STUFF TO DO. HOW ABOUT IF WE MEET AT THE ARCADE TONIGHT AROUND EIGHT?
SURE. SEE YOU THEN.
IF I DO HAVE TO FIGHT SPIDER-MAN, I'D LIKE THE ODDS TO BE STACKED JUST A BIT MORE IN MY FAVOR. AND I BELIEVE I KNOW JUST HOW TO DO IT...
THAT EVENING...
DEO CITY
RCAD
ND PINBALL HEAVEN
WOW, CHARLIE! YOU'RE GREAT--
-- I BET YOU COULD PLAY ALL NIGHT.
KNIGHTS
I'LL BET HE WILL, TOO. AND I'M GOING TO LEAVE YOU GUYS TO IT. I'M GOING TO BED.
NINJA Combat
OKAY, SEE YOU.
BLAST! I'D HOPED TO BEFRIEND THE GIRL AND GET TO HER NOTES! BUT PERHAPS THIS BOY CAN BE OF USE TO ME.

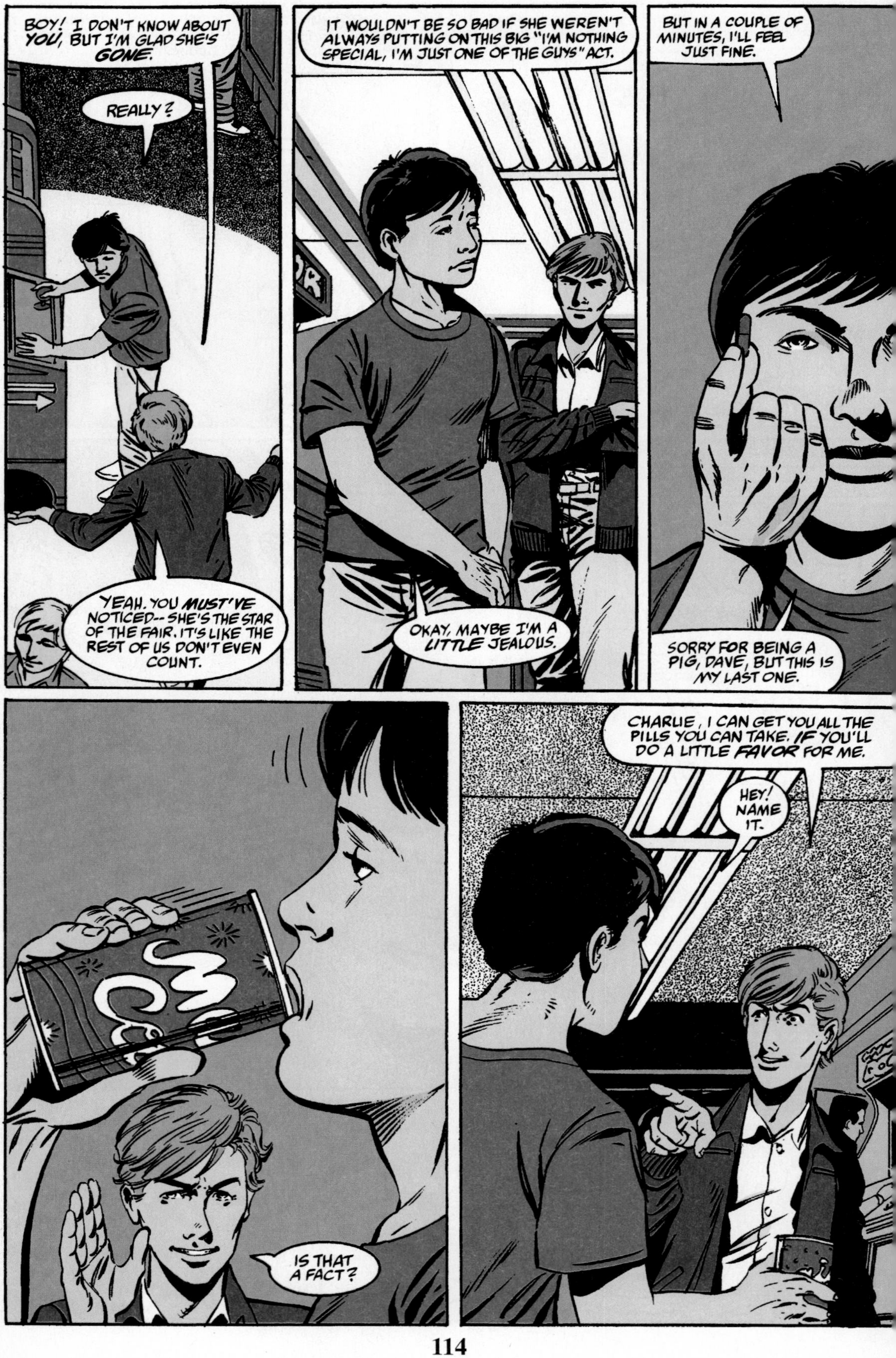
BOY! I DON'T KNOW ABOUT YOU, BUT I'M GLAD SHE'S GONE.
REALLY?
YEAH. YOU MUST'VE NOTICED-- SHE'S THE STAR OF THE FAIR. IT'S LIKE THE REST OF US DON'T EVEN COUNT.
IT WOULDN'T BE SO BAD IF SHE WEREN'T ALWAYS PUTTING ON THIS BIG "I'M NOTHING SPECIAL, I'M JUST ONE OF THE GUYS" ACT.
OKAY, MAYBE I'M A LITTLE JEALOUS.
BUT IN A COUPLE OF MINUTES, I'LL FEEL JUST FINE.
SORRY FOR BEING A PIG, DAVE, BUT THIS IS MY LAST ONE.
IS THAT A FACT?
CHARLIE, I CAN GET YOU ALL THE PILLS YOU CAN TAKE. IF YOU'LL DO A LITTLE FAVOR FOR ME.
HEY! NAME IT.

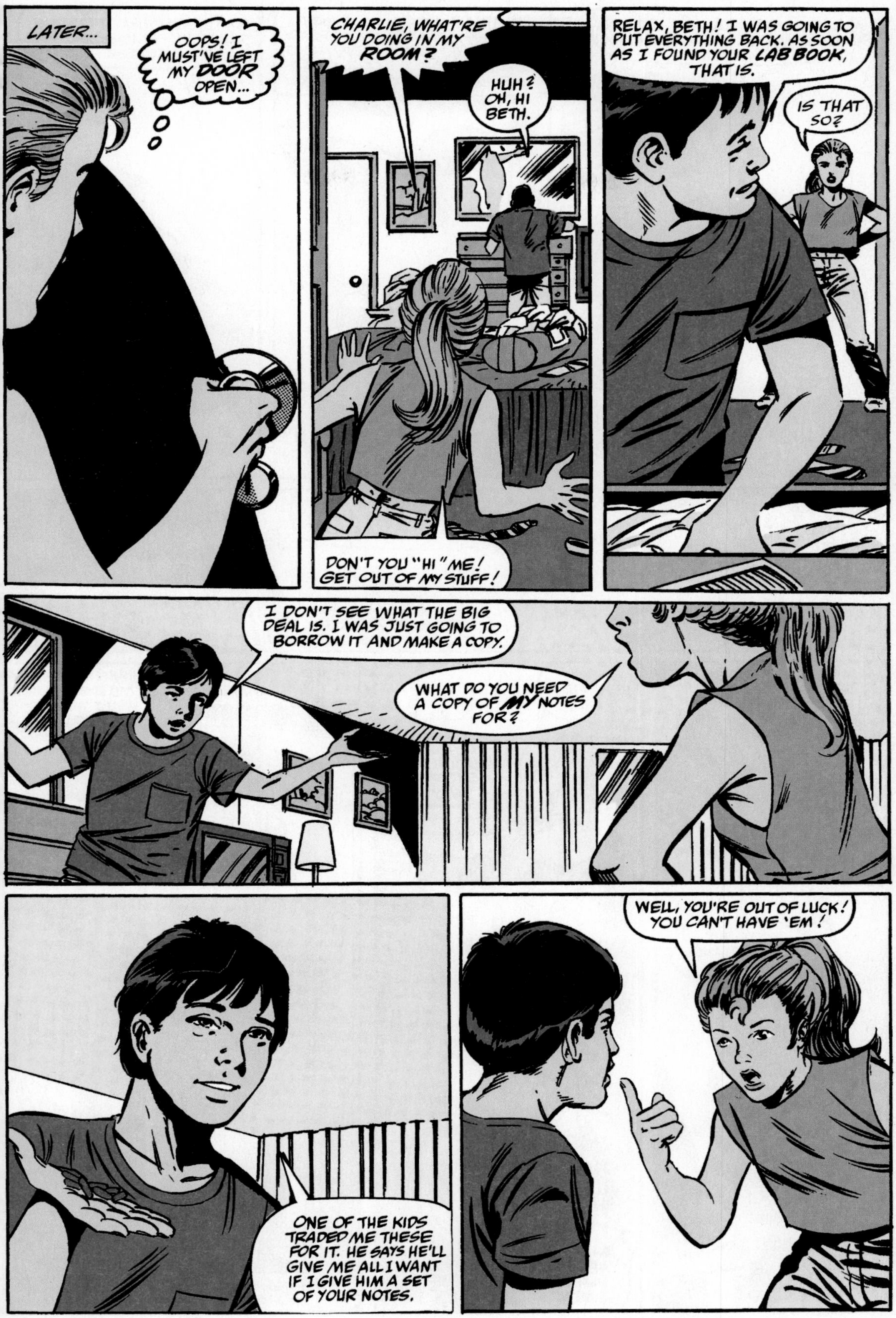
LATER...
OOPS! I MUST'VE LEFT MY DOOR OPEN...
CHARLIE, WHAT'RE YOU DOING IN MY ROOM?
HUH? OH, HI BETH.
DON'T YOU "HI" ME! GET OUT OF MY STUFF!
RELAX, BETH! I WAS GOING TO PUT EVERYTHING BACK. AS SOON AS I FOUND YOUR LAB BOOK, THAT IS.
IS THAT SO?
I DON'T SEE WHAT THE BIG DEAL IS. I WAS JUST GOING TO BORROW IT AND MAKE A COPY.
WHAT DO YOU NEED A COPY OF MY NOTES FOR?
ONE OF THE KIDS TRADED ME THESE FOR IT. HE SAYS HE'LL GIVE ME ALL I WANT IF I GIVE HIM A SET OF YOUR NOTES.
WELL, YOU'RE OUT OF LUCK! YOU CAN'T HAVE 'EM!

I'M NOT GONNA TELL MR. CARNEGIE. BUT I'D BETTER NOT CATCH YOU IN MY STUFF AGAIN.

I'M PRETTY SICK OF YOUR HIGH-AND-MIGHTY ATTITUDE. IT'S EASY FOR YOU TO BE MISS GOODY-TWO-SHOES. YOU'RE THE COOL SUPER-GENIUS. EVERYBODY LOVES *YOU*!

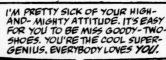

WHAT'S WRONG WITH TAKING SOMETHING TO MAKE *ME* FEEL A LITTLE BETTER?

ARE YOU TELLING ME THAT THOSE DRUGS REALLY MAKE YOU FEEL MORE *LOVED*?

YOU HAVE *NO* RIGHT TO TALK TO ME THAT WAY!

HOW ABOUT THIS THEN? IS IT COOL TO SELL OUT YOUR FRIENDS?

YOU DON'T UNDERSTAND *ANYTHING*!

WHOA! HEADS UP, CHARLIE.

WHY DON'T YOU JUST GET OUT OF MY WAY?

WELL, THAT MIGHT WORK *TOO*.

HI, BETH. WHAT'S WRONG WITH CHARLIE?

201

NOTHING. WE HAD A FIGHT.

SHE'S NOT TELLING ME EVERYTHING. AND I THINK I SEE WHY...

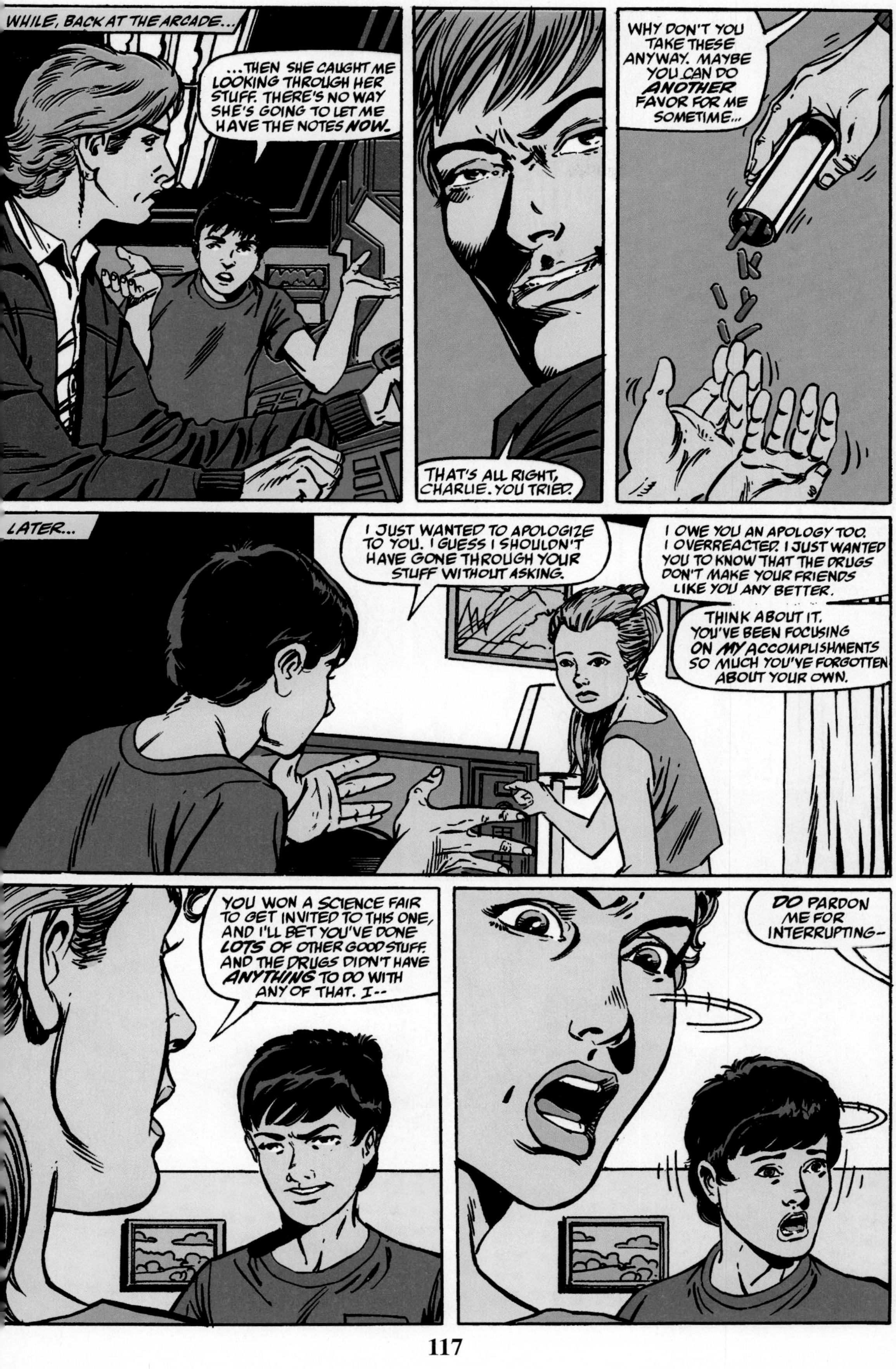
WHILE, BACK AT THE ARCADE...
...THEN SHE CAUGHT ME LOOKING THROUGH HER STUFF. THERE'S NO WAY SHE'S GOING TO LET ME HAVE THE NOTES NOW.
THAT'S ALL RIGHT, CHARLIE. YOU TRIED.
WHY DON'T YOU TAKE THESE ANYWAY. MAYBE YOU CAN DO ANOTHER FAVOR FOR ME SOMETIME...
LATER...
I JUST WANTED TO APOLOGIZE TO YOU. I GUESS I SHOULDN'T HAVE GONE THROUGH YOUR STUFF WITHOUT ASKING.
I OWE YOU AN APOLOGY TOO. I OVERREACTED. I JUST WANTED YOU TO KNOW THAT THE DRUGS DON'T MAKE YOUR FRIENDS LIKE YOU ANY BETTER.
THINK ABOUT IT. YOU'VE BEEN FOCUSING ON MY ACCOMPLISHMENTS SO MUCH YOU'VE FORGOTTEN ABOUT YOUR OWN.
YOU WON A SCIENCE FAIR TO GET INVITED TO THIS ONE, AND I'LL BET YOU'VE DONE LOTS OF OTHER GOOD STUFF. AND THE DRUGS DIDN'T HAVE ANYTHING TO DO WITH ANY OF THAT. I--
DO PARDON ME FOR INTERRUPTING--

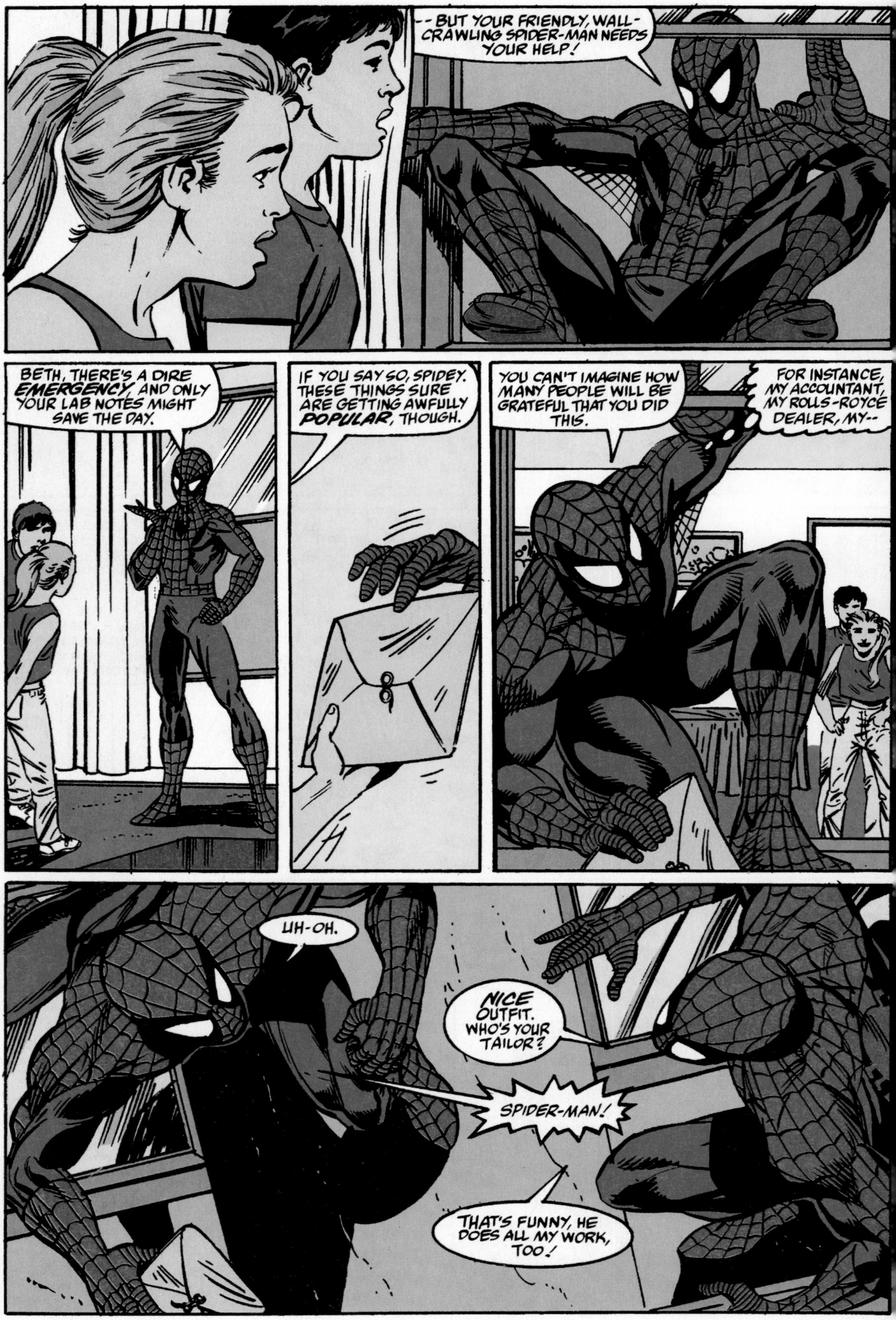
--BUT YOUR FRIENDLY, WALL-CRAWLING SPIDER-MAN NEEDS YOUR HELP!
BETH, THERE'S A DIRE EMERGENCY, AND ONLY YOUR LAB NOTES MIGHT SAVE THE DAY.
IF YOU SAY SO, SPIDEY. THESE THINGS SURE ARE GETTING AWFULLY POPULAR, THOUGH.
YOU CAN'T IMAGINE HOW MANY PEOPLE WILL BE GRATEFUL THAT YOU DID THIS.
FOR INSTANCE, MY ACCOUNTANT, MY ROLLS-ROYCE DEALER, MY--
UH-OH.
NICE OUTFIT. WHO'S YOUR TAILOR?
SPIDER-MAN!
THAT'S FUNNY, HE DOES ALL MY WORK, TOO!

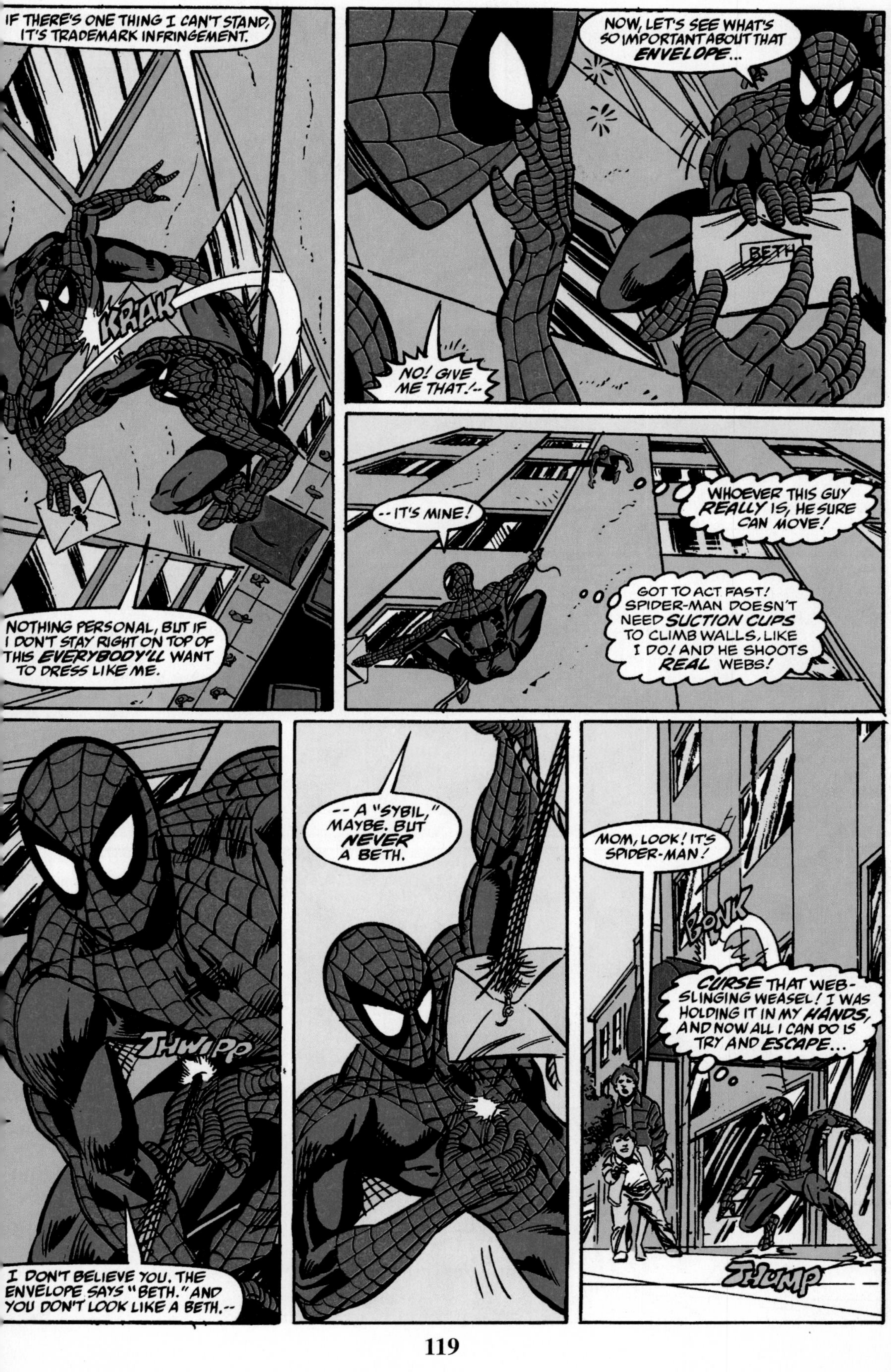
IF THERE'S ONE THING I CAN'T STAND, IT'S TRADEMARK INFRINGEMENT.
KRAK
NOTHING PERSONAL, BUT IF I DON'T STAY RIGHT ON TOP OF THIS EVERYBODY'LL WANT TO DRESS LIKE ME.
NOW, LET'S SEE WHAT'S SO IMPORTANT ABOUT THAT ENVELOPE...
BETH
NO! GIVE ME THAT!--
--IT'S MINE!
WHOEVER THIS GUY REALLY IS, HE SURE CAN MOVE!
GOT TO ACT FAST! SPIDER-MAN DOESN'T NEED SUCTION CUPS TO CLIMB WALLS, LIKE I DO! AND HE SHOOTS REAL WEBS!
THWIPP
I DON'T BELIEVE YOU. THE ENVELOPE SAYS "BETH." AND YOU DON'T LOOK LIKE A BETH.--
-- A "SYBIL," MAYBE. BUT NEVER A BETH.
MOM, LOOK! IT'S SPIDER-MAN!
BONK
CURSE THAT WEB-SLINGING WEASEL! I WAS HOLDING IT IN MY HANDS, AND NOW ALL I CAN DO IS TRY AND ESCAPE...
THUMP

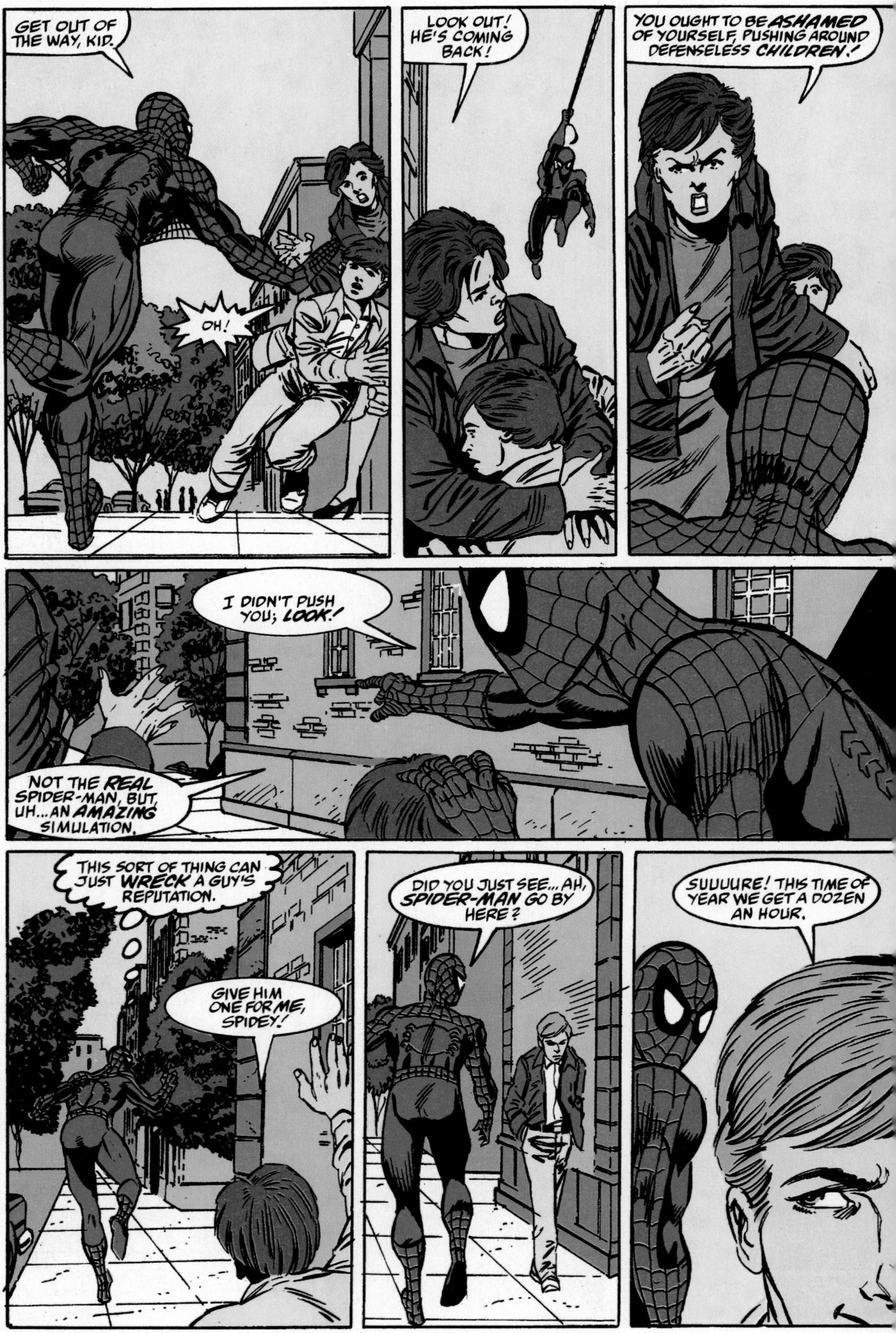
GET OUT OF THE WAY, KID.
OH!
LOOK OUT! HE'S COMING BACK!
YOU OUGHT TO BE ASHAMED OF YOURSELF, PUSHING AROUND DEFENSELESS CHILDREN!
I DIDN'T PUSH YOU; LOOK!
NOT THE REAL SPIDER-MAN, BUT, UH...AN AMAZING SIMULATION.
THIS SORT OF THING CAN JUST WRECK A GUY'S REPUTATION.
GIVE HIM ONE FOR ME, SPIDEY!
DID YOU JUST SEE... AH, SPIDER-MAN GO BY HERE?
SUUUURE! THIS TIME OF YEAR WE GET A DOZEN AN HOUR.

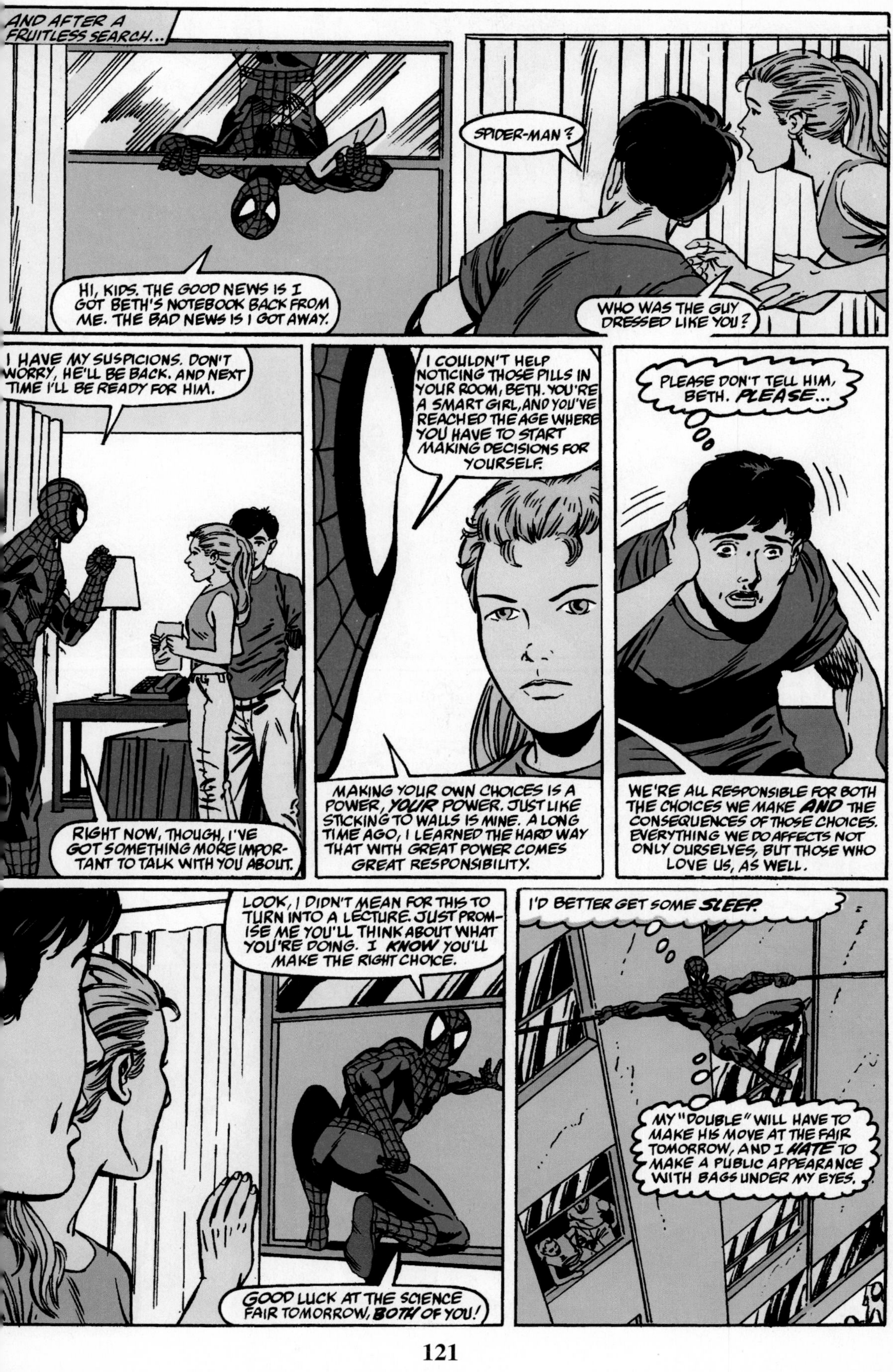
AND AFTER A FRUITLESS SEARCH...
HI, KIDS. THE GOOD NEWS IS I GOT BETH'S NOTEBOOK BACK FROM ME. THE BAD NEWS IS I GOT AWAY.
SPIDER-MAN?
WHO WAS THE GUY DRESSED LIKE YOU?
I HAVE MY SUSPICIONS. DON'T WORRY, HE'LL BE BACK. AND NEXT TIME I'LL BE READY FOR HIM.
RIGHT NOW, THOUGH, I'VE GOT SOMETHING MORE IMPORTANT TO TALK WITH YOU ABOUT.
I COULDN'T HELP NOTICING THOSE PILLS IN YOUR ROOM, BETH. YOU'RE A SMART GIRL, AND YOU'VE REACHED THE AGE WHERE YOU HAVE TO START MAKING DECISIONS FOR YOURSELF.
MAKING YOUR OWN CHOICES IS A POWER, YOUR POWER. JUST LIKE STICKING TO WALLS IS MINE. A LONG TIME AGO, I LEARNED THE HARD WAY THAT WITH GREAT POWER COMES GREAT RESPONSIBILITY.
PLEASE DON'T TELL HIM, BETH. PLEASE...
WE'RE ALL RESPONSIBLE FOR BOTH THE CHOICES WE MAKE AND THE CONSEQUENCES OF THOSE CHOICES. EVERYTHING WE DO AFFECTS NOT ONLY OURSELVES, BUT THOSE WHO LOVE US, AS WELL.
LOOK, I DIDN'T MEAN FOR THIS TO TURN INTO A LECTURE. JUST PROMISE ME YOU'LL THINK ABOUT WHAT YOU'RE DOING. I KNOW YOU'LL MAKE THE RIGHT CHOICE.
GOOD LUCK AT THE SCIENCE FAIR TOMORROW, BOTH OF YOU!
I'D BETTER GET SOME SLEEP.
MY "DOUBLE" WILL HAVE TO MAKE HIS MOVE AT THE FAIR TOMORROW, AND I HATE TO MAKE A PUBLIC APPEARANCE WITH BAGS UNDER MY EYES.

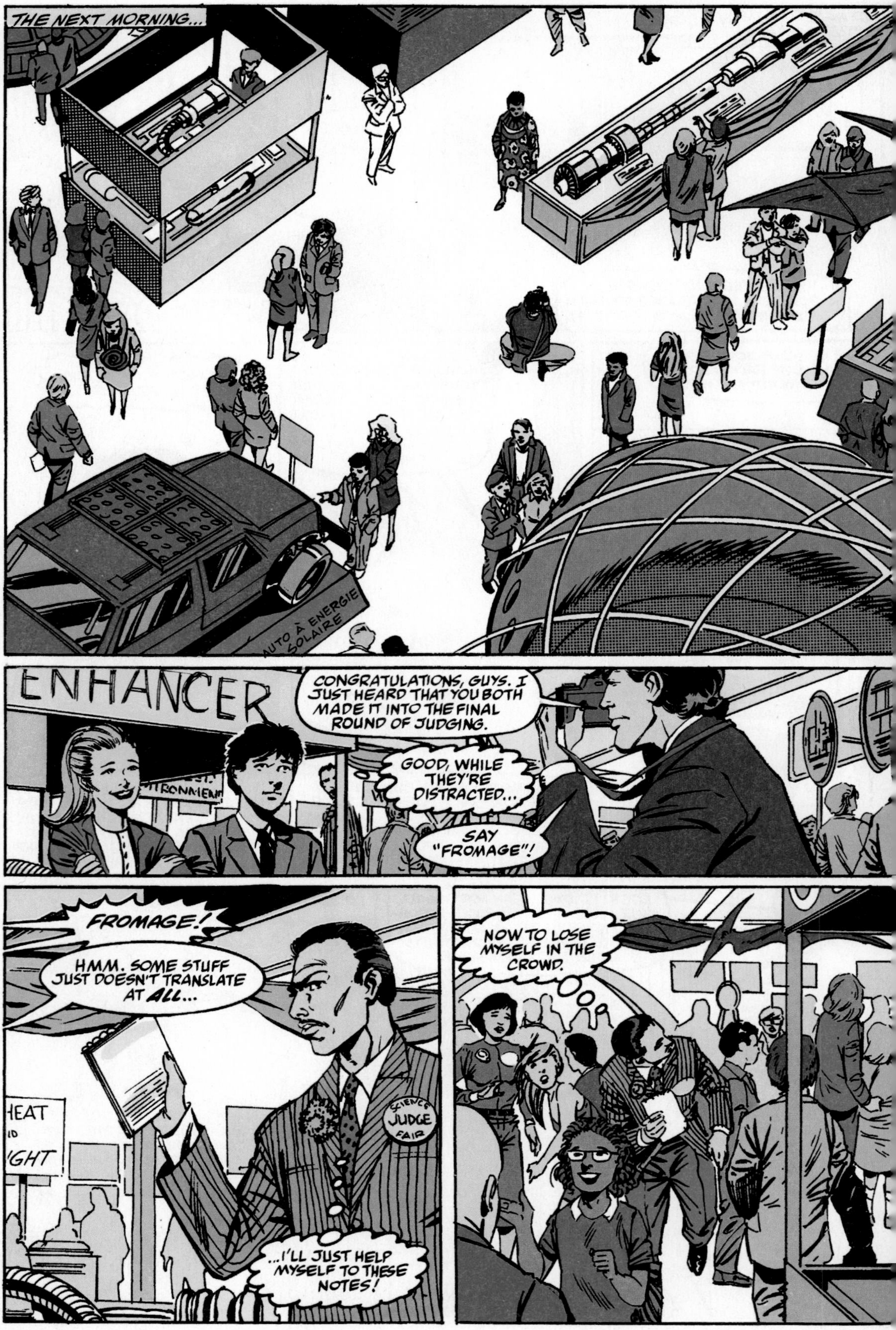
THE NEXT MORNING...
AUTO À ENERGIE SOLAIRE
ENHANCER
CONGRATULATIONS, GUYS. I JUST HEARD THAT YOU BOTH MADE IT INTO THE FINAL ROUND OF JUDGING.
GOOD, WHILE THEY'RE DISTRACTED...
SAY "FROMAGE"!
FROMAGE!
HMM. SOME STUFF JUST DOESN'T TRANSLATE AT ALL...
SCIENCE JUDGE FAIR
...I'LL JUST HELP MYSELF TO THESE NOTES!
NOW TO LOSE MYSELF IN THE CROWD.

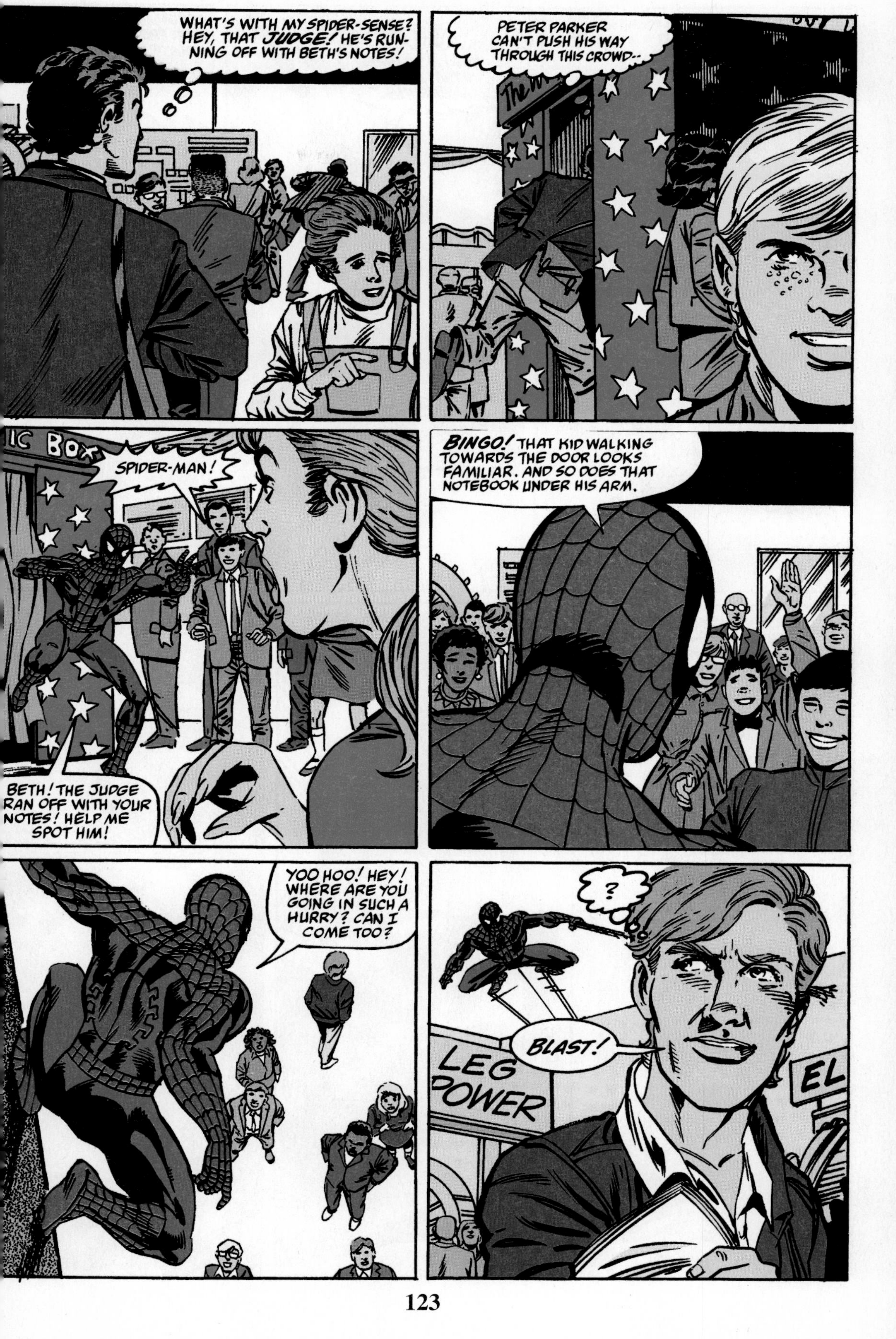
WHAT'S WITH MY SPIDER-SENSE? HEY, THAT JUDGE! HE'S RUNNING OFF WITH BETH'S NOTES!
PETER PARKER CAN'T PUSH HIS WAY THROUGH THIS CROWD--
SPIDER-MAN!
BETH! THE JUDGE RAN OFF WITH YOUR NOTES! HELP ME SPOT HIM!
BINGO! THAT KID WALKING TOWARDS THE DOOR LOOKS FAMILIAR. AND SO DOES THAT NOTEBOOK UNDER HIS ARM.
YOO HOO! HEY! WHERE ARE YOU GOING IN SUCH A HURRY? CAN I COME TOO?
?
BLAST!
LEG POWER

I DON'T KNOW WHY IT TOOK ME SO LONG TO FIGURE OUT WHO YOU REALLY ARE--

THWIPP

NO! I'M TRAPPED IN THAT ACCURSED WEBBING!

AFTER ALL, THE ONLY FOE I'VE EVER FACED WHO CAN IMPERSONATE ANYBODY IS *THE CHAMELEON.*

VERY WELL, SPIDER-MAN. THERE'S NO FURTHER NEED FOR THIS DISGUISE.

BUT YOU WILL SHORTLY DISCOVER THAT *CAPTURING* THE CHAMELEON AND *HOLDING* HIM--

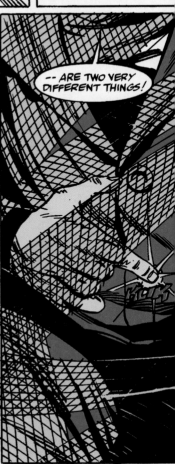

-- ARE TWO VERY DIFFERENT THINGS!

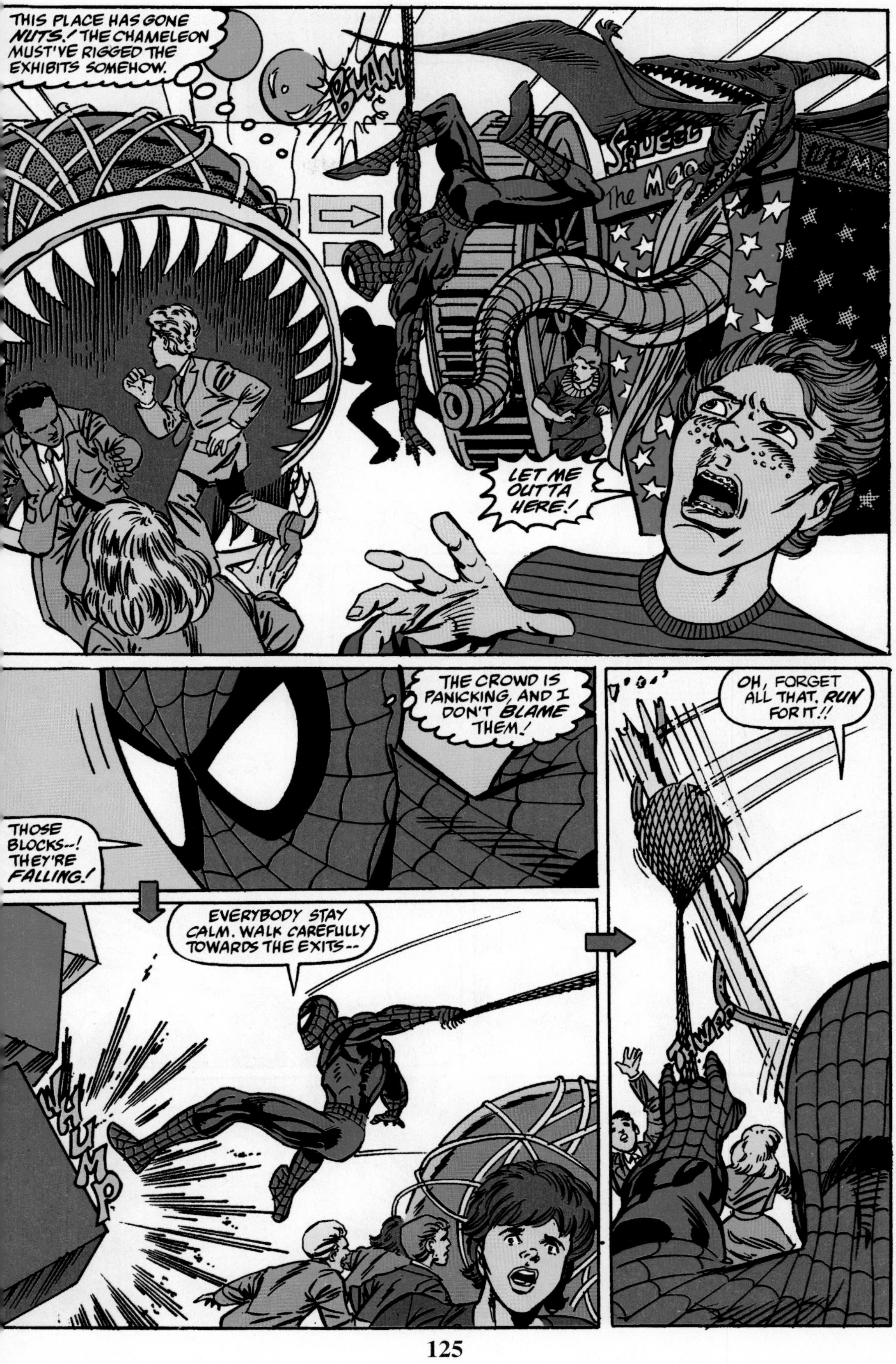
THIS PLACE HAS GONE NUTS.! THE CHAMELEON MUST'VE RIGGED THE EXHIBITS SOMEHOW.
LET ME OUTTA HERE!
THE CROWD IS PANICKING, AND I DON'T BLAME THEM!
THOSE BLOCKS--! THEY'RE FALLING!
EVERYBODY STAY CALM. WALK CAREFULLY TOWARDS THE EXITS--
WHUMP
OH, FORGET ALL THAT. RUN FOR IT!!

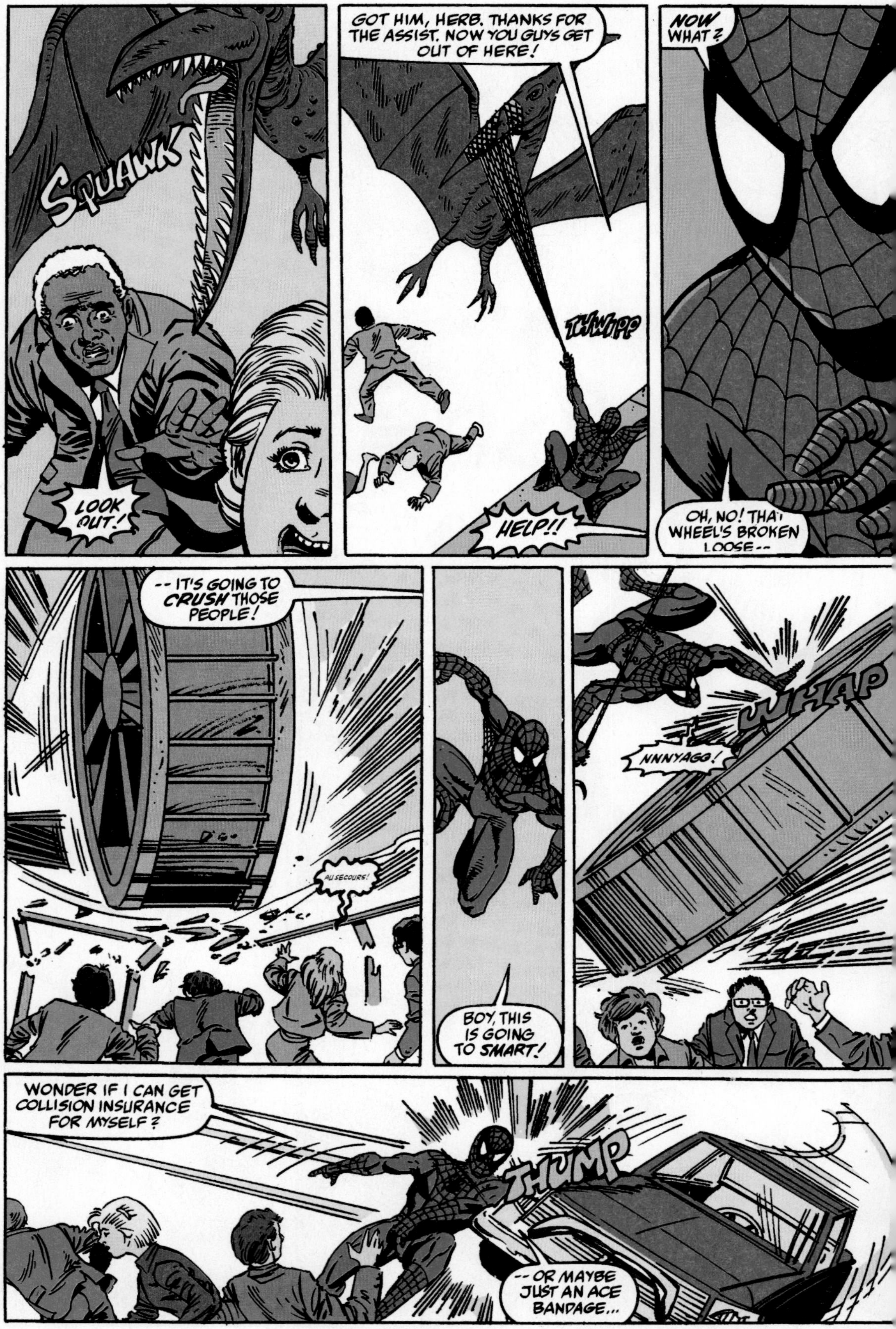
SQUAWK
LOOK OUT!
GOT HIM, HERB. THANKS FOR THE ASSIST. NOW YOU GUYS GET OUT OF HERE!
THWIPP
HELP!!
NOW WHAT?
OH, NO! THAT WHEEL'S BROKEN LOOSE--
--IT'S GOING TO CRUSH THOSE PEOPLE!
AU SECOURS!
BOY, THIS IS GOING TO SMART!
WHAP
NNNYAGG!
WONDER IF I CAN GET COLLISION INSURANCE FOR MYSELF?
THUMP
--OR MAYBE JUST AN ACE BANDAGE...

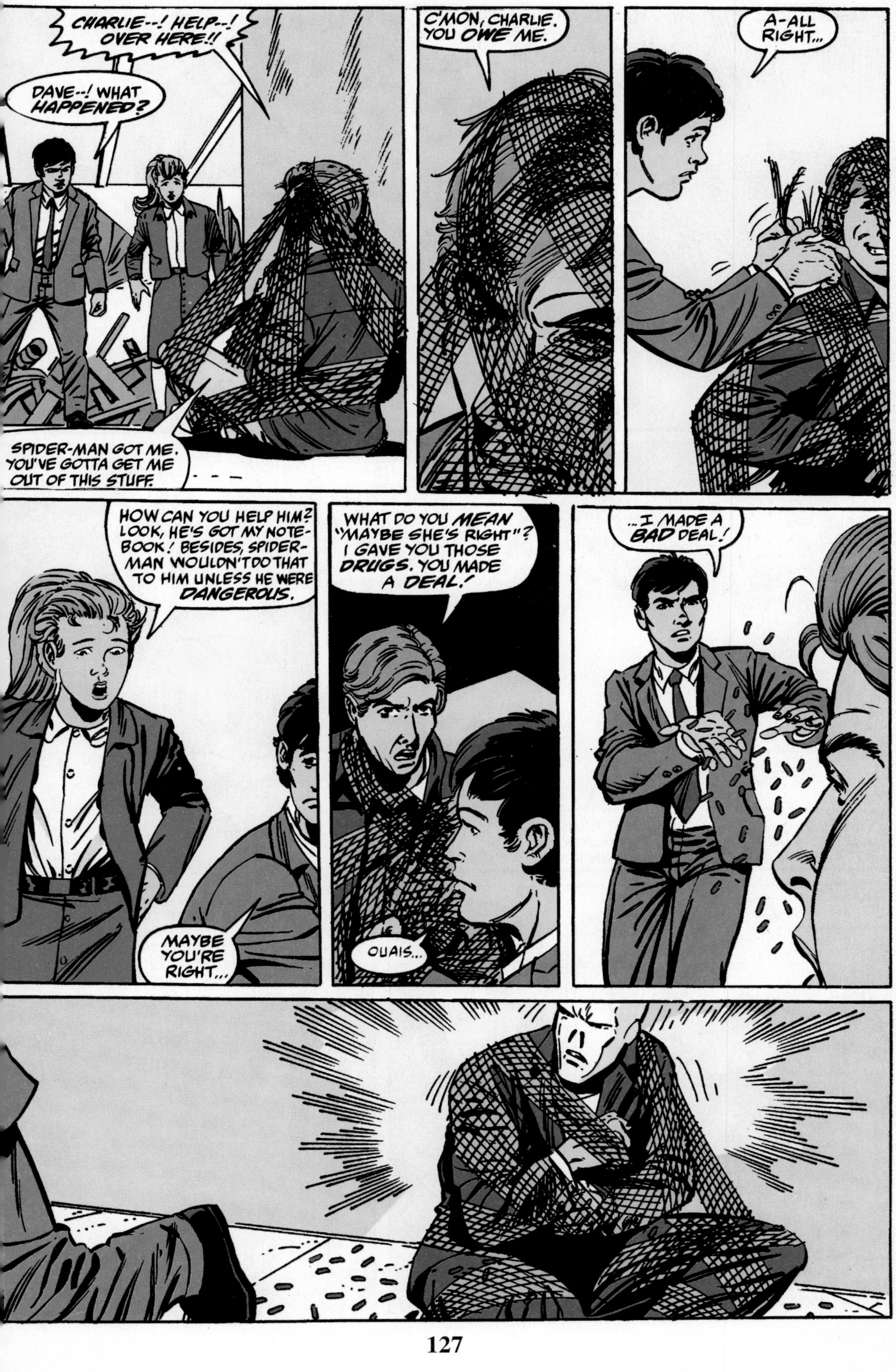
CHARLIE--! HELP--! OVER HERE!!
DAVE--! WHAT HAPPENED?
SPIDER-MAN GOT ME. YOU'VE GOTTA GET ME OUT OF THIS STUFF. - - -
C'MON, CHARLIE. YOU OWE ME.
A-ALL RIGHT...
HOW CAN YOU HELP HIM? LOOK, HE'S GOT MY NOTE-BOOK! BESIDES, SPIDER-MAN WOULDN'T DO THAT TO HIM UNLESS HE WERE DANGEROUS.
MAYBE YOU'RE RIGHT...
WHAT DO YOU MEAN "MAYBE SHE'S RIGHT"? I GAVE YOU THOSE DRUGS. YOU MADE A DEAL!
OUAIS...
...I MADE A BAD DEAL!

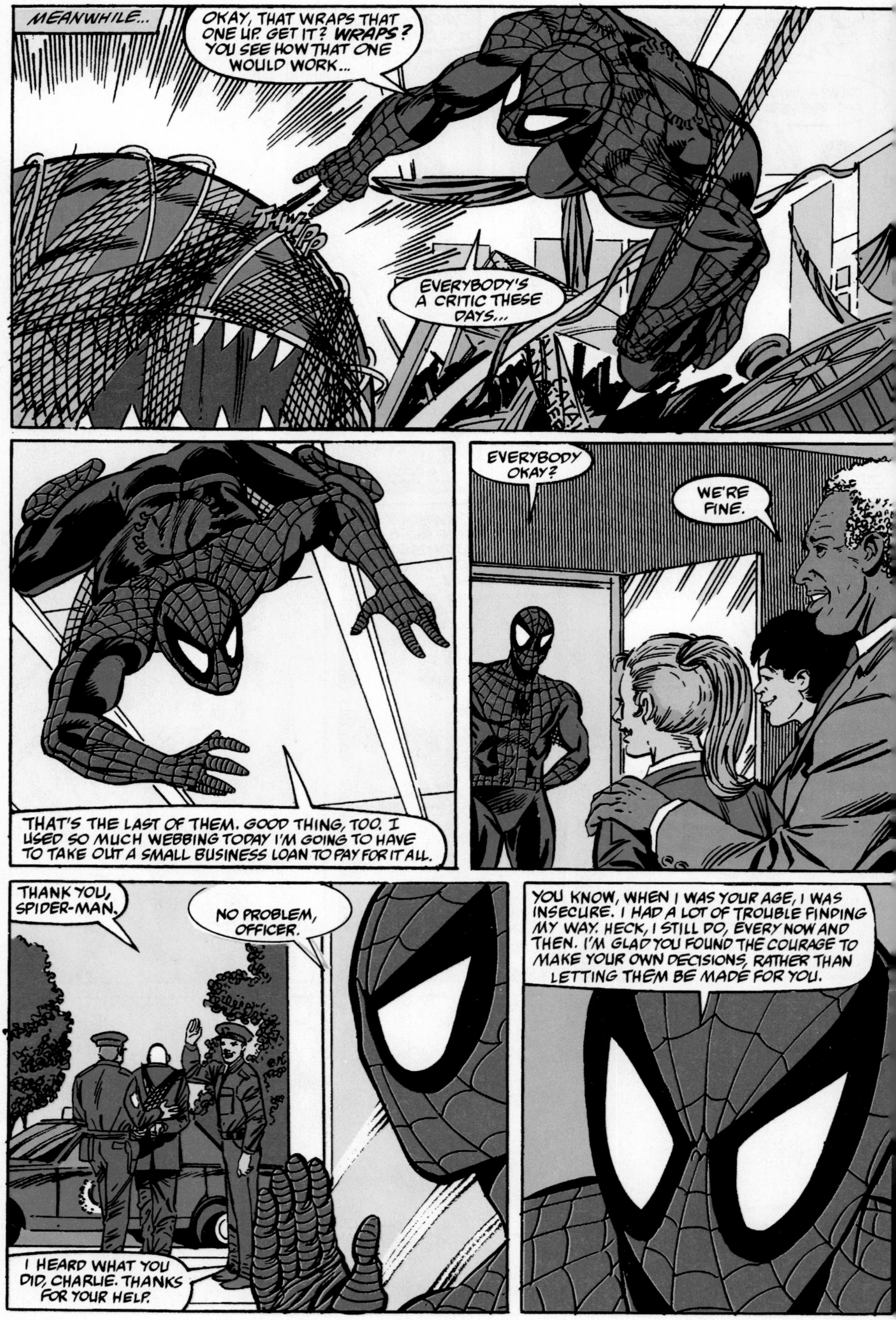
MEANWHILE...
OKAY, THAT WRAPS THAT ONE UP. GET IT? WRAPS? YOU SEE HOW THAT ONE WOULD WORK...
EVERYBODY'S A CRITIC THESE DAYS...
THAT'S THE LAST OF THEM. GOOD THING, TOO. I USED SO MUCH WEBBING TODAY I'M GOING TO HAVE TO TAKE OUT A SMALL BUSINESS LOAN TO PAY FOR IT ALL.
EVERYBODY OKAY?
WE'RE FINE.
THANK YOU, SPIDER-MAN.
NO PROBLEM, OFFICER.
I HEARD WHAT YOU DID, CHARLIE. THANKS FOR YOUR HELP.
YOU KNOW, WHEN I WAS YOUR AGE, I WAS INSECURE. I HAD A LOT OF TROUBLE FINDING MY WAY. HECK, I STILL DO, EVERY NOW AND THEN. I'M GLAD YOU FOUND THE COURAGE TO MAKE YOUR OWN DECISIONS, RATHER THAN LETTING THEM BE MADE FOR YOU.

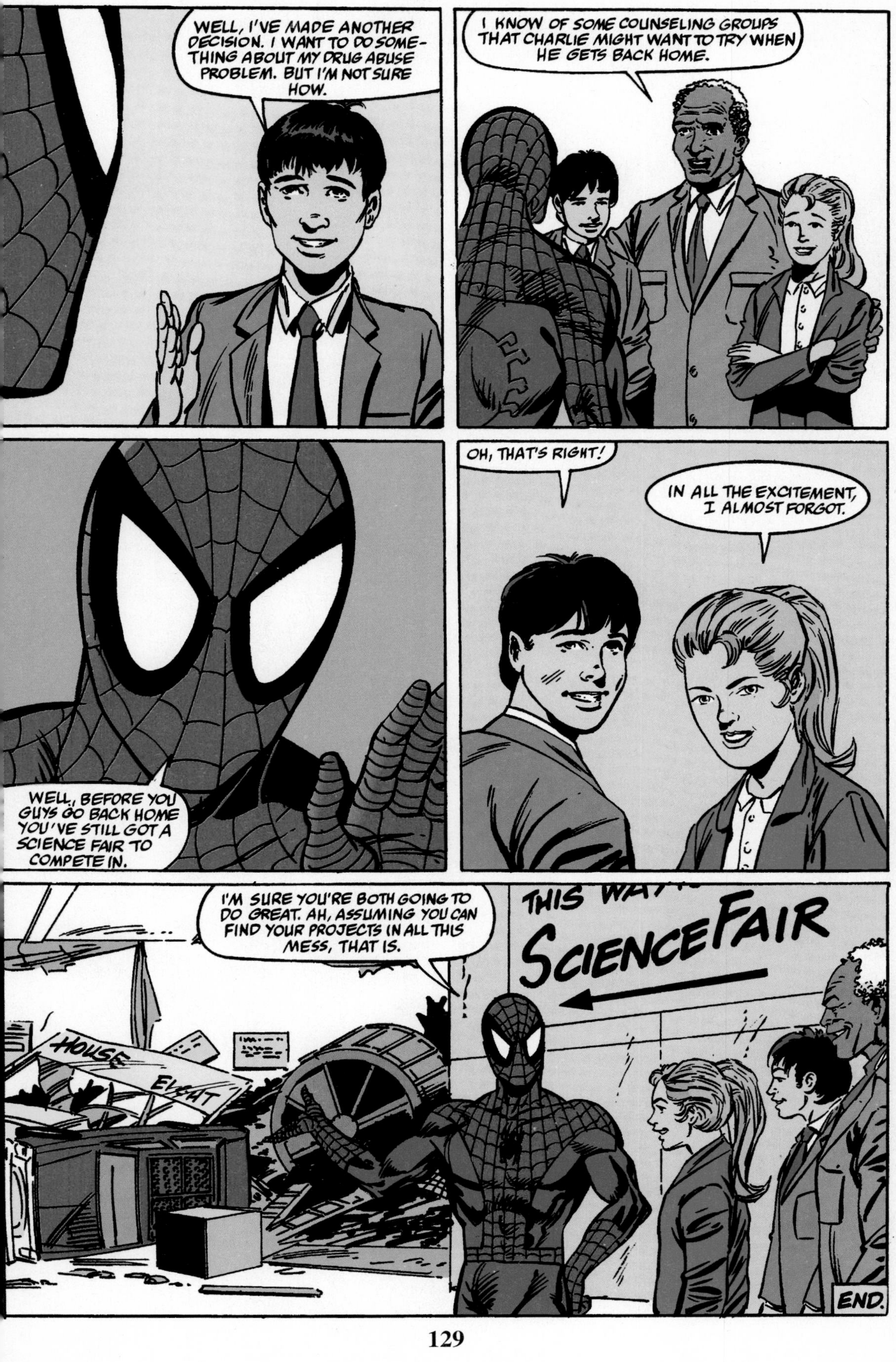
WELL, I'VE MADE ANOTHER DECISION. I WANT TO DO SOMETHING ABOUT MY DRUG ABUSE PROBLEM. BUT I'M NOT SURE HOW.
I KNOW OF SOME COUNSELING GROUPS THAT CHARLIE MIGHT WANT TO TRY WHEN HE GETS BACK HOME.
WELL, BEFORE YOU GUYS GO BACK HOME YOU'VE STILL GOT A SCIENCE FAIR TO COMPETE IN.
OH, THAT'S RIGHT!
IN ALL THE EXCITEMENT, I ALMOST FORGOT.
I'M SURE YOU'RE BOTH GOING TO DO GREAT. AH, ASSUMING YOU CAN FIND YOUR PROJECTS IN ALL THIS MESS, THAT IS.
SCIENCE FAIR
HOUSE
END.

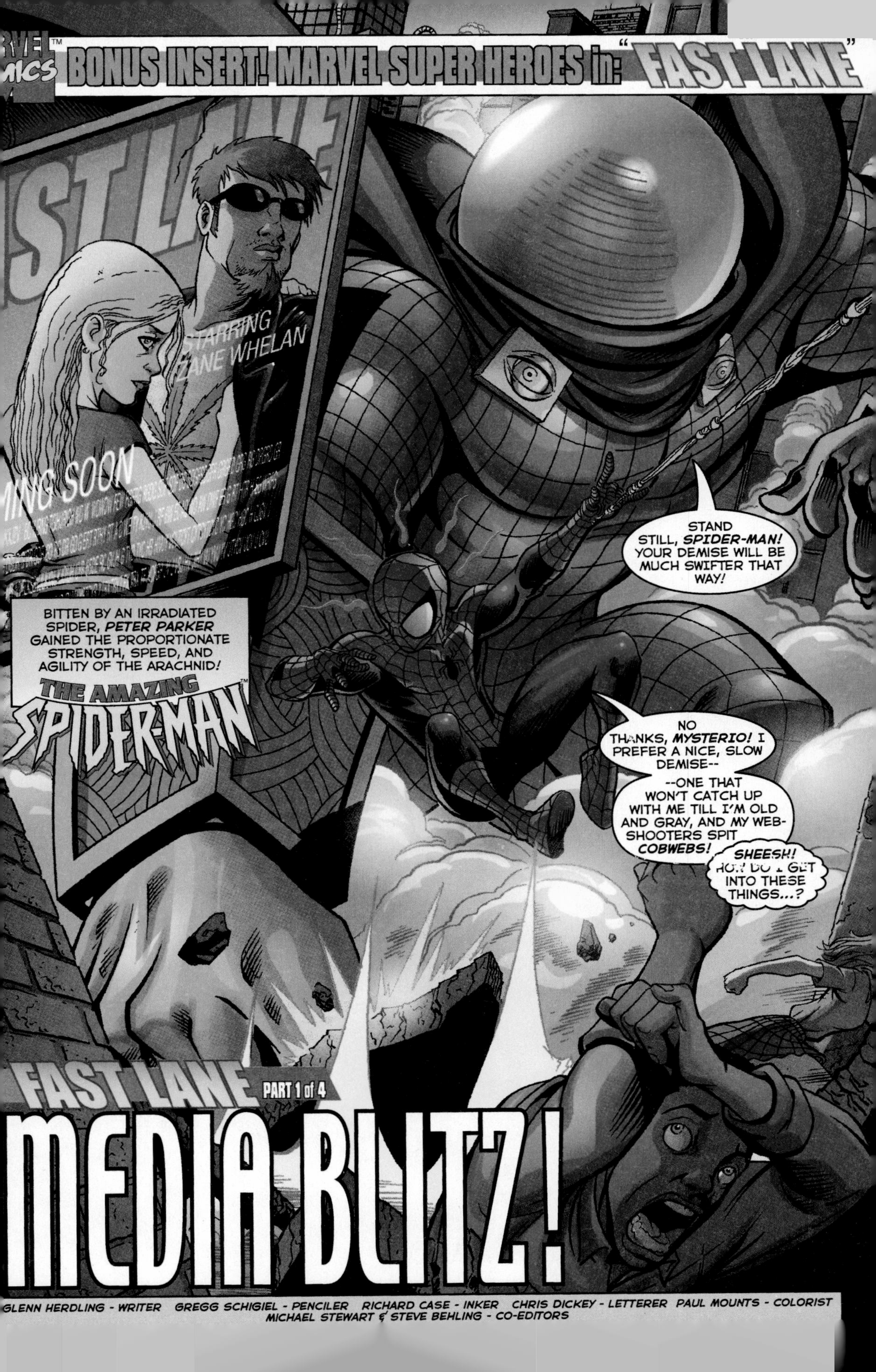

BONUS INSERT! MARVEL SUPER HEROES in: "FAST LANE"
STARRING ZANE WHELAN
COMING SOON
STAND STILL, SPIDER-MAN! YOUR DEMISE WILL BE MUCH SWIFTER THAT WAY!
BITTEN BY AN IRRADIATED SPIDER, PETER PARKER GAINED THE PROPORTIONATE STRENGTH, SPEED, AND AGILITY OF THE ARACHNID!
THE AMAZING SPIDER-MAN
NO THANKS, MYSTERIO! I PREFER A NICE, SLOW DEMISE--
--ONE THAT WON'T CATCH UP WITH ME TILL I'M OLD AND GRAY, AND MY WEB-SHOOTERS SPIT COBWEBS!
SHEESH! HOW DO I GET INTO THESE THINGS...?
FAST LANE PART 1 of 4
MEDIA BLITZ!
GLENN HERDLING - WRITER GREGG SCHIGIEL - PENCILER RICHARD CASE - INKER CHRIS DICKEY - LETTERER PAUL MOUNTS - COLORIST
MICHAEL STEWART & STEVE BEHLING - CO-EDITORS

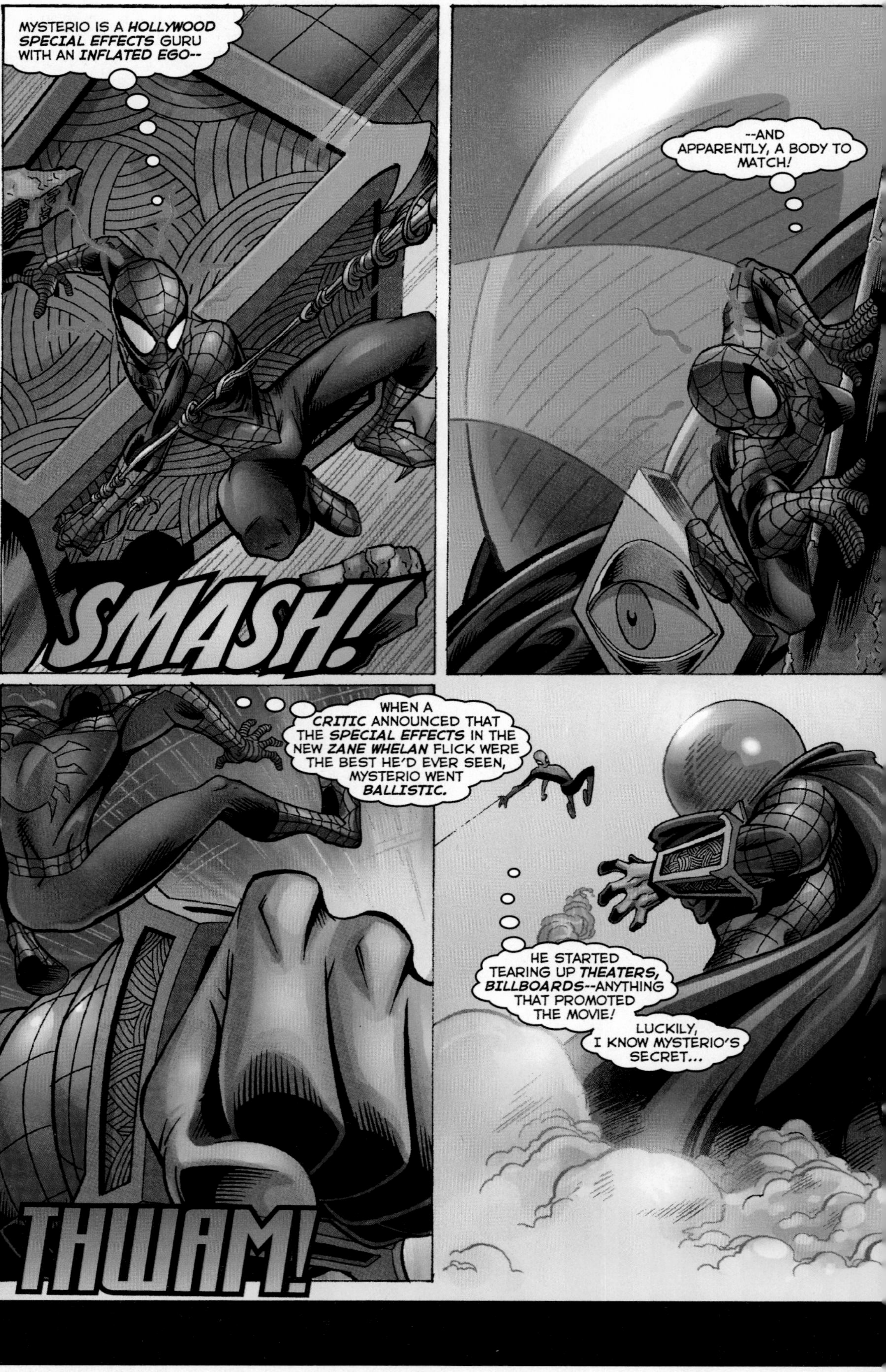
MYSTERIO IS A HOLLYWOOD SPECIAL EFFECTS GURU WITH AN INFLATED EGO--
SMASH!
--AND APPARENTLY, A BODY TO MATCH!
WHEN A CRITIC ANNOUNCED THAT THE SPECIAL EFFECTS IN THE NEW ZANE WHELAN FLICK WERE THE BEST HE'D EVER SEEN, MYSTERIO WENT BALLISTIC.
THWAM!
HE STARTED TEARING UP THEATERS, BILLBOARDS--ANYTHING THAT PROMOTED THE MOVIE!
LUCKILY, I KNOW MYSTERIO'S SECRET...

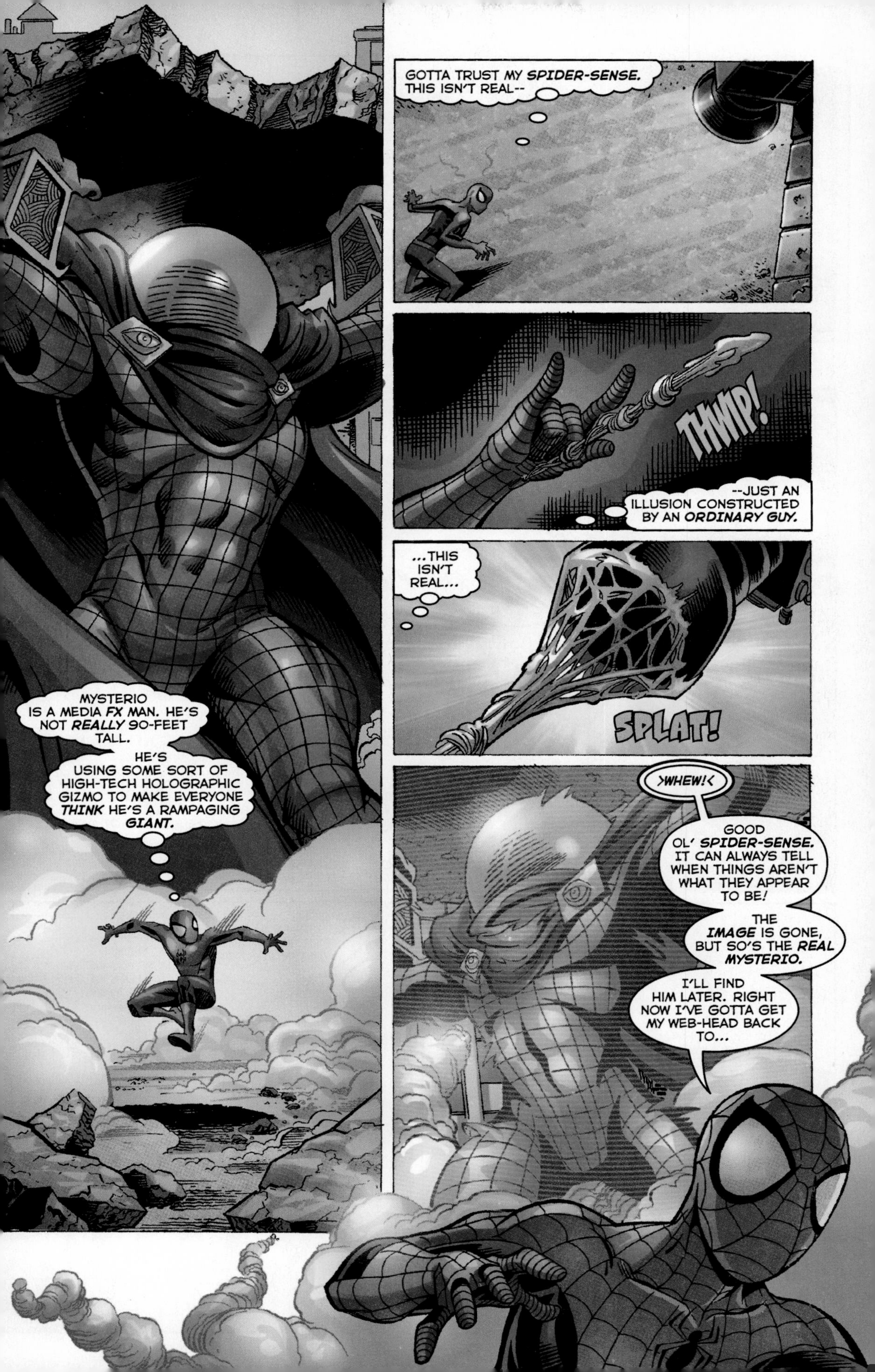
MYSTERIO IS A MEDIA *FX* MAN. HE'S NOT *REALLY* 90-FEET TALL.
HE'S USING SOME SORT OF HIGH-TECH HOLOGRAPHIC GIZMO TO MAKE EVERYONE *THINK* HE'S A RAMPAGING *GIANT.*
GOTTA TRUST MY *SPIDER-SENSE.* THIS ISN'T REAL--
THWIP!
--JUST AN ILLUSION CONSTRUCTED BY AN *ORDINARY GUY.*
...THIS ISN'T REAL...
SPLAT!
>WHEW!<
GOOD OL' *SPIDER-SENSE.* IT CAN ALWAYS TELL WHEN THINGS AREN'T WHAT THEY APPEAR TO BE!
THE *IMAGE* IS GONE, BUT SO'S THE *REAL MYSTERIO.*
I'LL FIND HIM LATER. RIGHT NOW I'VE GOTTA GET MY WEB-HEAD BACK TO...

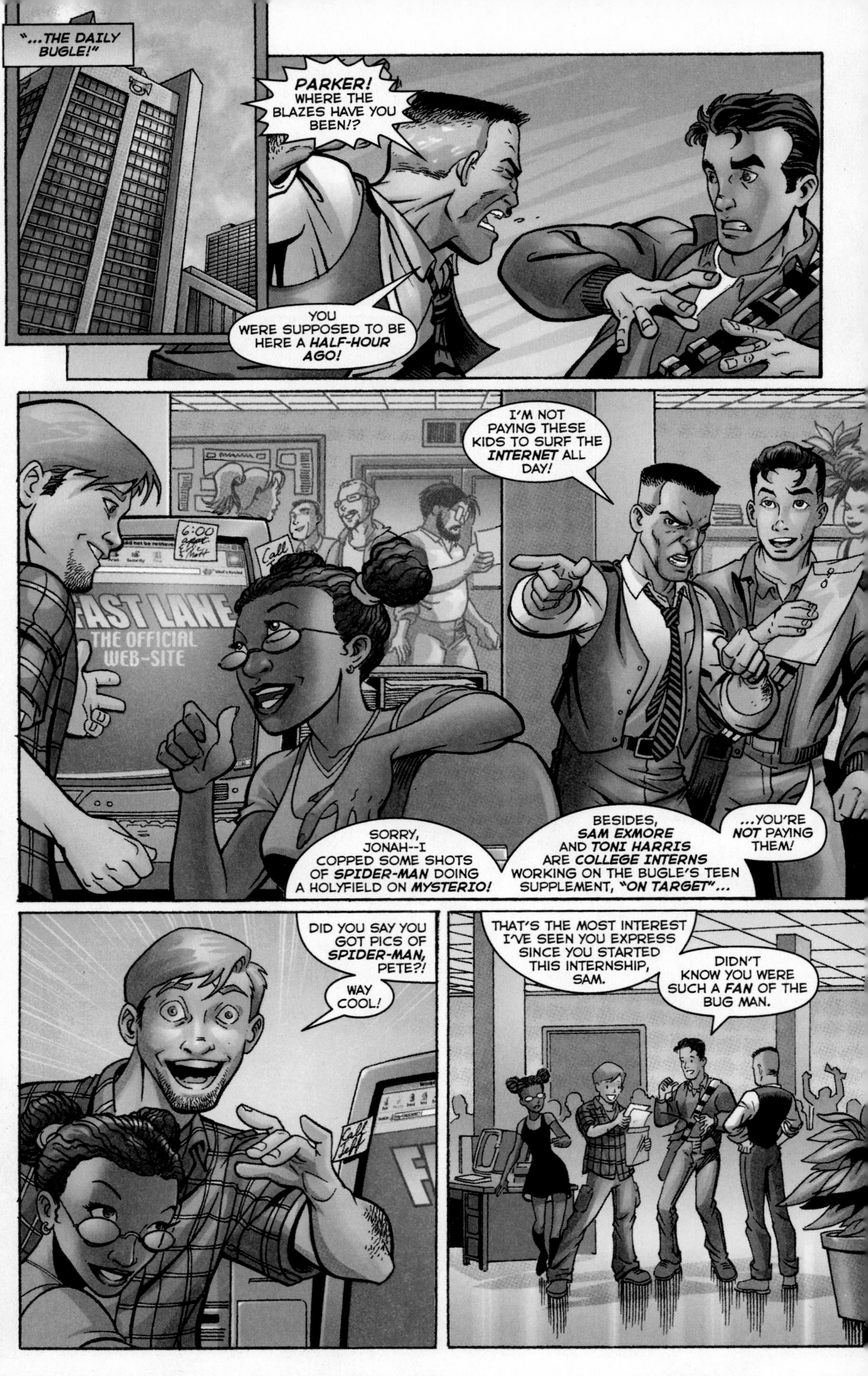
"...THE DAILY BUGLE!"
PARKER! WHERE THE BLAZES HAVE YOU BEEN!?
YOU WERE SUPPOSED TO BE HERE A HALF-HOUR AGO!
I'M NOT PAYING THESE KIDS TO SURF THE INTERNET ALL DAY!
FAST LANE THE OFFICIAL WEB-SITE
6:00 appt. Eric & Matt
Call
SORRY, JONAH--I COPPED SOME SHOTS OF SPIDER-MAN DOING A HOLYFIELD ON MYSTERIO!
BESIDES, SAM EXMORE AND TONI HARRIS ARE COLLEGE INTERNS WORKING ON THE BUGLE'S TEEN SUPPLEMENT, "ON TARGET"...
...YOU'RE NOT PAYING THEM!
DID YOU SAY YOU GOT PICS OF SPIDER-MAN, PETE?!
WAY COOL!
Call Jeff
THAT'S THE MOST INTEREST I'VE SEEN YOU EXPRESS SINCE YOU STARTED THIS INTERNSHIP, SAM.
DIDN'T KNOW YOU WERE SUCH A FAN OF THE BUG MAN.

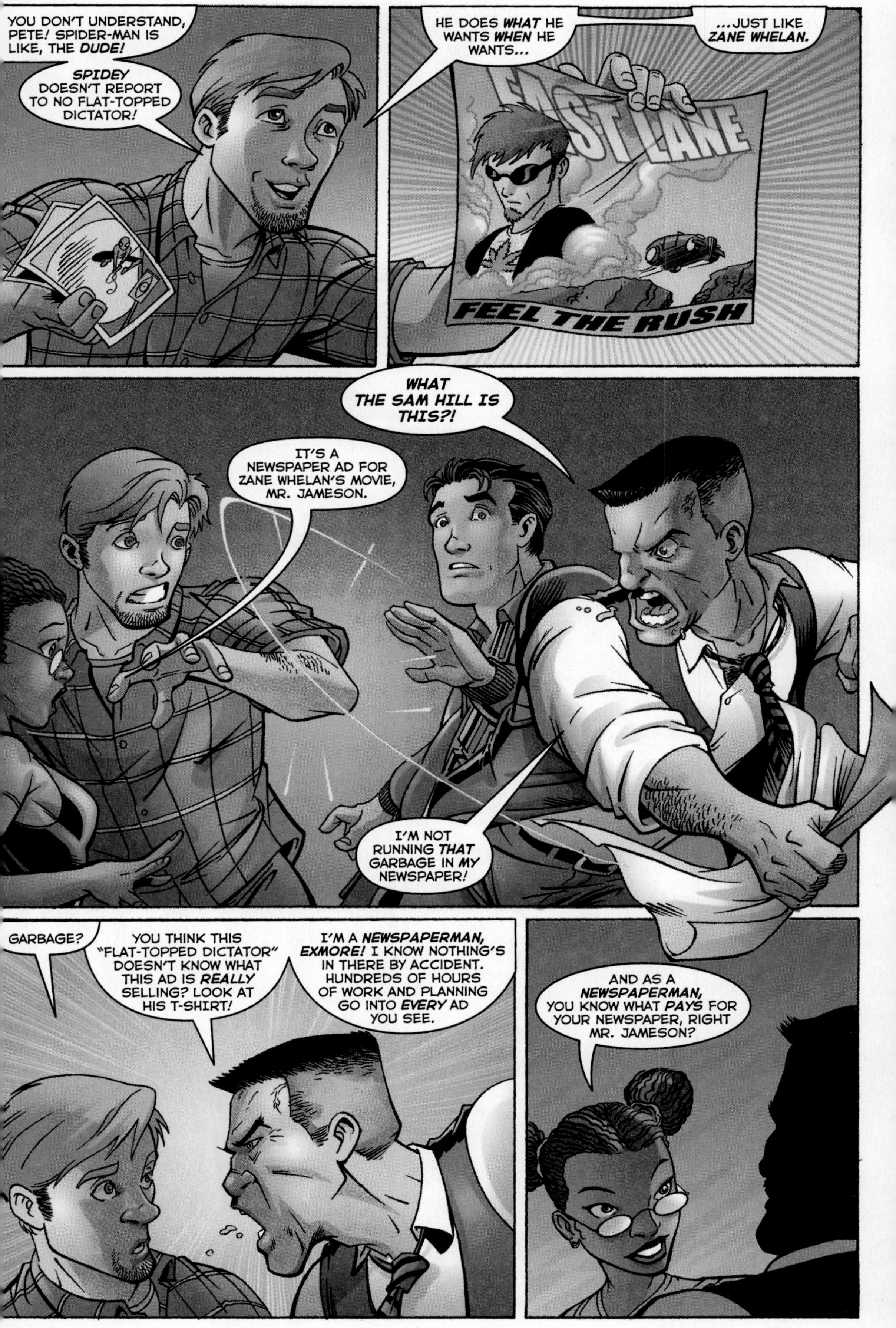
YOU DON'T UNDERSTAND, PETE! SPIDER-MAN IS LIKE, THE *DUDE!*
SPIDEY DOESN'T REPORT TO NO FLAT-TOPPED DICTATOR!
HE DOES *WHAT* HE WANTS *WHEN* HE WANTS...
...JUST LIKE *ZANE WHELAN.*
FEEL THE RUSH
WHAT THE SAM HILL IS THIS?!
IT'S A NEWSPAPER AD FOR ZANE WHELAN'S MOVIE, MR. JAMESON.
I'M NOT RUNNING *THAT* GARBAGE IN *MY* NEWSPAPER!
GARBAGE?
YOU THINK THIS "FLAT-TOPPED DICTATOR" DOESN'T KNOW WHAT THIS AD IS *REALLY* SELLING? LOOK AT HIS T-SHIRT!
I'M A *NEWSPAPERMAN, EXMORE!* I KNOW NOTHING'S IN THERE BY ACCIDENT. HUNDREDS OF HOURS OF WORK AND PLANNING GO INTO *EVERY* AD YOU SEE.
AND AS A *NEWSPAPERMAN,* YOU KNOW WHAT *PAYS* FOR YOUR NEWSPAPER, RIGHT MR. JAMESON?

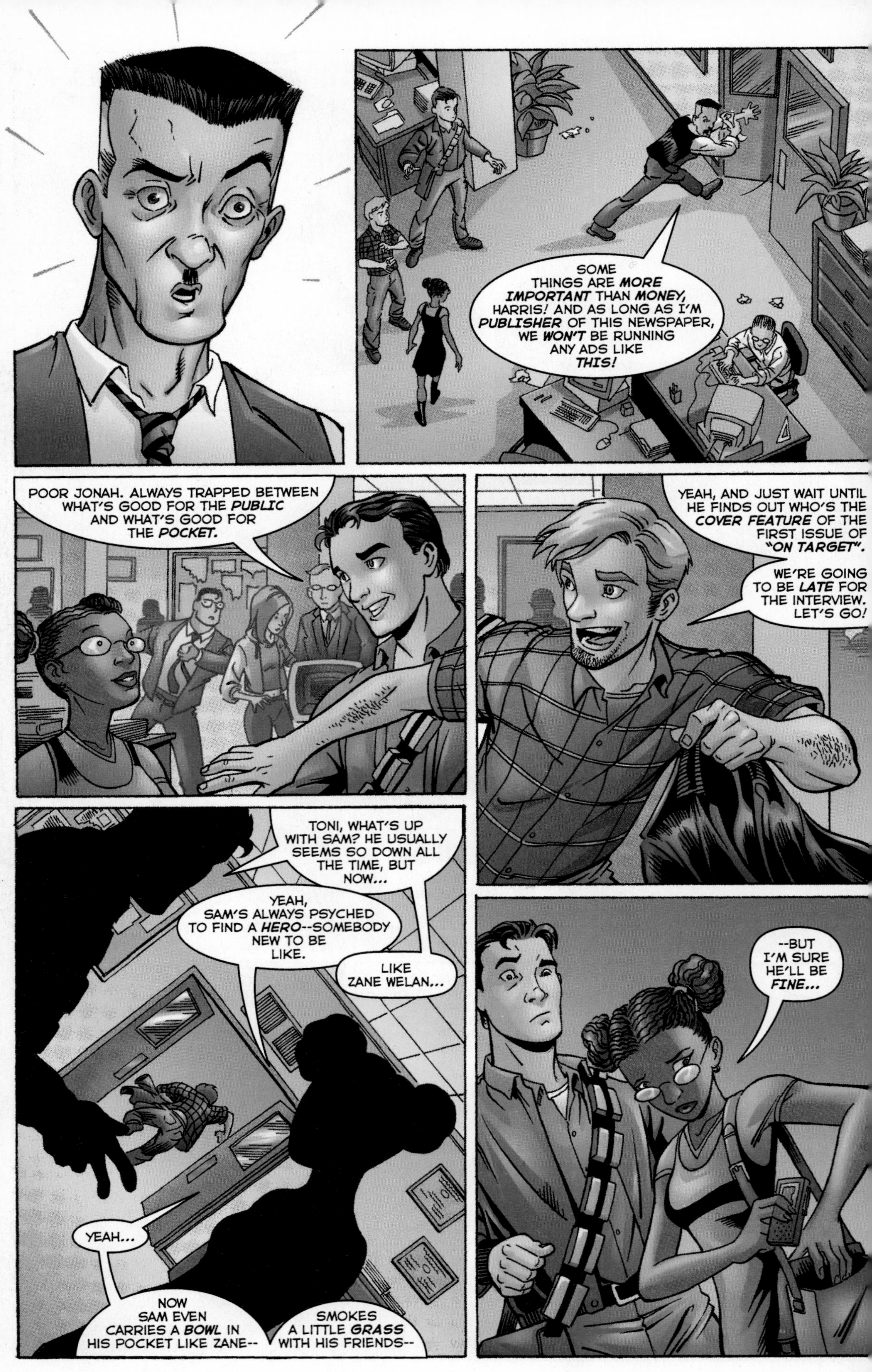
SOME THINGS ARE MORE IMPORTANT THAN MONEY, HARRIS! AND AS LONG AS I'M PUBLISHER OF THIS NEWSPAPER, WE WON'T BE RUNNING ANY ADS LIKE THIS!
POOR JONAH. ALWAYS TRAPPED BETWEEN WHAT'S GOOD FOR THE PUBLIC AND WHAT'S GOOD FOR THE POCKET.
YEAH, AND JUST WAIT UNTIL HE FINDS OUT WHO'S THE COVER FEATURE OF THE FIRST ISSUE OF "ON TARGET".
WE'RE GOING TO BE LATE FOR THE INTERVIEW. LET'S GO!
TONI, WHAT'S UP WITH SAM? HE USUALLY SEEMS SO DOWN ALL THE TIME, BUT NOW...
YEAH, SAM'S ALWAYS PSYCHED TO FIND A HERO--SOMEBODY NEW TO BE LIKE.
LIKE ZANE WELAN...
YEAH...
NOW SAM EVEN CARRIES A BOWL IN HIS POCKET LIKE ZANE--
SMOKES A LITTLE GRASS WITH HIS FRIENDS--
--BUT I'M SURE HE'LL BE FINE...

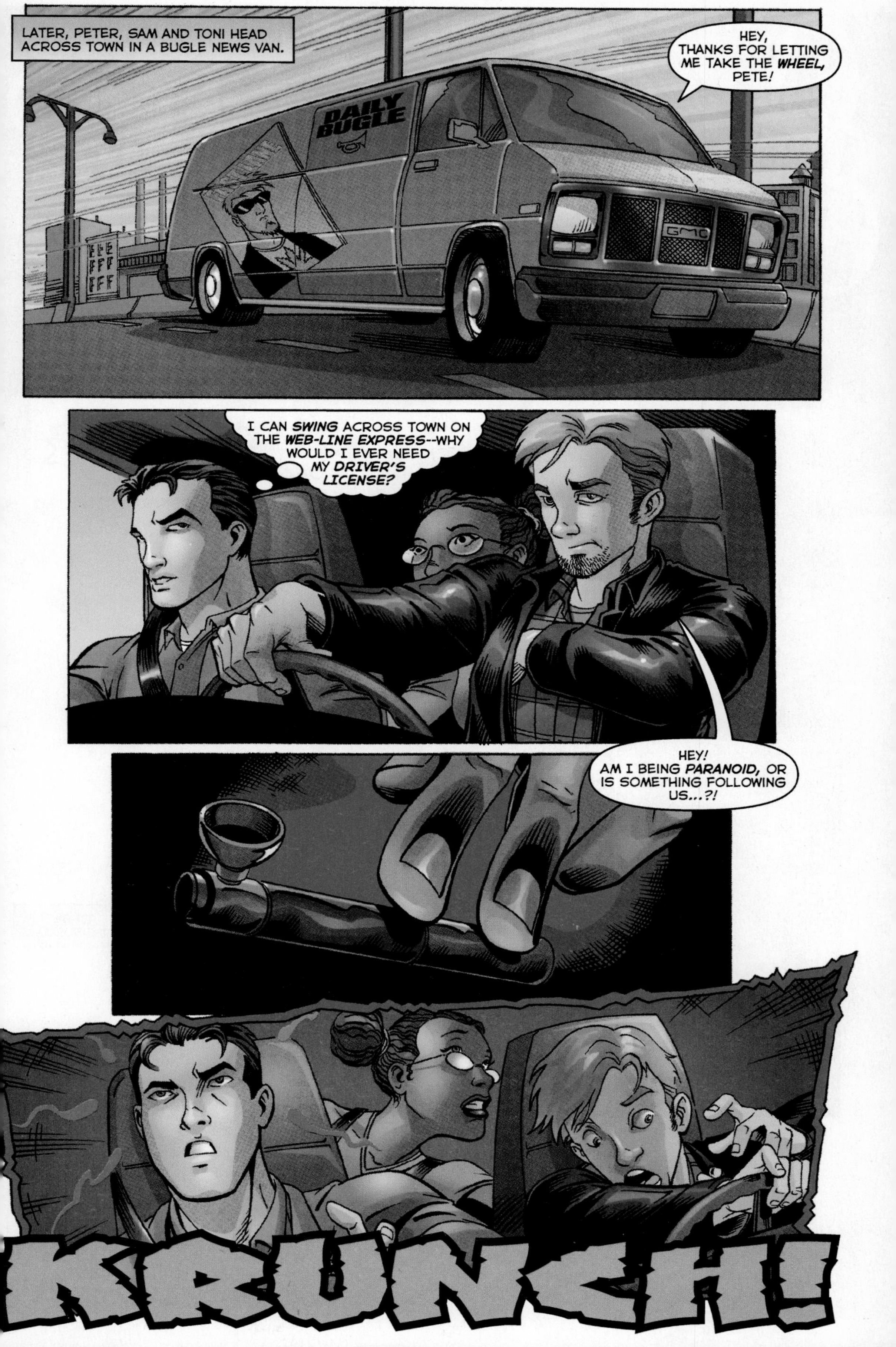

LATER, PETER, SAM AND TONI HEAD ACROSS TOWN IN A BUGLE NEWS VAN.
HEY, THANKS FOR LETTING ME TAKE THE *WHEEL,* PETE!
DAILY BUGLE
I CAN *SWING* ACROSS TOWN ON THE *WEB-LINE EXPRESS*--WHY WOULD I EVER NEED MY *DRIVER'S LICENSE?*
HEY! AM I BEING *PARANOID,* OR IS SOMETHING FOLLOWING US...?!
KRUNCH!

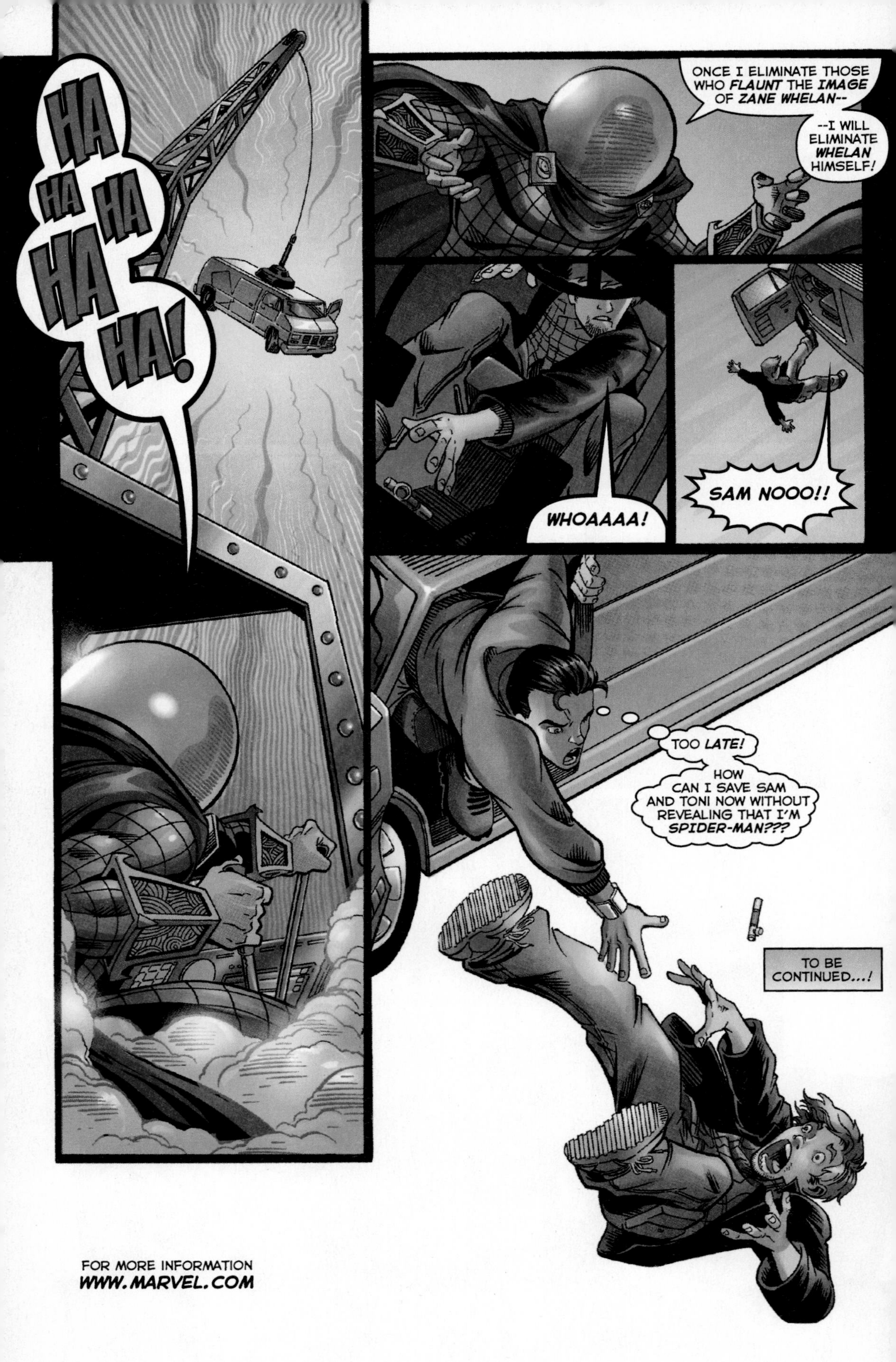
HA HA HA HA HA HA!
ONCE I ELIMINATE THOSE WHO FLAUNT THE IMAGE OF ZANE WHELAN--
--I WILL ELIMINATE WHELAN HIMSELF!
WHOAAAA!
SAM NOOO!!
TOO LATE!
HOW CAN I SAVE SAM AND TONI NOW WITHOUT REVEALING THAT I'M SPIDER-MAN???
TO BE CONTINUED...!

FOR MORE INFORMATION
WWW.MARVEL.COM

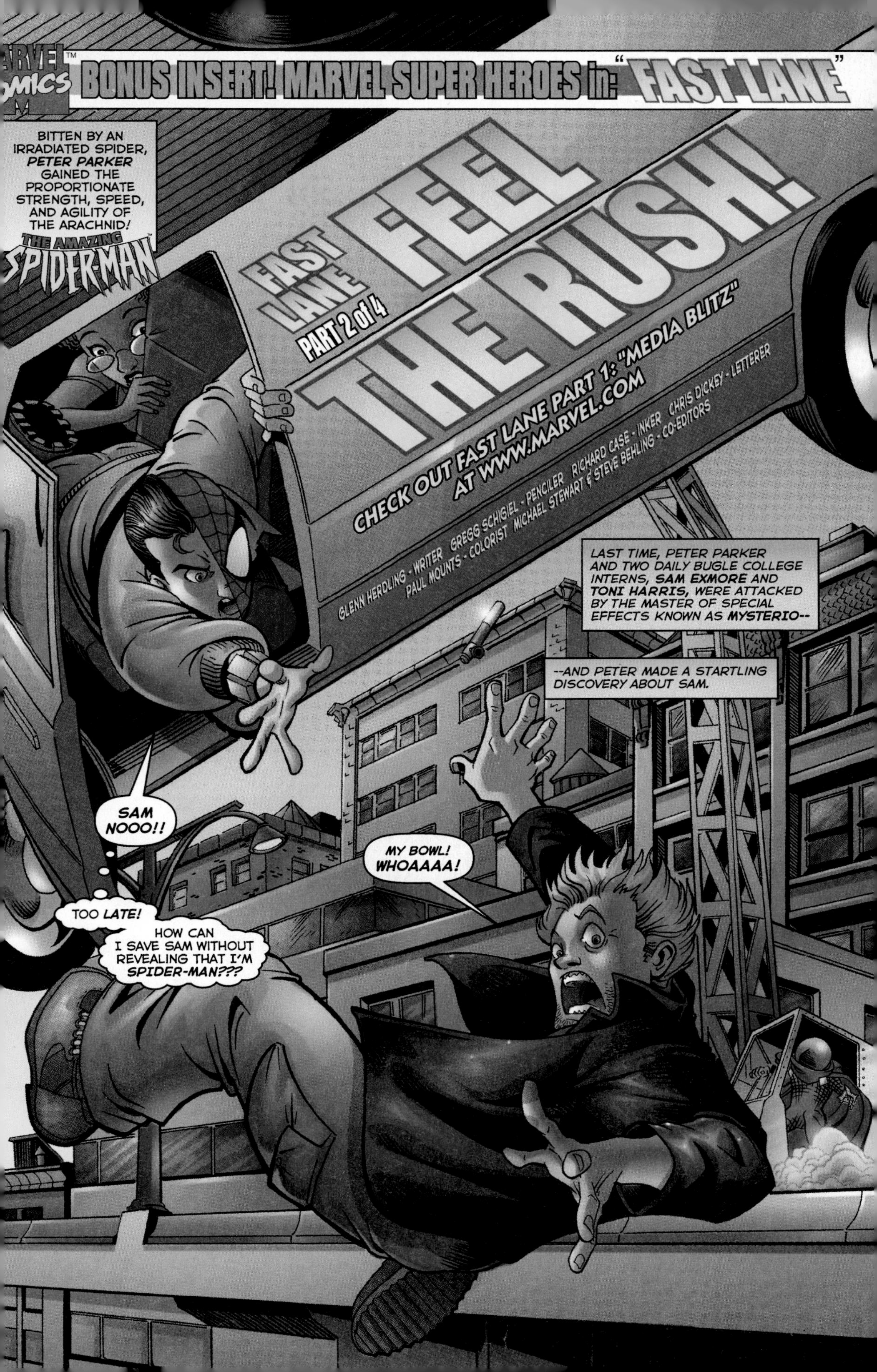

MARVEL COMICS
BONUS INSERT! MARVEL SUPER HEROES in: "FAST LANE"
BITTEN BY AN IRRADIATED SPIDER, PETER PARKER GAINED THE PROPORTIONATE STRENGTH, SPEED, AND AGILITY OF THE ARACHNID! THE AMAZING SPIDER-MAN
FAST LANE FEEL THE RUSH!
PART 2 of 4
CHECK OUT FAST LANE PART 1: "MEDIA BLITZ" AT WWW.MARVEL.COM
GLENN HERDLING - WRITER GREGG SCHIGIEL - PENCILER RICHARD CASE - INKER CHRIS DICKEY - LETTERER
PAUL MOUNTS - COLORIST MICHAEL STEWART & STEVE BEHLING - CO-EDITORS
LAST TIME, PETER PARKER AND TWO DAILY BUGLE COLLEGE INTERNS, SAM EXMORE AND TONI HARRIS, WERE ATTACKED BY THE MASTER OF SPECIAL EFFECTS KNOWN AS MYSTERIO--
--AND PETER MADE A STARTLING DISCOVERY ABOUT SAM.
SAM NOOO!!
MY BOWL! WHOAAAA!
TOO LATE!
HOW CAN I SAVE SAM WITHOUT REVEALING THAT I'M SPIDER-MAN???

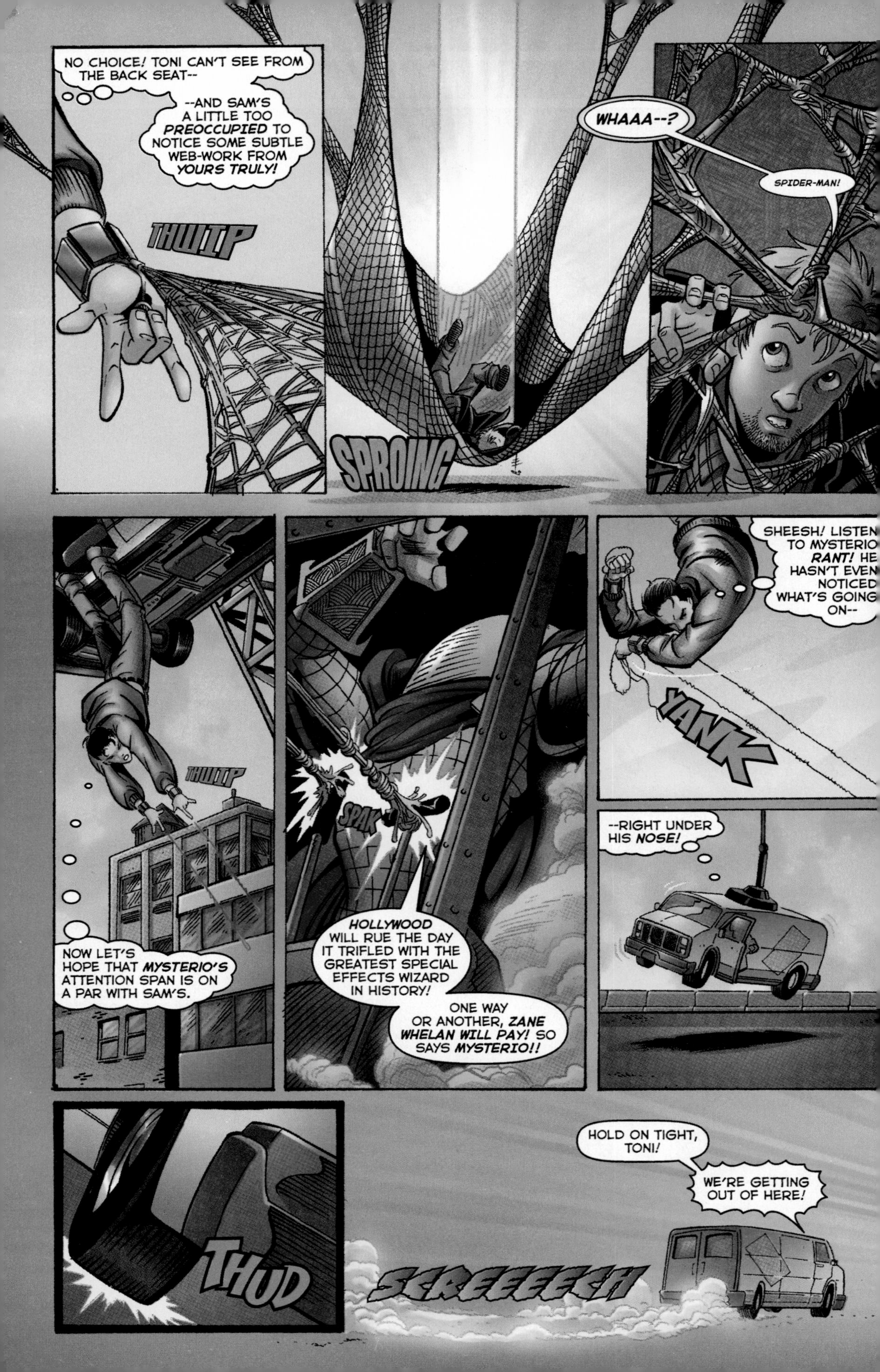

NO CHOICE! TONI CAN'T SEE FROM THE BACK SEAT--
--AND SAM'S A LITTLE TOO PREOCCUPIED TO NOTICE SOME SUBTLE WEB-WORK FROM YOURS TRULY!
THWIP
SPROING
WHAAA--?
SPIDER-MAN!
THWIP
NOW LET'S HOPE THAT MYSTERIO'S ATTENTION SPAN IS ON A PAR WITH SAM'S.
SPAK
HOLLYWOOD WILL RUE THE DAY IT TRIFLED WITH THE GREATEST SPECIAL EFFECTS WIZARD IN HISTORY!
ONE WAY OR ANOTHER, ZANE WHELAN WILL PAY! SO SAYS MYSTERIO!!
SHEESH! LISTEN TO MYSTERIO RANT! HE HASN'T EVEN NOTICED WHAT'S GOING ON--
YANK
--RIGHT UNDER HIS NOSE!
THUD
SCREEEEECH
HOLD ON TIGHT, TONI!
WE'RE GETTING OUT OF HERE!

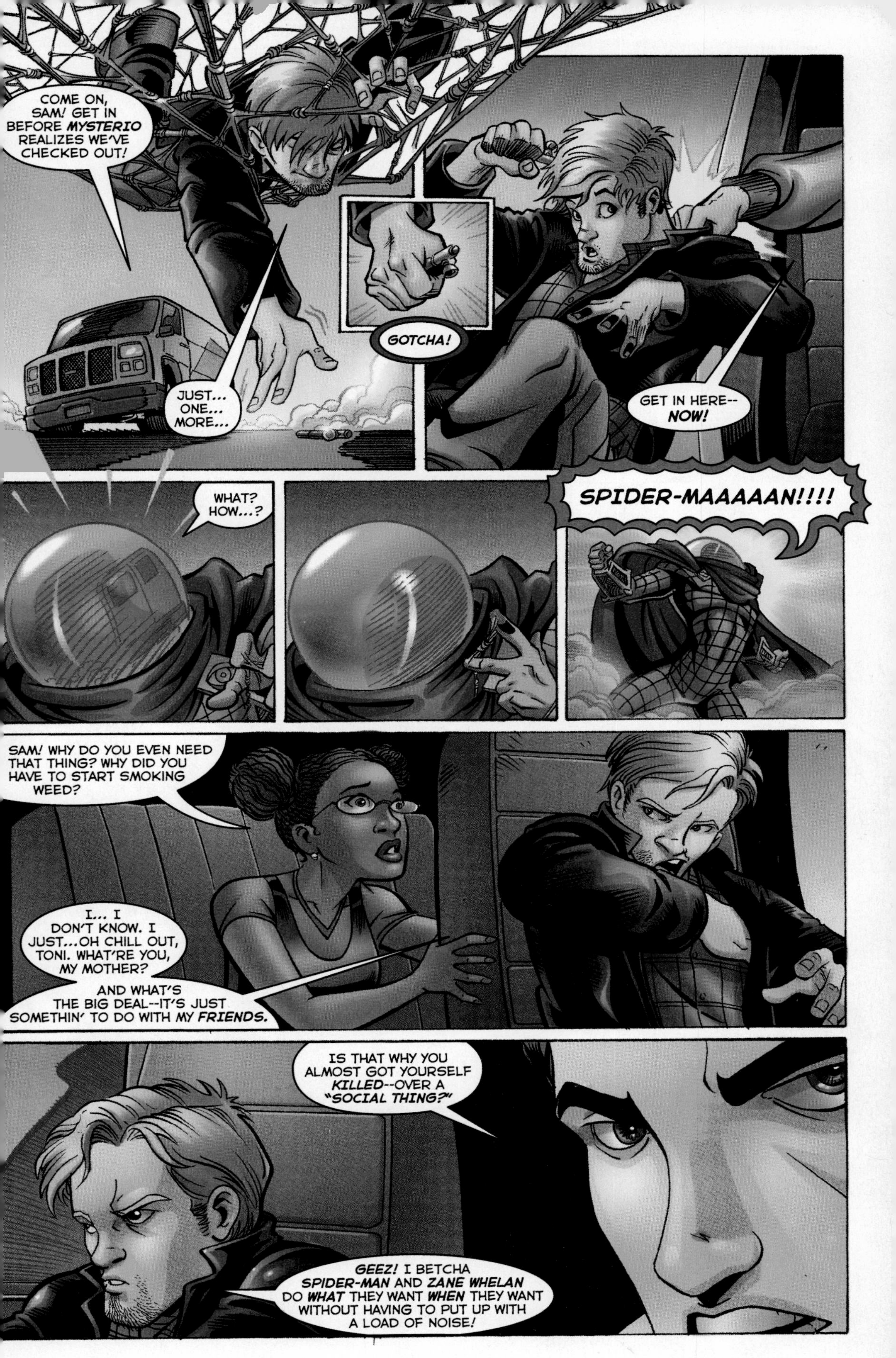
COME ON, SAM! GET IN BEFORE MYSTERIO REALIZES WE'VE CHECKED OUT!
JUST... ONE... MORE...
GOTCHA!
GET IN HERE-- NOW!
WHAT? HOW...?
SPIDER-MAAAAAN!!!!
SAM! WHY DO YOU EVEN NEED THAT THING? WHY DID YOU HAVE TO START SMOKING WEED?
I... I DON'T KNOW. I JUST...OH CHILL OUT, TONI. WHAT'RE YOU, MY MOTHER?
AND WHAT'S THE BIG DEAL--IT'S JUST SOMETHIN' TO DO WITH MY FRIENDS.
IS THAT WHY YOU ALMOST GOT YOURSELF KILLED--OVER A "SOCIAL THING?"
GEEZ! I BETCHA SPIDER-MAN AND ZANE WHELAN DO WHAT THEY WANT WHEN THEY WANT WITHOUT HAVING TO PUT UP WITH A LOAD OF NOISE!

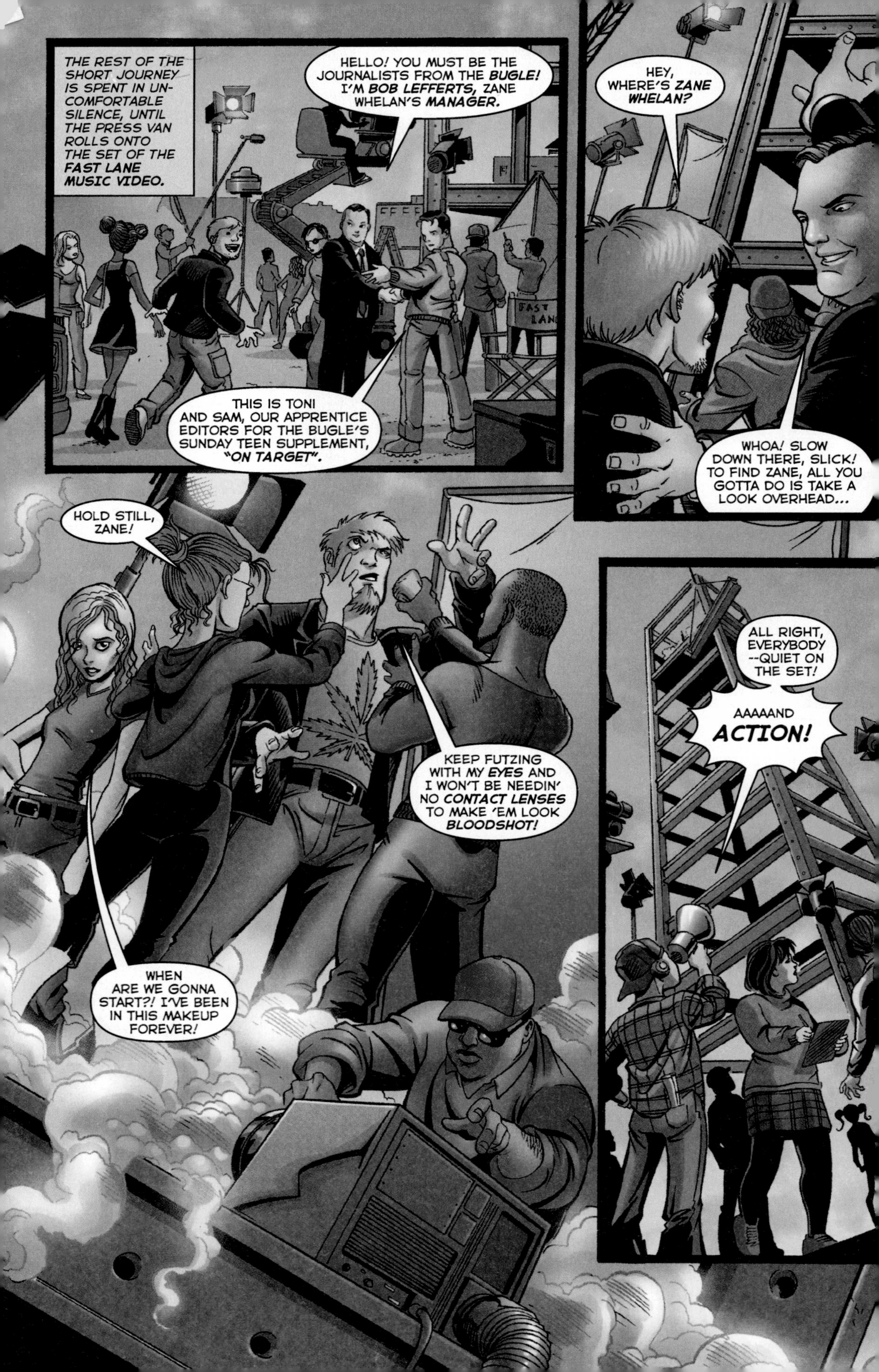
THE REST OF THE SHORT JOURNEY IS SPENT IN UN-COMFORTABLE SILENCE, UNTIL THE PRESS VAN ROLLS ONTO THE SET OF THE FAST LANE MUSIC VIDEO.
HELLO! YOU MUST BE THE JOURNALISTS FROM THE BUGLE! I'M BOB LEFFERTS, ZANE WHELAN'S MANAGER.
THIS IS TONI AND SAM, OUR APPRENTICE EDITORS FOR THE BUGLE'S SUNDAY TEEN SUPPLEMENT, "ON TARGET".
HEY, WHERE'S ZANE WHELAN?
WHOA! SLOW DOWN THERE, SLICK! TO FIND ZANE, ALL YOU GOTTA DO IS TAKE A LOOK OVERHEAD...
HOLD STILL, ZANE!
KEEP FUTZING WITH MY EYES AND I WON'T BE NEEDIN' NO CONTACT LENSES TO MAKE 'EM LOOK BLOODSHOT!
WHEN ARE WE GONNA START?! I'VE BEEN IN THIS MAKEUP FOREVER!
ALL RIGHT, EVERYBODY --QUIET ON THE SET!
AAAAAND ACTION!

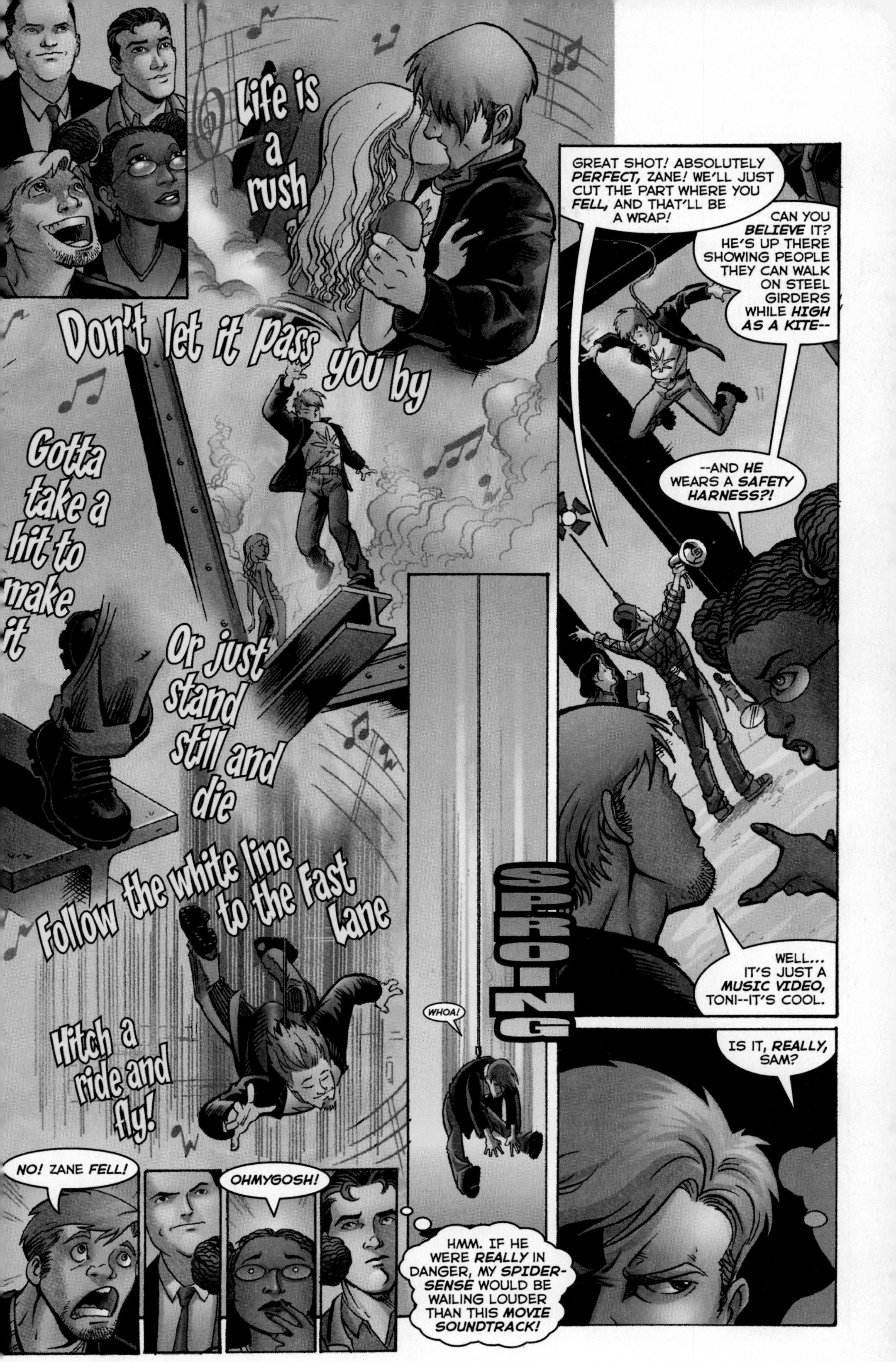
Life is a rush
Don't let it pass you by
Gotta take a hit to make it
Or just stand still and die
Follow the white line to the Fast Lane
Hitch a ride and fly!
GREAT SHOT! ABSOLUTELY PERFECT, ZANE! WE'LL JUST CUT THE PART WHERE YOU FELL, AND THAT'LL BE A WRAP!
CAN YOU BELIEVE IT? HE'S UP THERE SHOWING PEOPLE THEY CAN WALK ON STEEL GIRDERS WHILE HIGH AS A KITE--
--AND HE WEARS A SAFETY HARNESS?!
WELL... IT'S JUST A MUSIC VIDEO, TONI--IT'S COOL.
IS IT, REALLY, SAM?
SPROING
WHOA!
NO! ZANE FELL!
OHMYGOSH!
HMM. IF HE WERE REALLY IN DANGER, MY SPIDER-SENSE WOULD BE WAILING LOUDER THAN THIS MOVIE SOUNDTRACK!

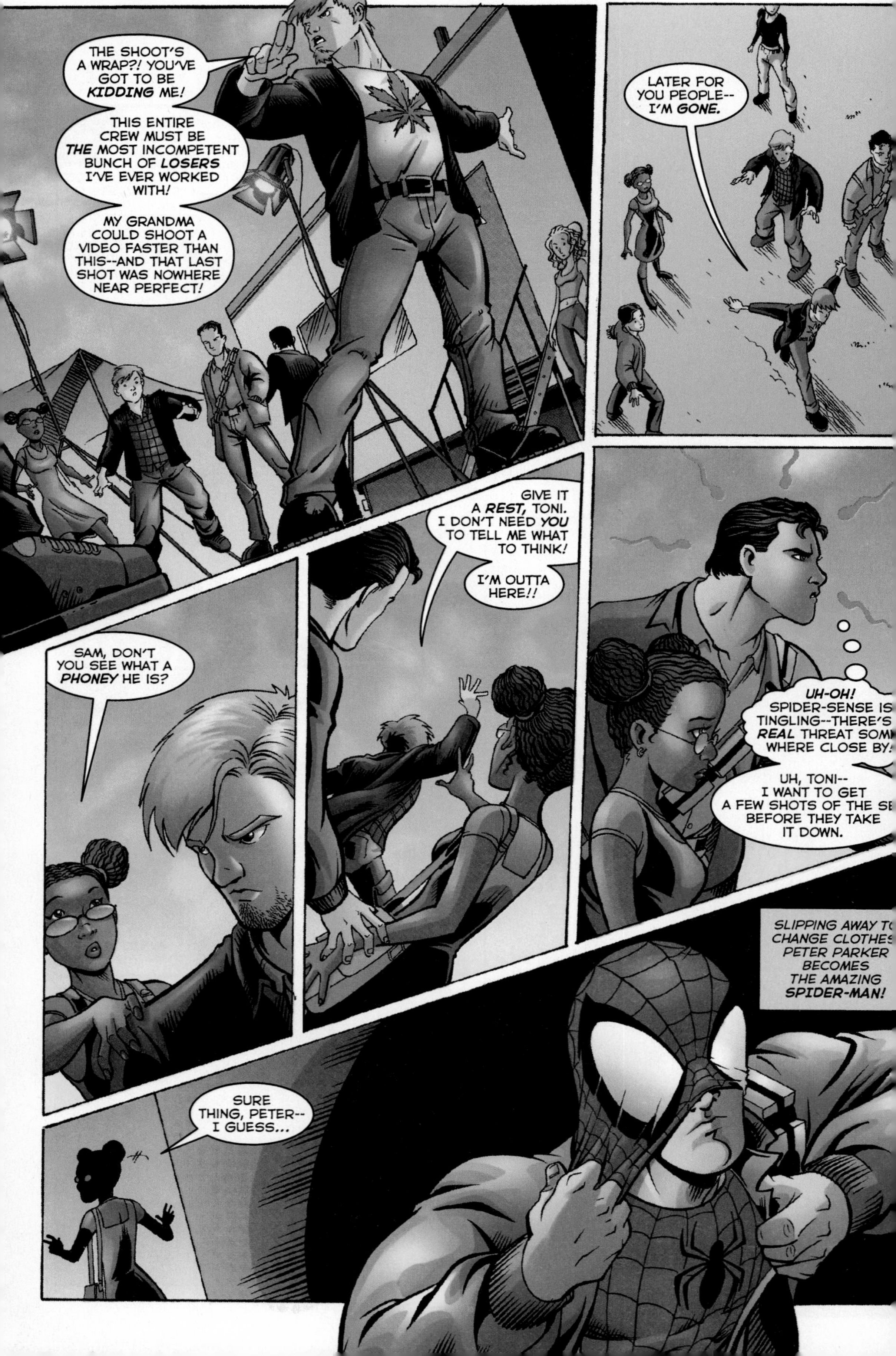
THE SHOOT'S A WRAP?! YOU'VE GOT TO BE KIDDING ME!
THIS ENTIRE CREW MUST BE THE MOST INCOMPETENT BUNCH OF LOSERS I'VE EVER WORKED WITH!
MY GRANDMA COULD SHOOT A VIDEO FASTER THAN THIS--AND THAT LAST SHOT WAS NOWHERE NEAR PERFECT!
LATER FOR YOU PEOPLE-- I'M GONE.
SAM, DON'T YOU SEE WHAT A PHONEY HE IS?
GIVE IT A REST, TONI. I DON'T NEED YOU TO TELL ME WHAT TO THINK!
I'M OUTTA HERE!!
UH-OH! SPIDER-SENSE IS TINGLING--THERE'S REAL THREAT SOM WHERE CLOSE BY!
UH, TONI-- I WANT TO GET A FEW SHOTS OF THE SE BEFORE THEY TAKE IT DOWN.
SURE THING, PETER-- I GUESS...
SLIPPING AWAY TO CHANGE CLOTHES PETER PARKER BECOMES THE AMAZING SPIDER-MAN!

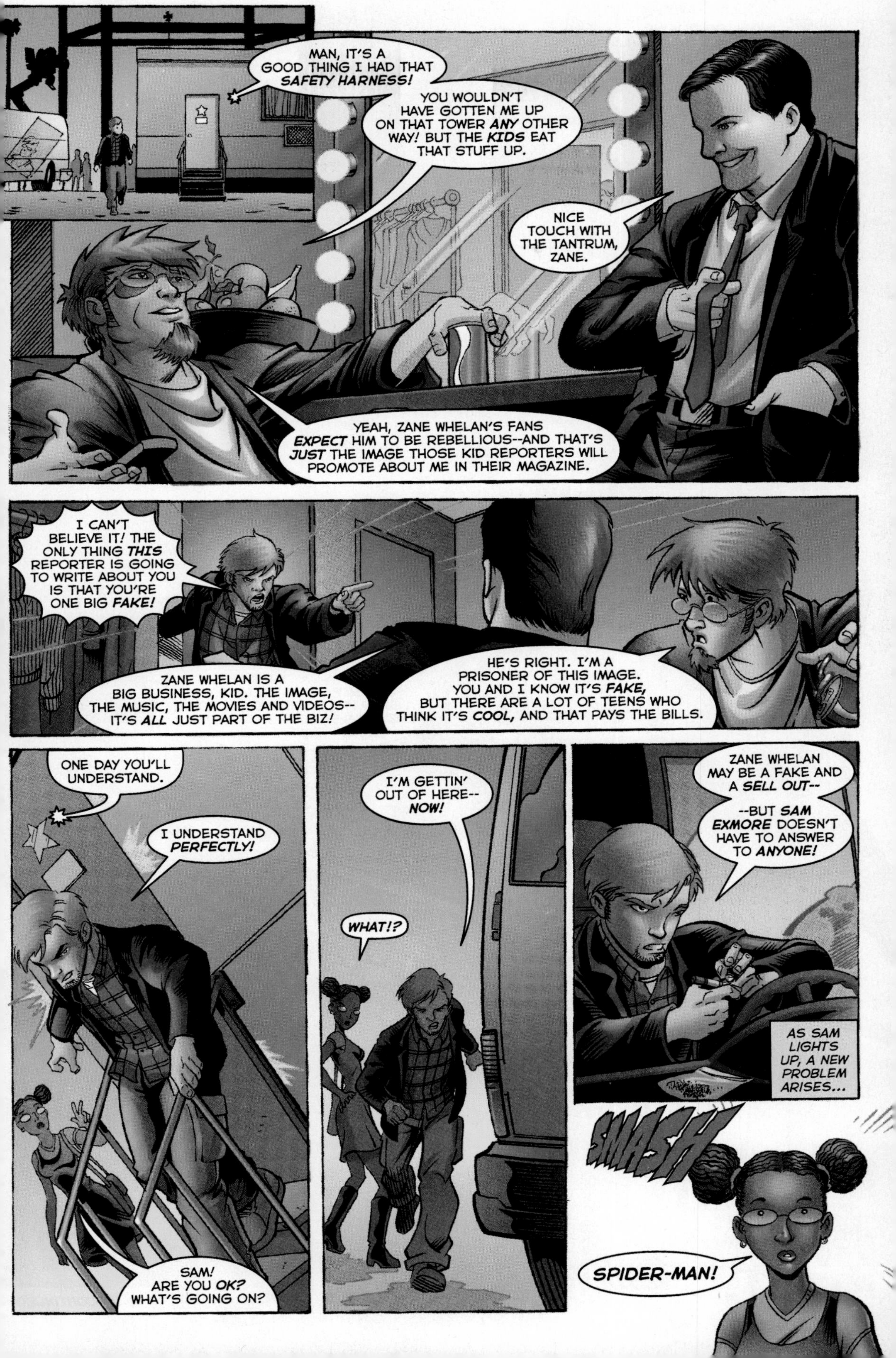
MAN, IT'S A GOOD THING I HAD THAT SAFETY HARNESS!
YOU WOULDN'T HAVE GOTTEN ME UP ON THAT TOWER ANY OTHER WAY! BUT THE KIDS EAT THAT STUFF UP.
NICE TOUCH WITH THE TANTRUM, ZANE.
YEAH, ZANE WHELAN'S FANS EXPECT HIM TO BE REBELLIOUS--AND THAT'S JUST THE IMAGE THOSE KID REPORTERS WILL PROMOTE ABOUT ME IN THEIR MAGAZINE.
I CAN'T BELIEVE IT! THE ONLY THING THIS REPORTER IS GOING TO WRITE ABOUT YOU IS THAT YOU'RE ONE BIG FAKE!
ZANE WHELAN IS A BIG BUSINESS, KID. THE IMAGE, THE MUSIC, THE MOVIES AND VIDEOS--IT'S ALL JUST PART OF THE BIZ!
HE'S RIGHT. I'M A PRISONER OF THIS IMAGE. YOU AND I KNOW IT'S FAKE, BUT THERE ARE A LOT OF TEENS WHO THINK IT'S COOL, AND THAT PAYS THE BILLS.
ONE DAY YOU'LL UNDERSTAND.
I UNDERSTAND PERFECTLY!
SAM! ARE YOU OK? WHAT'S GOING ON?
I'M GETTIN' OUT OF HERE--NOW!
WHAT!?
ZANE WHELAN MAY BE A FAKE AND A SELL OUT--
--BUT SAM EXMORE DOESN'T HAVE TO ANSWER TO ANYONE!
AS SAM LIGHTS UP, A NEW PROBLEM ARISES...
SMASH
SPIDER-MAN!

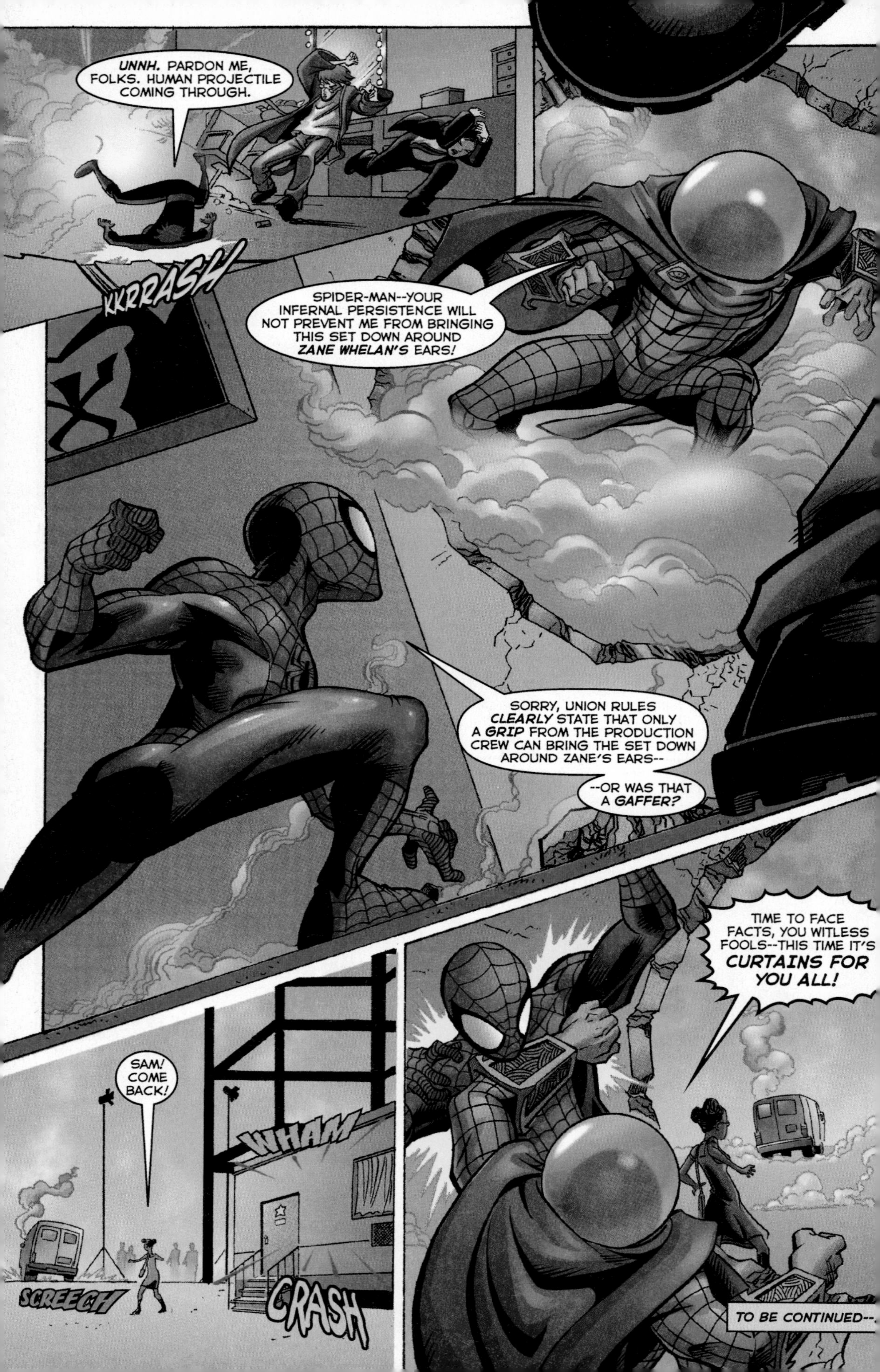
UNNH. PARDON ME, FOLKS. HUMAN PROJECTILE COMING THROUGH.
KKRRASH
SPIDER-MAN--YOUR INFERNAL PERSISTENCE WILL NOT PREVENT ME FROM BRINGING THIS SET DOWN AROUND ZANE WHELAN'S EARS!
SORRY, UNION RULES CLEARLY STATE THAT ONLY A GRIP FROM THE PRODUCTION CREW CAN BRING THE SET DOWN AROUND ZANE'S EARS--
--OR WAS THAT A GAFFER?
SAM! COME BACK!
WHAM
SCREECH
CRASH
TIME TO FACE FACTS, YOU WITLESS FOOLS--THIS TIME IT'S CURTAINS FOR YOU ALL!
TO BE CONTINUED--.

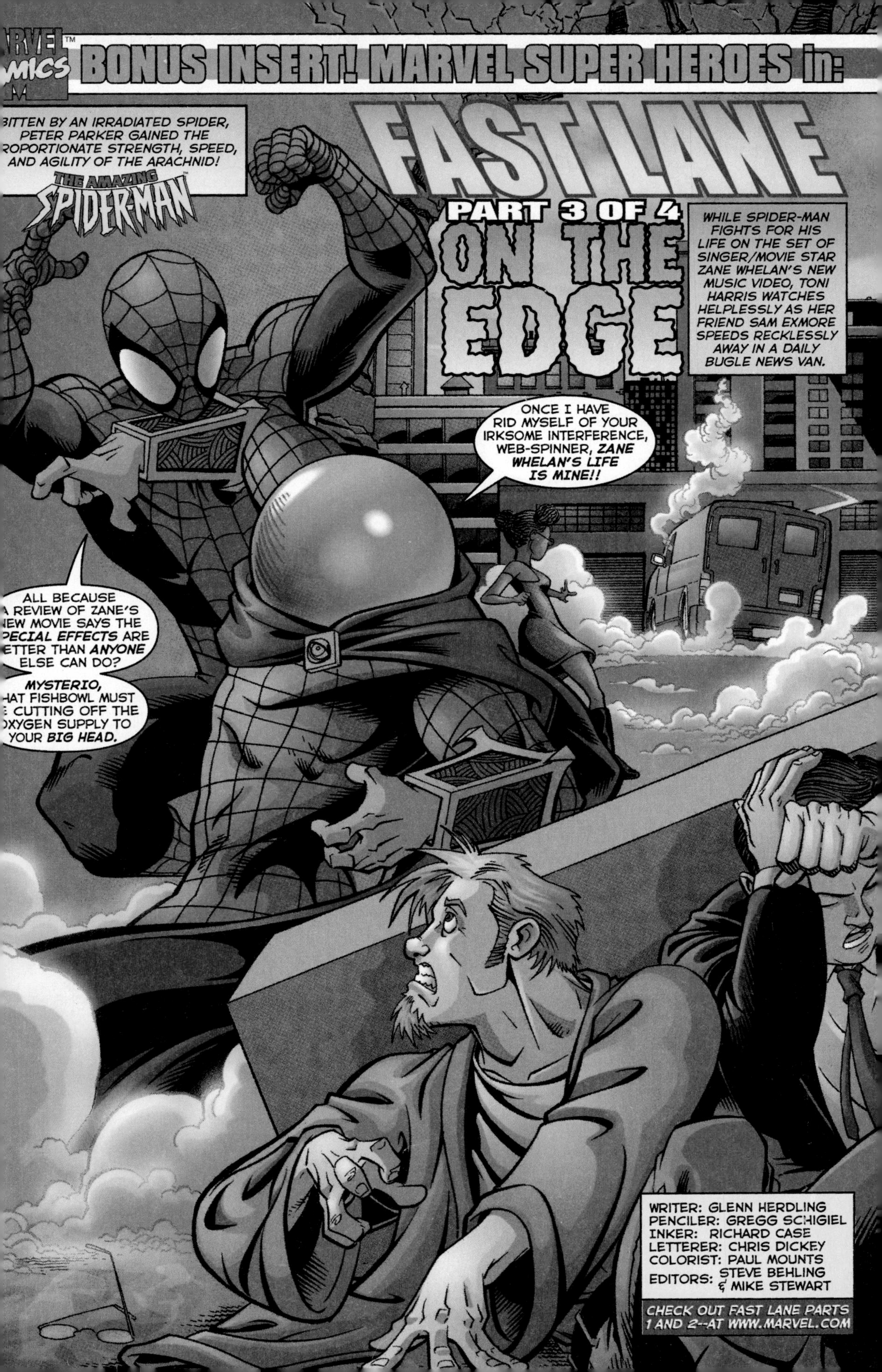
BONUS INSERT! MARVEL SUPER HEROES in:
FAST LANE
PART 3 OF 4
ON THE EDGE
BITTEN BY AN IRRADIATED SPIDER, PETER PARKER GAINED THE PROPORTIONATE STRENGTH, SPEED, AND AGILITY OF THE ARACHNID!
THE AMAZING SPIDER-MAN
WHILE SPIDER-MAN FIGHTS FOR HIS LIFE ON THE SET OF SINGER/MOVIE STAR ZANE WHELAN'S NEW MUSIC VIDEO, TONI HARRIS WATCHES HELPLESSLY AS HER FRIEND SAM EXMORE SPEEDS RECKLESSLY AWAY IN A DAILY BUGLE NEWS VAN.
ONCE I HAVE RID MYSELF OF YOUR IRKSOME INTERFERENCE, WEB-SPINNER, ZANE WHELAN'S LIFE IS MINE!!
ALL BECAUSE A REVIEW OF ZANE'S NEW MOVIE SAYS THE SPECIAL EFFECTS ARE BETTER THAN ANYONE ELSE CAN DO?
MYSTERIO, THAT FISHBOWL MUST BE CUTTING OFF THE OXYGEN SUPPLY TO YOUR BIG HEAD.
WRITER: GLENN HERDLING
PENCILER: GREGG SCHIGIEL
INKER: RICHARD CASE
LETTERER: CHRIS DICKEY
COLORIST: PAUL MOUNTS
EDITORS: STEVE BEHLING & MIKE STEWART
CHECK OUT FAST LANE PARTS 1 AND 2--AT WWW.MARVEL.COM

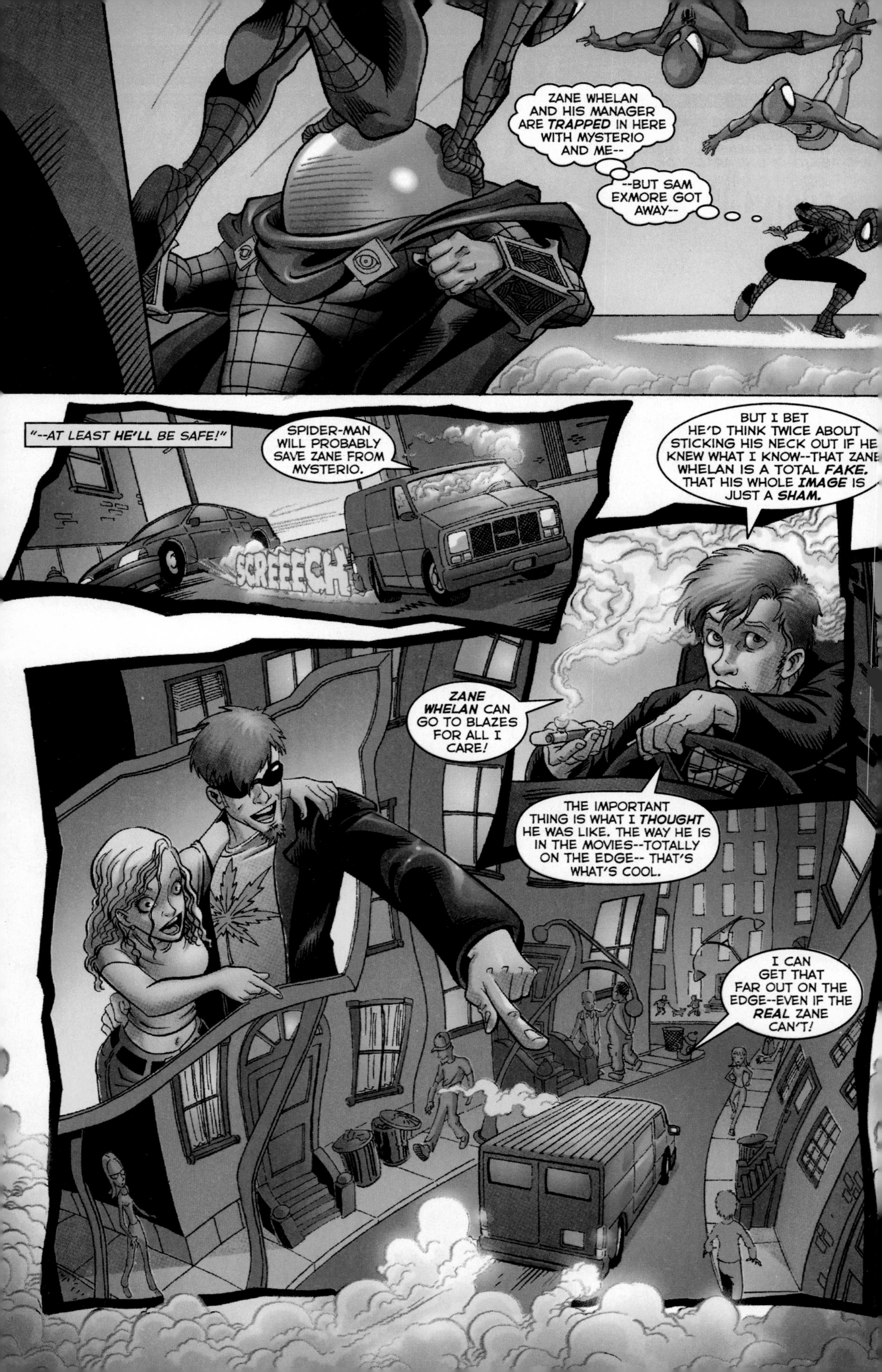
ZANE WHELAN AND HIS MANAGER ARE TRAPPED IN HERE WITH MYSTERIO AND ME--
--BUT SAM EXMORE GOT AWAY--
"--AT LEAST HE'LL BE SAFE!"
SPIDER-MAN WILL PROBABLY SAVE ZANE FROM MYSTERIO.
SCREEECH
BUT I BET HE'D THINK TWICE ABOUT STICKING HIS NECK OUT IF HE KNEW WHAT I KNOW--THAT ZANE WHELAN IS A TOTAL FAKE. THAT HIS WHOLE IMAGE IS JUST A SHAM.
ZANE WHELAN CAN GO TO BLAZES FOR ALL I CARE!
THE IMPORTANT THING IS WHAT I THOUGHT HE WAS LIKE. THE WAY HE IS IN THE MOVIES--TOTALLY ON THE EDGE-- THAT'S WHAT'S COOL.
I CAN GET THAT FAR OUT ON THE EDGE--EVEN IF THE REAL ZANE CAN'T!

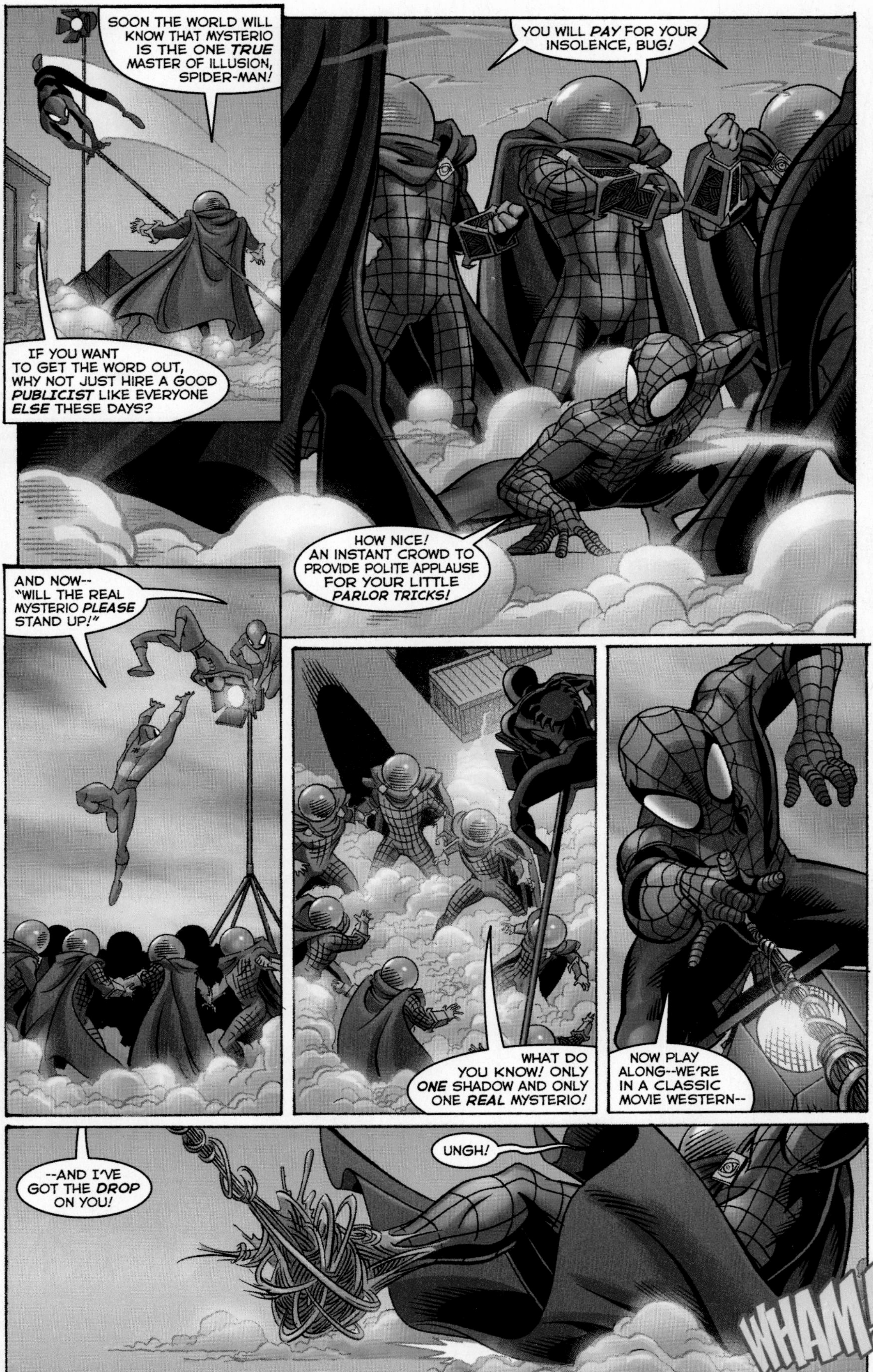
SOON THE WORLD WILL KNOW THAT MYSTERIO IS THE ONE TRUE MASTER OF ILLUSION, SPIDER-MAN!
IF YOU WANT TO GET THE WORD OUT, WHY NOT JUST HIRE A GOOD PUBLICIST LIKE EVERYONE ELSE THESE DAYS?
YOU WILL PAY FOR YOUR INSOLENCE, BUG!
HOW NICE! AN INSTANT CROWD TO PROVIDE POLITE APPLAUSE FOR YOUR LITTLE PARLOR TRICKS!
AND NOW-- "WILL THE REAL MYSTERIO PLEASE STAND UP!"
WHAT DO YOU KNOW! ONLY ONE SHADOW AND ONLY ONE REAL MYSTERIO!
NOW PLAY ALONG--WE'RE IN A CLASSIC MOVIE WESTERN--
--AND I'VE GOT THE DROP ON YOU!
UNGH!
WHAM!

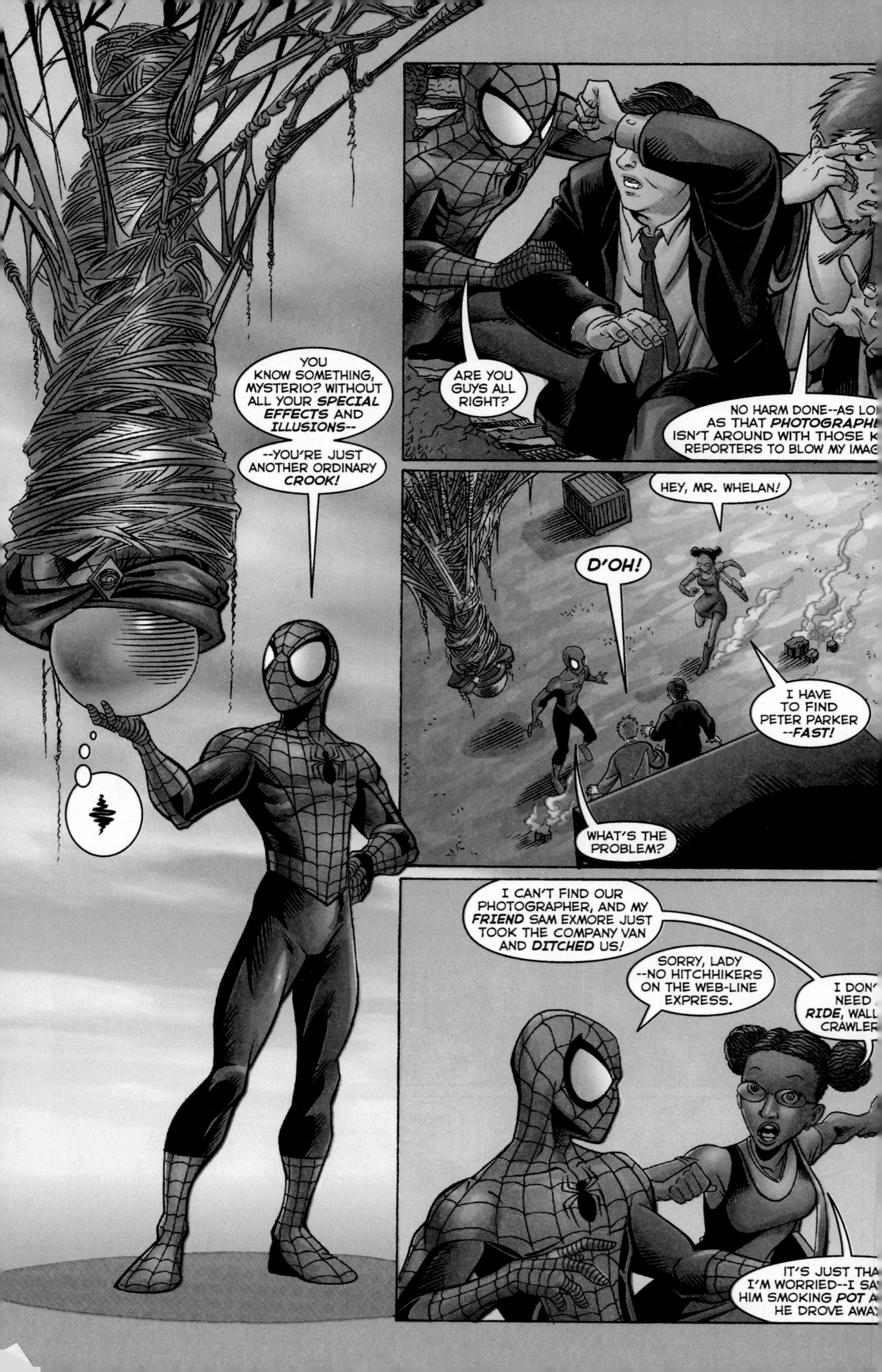
YOU KNOW SOMETHING, MYSTERIO? WITHOUT ALL YOUR SPECIAL EFFECTS AND ILLUSIONS--
--YOU'RE JUST ANOTHER ORDINARY CROOK!
ARE YOU GUYS ALL RIGHT?
NO HARM DONE--AS LO
AS THAT PHOTOGRAPHE
ISN'T AROUND WITH THOSE K
REPORTERS TO BLOW MY IMAG
HEY, MR. WHELAN!
D'OH!
I HAVE TO FIND PETER PARKER --FAST!
WHAT'S THE PROBLEM?
I CAN'T FIND OUR PHOTOGRAPHER, AND MY FRIEND SAM EXMORE JUST TOOK THE COMPANY VAN AND DITCHED US!
SORRY, LADY --NO HITCHHIKERS ON THE WEB-LINE EXPRESS.
I DON' NEED RIDE, WALL CRAWLER
IT'S JUST THA I'M WORRIED--I SA HIM SMOKING POT A HE DROVE AWAY

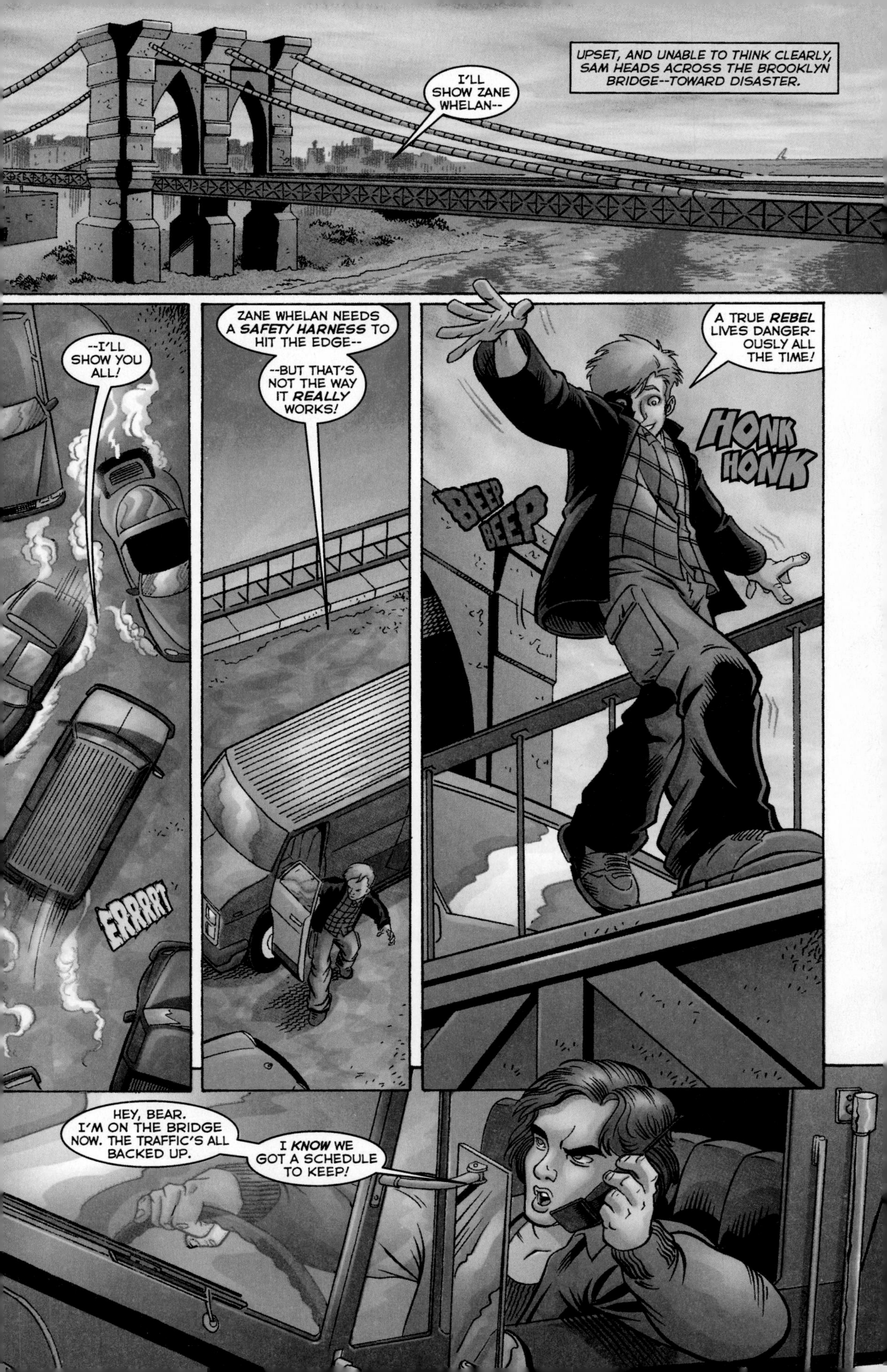

UPSET, AND UNABLE TO THINK CLEARLY, SAM HEADS ACROSS THE BROOKLYN BRIDGE--TOWARD DISASTER.
I'LL SHOW ZANE WHELAN--
--I'LL SHOW YOU ALL!
ERRRRT
ZANE WHELAN NEEDS A SAFETY HARNESS TO HIT THE EDGE--
--BUT THAT'S NOT THE WAY IT REALLY WORKS!
A TRUE REBEL LIVES DANGER-OUSLY ALL THE TIME!
HONK HONK
BEEP BEEP
HEY, BEAR. I'M ON THE BRIDGE NOW. THE TRAFFIC'S ALL BACKED UP.
I KNOW WE GOT A SCHEDULE TO KEEP!

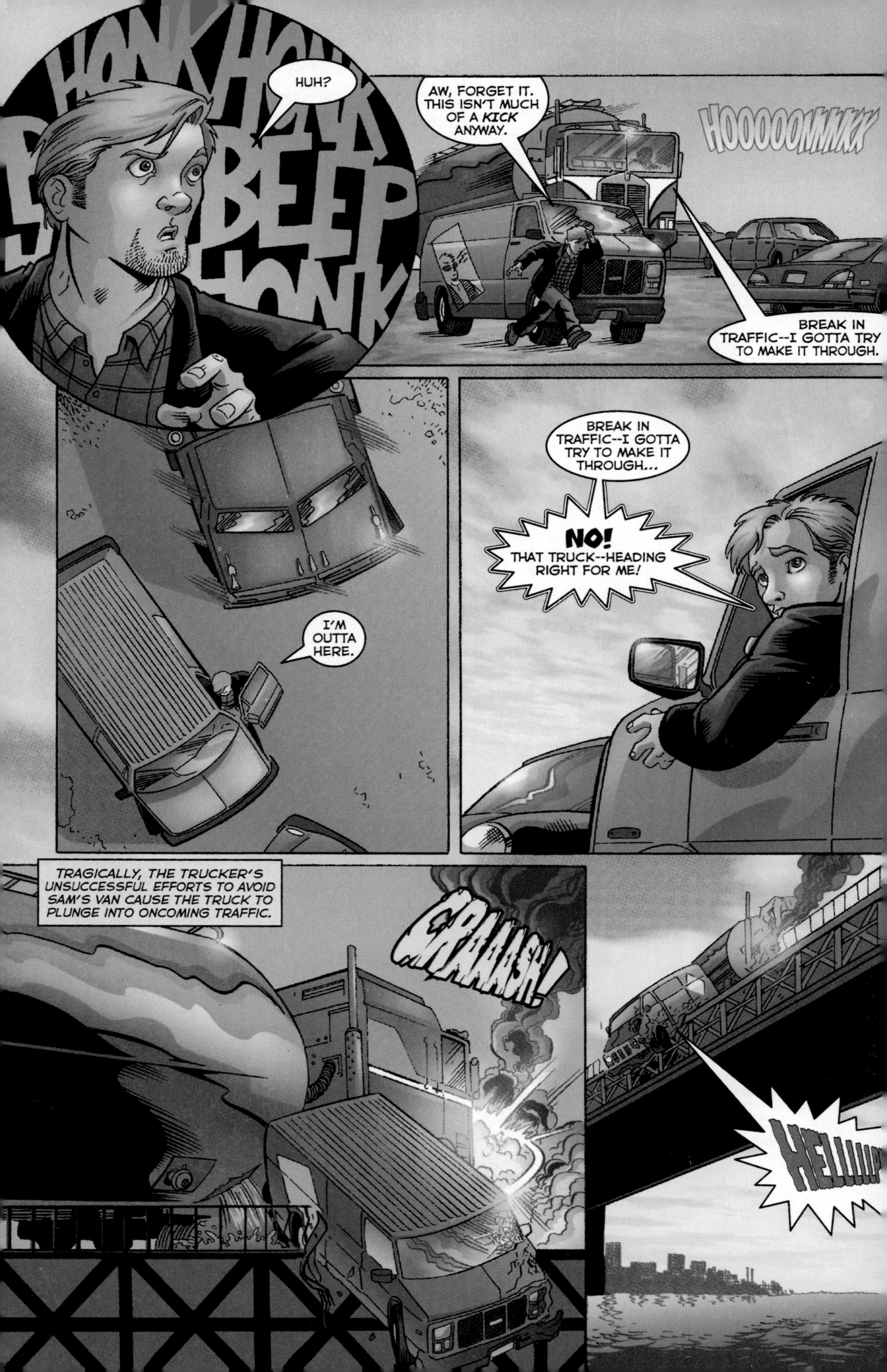
HONK HONK
BEEP
HONK
HUH?
AW, FORGET IT. THIS ISN'T MUCH OF A KICK ANYWAY.
HOOOOONNNKK
BREAK IN TRAFFIC--I GOTTA TRY TO MAKE IT THROUGH.
I'M OUTTA HERE.
BREAK IN TRAFFIC--I GOTTA TRY TO MAKE IT THROUGH...
NO! THAT TRUCK--HEADING RIGHT FOR ME!
TRAGICALLY, THE TRUCKER'S UNSUCCESSFUL EFFORTS TO AVOID SAM'S VAN CAUSE THE TRUCK TO PLUNGE INTO ONCOMING TRAFFIC.
CRAAASH!
HELLLLP

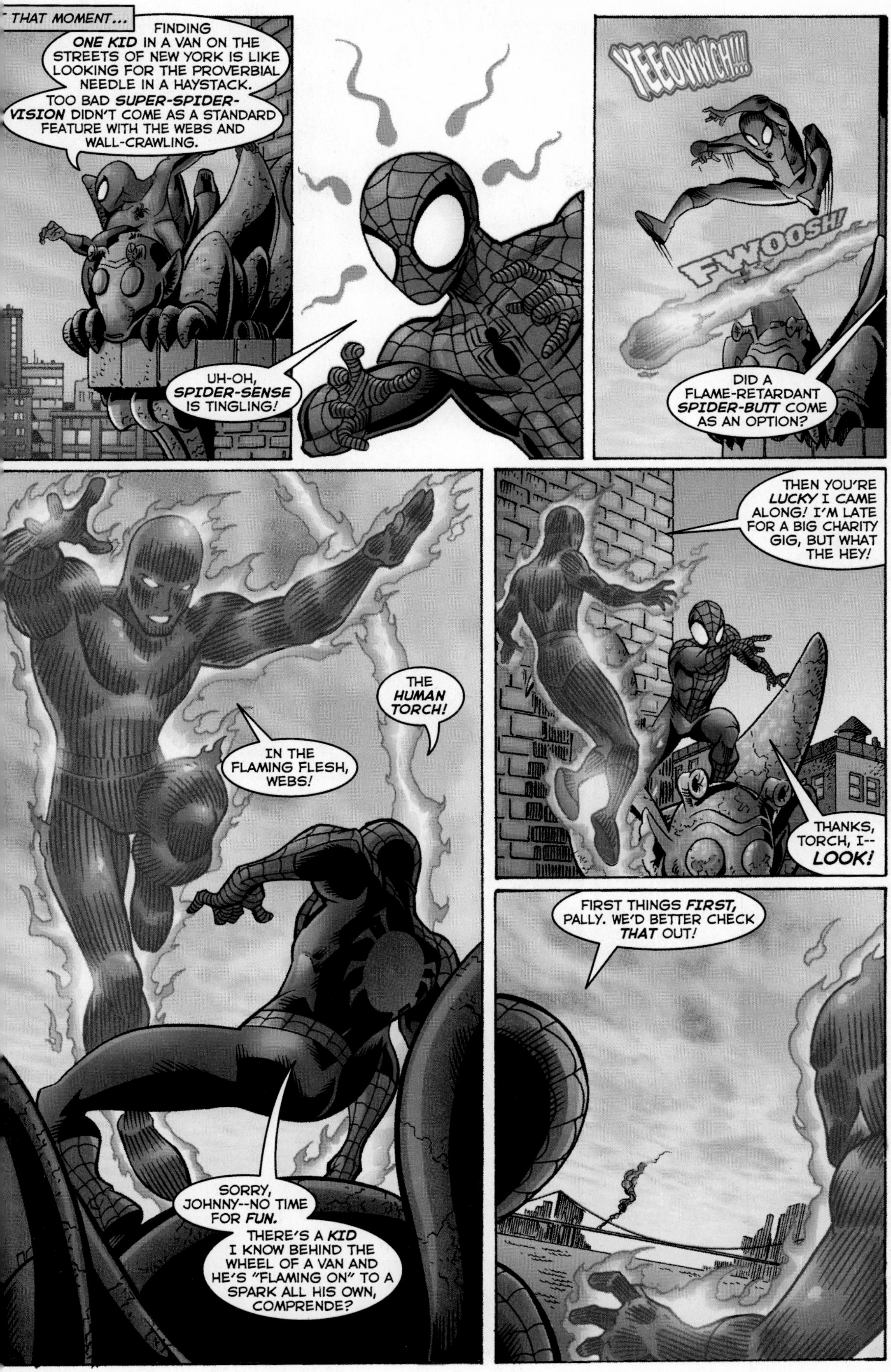

T THAT MOMENT...
FINDING ONE KID IN A VAN ON THE STREETS OF NEW YORK IS LIKE LOOKING FOR THE PROVERBIAL NEEDLE IN A HAYSTACK.
TOO BAD SUPER-SPIDER-VISION DIDN'T COME AS A STANDARD FEATURE WITH THE WEBS AND WALL-CRAWLING.
UH-OH, SPIDER-SENSE IS TINGLING!
YEEOWWCH!!!
FWOOSH!
DID A FLAME-RETARDANT SPIDER-BUTT COME AS AN OPTION?
THE HUMAN TORCH!
IN THE FLAMING FLESH, WEBS!
SORRY, JOHNNY--NO TIME FOR FUN.
THERE'S A KID I KNOW BEHIND THE WHEEL OF A VAN AND HE'S "FLAMING ON" TO A SPARK ALL HIS OWN, COMPRENDE?
THEN YOU'RE LUCKY I CAME ALONG! I'M LATE FOR A BIG CHARITY GIG, BUT WHAT THE HEY!
THANKS, TORCH, I-- LOOK!
FIRST THINGS FIRST, PALLY. WE'D BETTER CHECK THAT OUT!

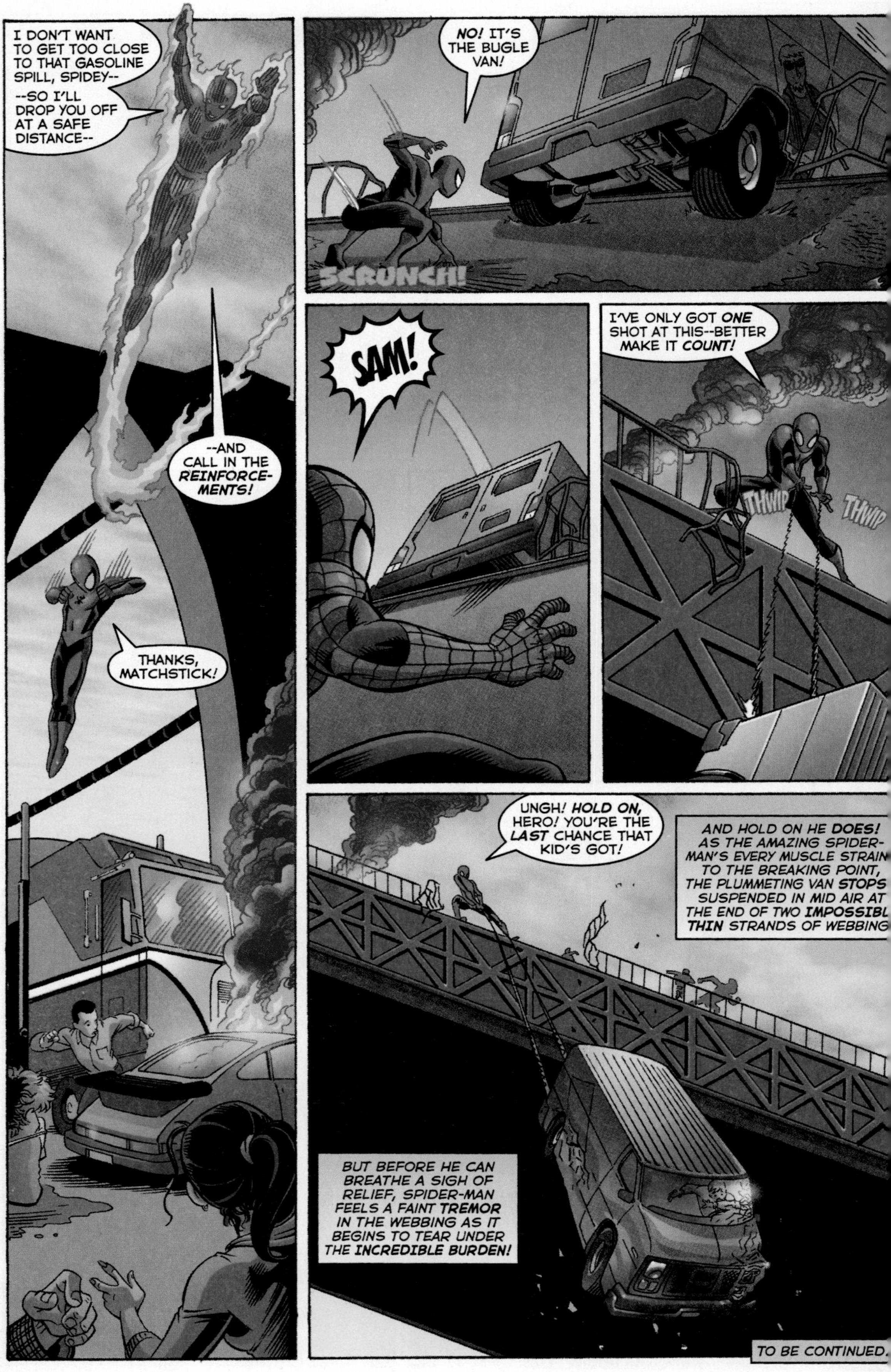
I DON'T WANT TO GET TOO CLOSE TO THAT GASOLINE SPILL, SPIDEY--
--SO I'LL DROP YOU OFF AT A SAFE DISTANCE--
--AND CALL IN THE REINFORCE-MENTS!
THANKS, MATCHSTICK!
NO! IT'S THE BUGLE VAN!
SCRUNCH!
SAM!
I'VE ONLY GOT ONE SHOT AT THIS--BETTER MAKE IT COUNT!
THWIP
THWIP
UNGH! HOLD ON, HERO! YOU'RE THE LAST CHANCE THAT KID'S GOT!
AND HOLD ON HE DOES! AS THE AMAZING SPIDER-MAN'S EVERY MUSCLE STRAIN TO THE BREAKING POINT, THE PLUMMETING VAN STOPS SUSPENDED IN MID AIR AT THE END OF TWO IMPOSSIBL THIN STRANDS OF WEBBING
BUT BEFORE HE CAN BREATHE A SIGH OF RELIEF, SPIDER-MAN FEELS A FAINT TREMOR IN THE WEBBING AS IT BEGINS TO TEAR UNDER THE INCREDIBLE BURDEN!
TO BE CONTINUED.

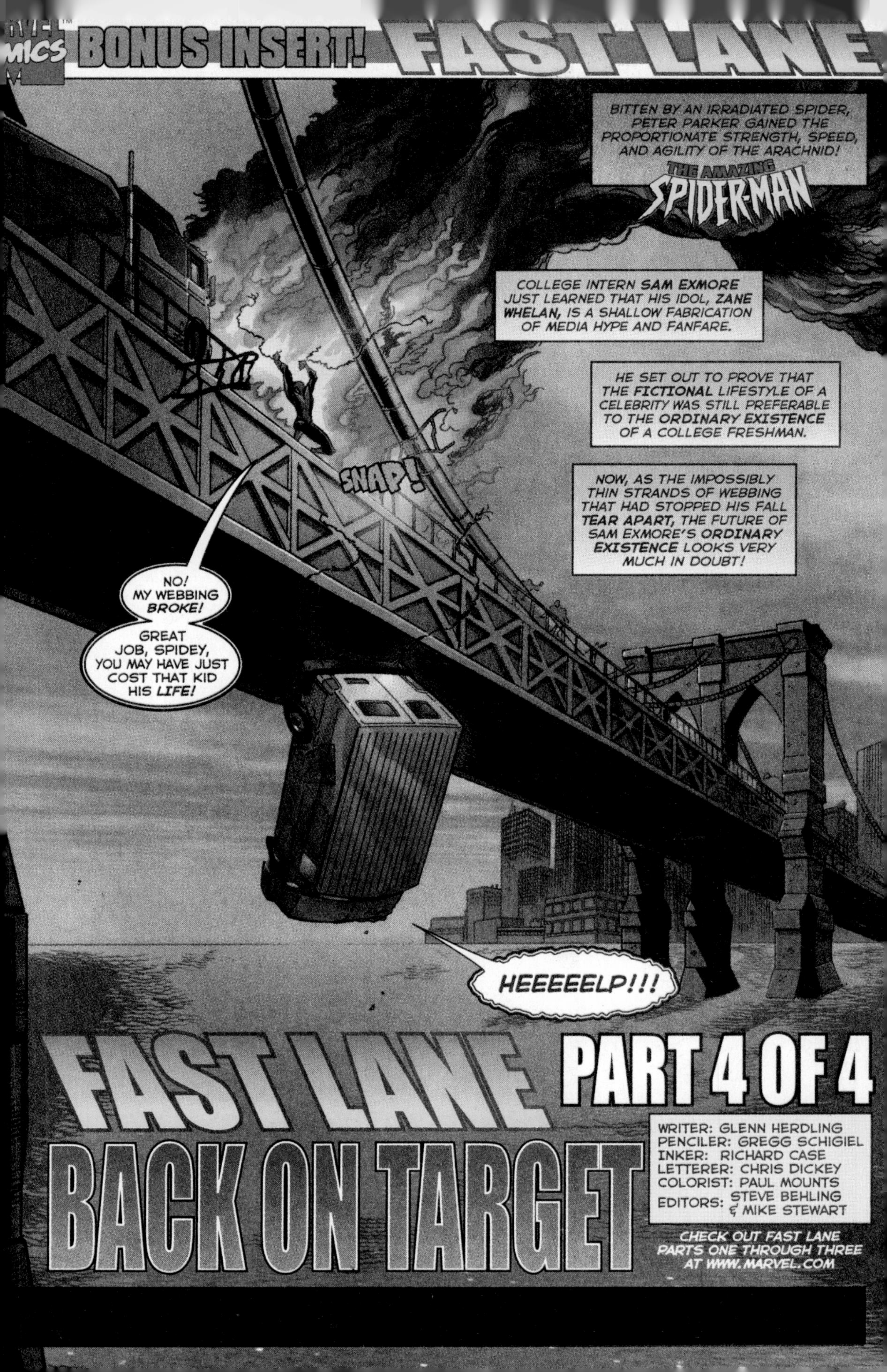
MARVEL COMICS
BONUS INSERT!
FAST LANE
BITTEN BY AN IRRADIATED SPIDER, PETER PARKER GAINED THE PROPORTIONATE STRENGTH, SPEED, AND AGILITY OF THE ARACHNID!
THE AMAZING SPIDER-MAN
COLLEGE INTERN SAM EXMORE JUST LEARNED THAT HIS IDOL, ZANE WHELAN, IS A SHALLOW FABRICATION OF MEDIA HYPE AND FANFARE.
HE SET OUT TO PROVE THAT THE FICTIONAL LIFESTYLE OF A CELEBRITY WAS STILL PREFERABLE TO THE ORDINARY EXISTENCE OF A COLLEGE FRESHMAN.
NOW, AS THE IMPOSSIBLY THIN STRANDS OF WEBBING THAT HAD STOPPED HIS FALL TEAR APART, THE FUTURE OF SAM EXMORE'S ORDINARY EXISTENCE LOOKS VERY MUCH IN DOUBT!
SNAP!
NO! MY WEBBING BROKE!
GREAT JOB, SPIDEY, YOU MAY HAVE JUST COST THAT KID HIS LIFE!
HEEEEELP!!!
FAST LANE PART 4 OF 4
BACK ON TARGET
WRITER: GLENN HERDLING
PENCILER: GREGG SCHIGIEL
INKER: RICHARD CASE
LETTERER: CHRIS DICKEY
COLORIST: PAUL MOUNTS
EDITORS: STEVE BEHLING & MIKE STEWART
CHECK OUT FAST LANE PARTS ONE THROUGH THREE AT WWW.MARVEL.COM

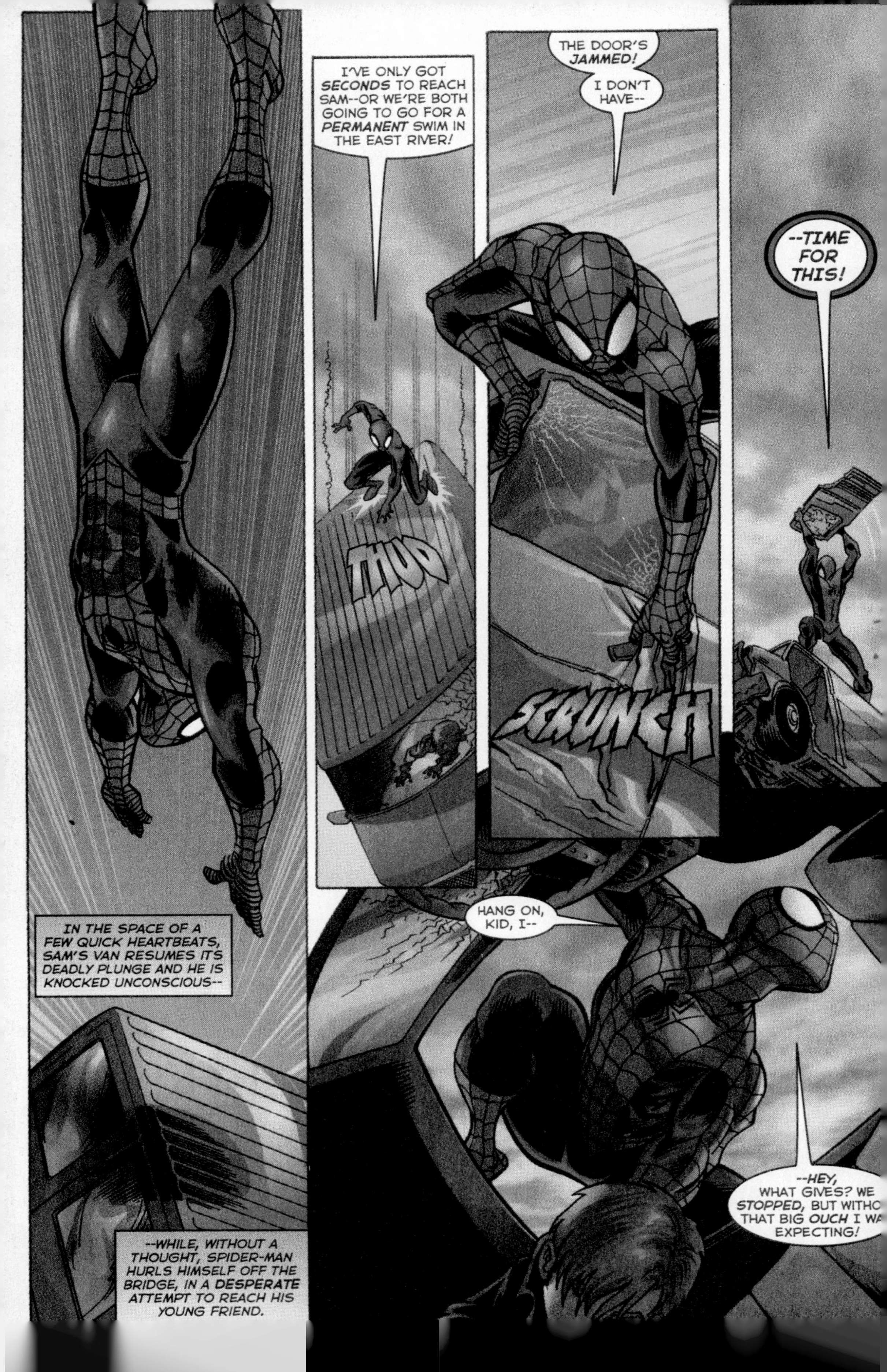

IN THE SPACE OF A FEW QUICK HEARTBEATS, SAM'S VAN RESUMES ITS DEADLY PLUNGE AND HE IS KNOCKED UNCONSCIOUS--
--WHILE, WITHOUT A THOUGHT, SPIDER-MAN HURLS HIMSELF OFF THE BRIDGE, IN A DESPERATE ATTEMPT TO REACH HIS YOUNG FRIEND.
I'VE ONLY GOT SECONDS TO REACH SAM--OR WE'RE BOTH GOING TO GO FOR A PERMANENT SWIM IN THE EAST RIVER!
THUD
THE DOOR'S JAMMED!
I DON'T HAVE--
SCRUNCH
--TIME FOR THIS!
HANG ON, KID, I--
--HEY, WHAT GIVES? WE STOPPED, BUT WITHO THAT BIG OUCH I WA EXPECTING!

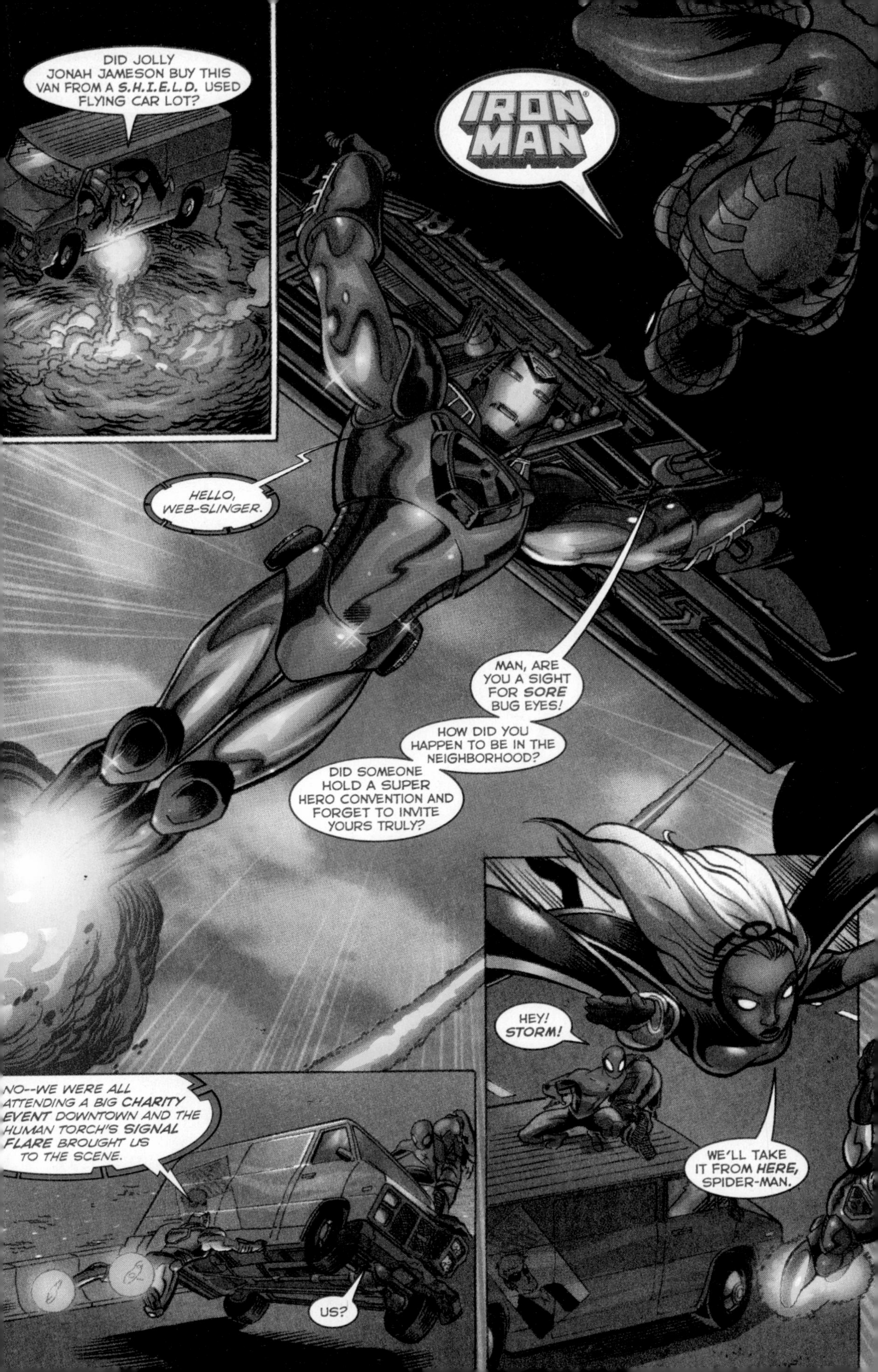

DID JOLLY JONAH JAMESON BUY THIS VAN FROM A S.H.I.E.L.D. USED FLYING CAR LOT?
IRON MAN
HELLO, WEB-SLINGER.
MAN, ARE YOU A SIGHT FOR SORE BUG EYES!
HOW DID YOU HAPPEN TO BE IN THE NEIGHBORHOOD?
DID SOMEONE HOLD A SUPER HERO CONVENTION AND FORGET TO INVITE YOURS TRULY?
NO--WE WERE ALL ATTENDING A BIG CHARITY EVENT DOWNTOWN AND THE HUMAN TORCH'S SIGNAL FLARE BROUGHT US TO THE SCENE.
US?
HEY! STORM!
WE'LL TAKE IT FROM HERE, SPIDER-MAN.

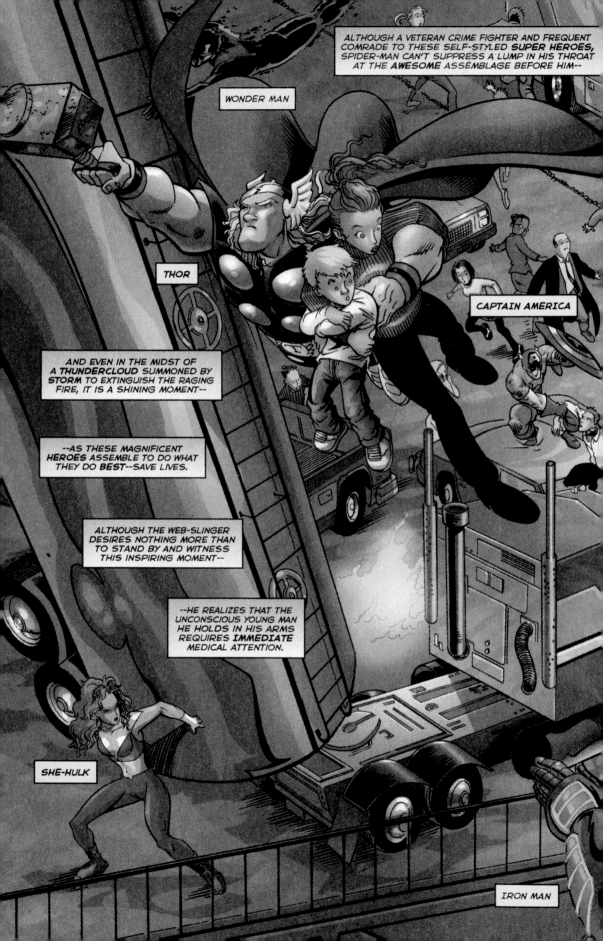

ALTHOUGH A VETERAN CRIME FIGHTER AND FREQUENT COMRADE TO THESE SELF-STYLED *SUPER HEROES*, SPIDER-MAN CAN'T SUPPRESS A LUMP IN HIS THROAT AT THE *AWESOME* ASSEMBLAGE BEFORE HIM--

WONDER MAN

THOR

CAPTAIN AMERICA

AND EVEN IN THE MIDST OF A *THUNDERCLOUD* SUMMONED BY *STORM* TO EXTINGUISH THE RAGING FIRE, IT IS A SHINING MOMENT--

--AS THESE MAGNIFICENT *HEROES* ASSEMBLE TO DO WHAT THEY DO *BEST*--SAVE LIVES.

ALTHOUGH THE WEB-SLINGER DESIRES NOTHING MORE THAN TO STAND BY AND WITNESS THIS INSPIRING MOMENT--

--HE REALIZES THAT THE UNCONSCIOUS YOUNG MAN HE HOLDS IN HIS ARMS REQUIRES *IMMEDIATE* MEDICAL ATTENTION.

SHE-HULK

IRON MAN

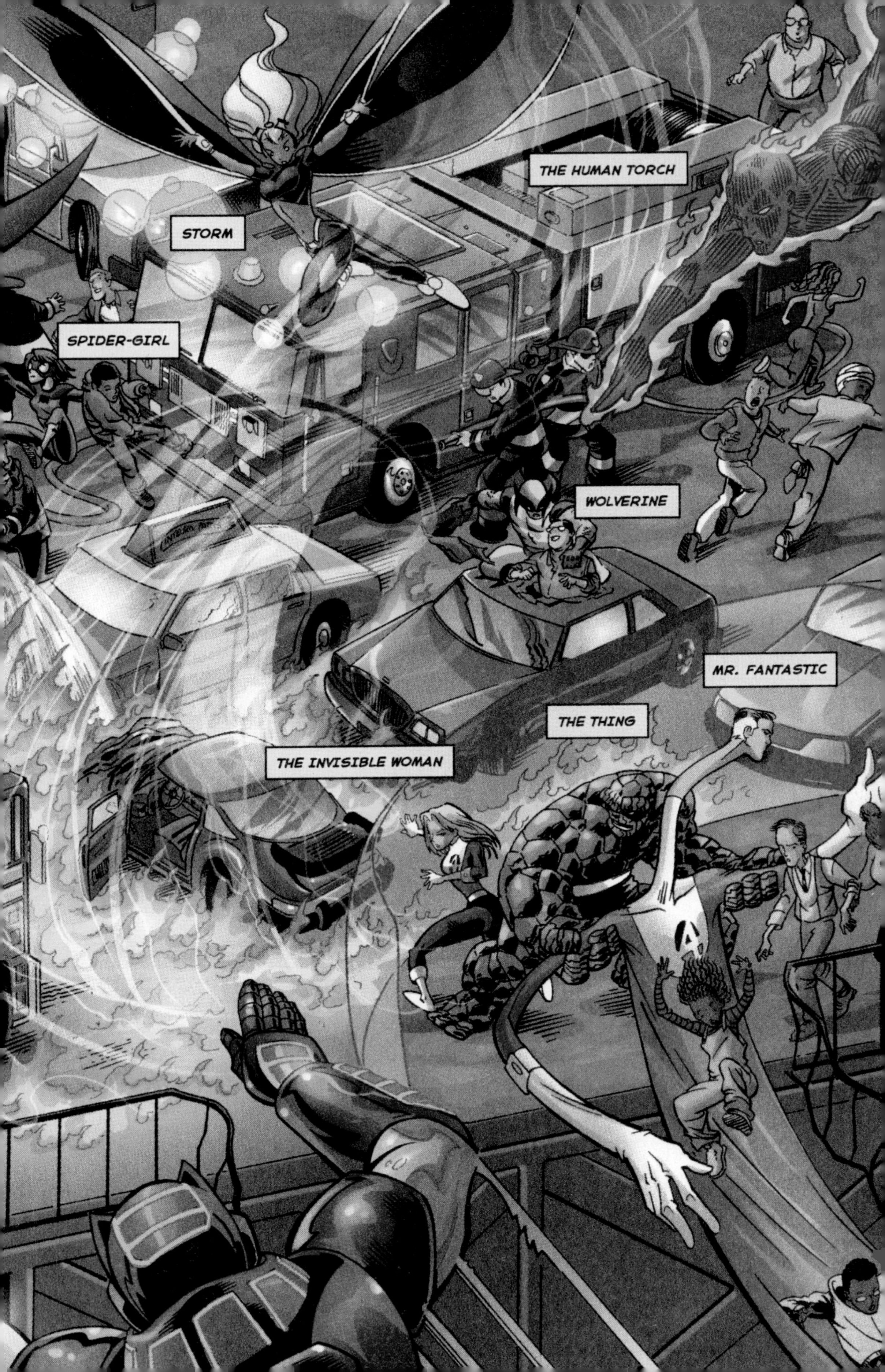
STORM
THE HUMAN TORCH
SPIDER-GIRL
WOLVERINE
MR. FANTASTIC
THE THING
THE INVISIBLE WOMAN

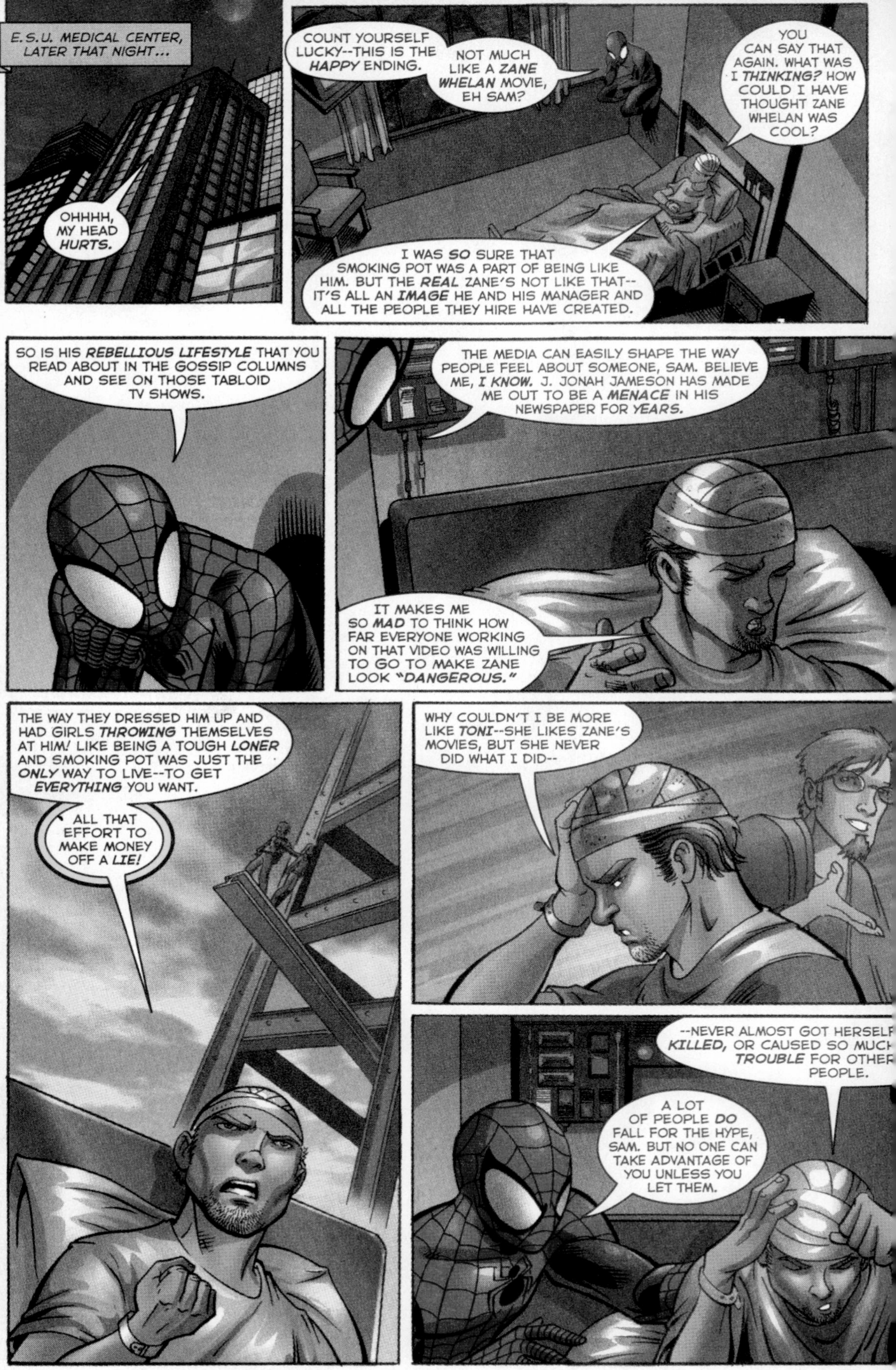
E.S.U. MEDICAL CENTER, LATER THAT NIGHT...
OHHHH, MY HEAD HURTS.
COUNT YOURSELF LUCKY--THIS IS THE HAPPY ENDING.
NOT MUCH LIKE A ZANE WHELAN MOVIE, EH SAM?
YOU CAN SAY THAT AGAIN. WHAT WAS I THINKING? HOW COULD I HAVE THOUGHT ZANE WHELAN WAS COOL?
I WAS SO SURE THAT SMOKING POT WAS A PART OF BEING LIKE HIM. BUT THE REAL ZANE'S NOT LIKE THAT--IT'S ALL AN IMAGE HE AND HIS MANAGER AND ALL THE PEOPLE THEY HIRE HAVE CREATED.
SO IS HIS REBELLIOUS LIFESTYLE THAT YOU READ ABOUT IN THE GOSSIP COLUMNS AND SEE ON THOSE TABLOID TV SHOWS.
THE MEDIA CAN EASILY SHAPE THE WAY PEOPLE FEEL ABOUT SOMEONE, SAM. BELIEVE ME, I KNOW. J. JONAH JAMESON HAS MADE ME OUT TO BE A MENACE IN HIS NEWSPAPER FOR YEARS.
IT MAKES ME SO MAD TO THINK HOW FAR EVERYONE WORKING ON THAT VIDEO WAS WILLING TO GO TO MAKE ZANE LOOK "DANGEROUS."
THE WAY THEY DRESSED HIM UP AND HAD GIRLS THROWING THEMSELVES AT HIM! LIKE BEING A TOUGH LONER AND SMOKING POT WAS JUST THE ONLY WAY TO LIVE--TO GET EVERYTHING YOU WANT.
ALL THAT EFFORT TO MAKE MONEY OFF A LIE!
WHY COULDN'T I BE MORE LIKE TONI--SHE LIKES ZANE'S MOVIES, BUT SHE NEVER DID WHAT I DID--
--NEVER ALMOST GOT HERSELF KILLED, OR CAUSED SO MUCH TROUBLE FOR OTHER PEOPLE.
A LOT OF PEOPLE DO FALL FOR THE HYPE, SAM. BUT NO ONE CAN TAKE ADVANTAGE OF YOU UNLESS YOU LET THEM.

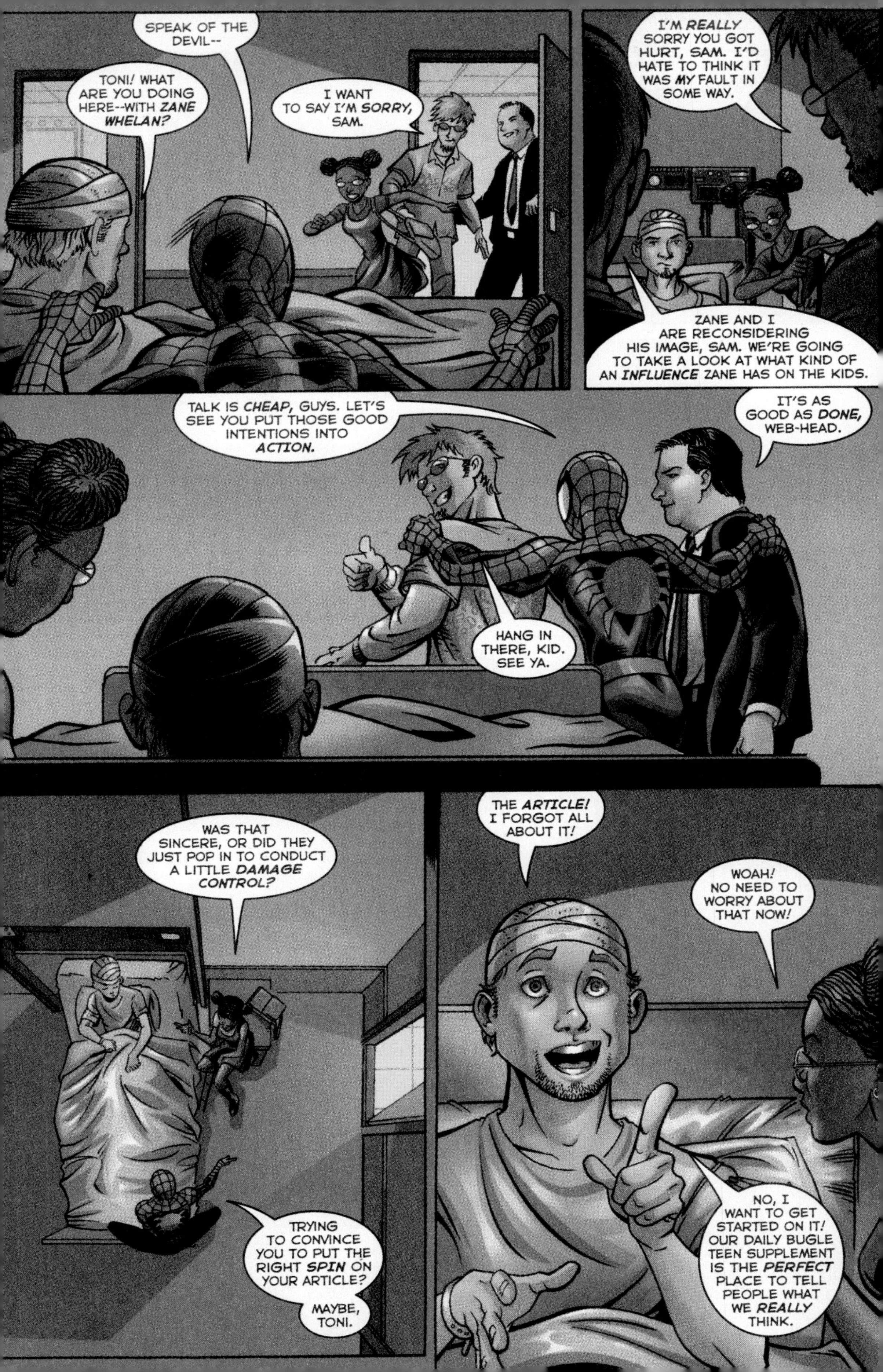
SPEAK OF THE DEVIL--
TONI! WHAT ARE YOU DOING HERE--WITH ZANE WHELAN?
I WANT TO SAY I'M SORRY, SAM.
I'M REALLY SORRY YOU GOT HURT, SAM. I'D HATE TO THINK IT WAS MY FAULT IN SOME WAY.
ZANE AND I ARE RECONSIDERING HIS IMAGE, SAM. WE'RE GOING TO TAKE A LOOK AT WHAT KIND OF AN INFLUENCE ZANE HAS ON THE KIDS.
TALK IS CHEAP, GUYS. LET'S SEE YOU PUT THOSE GOOD INTENTIONS INTO ACTION.
IT'S AS GOOD AS DONE, WEB-HEAD.
HANG IN THERE, KID. SEE YA.
WAS THAT SINCERE, OR DID THEY JUST POP IN TO CONDUCT A LITTLE DAMAGE CONTROL?
TRYING TO CONVINCE YOU TO PUT THE RIGHT SPIN ON YOUR ARTICLE?
MAYBE, TONI.
THE ARTICLE! I FORGOT ALL ABOUT IT!
WOAH! NO NEED TO WORRY ABOUT THAT NOW!
NO, I WANT TO GET STARTED ON IT! OUR DAILY BUGLE TEEN SUPPLEMENT IS THE PERFECT PLACE TO TELL PEOPLE WHAT WE REALLY THINK.

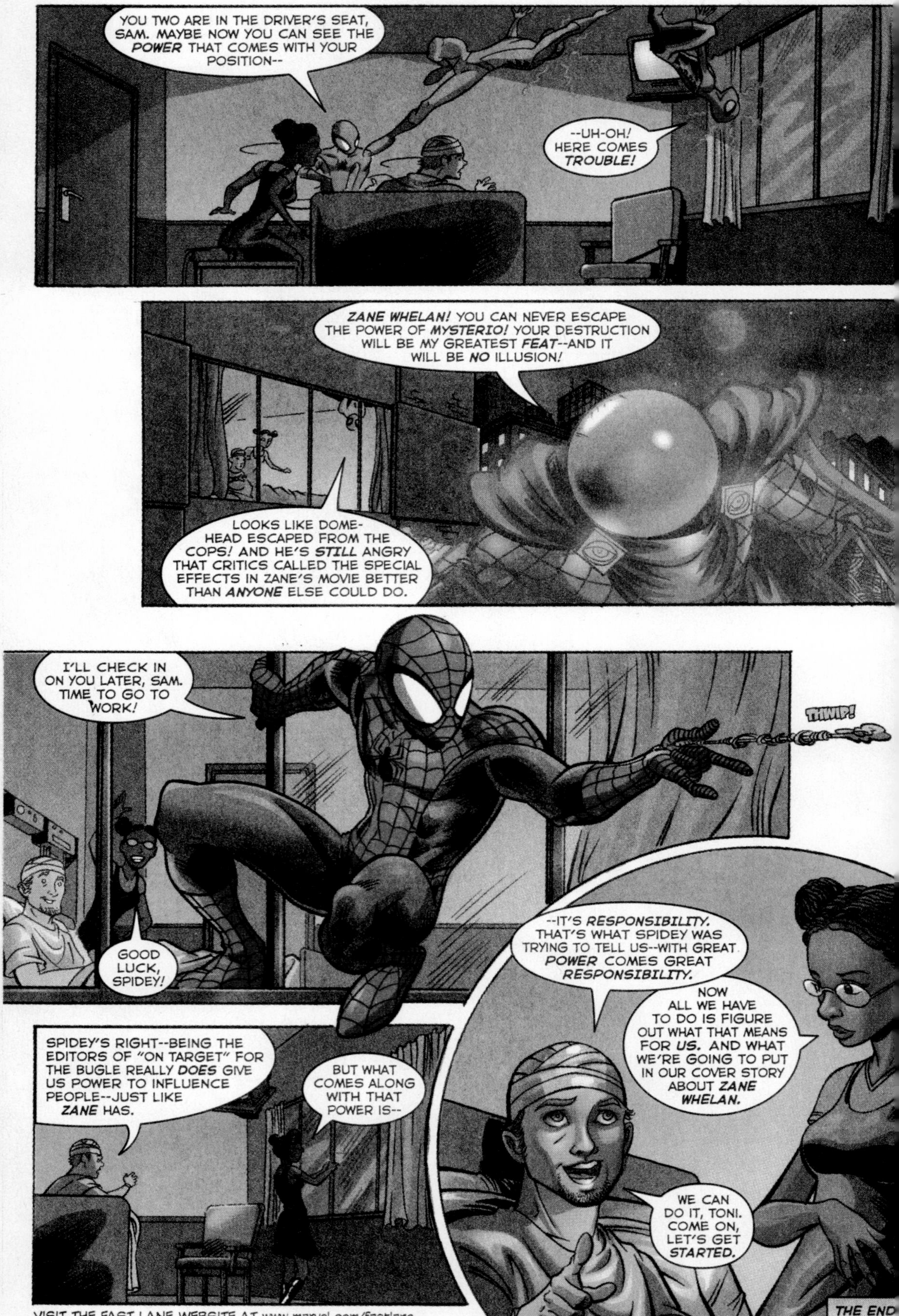
YOU TWO ARE IN THE DRIVER'S SEAT, SAM. MAYBE NOW YOU CAN SEE THE POWER THAT COMES WITH YOUR POSITION--
--UH-OH! HERE COMES TROUBLE!
ZANE WHELAN! YOU CAN NEVER ESCAPE THE POWER OF MYSTERIO! YOUR DESTRUCTION WILL BE MY GREATEST FEAT--AND IT WILL BE NO ILLUSION!
LOOKS LIKE DOME-HEAD ESCAPED FROM THE COPS! AND HE'S STILL ANGRY THAT CRITICS CALLED THE SPECIAL EFFECTS IN ZANE'S MOVIE BETTER THAN ANYONE ELSE COULD DO.
I'LL CHECK IN ON YOU LATER, SAM. TIME TO GO TO WORK!
THWIP!
GOOD LUCK, SPIDEY!
SPIDEY'S RIGHT--BEING THE EDITORS OF "ON TARGET" FOR THE BUGLE REALLY DOES GIVE US POWER TO INFLUENCE PEOPLE--JUST LIKE ZANE HAS.
BUT WHAT COMES ALONG WITH THAT POWER IS--
--IT'S RESPONSIBILITY. THAT'S WHAT SPIDEY WAS TRYING TO TELL US--WITH GREAT POWER COMES GREAT RESPONSIBILITY.
NOW ALL WE HAVE TO DO IS FIGURE OUT WHAT THAT MEANS FOR US. AND WHAT WE'RE GOING TO PUT IN OUR COVER STORY ABOUT ZANE WHELAN.
WE CAN DO IT, TONI. COME ON, LET'S GET STARTED.
THE END

VISIT THE FAST LANE WEBSITE AT www.marvel.com/fastlane
FOR ALCOHOL AND DRUG INFORMATION CALL 1-800-788-2800

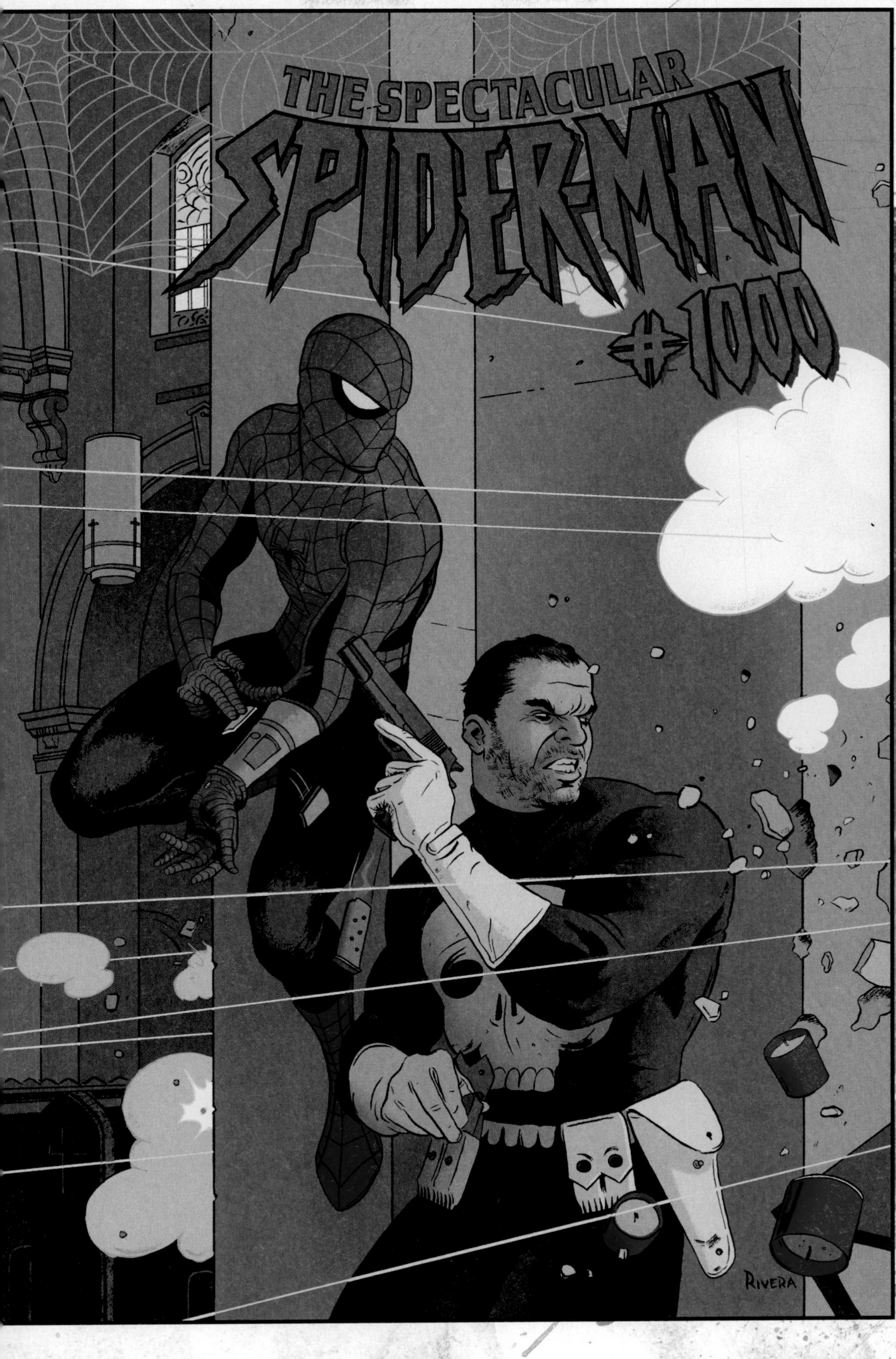
THE SPECTACULAR
SPIDER-MAN
#1000
RIVERA

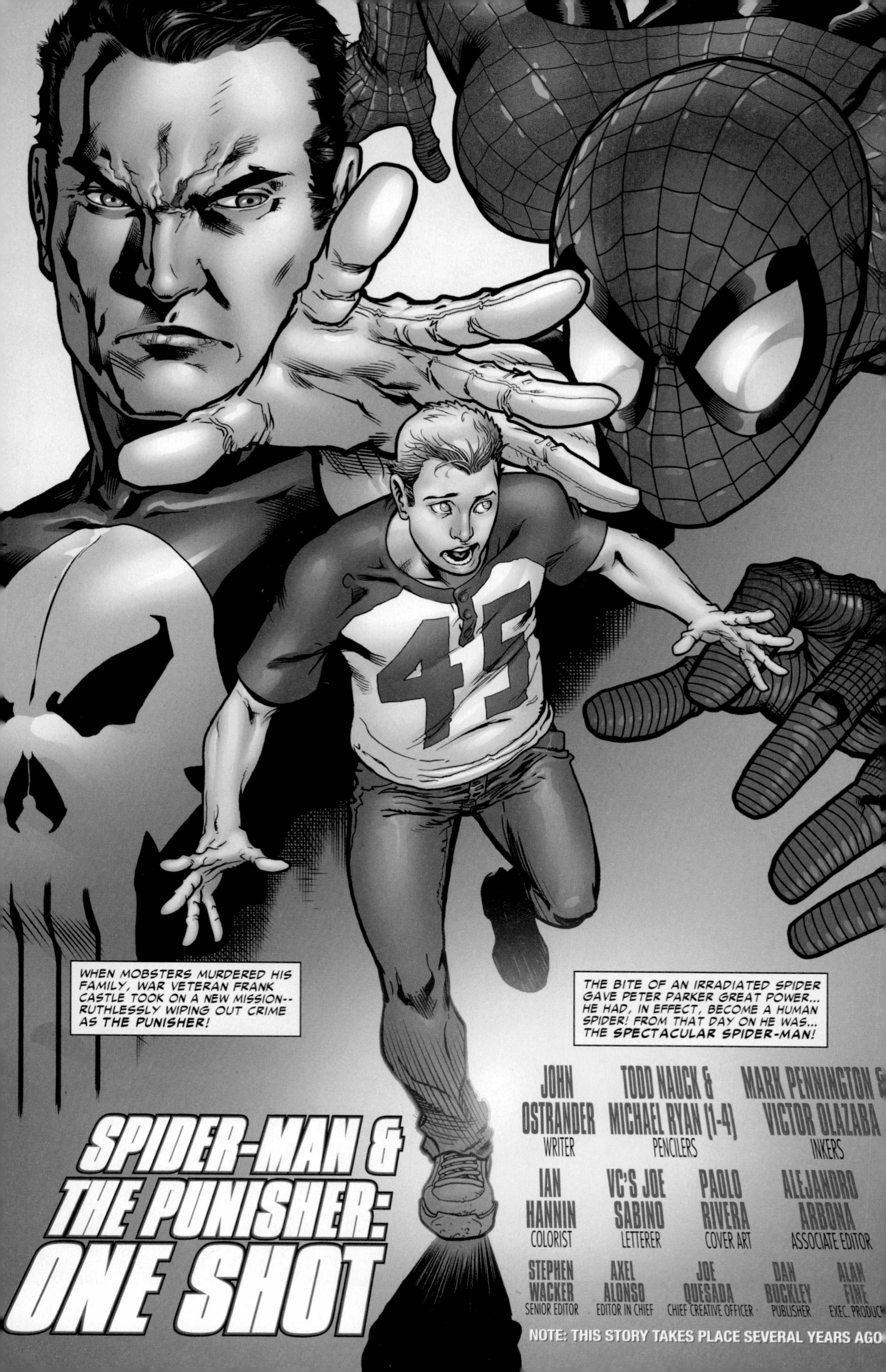
WHEN MOBSTERS MURDERED HIS FAMILY, WAR VETERAN FRANK CASTLE TOOK ON A NEW MISSION--RUTHLESSLY WIPING OUT CRIME AS THE PUNISHER!
THE BITE OF AN IRRADIATED SPIDER GAVE PETER PARKER GREAT POWER... HE HAD, IN EFFECT, BECOME A HUMAN SPIDER! FROM THAT DAY ON HE WAS... THE SPECTACULAR SPIDER-MAN!
45
SPIDER-MAN & THE PUNISHER: ONE SHOT
JOHN OSTRANDER WRITER
TODD NAUCK & MICHAEL RYAN (1-4) PENCILERS
MARK PENNINGTON & VICTOR OLAZABA INKERS
IAN HANNIN COLORIST
VC'S JOE SABINO LETTERER
PAOLO RIVERA COVER ART
ALEJANDRO ARBONA ASSOCIATE EDITOR
STEPHEN WACKER SENIOR EDITOR
AXEL ALONSO EDITOR IN CHIEF
JOE QUESADA CHIEF CREATIVE OFFICER
DAN BUCKLEY PUBLISHER
ALAN FINE EXEC. PRODUC
NOTE: THIS STORY TAKES PLACE SEVERAL YEARS AGO

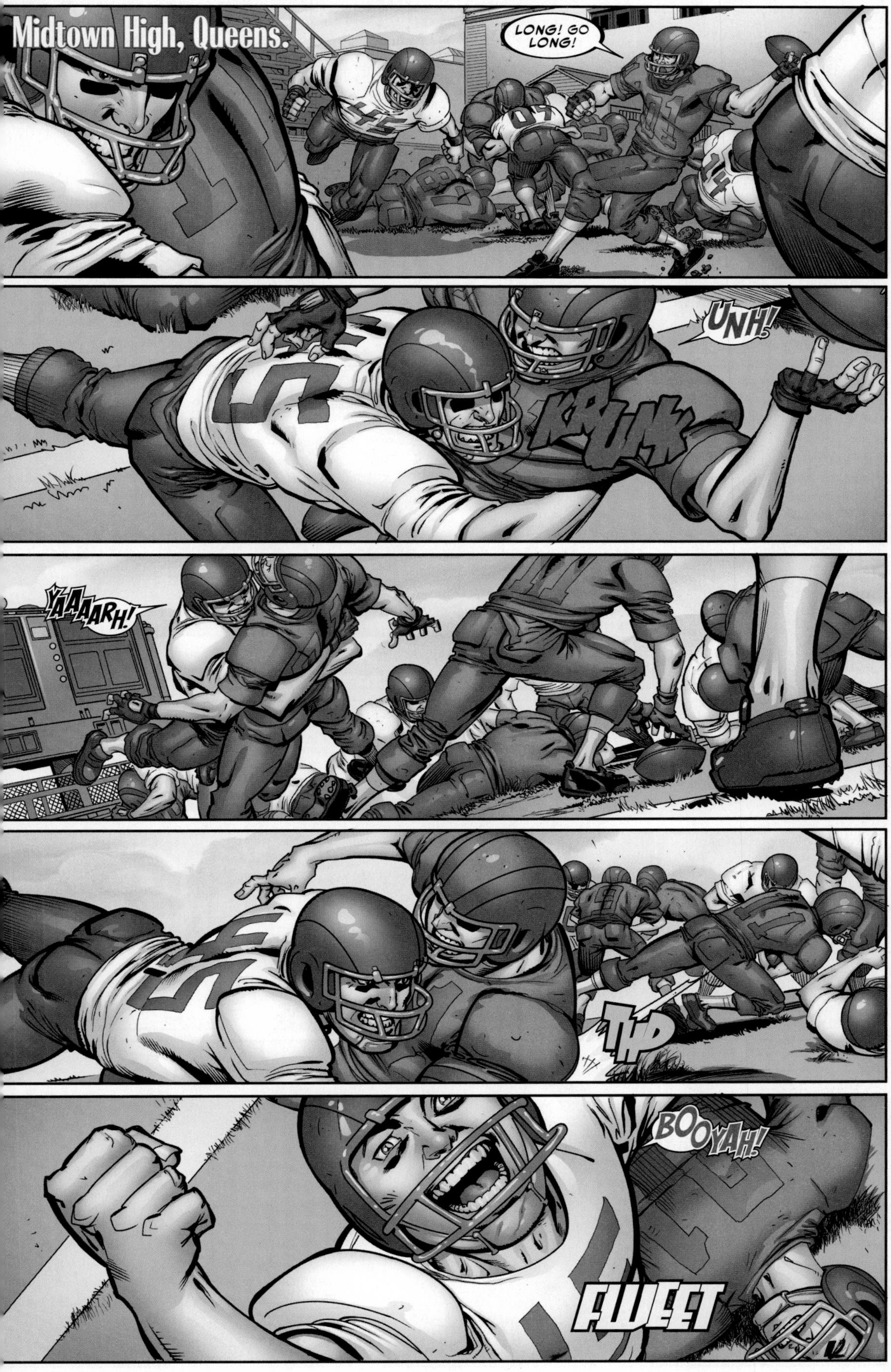
Midtown High, Queens.
LONG! GO LONG!
UNH!
KRUNK
YAAAARH!
THP
BOOYAH!
FWEET

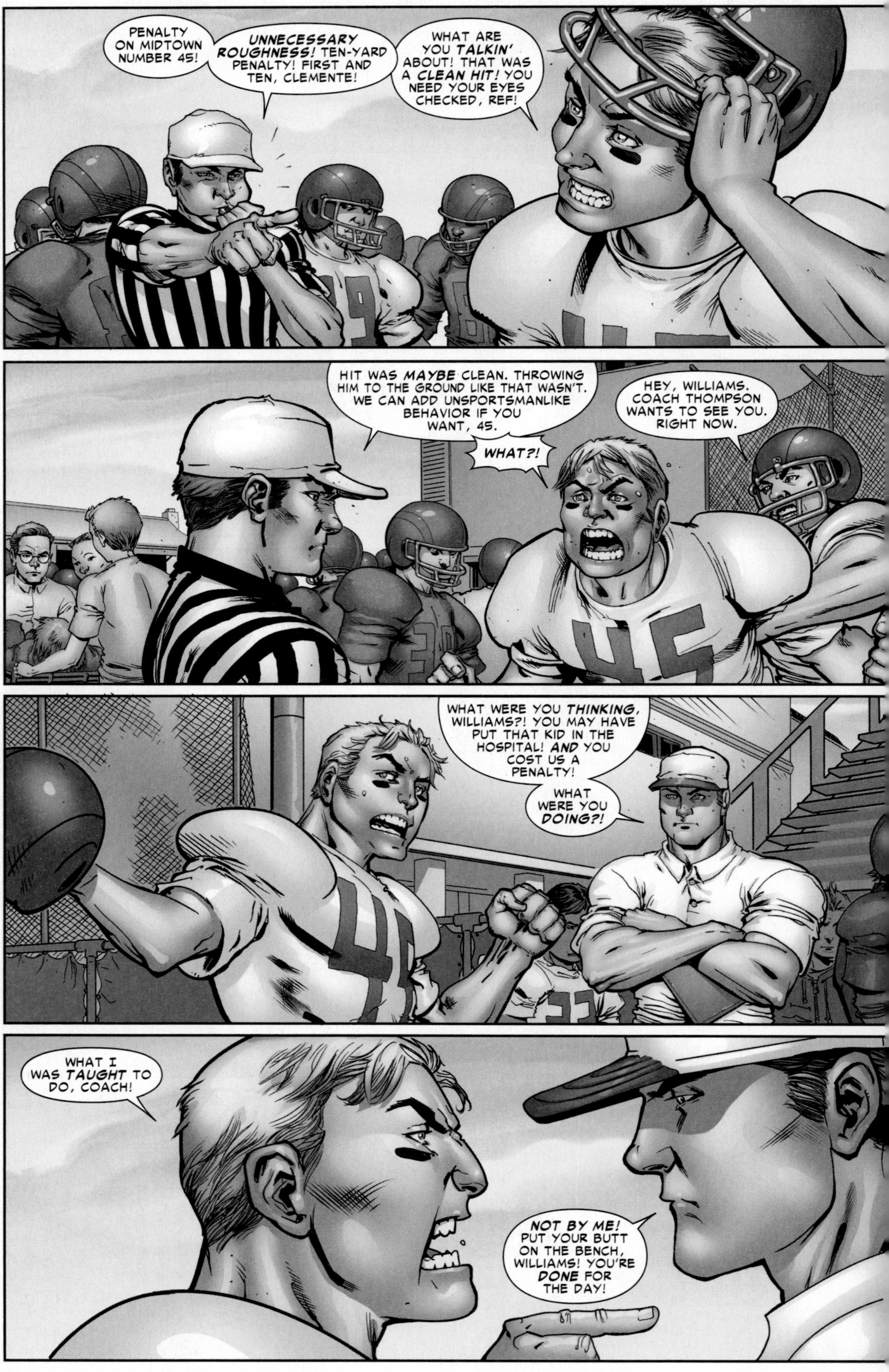
PENALTY ON MIDTOWN NUMBER 45!
UNNECESSARY ROUGHNESS! TEN-YARD PENALTY! FIRST AND TEN, CLEMENTE!
WHAT ARE YOU TALKIN' ABOUT! THAT WAS A CLEAN HIT! YOU NEED YOUR EYES CHECKED, REF!
HIT WAS MAYBE CLEAN. THROWING HIM TO THE GROUND LIKE THAT WASN'T. WE CAN ADD UNSPORTSMANLIKE BEHAVIOR IF YOU WANT, 45.
WHAT?!
HEY, WILLIAMS. COACH THOMPSON WANTS TO SEE YOU. RIGHT NOW.
WHAT WERE YOU THINKING, WILLIAMS?! YOU MAY HAVE PUT THAT KID IN THE HOSPITAL! AND YOU COST US A PENALTY!
WHAT WERE YOU DOING?!
WHAT I WAS TAUGHT TO DO, COACH!
NOT BY ME! PUT YOUR BUTT ON THE BENCH, WILLIAMS! YOU'RE DONE FOR THE DAY!

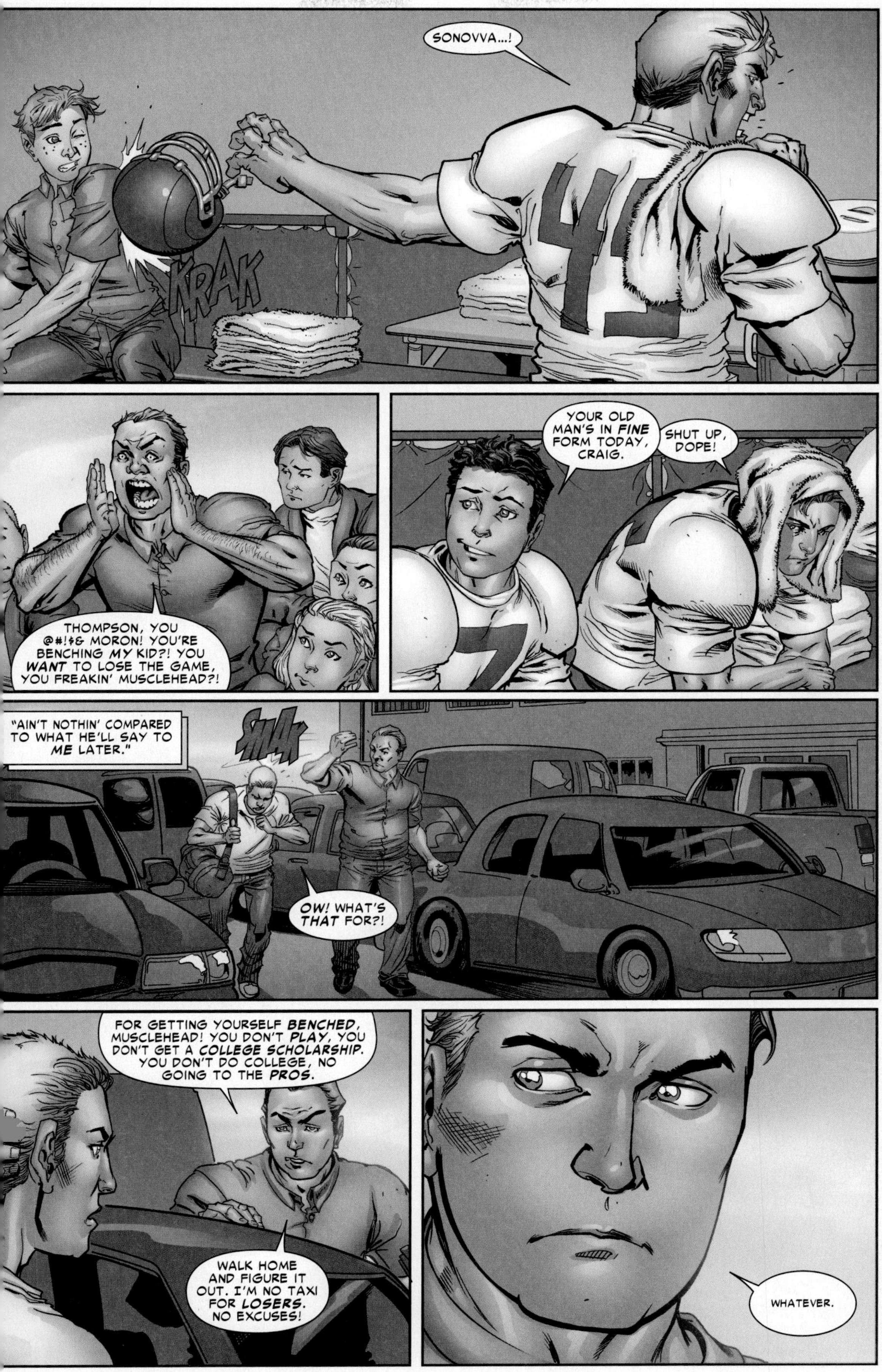
SONOVVA...!
KRAK
THOMPSON, YOU @#!$& MORON! YOU'RE BENCHING MY KID?! YOU WANT TO LOSE THE GAME, YOU FREAKIN' MUSCLEHEAD?!
YOUR OLD MAN'S IN FINE FORM TODAY, CRAIG.
SHUT UP, DOPE!
"AIN'T NOTHIN' COMPARED TO WHAT HE'LL SAY TO ME LATER."
SMAK
OW! WHAT'S THAT FOR?!
FOR GETTING YOURSELF BENCHED, MUSCLEHEAD! YOU DON'T PLAY, YOU DON'T GET A COLLEGE SCHOLARSHIP. YOU DON'T DO COLLEGE, NO GOING TO THE PROS.
WALK HOME AND FIGURE IT OUT. I'M NO TAXI FOR LOSERS. NO EXCUSES!
WHATEVER.

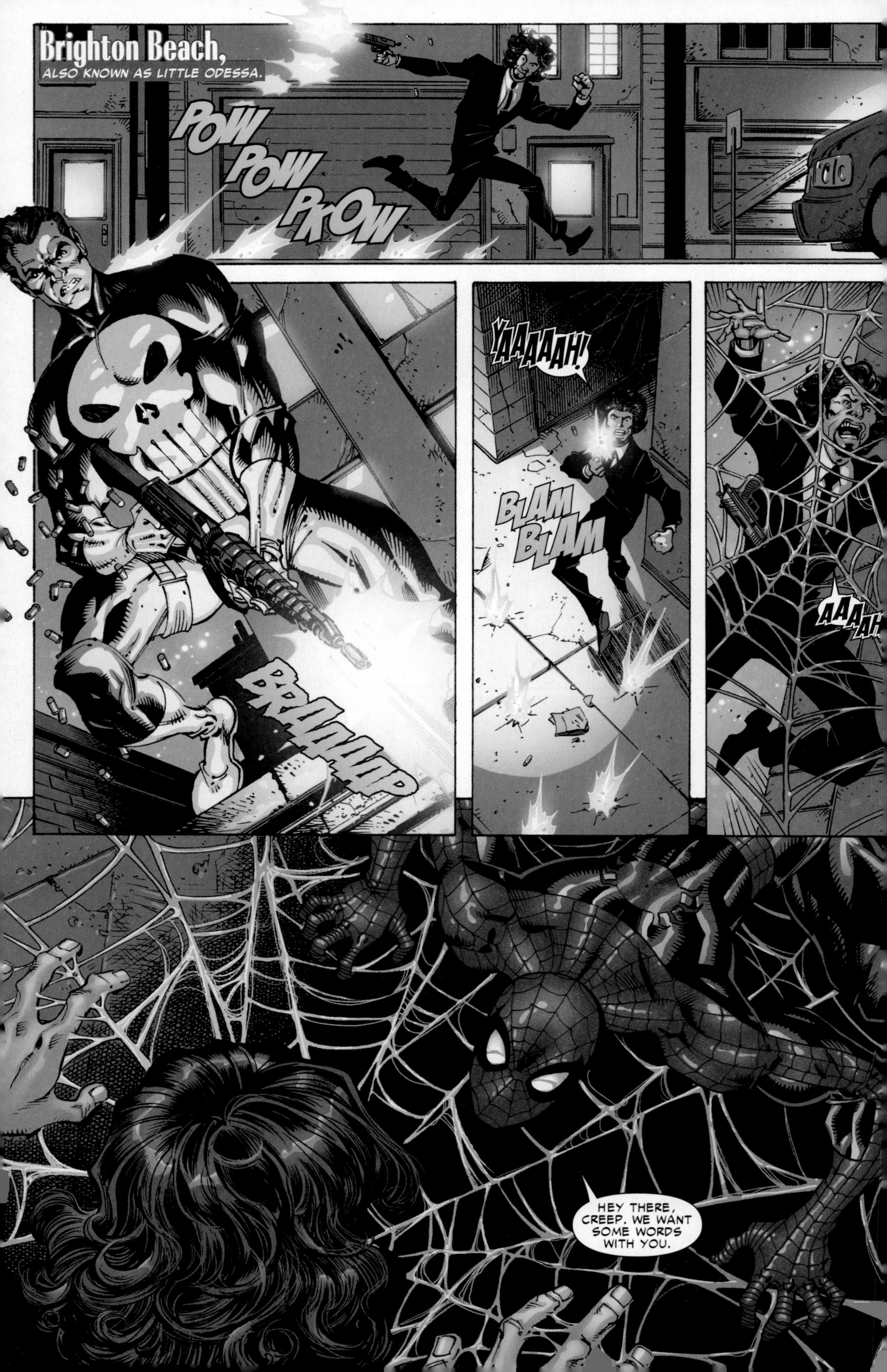
Brighton Beach,
ALSO KNOWN AS LITTLE ODESSA.
POW POW PKOW
BRAAAAP
YAAAAAH!
BLAM BLAM
AAAAH
HEY THERE, CREEP. WE WANT SOME WORDS WITH YOU.

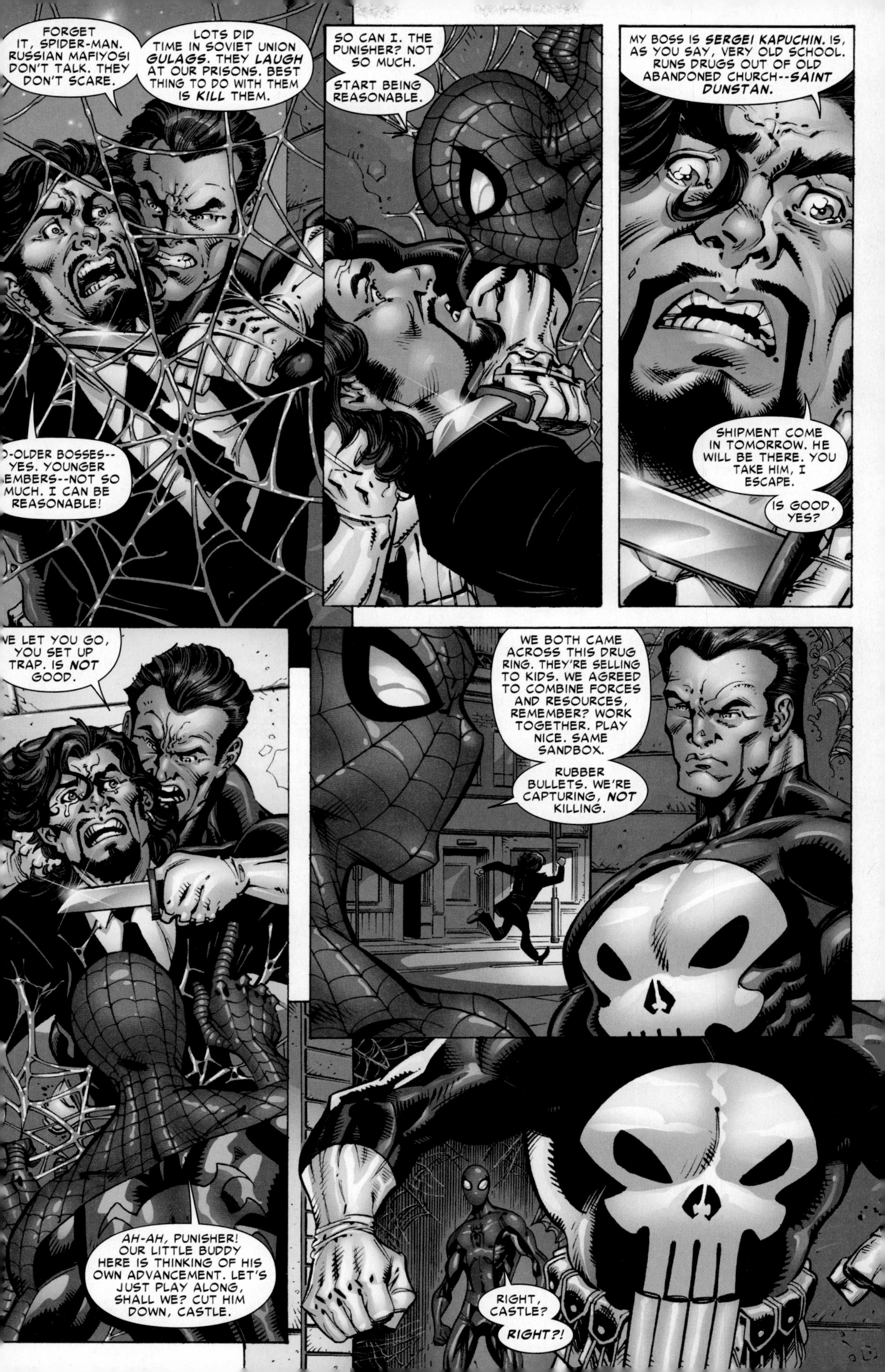
FORGET IT, SPIDER-MAN. RUSSIAN MAFIYOSI DON'T TALK. THEY DON'T SCARE.
LOTS DID TIME IN SOVIET UNION GULAGS. THEY LAUGH AT OUR PRISONS. BEST THING TO DO WITH THEM IS KILL THEM.
SO CAN I. THE PUNISHER? NOT SO MUCH.
START BEING REASONABLE.
MY BOSS IS SERGEI KAPUCHIN. IS, AS YOU SAY, VERY OLD SCHOOL. RUNS DRUGS OUT OF OLD ABANDONED CHURCH--SAINT DUNSTAN.
-OLDER BOSSES--YES. YOUNGER EMBERS--NOT SO MUCH. I CAN BE REASONABLE!
SHIPMENT COME IN TOMORROW. HE WILL BE THERE. YOU TAKE HIM, I ESCAPE.
IS GOOD, YES?
E LET YOU GO, YOU SET UP TRAP. IS NOT GOOD.
WE BOTH CAME ACROSS THIS DRUG RING. THEY'RE SELLING TO KIDS. WE AGREED TO COMBINE FORCES AND RESOURCES, REMEMBER? WORK TOGETHER. PLAY NICE. SAME SANDBOX.
RUBBER BULLETS. WE'RE CAPTURING, NOT KILLING.
AH-AH, PUNISHER! OUR LITTLE BUDDY HERE IS THINKING OF HIS OWN ADVANCEMENT. LET'S JUST PLAY ALONG, SHALL WE? CUT HIM DOWN, CASTLE.
RIGHT, CASTLE?
RIGHT?!

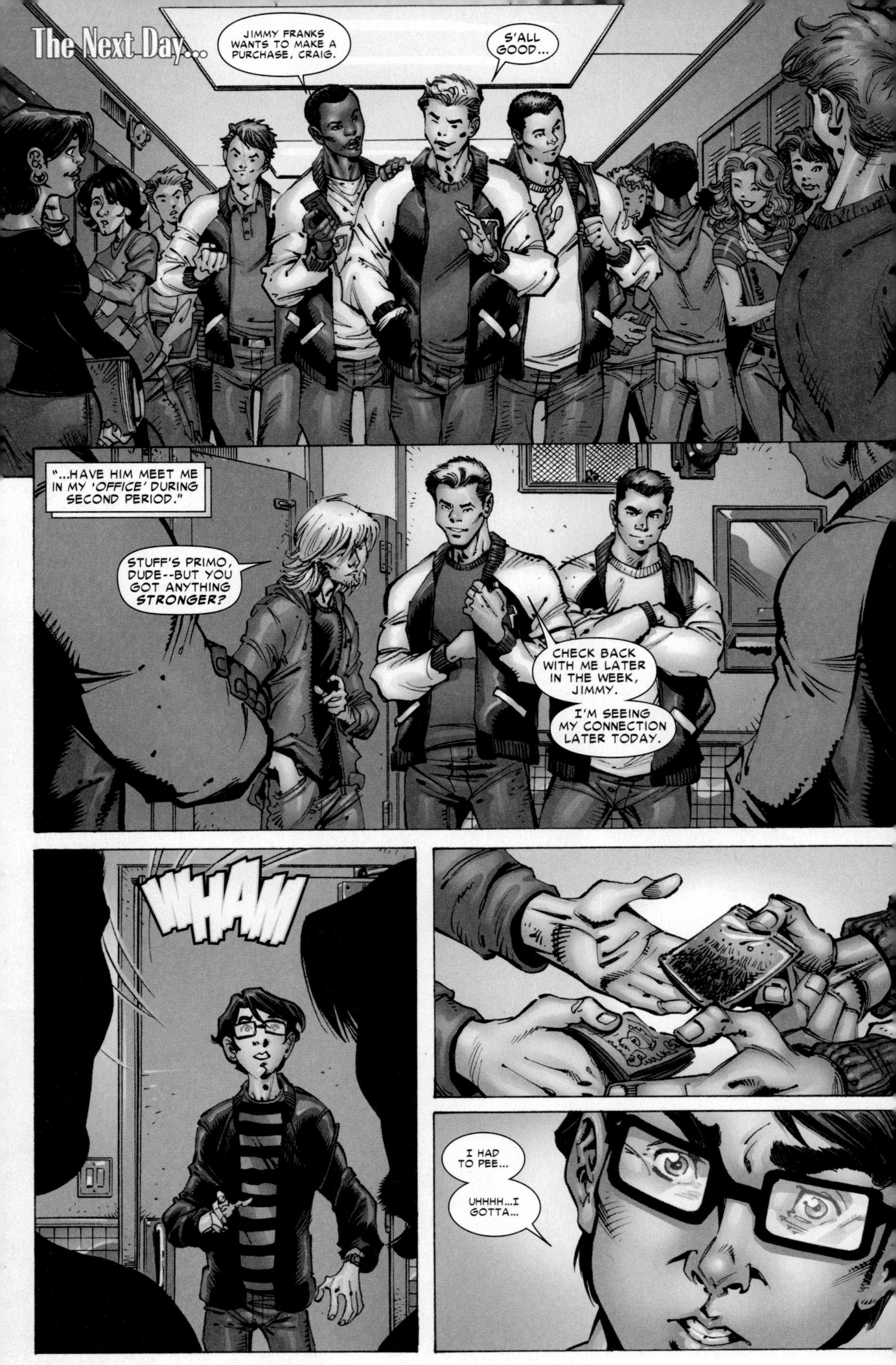
The Next Day...
JIMMY FRANKS WANTS TO MAKE A PURCHASE, CRAIG.
S'ALL GOOD...
"...HAVE HIM MEET ME IN MY 'OFFICE' DURING SECOND PERIOD."
STUFF'S PRIMO, DUDE--BUT YOU GOT ANYTHING STRONGER?
CHECK BACK WITH ME LATER IN THE WEEK, JIMMY.
I'M SEEING MY CONNECTION LATER TODAY.
WHAM
I HAD TO PEE...
UHHHH...I GOTTA...

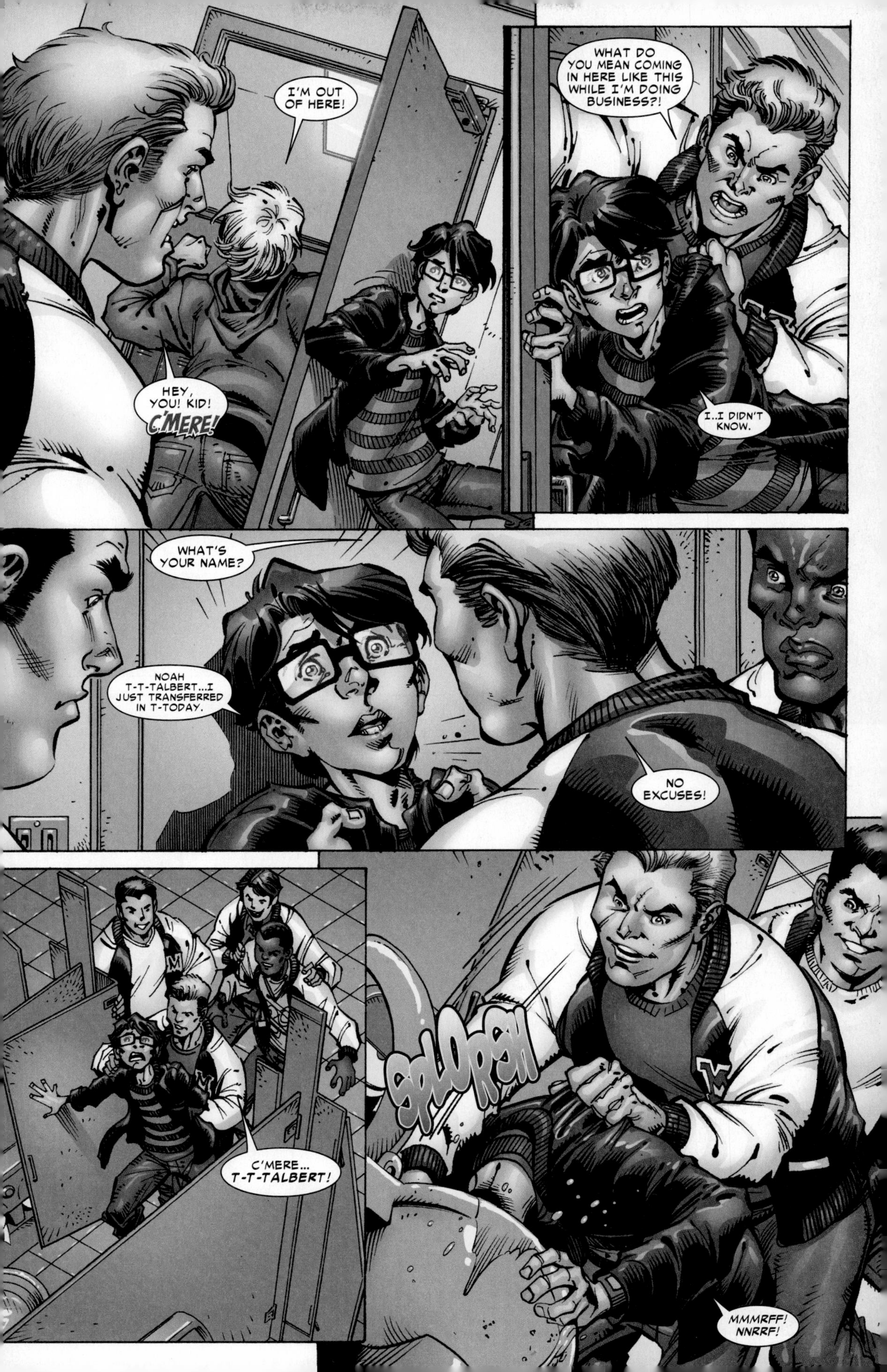
I'M OUT OF HERE!
HEY, YOU! KID! C'MERE!
WHAT DO YOU MEAN COMING IN HERE LIKE THIS WHILE I'M DOING BUSINESS?!
I..I DIDN'T KNOW.
WHAT'S YOUR NAME?
NOAH T-T-TALBERT...I JUST TRANSFERRED IN T-TODAY.
NO EXCUSES!
C'MERE... T-T-TALBERT!
SPLOOSH
MMMRFF! NNRRF!

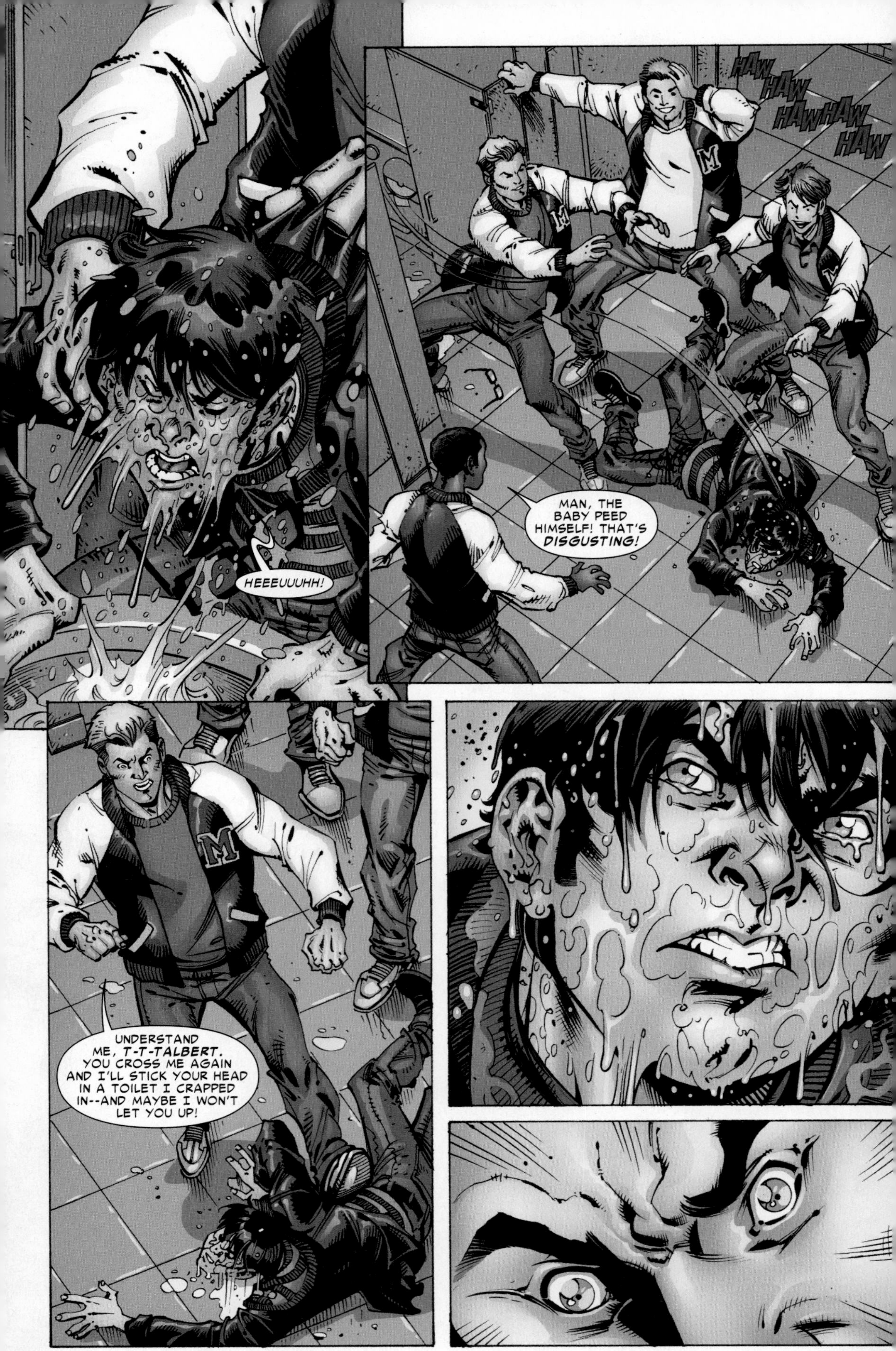
HEEEUUUHH!
HAW HAW HAW HAW HAW
MAN, THE BABY PEED HIMSELF! THAT'S *DISGUSTING!*
UNDERSTAND ME, *T-T-TALBERT.* YOU CROSS ME AGAIN AND I'LL STICK YOUR HEAD IN A TOILET I CRAPPED IN--AND MAYBE I WON'T LET YOU UP!

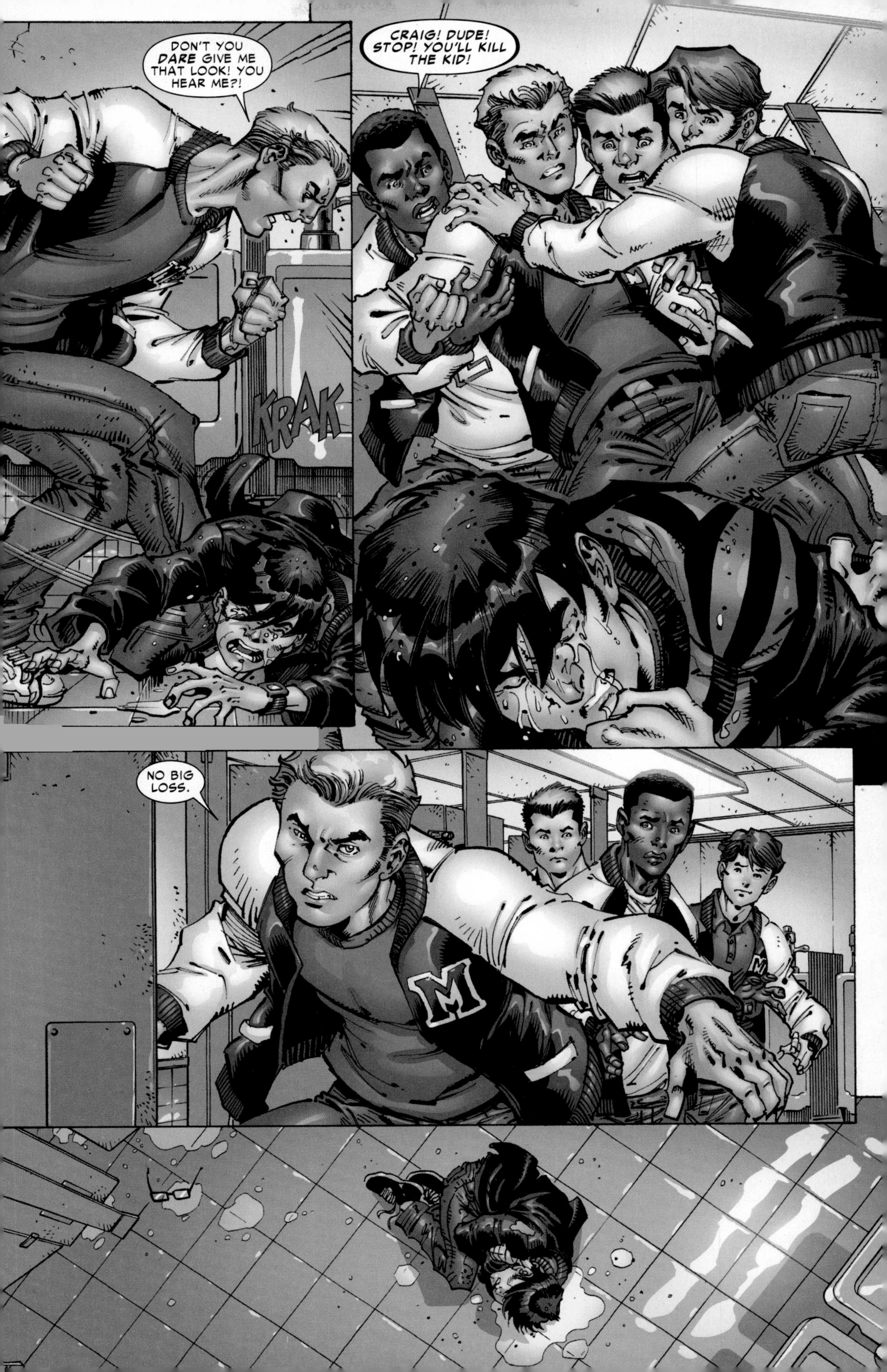
DON'T YOU DARE GIVE ME THAT LOOK! YOU HEAR ME?!
KRAK
CRAIG! DUDE! STOP! YOU'LL KILL THE KID!
NO BIG LOSS.

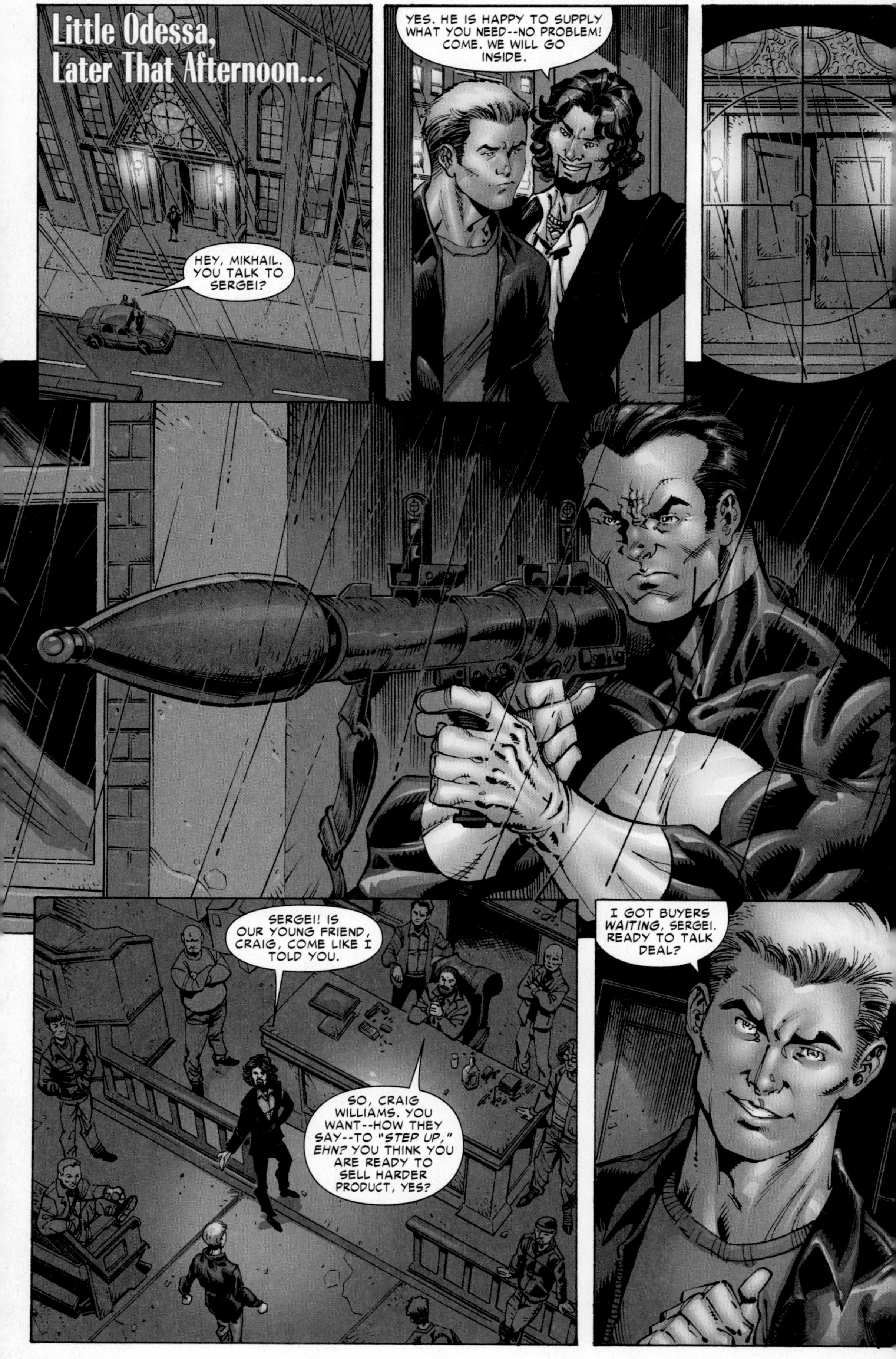
Little Odessa, Later That Afternoon...
HEY, MIKHAIL. YOU TALK TO SERGEI?
YES. HE IS HAPPY TO SUPPLY WHAT YOU NEED--NO PROBLEM! COME. WE WILL GO INSIDE.
SERGEI! IS OUR YOUNG FRIEND, CRAIG, COME LIKE I TOLD YOU.
SO, CRAIG WILLIAMS. YOU WANT--HOW THEY SAY--TO "STEP UP," EHN? YOU THINK YOU ARE READY TO SELL HARDER PRODUCT, YES?
I GOT BUYERS WAITING, SERGEI. READY TO TALK DEAL?

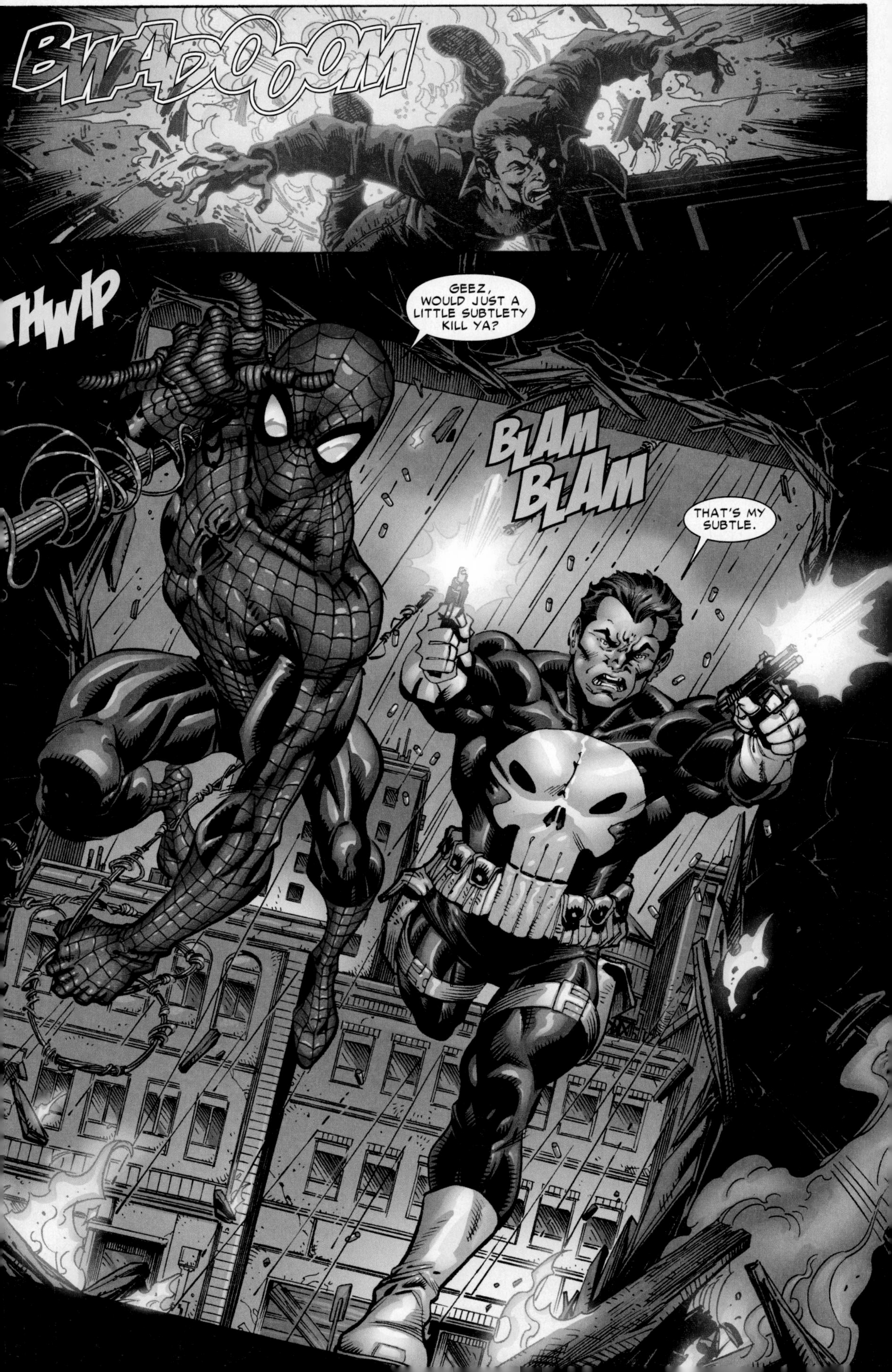
BWADOOOM
THWIP
GEEZ, WOULD JUST A LITTLE SUBTLETY KILL YA?
BLAM BLAM
THAT'S MY SUBTLE.

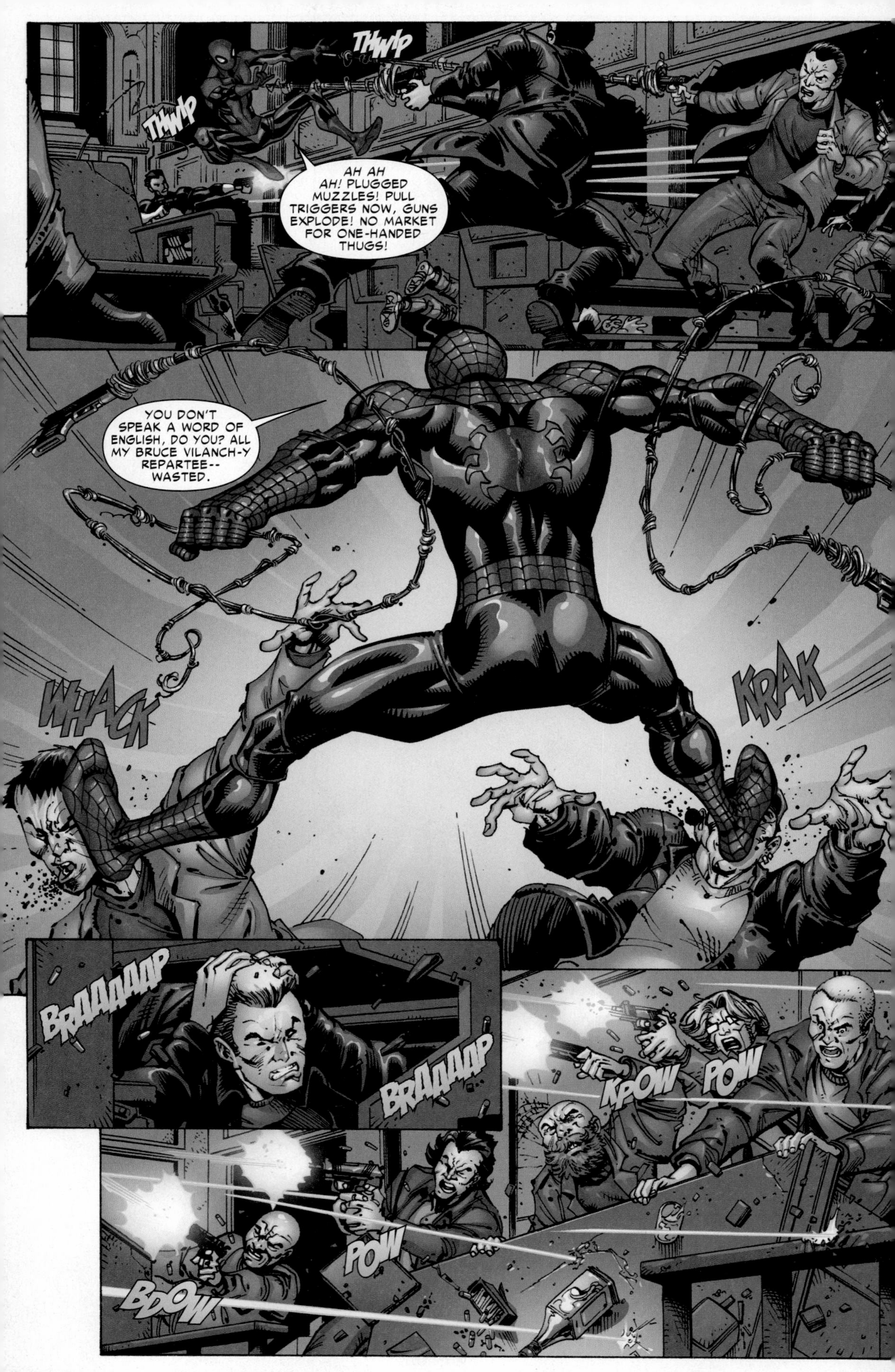

THWIP
THWIP
AH AH AH! PLUGGED MUZZLES! PULL TRIGGERS NOW, GUNS EXPLODE! NO MARKET FOR ONE-HANDED THUGS!
YOU DON'T SPEAK A WORD OF ENGLISH, DO YOU? ALL MY BRUCE VILANCH-Y REPARTEE--WASTED.
WHACK
KRAK
BRAAAAAP
BRAAAAP
KPOW
POW
POW
BDOW

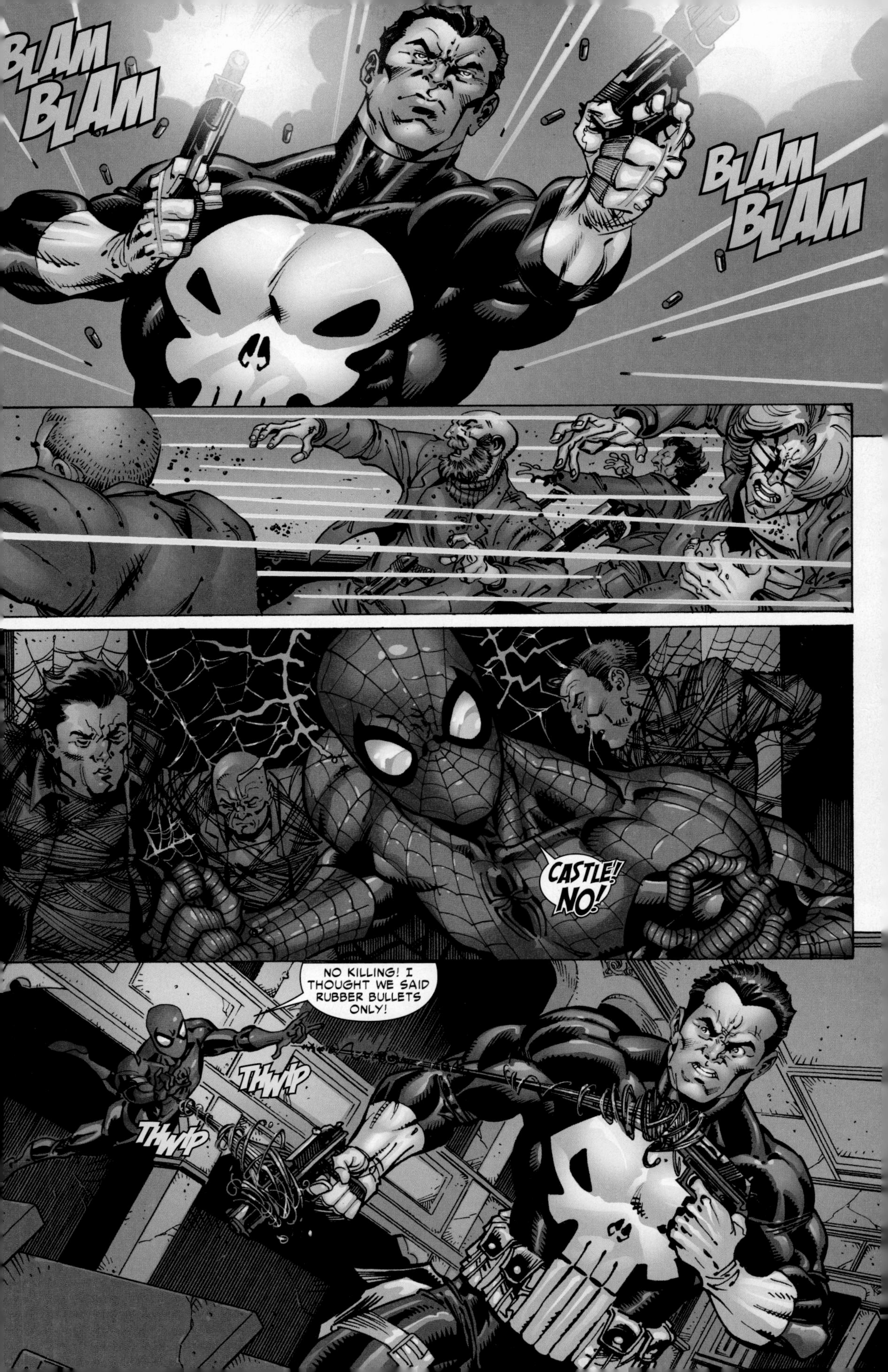
BLAM
BLAM
BLAM
BLAM
CASTLE! NO!
NO KILLING! I THOUGHT WE SAID RUBBER BULLETS ONLY!
THWIP
THWIP

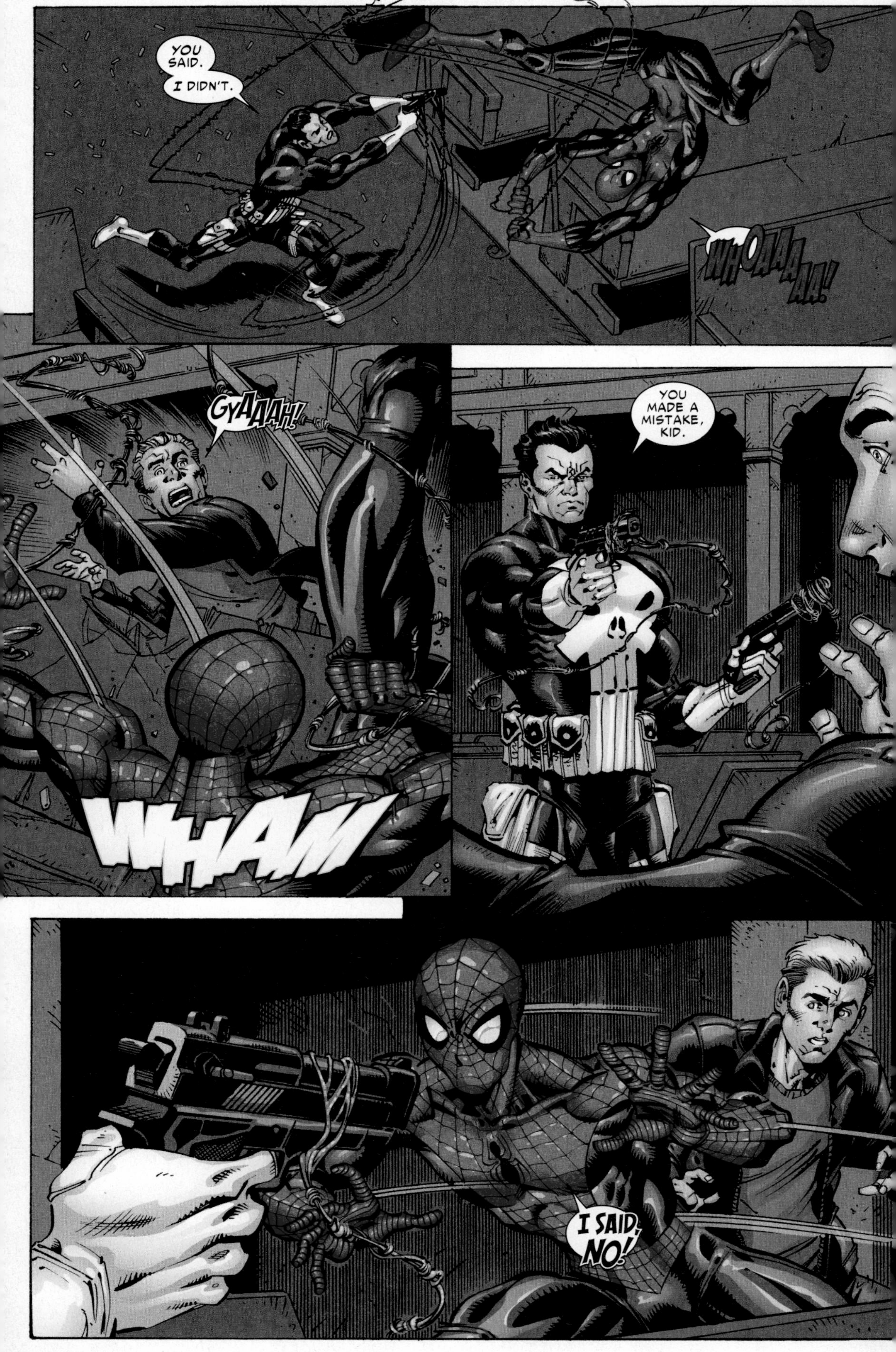
YOU SAID.
I DIDN'T.
WHOAAAAA!
GYAAAH!
WHAM
YOU MADE A MISTAKE, KID.
I SAID, NO!

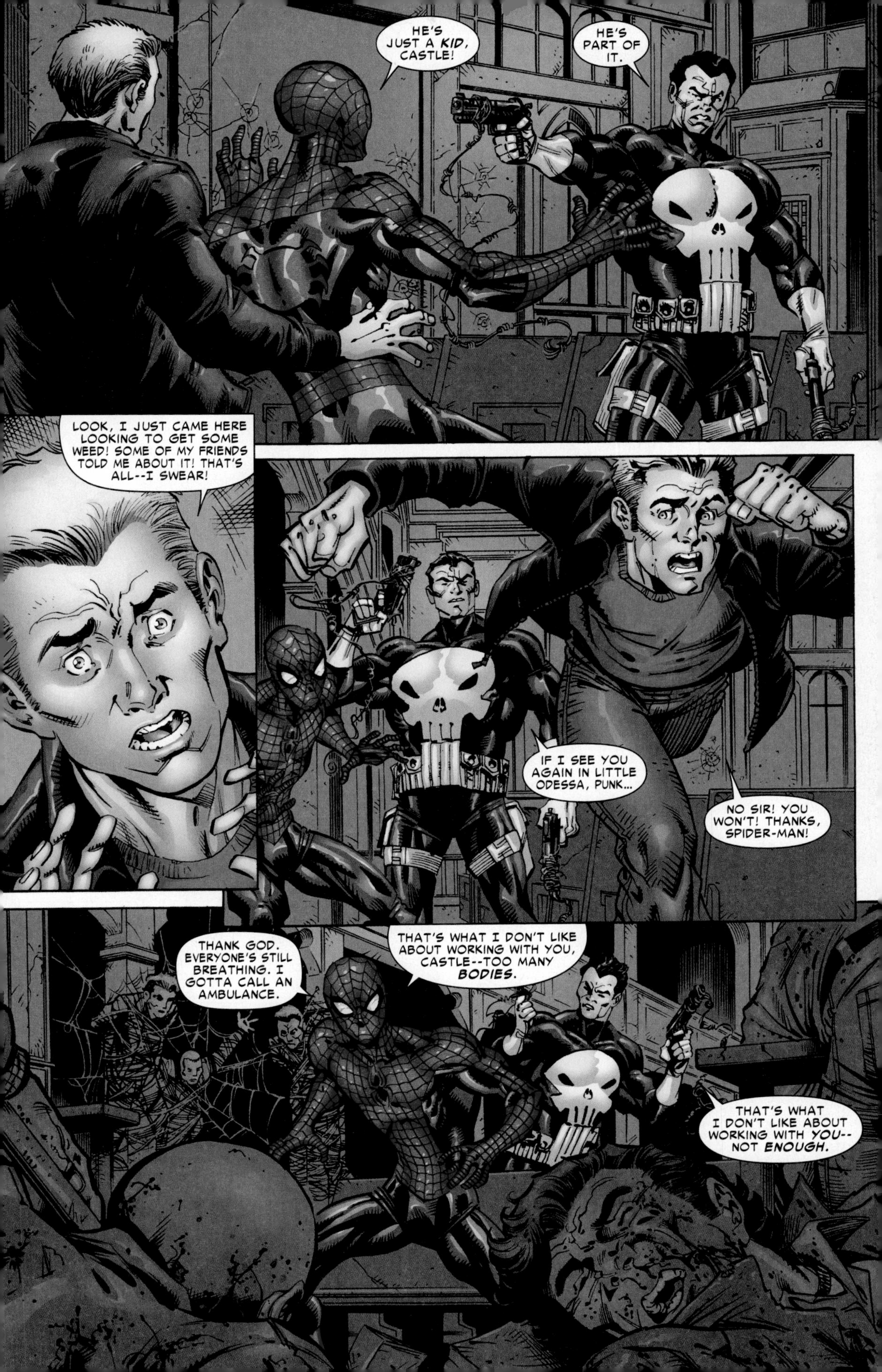

HE'S JUST A *KID*, CASTLE!
HE'S PART OF IT.
LOOK, I JUST CAME HERE LOOKING TO GET SOME WEED! SOME OF MY FRIENDS TOLD ME ABOUT IT! THAT'S ALL--I SWEAR!
IF I SEE YOU AGAIN IN LITTLE ODESSA, PUNK...
NO SIR! YOU WON'T! THANKS, SPIDER-MAN!
THANK GOD. EVERYONE'S STILL BREATHING. I GOTTA CALL AN AMBULANCE.
THAT'S WHAT I DON'T LIKE ABOUT WORKING WITH YOU, CASTLE--TOO MANY *BODIES*.
THAT'S WHAT I DON'T LIKE ABOUT WORKING WITH *YOU*--NOT *ENOUGH*.

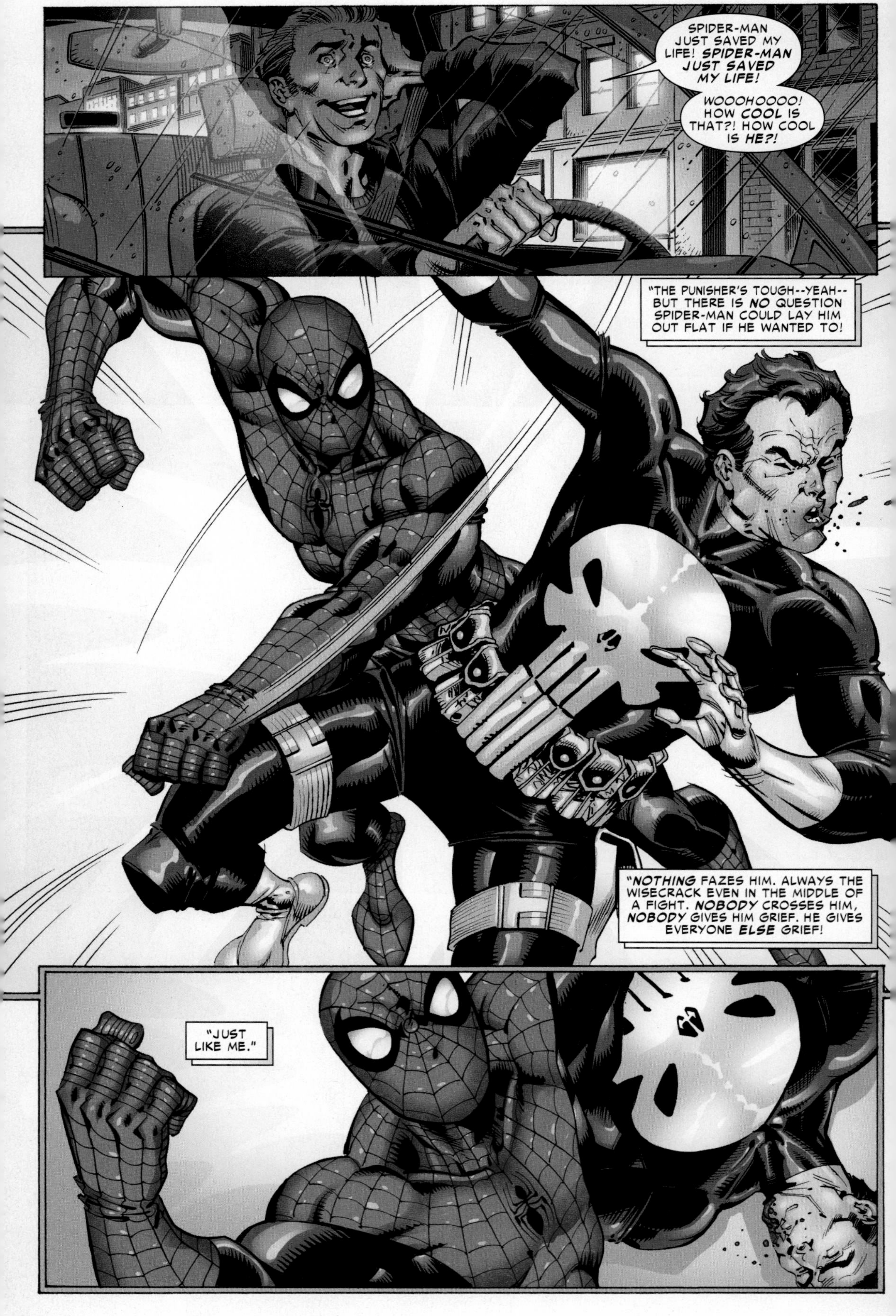
SPIDER-MAN JUST SAVED MY LIFE! SPIDER-MAN JUST SAVED MY LIFE!
WOOOHOOOO! HOW COOL IS THAT?! HOW COOL IS HE?!
"THE PUNISHER'S TOUGH--YEAH--BUT THERE IS NO QUESTION SPIDER-MAN COULD LAY HIM OUT FLAT IF HE WANTED TO!
"NOTHING FAZES HIM. ALWAYS THE WISECRACK EVEN IN THE MIDDLE OF A FIGHT. NOBODY CROSSES HIM, NOBODY GIVES HIM GRIEF. HE GIVES EVERYONE ELSE GRIEF!
"JUST LIKE ME."

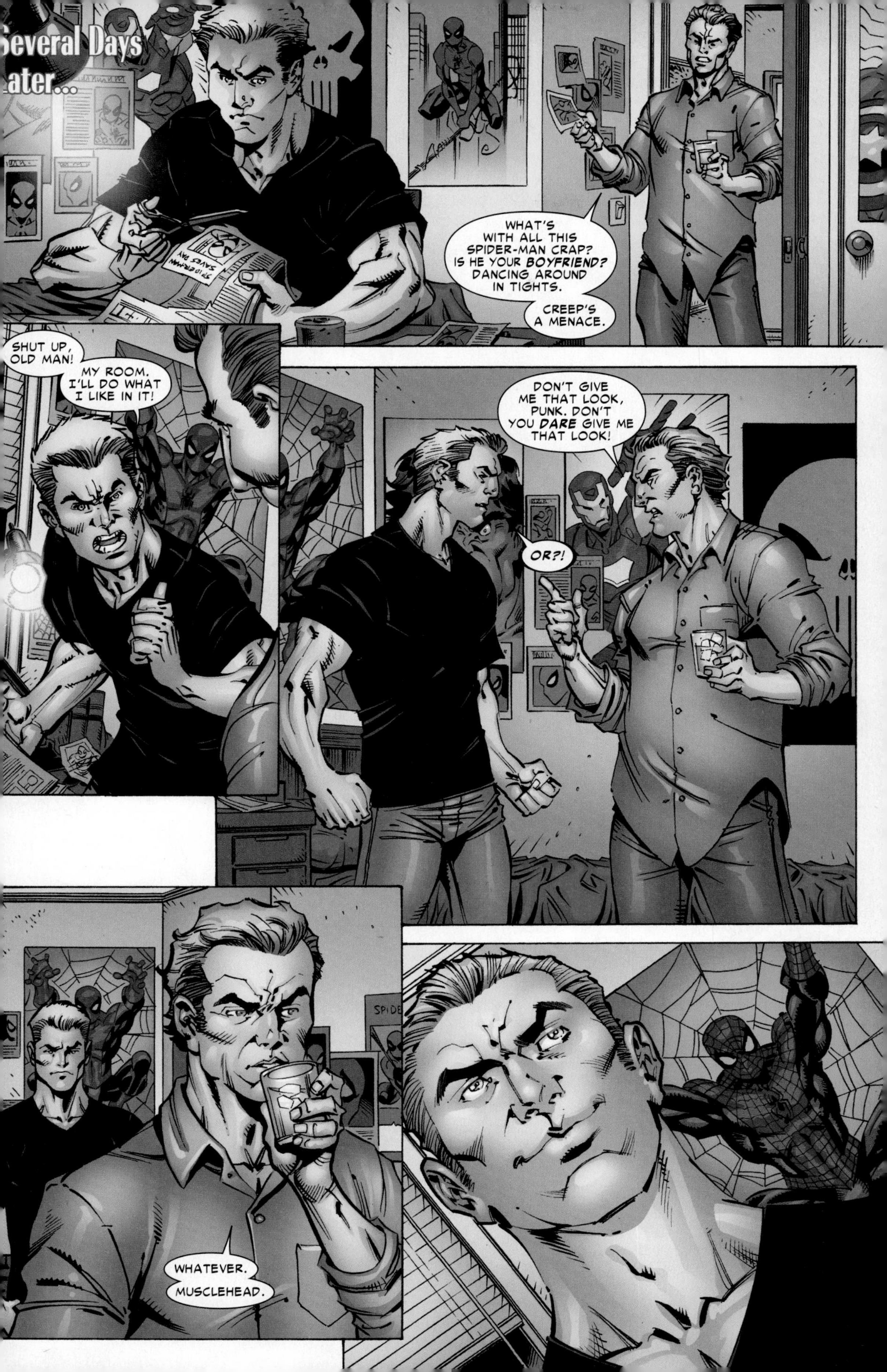
Several Days Later...
SPIDER-MAN SAVES DAY
WHAT'S WITH ALL THIS SPIDER-MAN CRAP? IS HE YOUR BOYFRIEND? DANCING AROUND IN TIGHTS.
CREEP'S A MENACE.
SHUT UP, OLD MAN!
MY ROOM. I'LL DO WHAT I LIKE IN IT!
DON'T GIVE ME THAT LOOK, PUNK. DON'T YOU DARE GIVE ME THAT LOOK!
OR?!
WHATEVER.
MUSCLEHEAD.

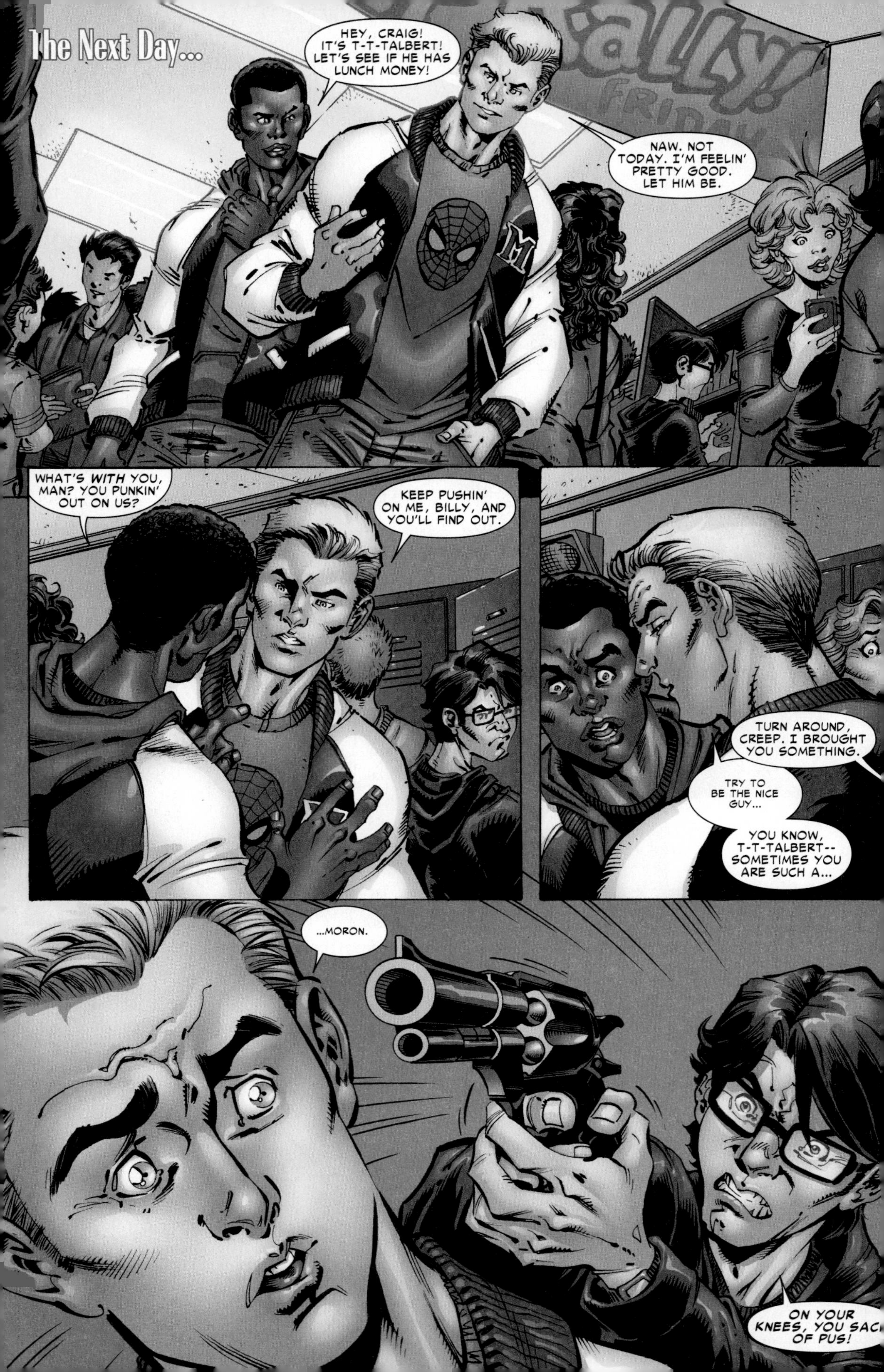
The Next Day...
HEY, CRAIG! IT'S T-T-TALBERT! LET'S SEE IF HE HAS LUNCH MONEY!
NAW. NOT TODAY. I'M FEELIN' PRETTY GOOD. LET HIM BE.
WHAT'S WITH YOU, MAN? YOU PUNKIN' OUT ON US?
KEEP PUSHIN' ON ME, BILLY, AND YOU'LL FIND OUT.
TURN AROUND, CREEP. I BROUGHT YOU SOMETHING.
TRY TO BE THE NICE GUY...
YOU KNOW, T-T-TALBERT-- SOMETIMES YOU ARE SUCH A...
...MORON.
ON YOUR KNEES, YOU SAC OF PUS!

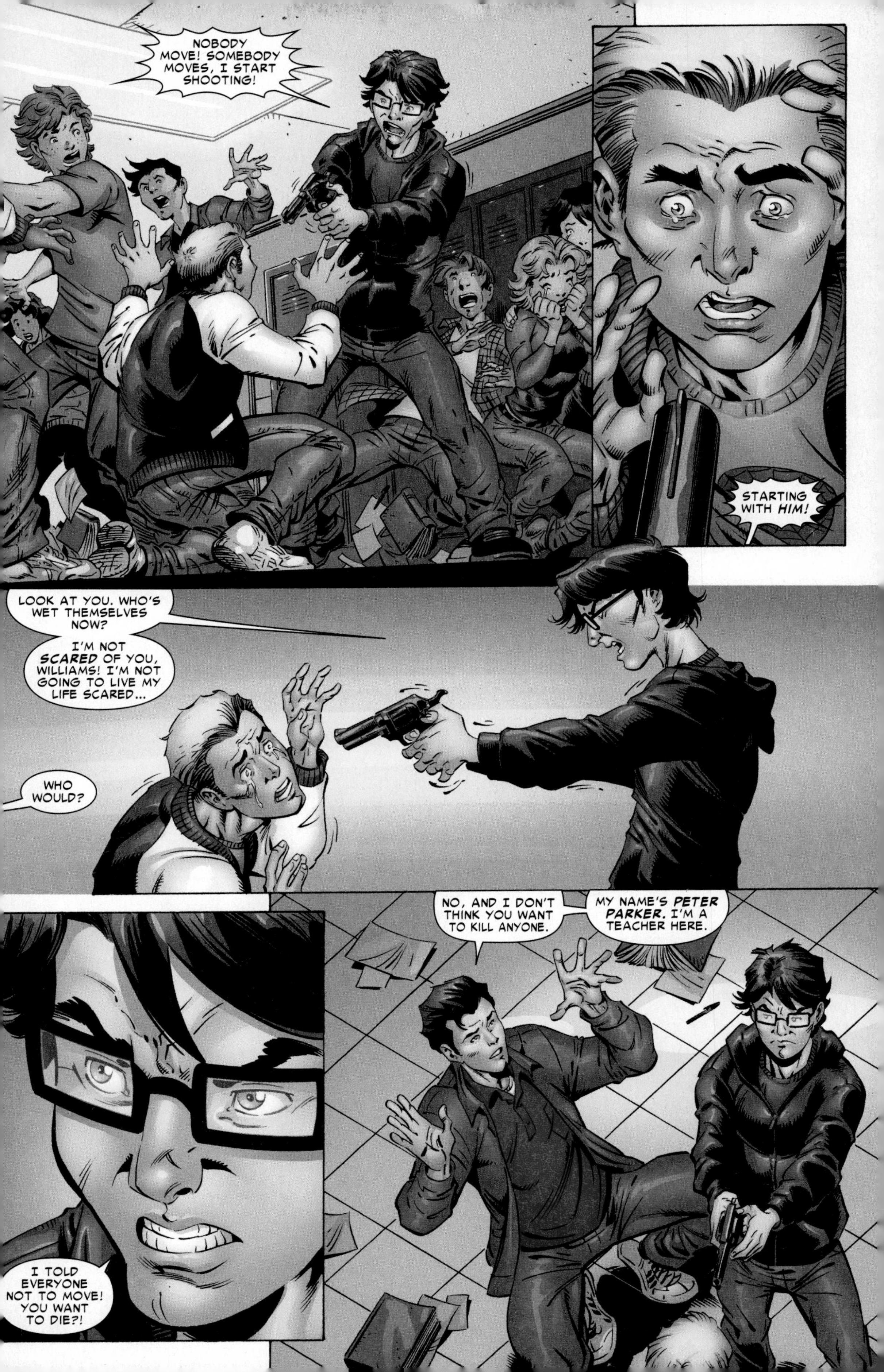
NOBODY MOVE! SOMEBODY MOVES, I START SHOOTING!
STARTING WITH HIM!
LOOK AT YOU. WHO'S WET THEMSELVES NOW?
I'M NOT SCARED OF YOU, WILLIAMS! I'M NOT GOING TO LIVE MY LIFE SCARED...
WHO WOULD?
I TOLD EVERYONE NOT TO MOVE! YOU WANT TO DIE?!
NO, AND I DON'T THINK YOU WANT TO KILL ANYONE.
MY NAME'S PETER PARKER. I'M A TEACHER HERE.

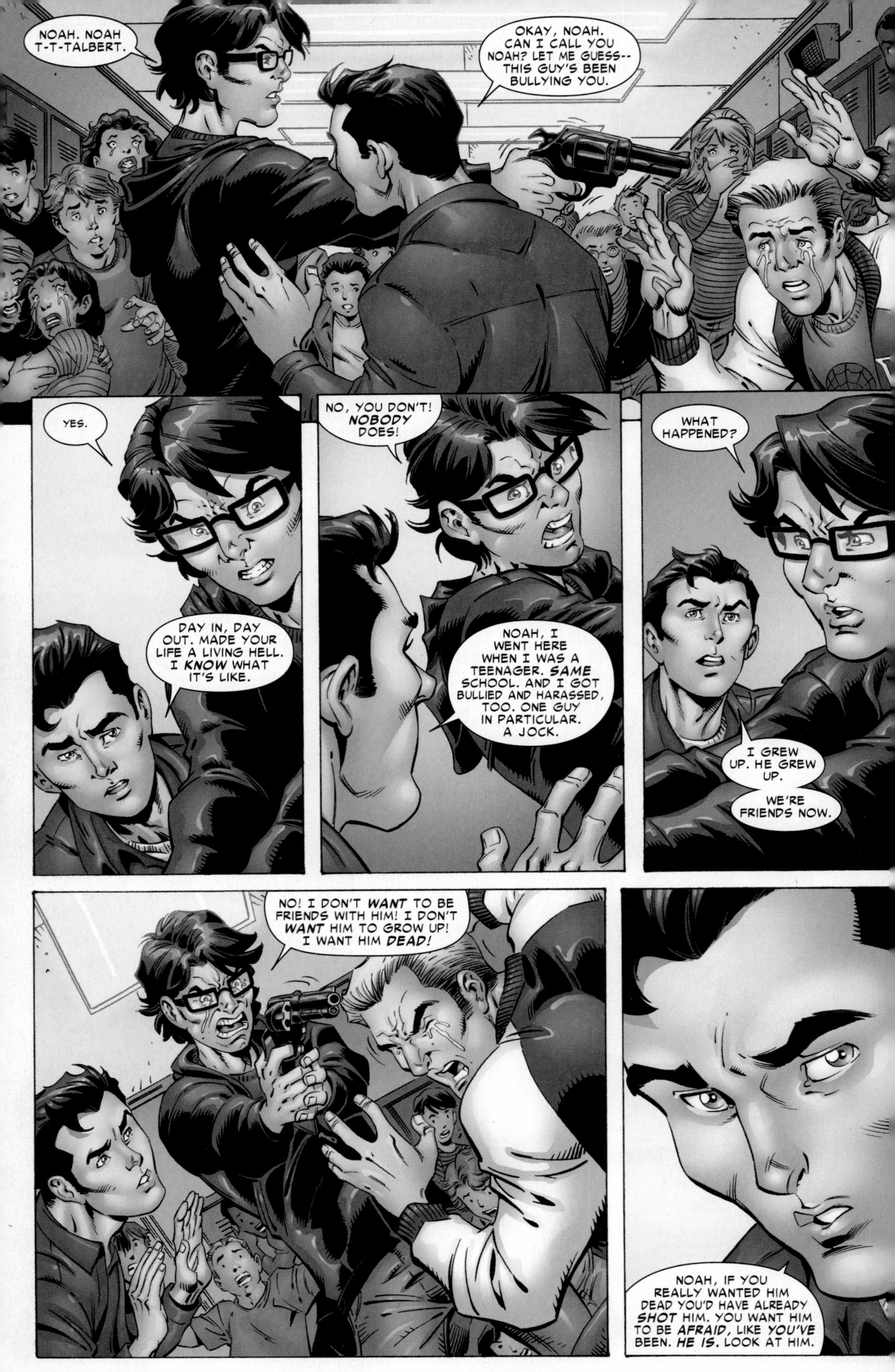
NOAH. NOAH T-T-TALBERT.
OKAY, NOAH. CAN I CALL YOU NOAH? LET ME GUESS-- THIS GUY'S BEEN BULLYING YOU.
YES.
DAY IN, DAY OUT. MADE YOUR LIFE A LIVING HELL. I KNOW WHAT IT'S LIKE.
NO, YOU DON'T! NOBODY DOES!
NOAH, I WENT HERE WHEN I WAS A TEENAGER. SAME SCHOOL. AND I GOT BULLIED AND HARASSED, TOO. ONE GUY IN PARTICULAR. A JOCK.
WHAT HAPPENED?
I GREW UP. HE GREW UP.
WE'RE FRIENDS NOW.
NO! I DON'T WANT TO BE FRIENDS WITH HIM! I DON'T WANT HIM TO GROW UP! I WANT HIM DEAD!
NOAH, IF YOU REALLY WANTED HIM DEAD YOU'D HAVE ALREADY SHOT HIM. YOU WANT HIM TO BE AFRAID, LIKE YOU'VE BEEN. HE IS. LOOK AT HIM.

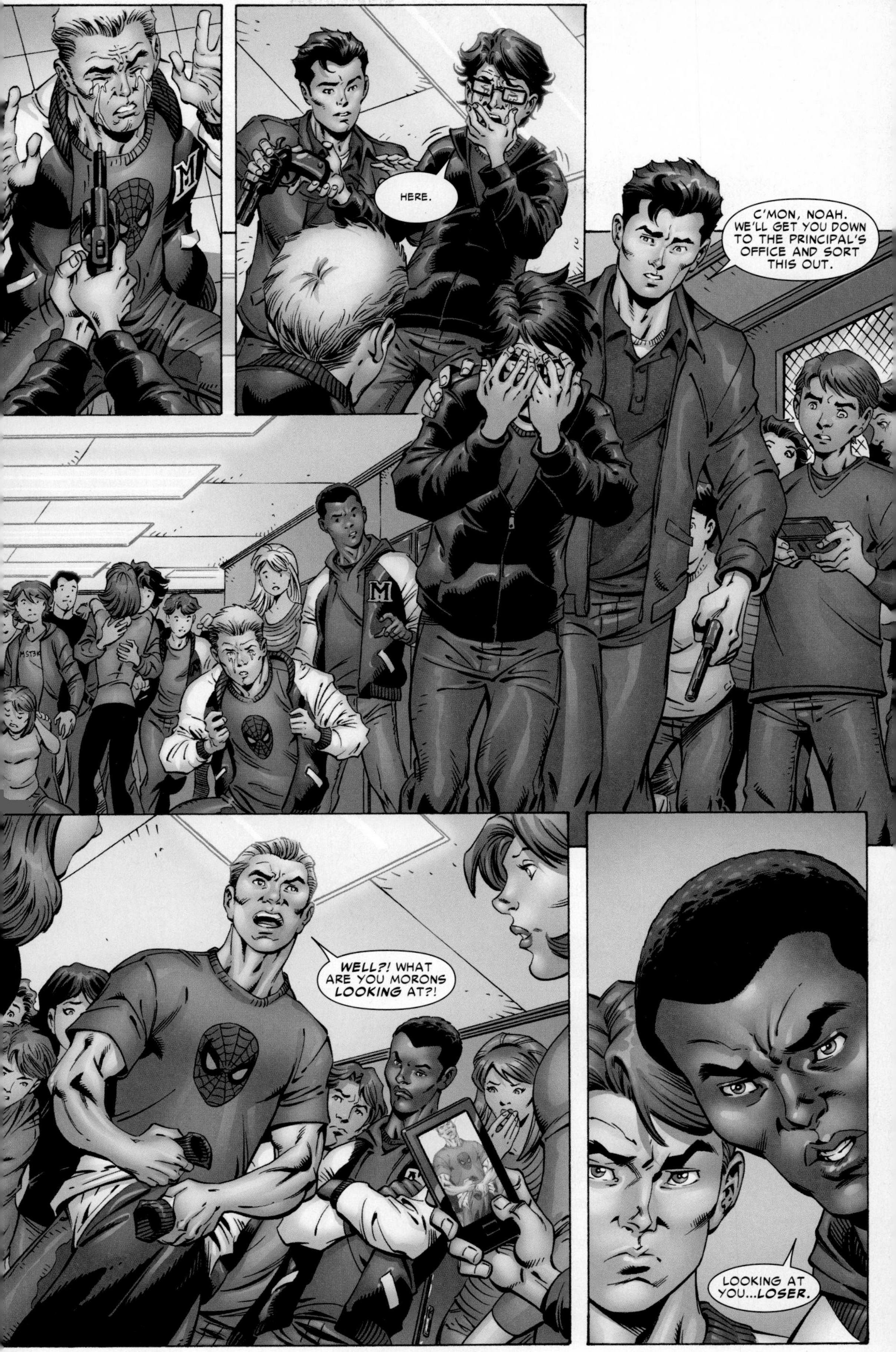
HERE.
C'MON, NOAH. WE'LL GET YOU DOWN TO THE PRINCIPAL'S OFFICE AND SORT THIS OUT.
WELL?! WHAT ARE YOU MORONS LOOKING AT?!
LOOKING AT YOU...LOSER.

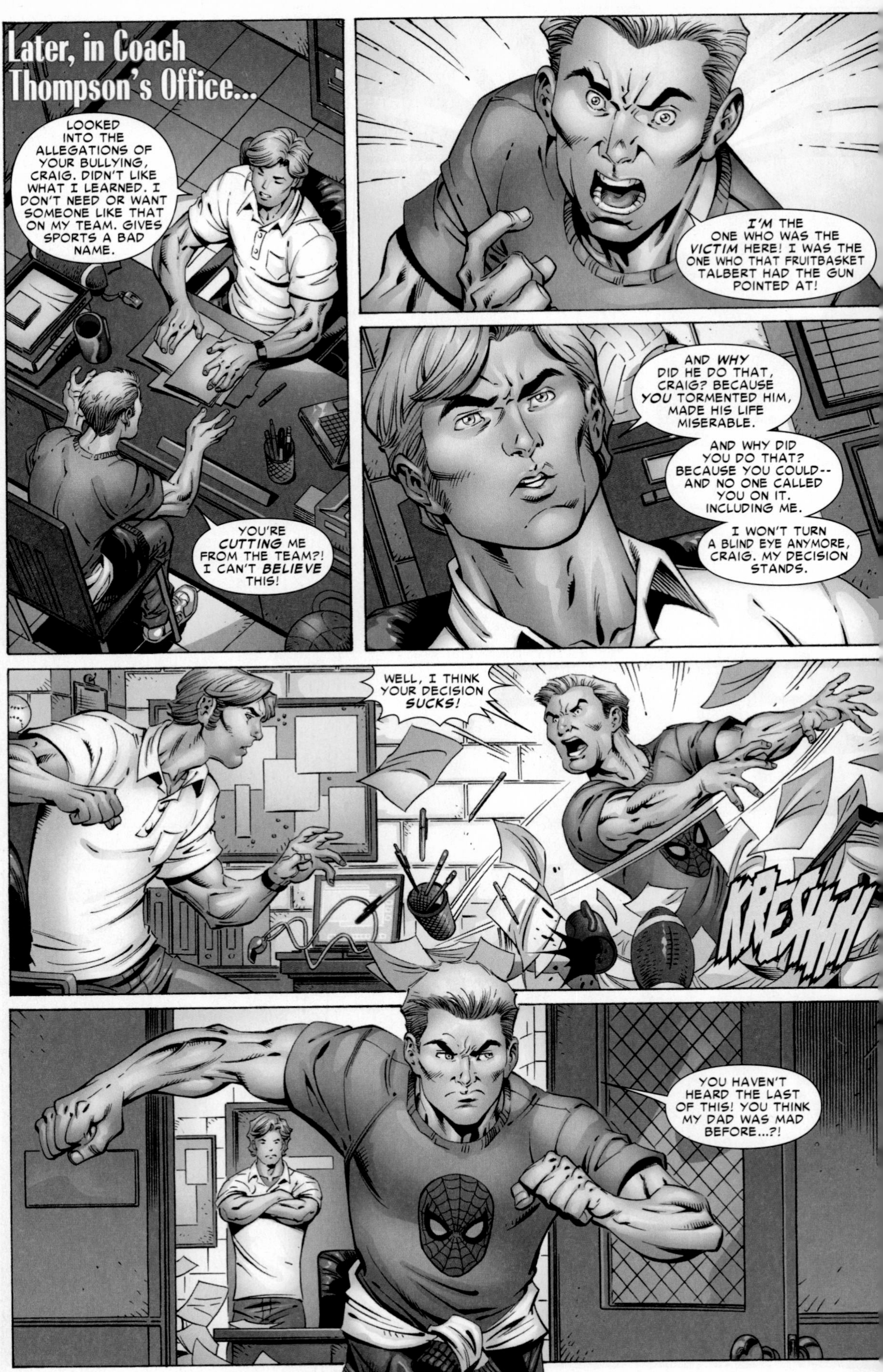

Later, in Coach Thompson's Office...
LOOKED INTO THE ALLEGATIONS OF YOUR BULLYING, CRAIG. DIDN'T LIKE WHAT I LEARNED. I DON'T NEED OR WANT SOMEONE LIKE THAT ON MY TEAM. GIVES SPORTS A BAD NAME.
YOU'RE CUTTING ME FROM THE TEAM?! I CAN'T BELIEVE THIS!
I'M THE ONE WHO WAS THE VICTIM HERE! I WAS THE ONE WHO THAT FRUITBASKET TALBERT HAD THE GUN POINTED AT!
AND WHY DID HE DO THAT, CRAIG? BECAUSE YOU TORMENTED HIM, MADE HIS LIFE MISERABLE.
AND WHY DID YOU DO THAT? BECAUSE YOU COULD-- AND NO ONE CALLED YOU ON IT. INCLUDING ME.
I WON'T TURN A BLIND EYE ANYMORE, CRAIG. MY DECISION STANDS.
WELL, I THINK YOUR DECISION SUCKS!
KRESHHH
YOU HAVEN'T HEARD THE LAST OF THIS! YOU THINK MY DAD WAS MAD BEFORE...?!

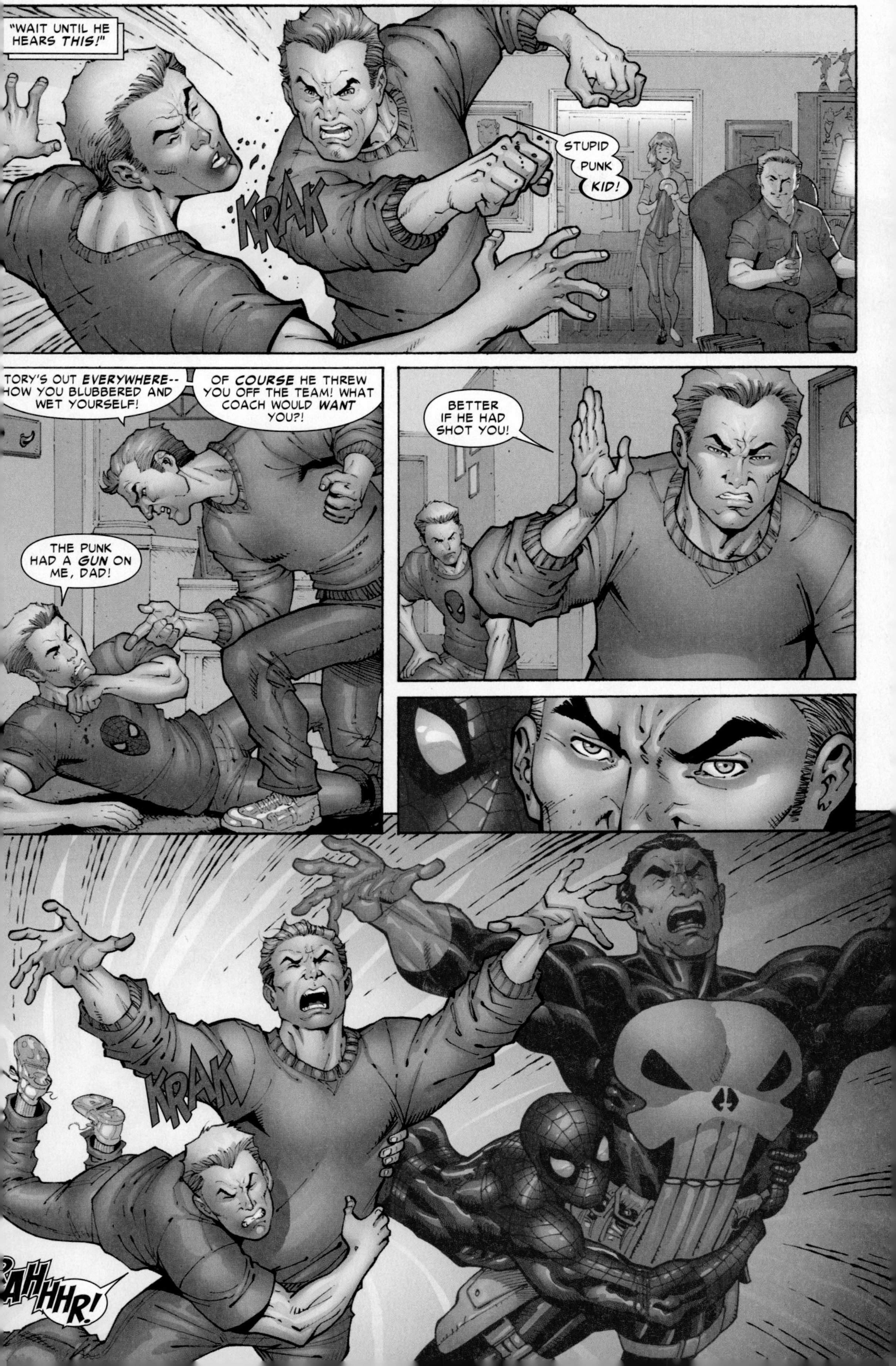
"WAIT UNTIL HE HEARS THIS!"
STUPID PUNK KID!
KRAK
TORY'S OUT EVERYWHERE-- HOW YOU BLUBBERED AND WET YOURSELF!
OF COURSE HE THREW YOU OFF THE TEAM! WHAT COACH WOULD WANT YOU?!
THE PUNK HAD A GUN ON ME, DAD!
BETTER IF HE HAD SHOT YOU!
KRAK
AHHHR!

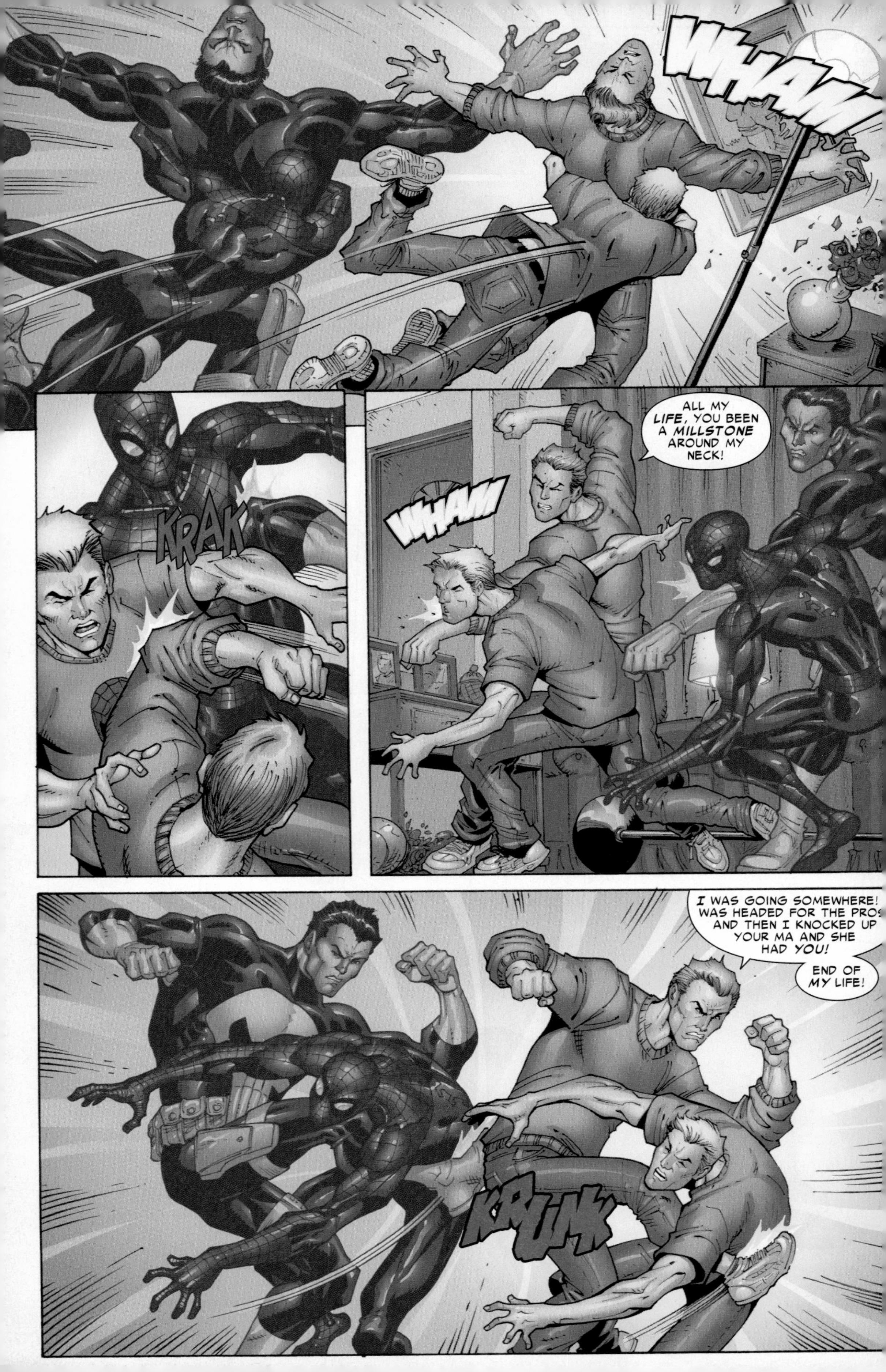
WHAM
KRAK
ALL MY LIFE, YOU BEEN A MILLSTONE AROUND MY NECK!
WHAM
I WAS GOING SOMEWHERE! WAS HEADED FOR THE PROS AND THEN I KNOCKED UP YOUR MA AND SHE HAD YOU!
END OF MY LIFE!
KRUNK

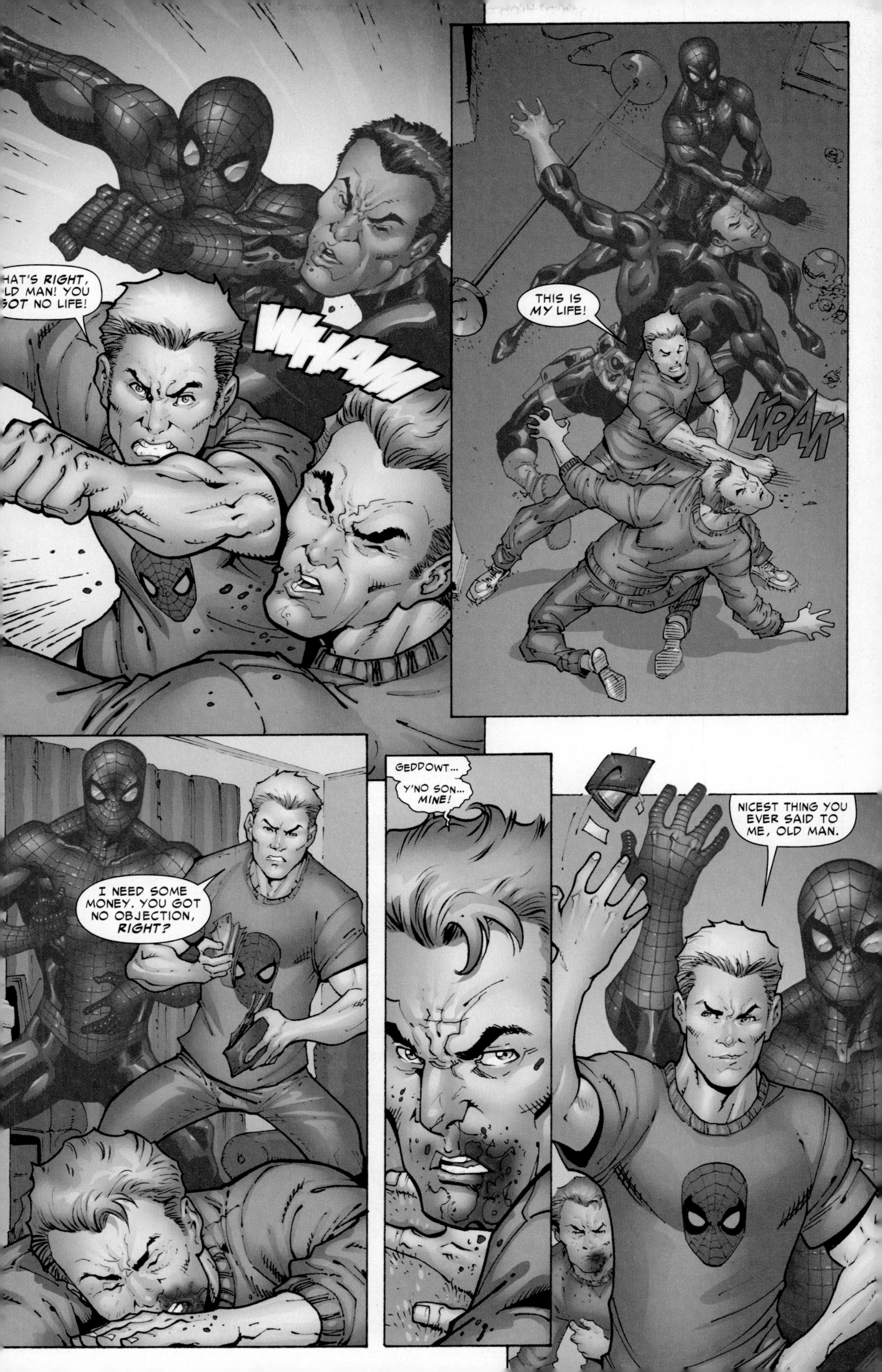
HAT'S RIGHT, LD MAN! YOU GOT NO LIFE!
WHAM
THIS IS MY LIFE!
KRAK
I NEED SOME MONEY. YOU GOT NO OBJECTION, RIGHT?
GEDDOWT...
Y'NO SON... MINE!
NICEST THING YOU EVER SAID TO ME, OLD MAN.

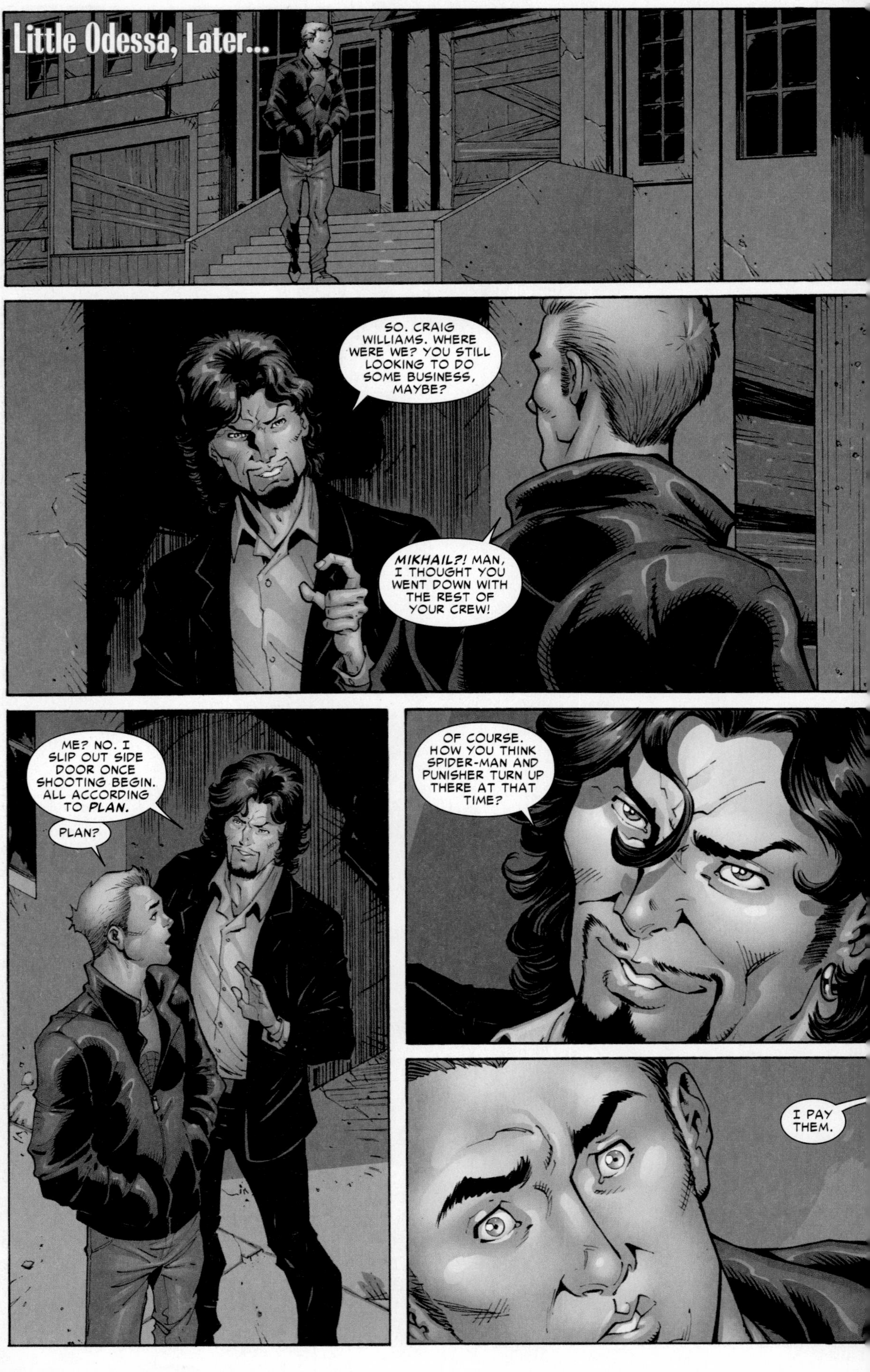

Little Odessa, Later...
SO. CRAIG WILLIAMS. WHERE WERE WE? YOU STILL LOOKING TO DO SOME BUSINESS, MAYBE?
MIKHAIL?! MAN, I THOUGHT YOU WENT DOWN WITH THE REST OF YOUR CREW!
ME? NO. I SLIP OUT SIDE DOOR ONCE SHOOTING BEGIN. ALL ACCORDING TO PLAN.
PLAN?
OF COURSE. HOW YOU THINK SPIDER-MAN AND PUNISHER TURN UP THERE AT THAT TIME?
I PAY THEM.

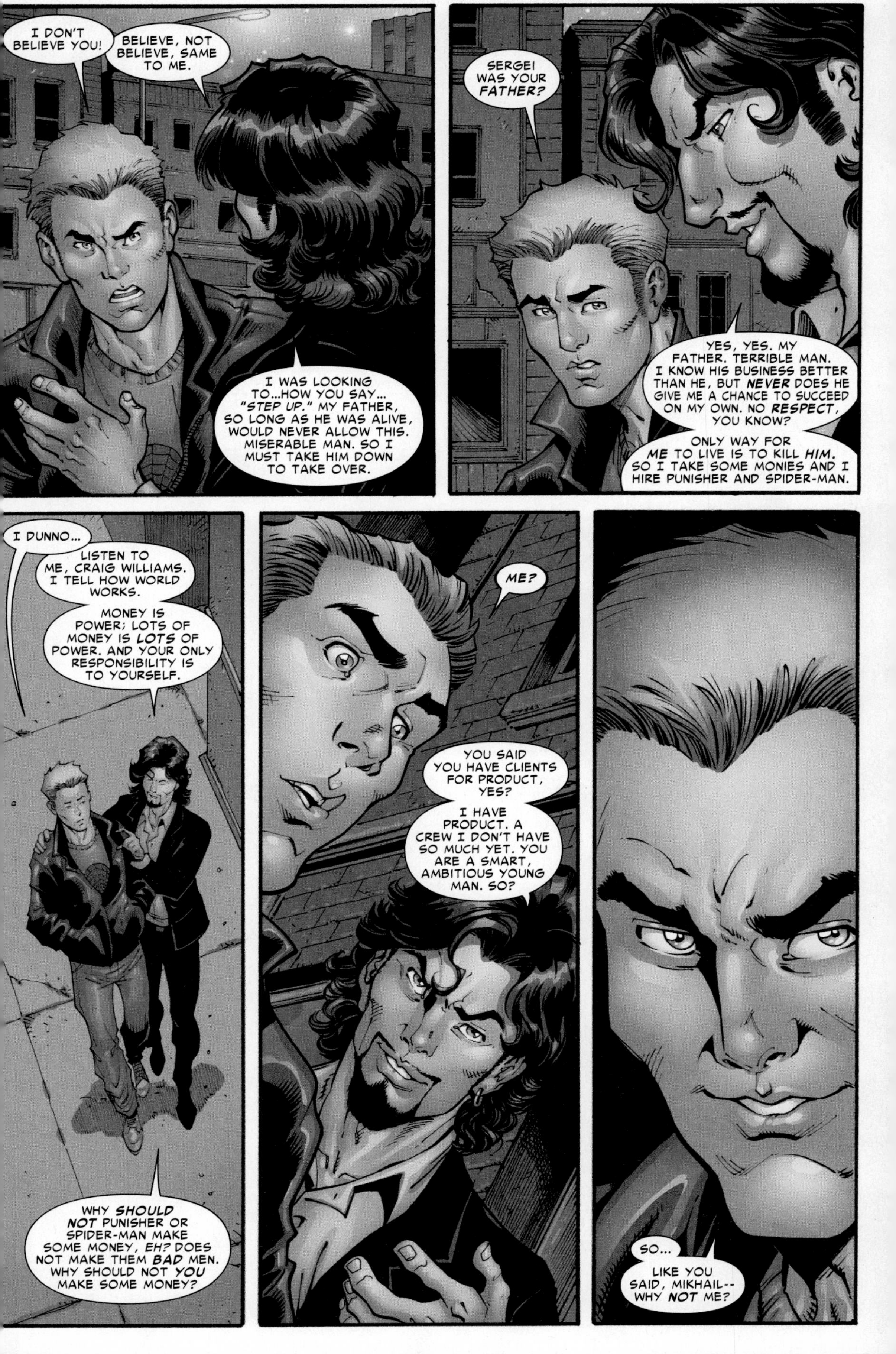
I DON'T BELIEVE YOU!
BELIEVE, NOT BELIEVE, SAME TO ME.
I WAS LOOKING TO...HOW YOU SAY... "STEP UP." MY FATHER, SO LONG AS HE WAS ALIVE, WOULD NEVER ALLOW THIS. MISERABLE MAN. SO I MUST TAKE HIM DOWN TO TAKE OVER.
SERGEI WAS YOUR FATHER?
YES, YES. MY FATHER. TERRIBLE MAN. I KNOW HIS BUSINESS BETTER THAN HE, BUT NEVER DOES HE GIVE ME A CHANCE TO SUCCEED ON MY OWN. NO RESPECT, YOU KNOW?
ONLY WAY FOR ME TO LIVE IS TO KILL HIM. SO I TAKE SOME MONIES AND I HIRE PUNISHER AND SPIDER-MAN.
I DUNNO...
LISTEN TO ME, CRAIG WILLIAMS. I TELL HOW WORLD WORKS.
MONEY IS POWER; LOTS OF MONEY IS LOTS OF POWER. AND YOUR ONLY RESPONSIBILITY IS TO YOURSELF.
WHY SHOULD NOT PUNISHER OR SPIDER-MAN MAKE SOME MONEY, EH? DOES NOT MAKE THEM BAD MEN. WHY SHOULD NOT YOU MAKE SOME MONEY?
ME?
YOU SAID YOU HAVE CLIENTS FOR PRODUCT, YES?
I HAVE PRODUCT. A CREW I DON'T HAVE SO MUCH YET. YOU ARE A SMART, AMBITIOUS YOUNG MAN. SO?
SO...
LIKE YOU SAID, MIKHAIL-- WHY NOT ME?

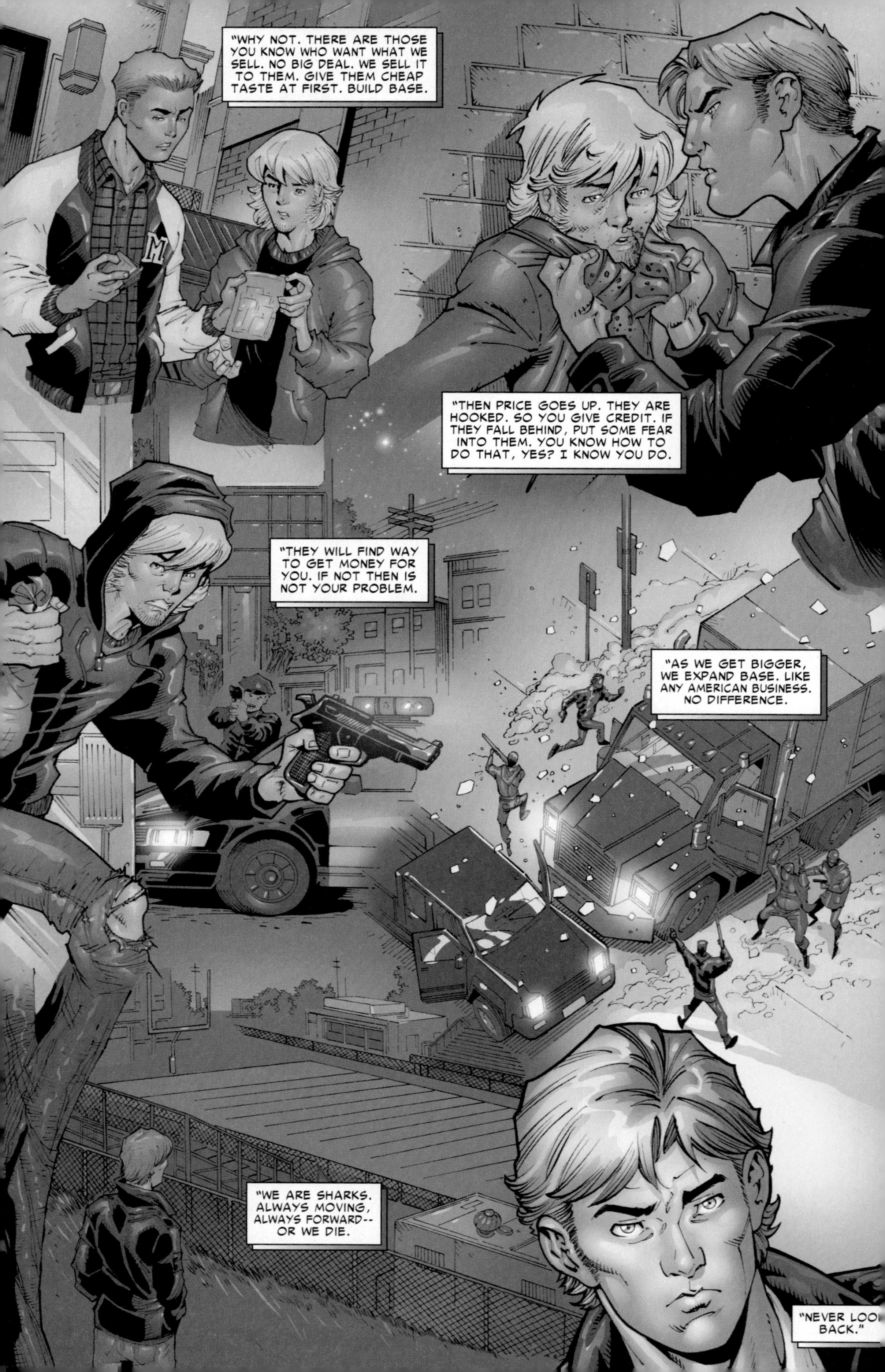
"WHY NOT. THERE ARE THOSE YOU KNOW WHO WANT WHAT WE SELL. NO BIG DEAL. WE SELL IT TO THEM. GIVE THEM CHEAP TASTE AT FIRST. BUILD BASE.
"THEN PRICE GOES UP. THEY ARE HOOKED. SO YOU GIVE CREDIT. IF THEY FALL BEHIND, PUT SOME FEAR INTO THEM. YOU KNOW HOW TO DO THAT, YES? I KNOW YOU DO.
"THEY WILL FIND WAY TO GET MONEY FOR YOU. IF NOT THEN IS NOT YOUR PROBLEM.
"AS WE GET BIGGER, WE EXPAND BASE. LIKE ANY AMERICAN BUSINESS. NO DIFFERENCE.
"WE ARE SHARKS. ALWAYS MOVING, ALWAYS FORWARD-- OR WE DIE.
"NEVER LOO BACK."

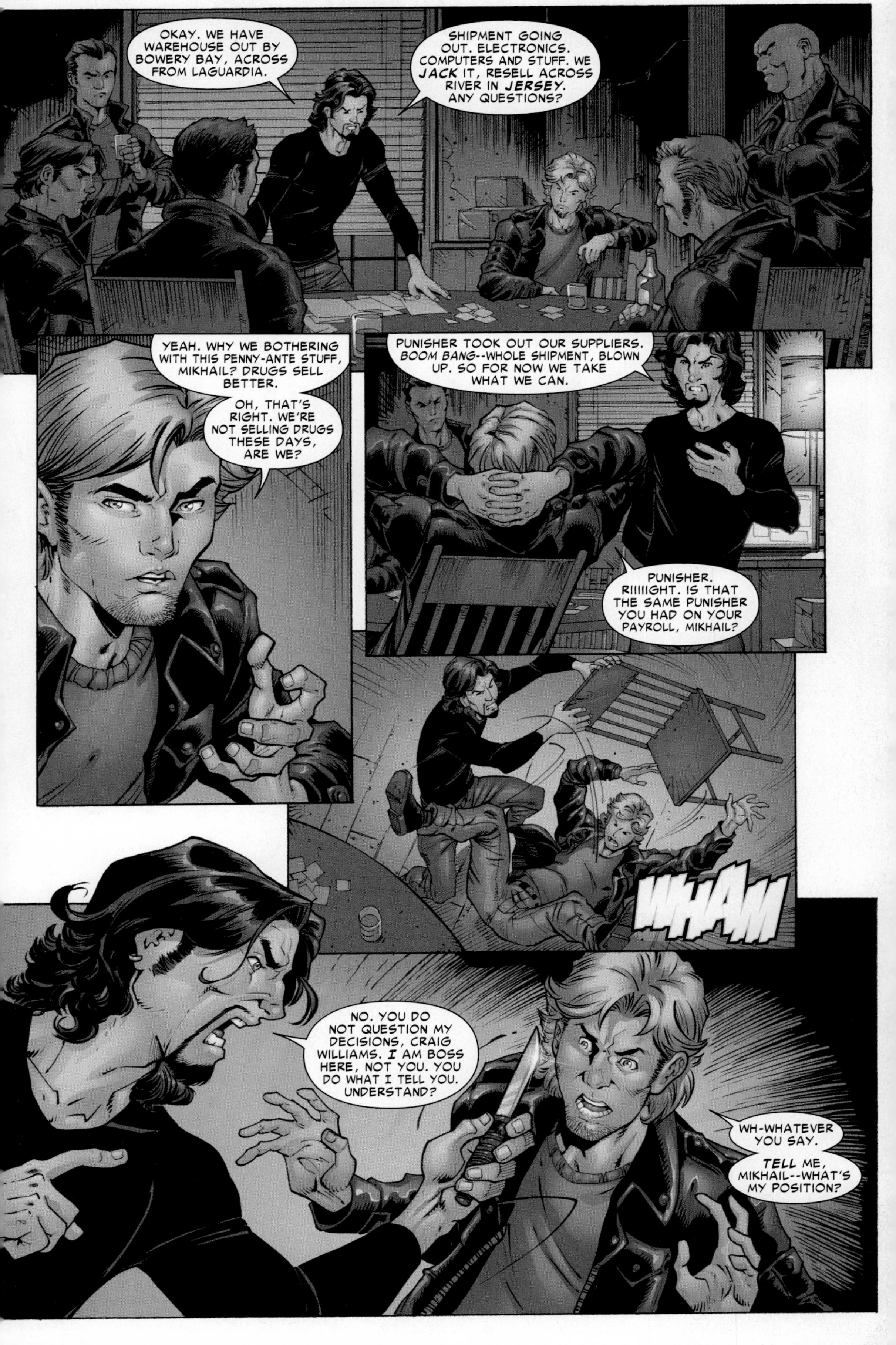
OKAY. WE HAVE WAREHOUSE OUT BY BOWERY BAY, ACROSS FROM LAGUARDIA.
SHIPMENT GOING OUT. ELECTRONICS. COMPUTERS AND STUFF. WE JACK IT, RESELL ACROSS RIVER IN JERSEY. ANY QUESTIONS?
YEAH. WHY WE BOTHERING WITH THIS PENNY-ANTE STUFF, MIKHAIL? DRUGS SELL BETTER.
OH, THAT'S RIGHT. WE'RE NOT SELLING DRUGS THESE DAYS, ARE WE?
PUNISHER TOOK OUT OUR SUPPLIERS. BOOM BANG--WHOLE SHIPMENT, BLOWN UP. SO FOR NOW WE TAKE WHAT WE CAN.
PUNISHER. RIIIIIGHT. IS THAT THE SAME PUNISHER YOU HAD ON YOUR PAYROLL, MIKHAIL?
WHAM
NO. YOU DO NOT QUESTION MY DECISIONS, CRAIG WILLIAMS. I AM BOSS HERE, NOT YOU. YOU DO WHAT I TELL YOU. UNDERSTAND?
WH-WHATEVER YOU SAY.
TELL ME, MIKHAIL--WHAT'S MY POSITION?

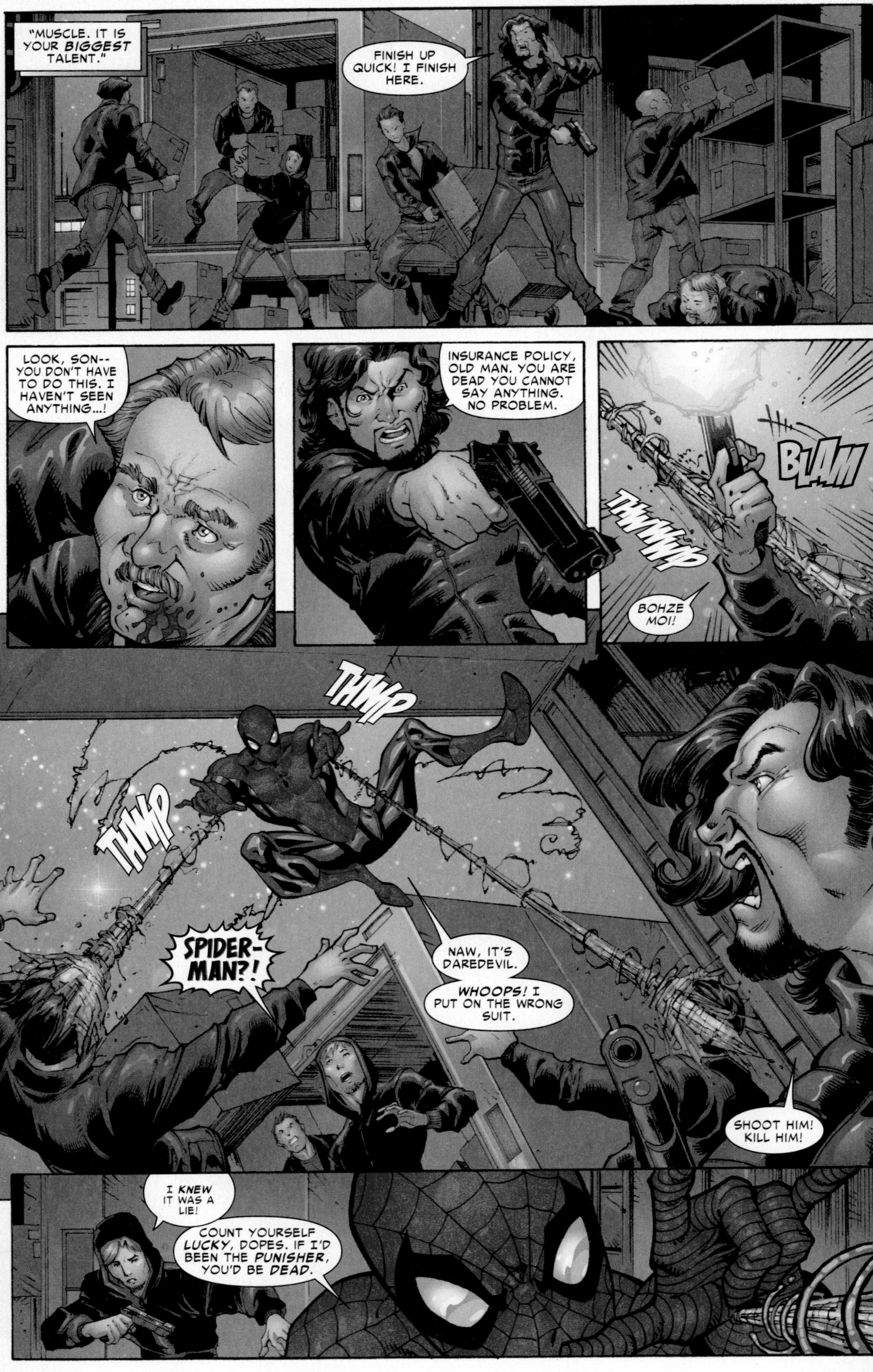
"MUSCLE. IT IS YOUR BIGGEST TALENT."
FINISH UP QUICK! I FINISH HERE.
LOOK, SON-- YOU DON'T HAVE TO DO THIS. I HAVEN'T SEEN ANYTHING...!
INSURANCE POLICY, OLD MAN. YOU ARE DEAD YOU CANNOT SAY ANYTHING. NO PROBLEM.
BLAM
THWWWP
BOHZE MOI!
THWP
THWP
SPIDER-MAN?!
NAW, IT'S DAREDEVIL.
WHOOPS! I PUT ON THE WRONG SUIT.
SHOOT HIM! KILL HIM!
I KNEW IT WAS A LIE!
COUNT YOURSELF LUCKY, DOPES. IF I'D BEEN THE PUNISHER, YOU'D BE DEAD.

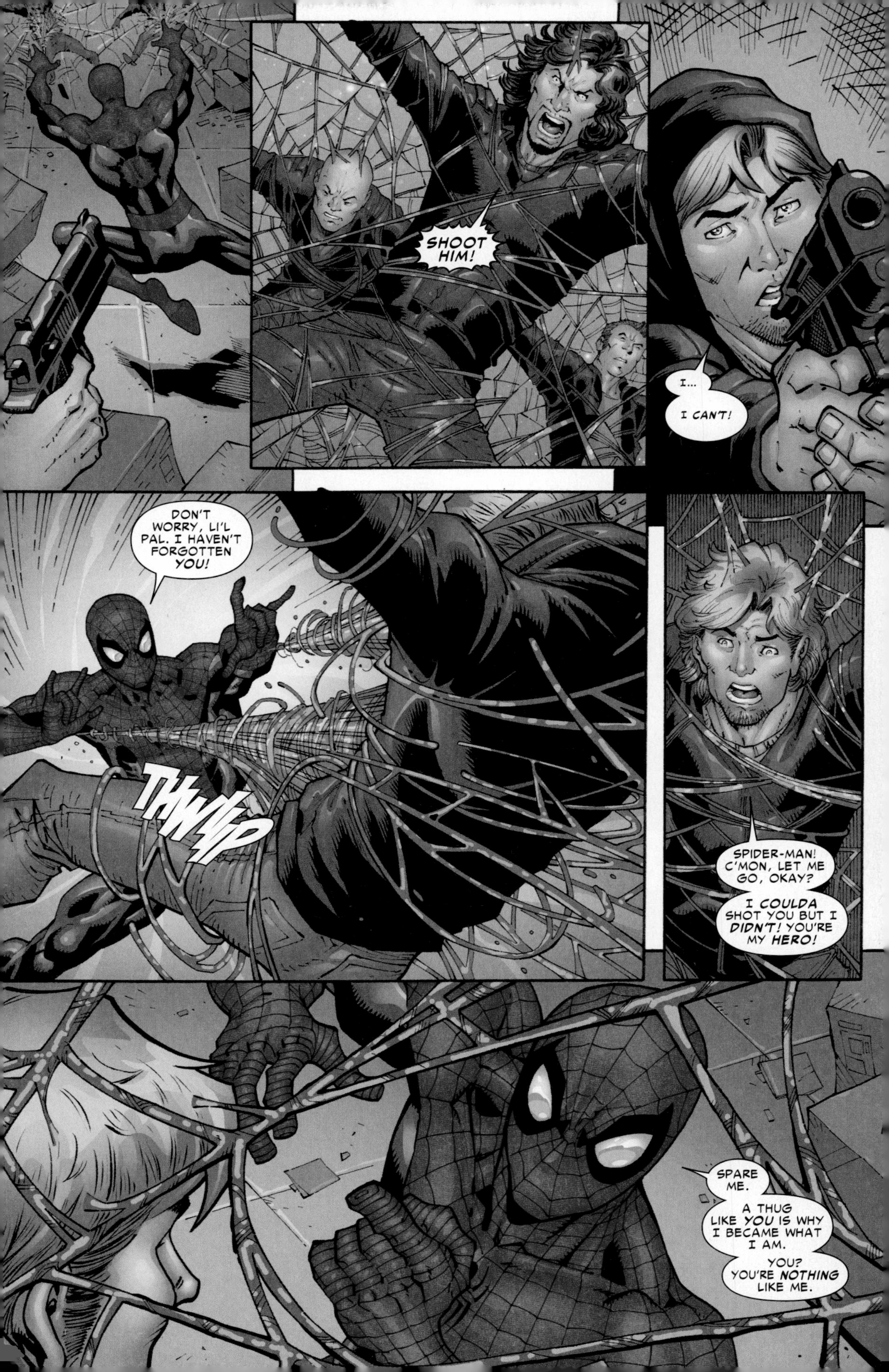
SHOOT HIM!
I...
I CAN'T!
DON'T WORRY, LI'L PAL. I HAVEN'T FORGOTTEN YOU!
THWIP
SPIDER-MAN! C'MON, LET ME GO, OKAY?
I COULDA SHOT YOU BUT I DIDN'T! YOU'RE MY HERO!
SPARE ME.
A THUG LIKE YOU IS WHY I BECAME WHAT I AM.
YOU? YOU'RE NOTHING LIKE ME.

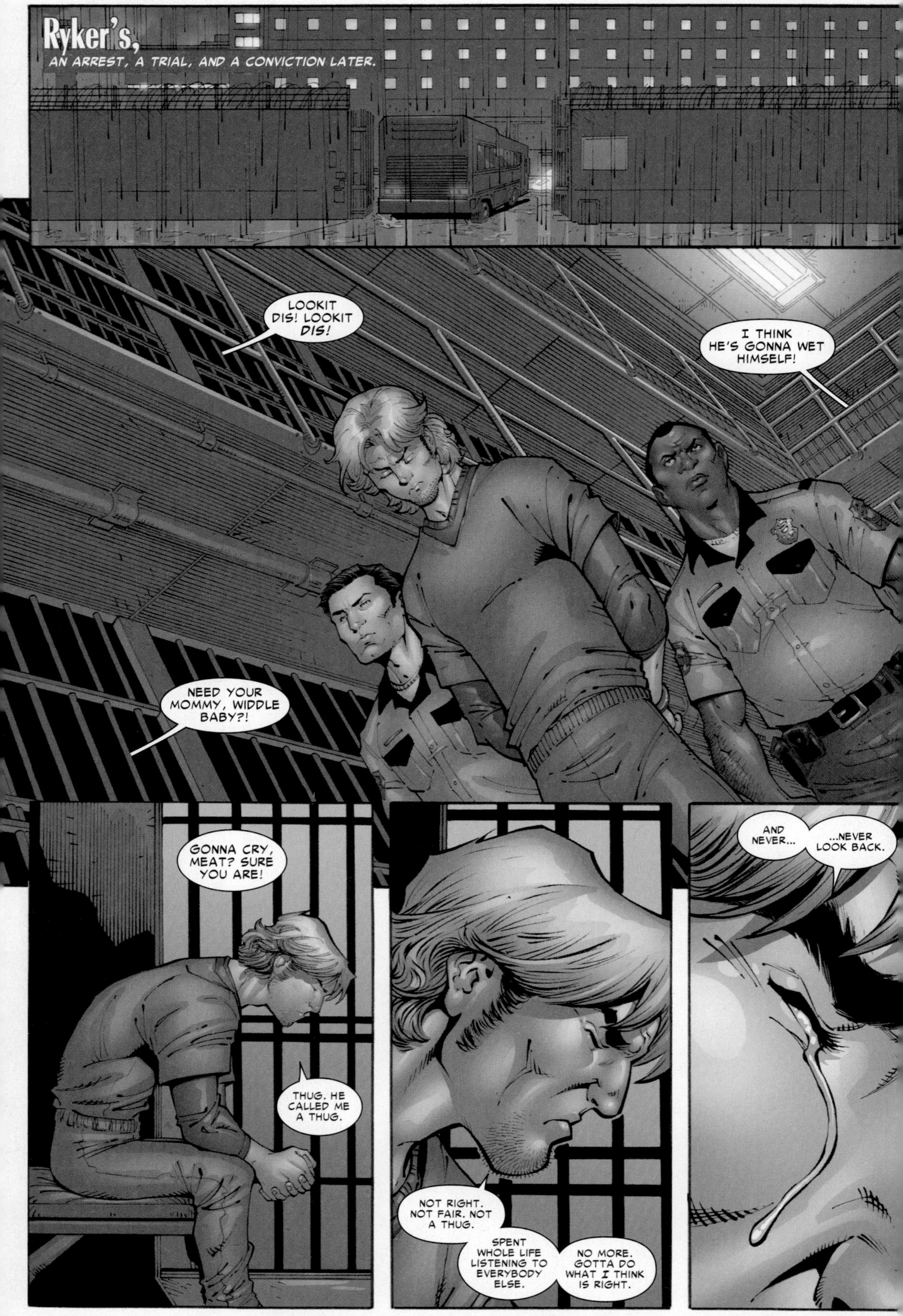
Ryker's,
AN ARREST, A TRIAL, AND A CONVICTION LATER.
LOOKIT DIS! LOOKIT DIS!
I THINK HE'S GONNA WET HIMSELF!
NEED YOUR MOMMY, WIDDLE BABY?!
GONNA CRY, MEAT? SURE YOU ARE!
THUG. HE CALLED ME A THUG.
NOT RIGHT. NOT FAIR. NOT A THUG.
SPENT WHOLE LIFE LISTENING TO EVERYBODY ELSE.
NO MORE. GOTTA DO WHAT *I* THINK IS RIGHT.
AND NEVER...
...NEVER LOOK BACK.

"I THINK OF A HERO AS SOMEONE WHO UNDERSTANDS THE DEGREE OF RESPONSIBILITY THAT COMES WITH HIS FREEDOM." **BOB DYLAN**

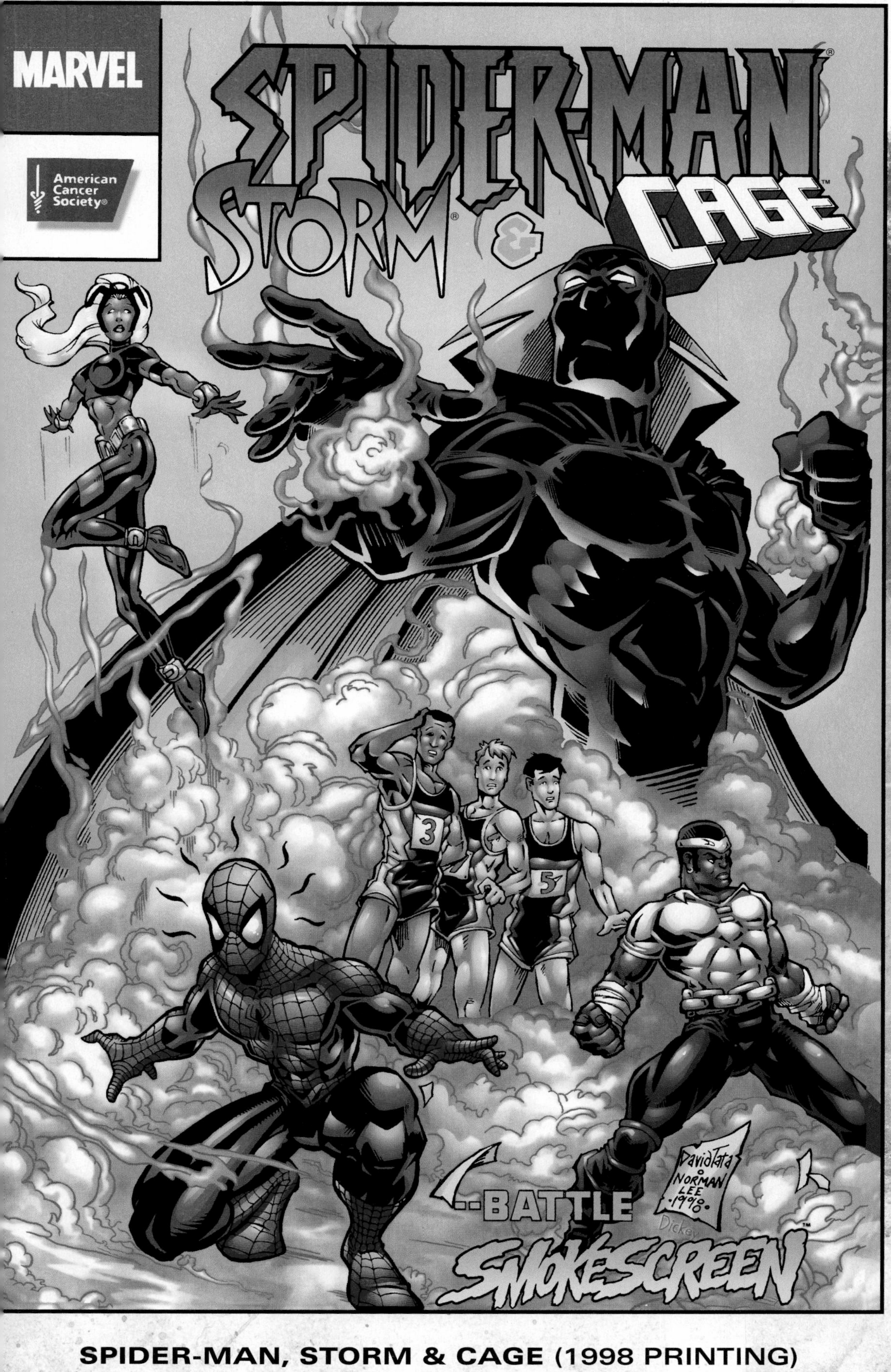
MARVEL
American Cancer Society
SPIDER-MAN
STORM & CAGE
...BATTLE
SMOKESCREEN
David Tata
NORMAN LEE 1996
Dickey

SPIDER-MAN, STORM & CAGE (1998 PRINTING)

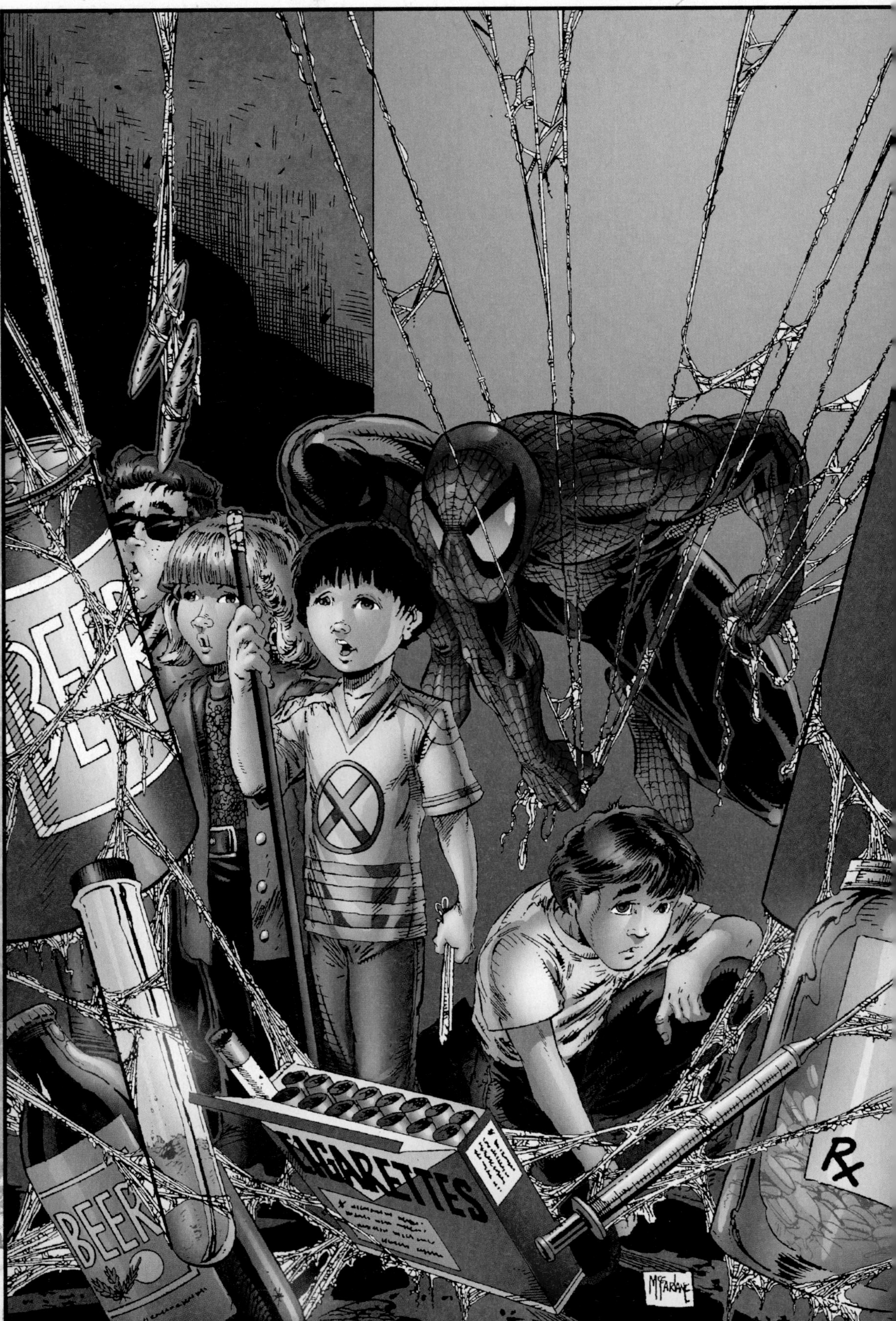
BEER
CIGARETTES
BEER
RX
McFARLANE

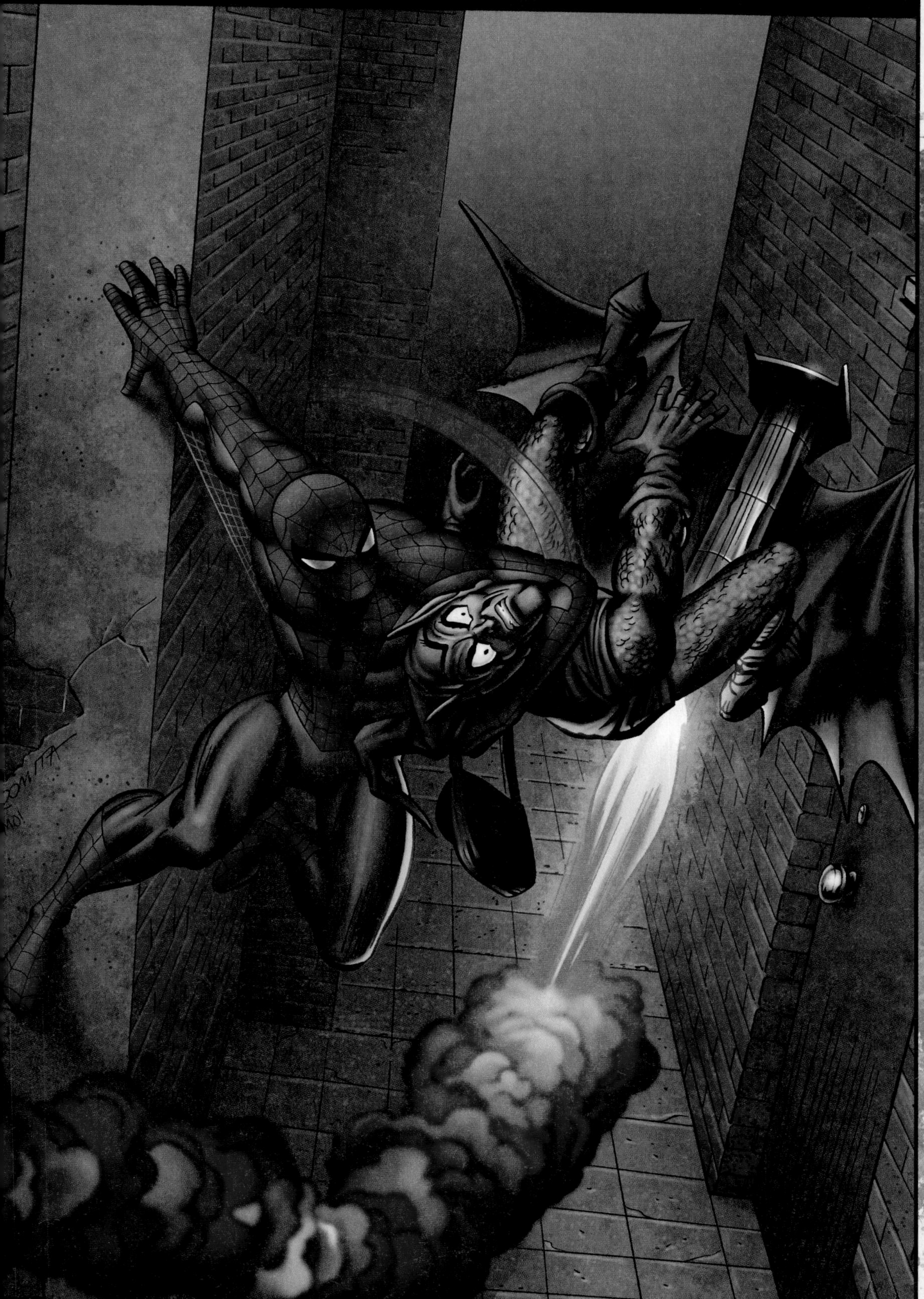